Celebrating the Commonplace

by Doug Rasmusson

Drawings by Delmar Holdgrafer
Cover design and painting by Avis Brandt

Louise and Doug Rasmusson

Round Table at By-Lo

First edition, 1999

Library of Congress catalog card number 99-93803
ISBN 0-9659896-1-5
12345678910

Asgard Publishing
P.O. Box 454
Hancock, Minnesota 56244
            Phone: (320)392-5634
            E-mail: drasm@info-link.net

Dedication

I suppose there are people who get a book printed all by themselves, but such is certainly not the case with me. Without the encouragement of the folks at the papers in Hancock and Morris and an occasional comment from friends and acquaintances this and the last book would never have happened.

Carol Oen and the good wife Louise have spent a lot of time editing text and holding my feet to the fire so I give them full credit for getting this book out. Carol knows about two hundred percent more about computers than I, and this knowledge was very important. I occasionally find myself staring at a blank screen with a mind that is equally blank.

Avis and Delmar I must thank for the artwork, and I am grateful to all the people whose antics give me material to write about.

Doug Rasmusson
Retired Farmer, Active Author

Introduction

This short piece is an attempt to sell you on the idea that you should buy this book and read it. Well, buy it anyway. The things in the book have their roots in the round table, a universal place where people gather and exchange ideas or whatever. My most used round table is located in The Owl's Nest in Hancock, but there is another across the street in the Senior Citizens Center and I have noticed and made use of others in many, many other towns.

The first book sold out the first printing, and while a good share of the second run remains in my garage, I am optimistic enough to try again with new material, a new cover, but the same old help from friends. It would have been out sooner but I spent a good share of last winter dividing my time between the hospital, my recliner and the doctor's office.

That last was my attempt to elicit sympathy. Now I will try to appeal to your reason. This book is admirably sized to fit atop the tank on your toilet; the stories are of an appropriate length to fit the occasion, so it is a practical book, meant to fill a need.

Table of Contents

Celebrating –Commonplace	1
Poetry	2
King David	4
Stone House & Last Big Pine	5
Baseball	7
Mutual Aid	10
The Sad Sack	12
The Winner	12
Skinny Santas	13
Sheep Dogs	14
The Silage Basket	15
Manure Tour	16
Corsets and Girdles	19
My Right Knee	20
Hearing Aids	20
North Dakota, Still There?	21
Old Guys in Orbit	22
Raising Children	23
Reader's Digest	25
Plugging the Book	26
Pigs	29
Senior Citizens	30
Sex, Sex, Sex	31
Colonoscopy	32
No Accounting for Taste	33
Teeth	34
Back in the Old Country	35
Titanic	36
Water Skiing for Fitness	39
Valentine's Day	40
Whales and Asteroids	41
Signs of Spring	42
Frost Boils	43
On Paying Attention	44
Dear Ann	45
The Luddites	46
The Summer Olympics	47
The Cat	48
Mad Cow Disease	51
Checking Our Mail	52
Renewing Acquaintances	54
Taking the Heat	55
Art in the Hinterlands	56
Mountain Climbing	57
Some Favorite Adages	58
Winter is Coming	59
Tough on Cars	63
How Brains Work	64
Good Old Formerly	65
My List	67
Mystic Lake	67
Stuff	68
Getting Dry	71
Haircuts	72
Having Faith	73
Learning Life's Lessons`	74
New Things	75
Unmodern Math	76
Per Diem	77
Minutes of my Meetings	81
What Do Names Mean	82
Mother Nature	84
Computer Complaints	85
Life Is Improving	86
New Year's Eve	87
New Year's Day	88
Palm Sunday	89
Nose Hair and Baseball	91
Oatmeal	92
Thoughts on Aging	93
The Organ Transplant	94
A Warmer Spell	95
Finding a Mate	96
My Chicken Dream	99
Use It All Up	100
National Endowment—Arts	102
A New Suit of Clothes	102
Riding the Waves	104

Speed	105	To Spring	133
How to Gather a Crowd	106	My Brush with Royalty	135
Pant Legs	109	Iowa Stories	137
Paul Harvey	110	Our Things	138
Peace at Last	110	This House	140
Governor Perpich	111	Toy Show	141
Second Guesses	112	Bicycles across Minnesota	143
Stranger in Town	113	Hope for the Future	144
Tough Luck	114	Broken Leg	146
Pickup	117	Two Poems to Buffet	147
Prairie Pioneer Days	118	Pigs and Cornshellers	149
The Predestinarian	118	The Turkey	150
Problems	119	Growing Older	151
Prozacville, USA	120	Solutions	153
Symmetry	121	Sweet Corn Time	154
Powerball	123	Rover	157
Eat More Geese	125	Temptation	158
Prunes	126	A Fair Tax	159
Radio	127	Party Line Telephones	160
Respect	128	Hubble Space Telescope	161
Reunion	129	Term Limits	162
Roosevelt and Hoover	130	Uncle Adolph	164
The Routine	131		

Illustrations by Delmar Holdgrafer

Baseball	6
Corsets and Girdles	18
Pigs	28
Water Skiing for Fitness	38
Mad Cow Disease	50
Tough on Cars	62
Getting Dry	70
Minutes of My Meetings	80
Nose Hair and Baseball	90
My Chicken Dream	98
Pant Legs	108
Pickup	116
Eat More Geese	124
My Brush with Royalty	134
Pigs and Cornshellers	148
Rover	156

Celebrating the Commonplace

For several years now I have been writing these things, short little stories about nothing much. It's gotten to be a habit, and it seems I can get something down on paper even if I really don't have anything important to say. I don't find it difficult, even a bird in a cage can do that much. I have no great aspirations. I do not expect to write the great American novel or anything like that. I figured I had just found a hobby that I could handle, one that did not require agility or endurance and could be done sitting down. Another occupation for my retirement years.

What I have been reading about and hearing on radio and television lately makes me wonder about just what is important. The greater part of what I hear does not affect me or mine.

What happens close to home, the things that affect us, our neighbors, family, and close friends are discounted as unimportant. We have been trained to think that in the general scheme of things these incidents don't amount to much. The prestigious, the spectacular, and the sensational get more attention in the media.

Now when a group gets together, they may talk about personal or neighborhood occurrences, but they will also talk about the spectacular, the dramatic and the exciting even if in the long run it matters little to them and theirs. I blame the media for this. They say they are only satisfying this insatiable need to know that the public has, but the best that can be said of this is that it is only entertainment, and not very good entertainment at that.

We go through months of media frenzy with any scandal. None of this stuff is as important as the price of grain, the weather, or what happened at school today with your kids. That's the important stuff.

1

Poetry

All my life I have had a tendency to versify. Not all the time, only on occasion. I have considered this more of an affliction than a gift and have tried to keep the habit under control. Now that I am growing old I worry less about appearances and what others think of me so I do it a little more and am more open about it. Also, I find others share this tendency to remember poems and even once in a while come up with one of their own. Everybody remembers a little poetry, maybe a nasty limerick or something innocent from childhood, or maybe something they saw written on the wall of an outhouse. Poetry comes in all shapes and sizes.

I suppose the tendency to do this kind of stuff may be inherited. Walt Erickson gave me a poem he found in some of his father's stuff. It was written in indelible pencil, if any of you are old enough to remember that sort of thing, and the signature at the end was "By August Rasmusson", my father. It was dated 1912. What the heck, if dad could do it, why shouldn't I?

A few of the survivors, classes of '43, '44 and '45 of Hancock High got together for a potluck dinner and a little reminiscing this summer. Erland Charles recited a poem he recalled that I had written back when the world was young and we were too. A couple of others also claimed to remember, but they had no proof as Erland spoke first. I don't know whether I should be flattered or embarrassed by this. It just goes to show how these things stick in one's mind.

I have heard Otto Shaefer recite poems he had learned back in the twenties for school programs. He is a practical person, why should this useless thing stick in his mind?

I met an old fellow once who makes his living teaching and writing poetry. Not a good living, as you could well imagine, but his needs are simple and he gets along.

I mentioned to him the incredible length of Longfellow's epic poem *Hiawatha* and how no one should be expected to read the whole thing, all fifty-six pages, in one sitting. He differed with me and recited a page or two of his favorite part, the building of the canoe, from memory. All I can remember is "By the shore of Gitche Gumee, by shining Big-Sea-Water" but he had "Give me of your bark, O birch tree! Of your yellow bark, O birch tree" and a whole lot more down pat.

Things may change now, however. We are getting into a technical age with less emphasis on the written word, less attention to memorization; we depend on computers and the Internet more and more every day. For example, my spell-checker on this machine is not familiar with the word "Hiawatha", and draws a wavy red line under it, but has no suggestions about how it should be spelled.

King David

King David now had grown old
And complained that he was always cold.
He had cold hands, he had cold feet,
The palace had no central heat.
At night he piled the blankets high,
"But still I shiver!" he would sigh.

Then his ministers of state,
Who knew their jobs, their very fate
Depended on him feeling good,
Decided it was time they should
Find the King a nice new nurse.
What the heck, they could do worse.

They got Abishag the Shunimite
With face so fair and smile so bright
To use her soft and lovely form
King David's ancient bones to warm.
She nursed him, saw that he was fed
And every night she shared his bed.

She kept the old boy good and hot
Even though he knew her not.

Now this may be a little silly
But lately I've been somewhat chilly.
Now in the autumn of my life
Do you suppose a younger wife?

But Louise says her idea's better,
She'll knit me a heavy sweater.

The Stone House and the Last Big Pine

The old man told me that his father
And his uncles built the house.
In summer, to farm, they would have
To move the many, many rocks,
So used some to form the walls.

In winter, they cut the Wisconsin Pine
That built the cities.
But summers they farmed
And built the house.

Two stories, square, no foolishness,
And from the upper windows,
You can see where every rock came from.
And rocks enough are left in
Just that small space
To build a dozen more.

If you would go now from there
Toward Hayward, you could see
The old pine tree that's left.
It's not the biggest, tallest
Of the many that were taken,
It's just the last.

WHEN WORK WAS A JOB AND BASEBALL WAS FUN

Baseball

Spring is just around the corner. The newspapers are talking about baseball, and I got to thinking about the game here in this area. I mentioned this to Jim Morrison, saying how nice it would be if someone from the paper would talk to some of the old timers around here about the game, and collect some of the stories. Make kind of an historical document, a record of the sport. He said, "You do it, we all got jobs." I explained that I am not qualified to do this. Fact and fancy seem to merge in my mind, and details get lost. I have a tendency to substitute imagination for actual incidents. "What's your point?" he inquires. I go on further about my inadequacies. He says, "Try it."

My interest in baseball was never as intense as my father-in-law's or his youngest daughter's. Louise and he debated the merits of the clubs and the players. His favorites were the Chicago Cubs, while Louise was a Yankee fan. Ed was from the Madison, Wisconsin area before moving to North Dakota, and he maintained an interest in the Cubs throughout his life.

When the Senators came to Minnesota, became the Twins, and television came out of the snowstorm stage, Ed would watch them play with some interest, but when they were losing, he would shut off the TV and mumble, "I've always been a National League man." Ed spent his later winters in a motel near the Cubs' spring training facility in Mesa, Arizona, and watched every exhibition game and most morning practices. He and his two brothers had played the game in Wisconsin and later in North Dakota. His old heavy woolen uniform and catcher's mitt are in the museum in Alexander, North Dakota.

In my position as a polite son-in-law, I had to listen to a lot of stories by Ed, and a lot of them were about baseball. The

7

kind of baseball that was played on Sunday afternoons in nearly every town in America in the summertime. One assumes that time will polish some of the rough edges off the memories, make things seem a little nicer than they really were, so when Ed told me about Lewis "Moose" Studlien, his cousin from Hoffman, Minnesota, I discounted it about half. Ed said Lewis was good, so good in fact that he had a contract offered to him by the Chicago Cubs.

It was after Ed had died that I went with Louise to a family reunion in The Cities, and I met this Studlien. I mentioned that I remembered hearing he had played a lot of ball around West Central Minnesota, and that he had been offered a chance to play professionally. He said sure, he had several offers, but you want to remember what it was like in the twenties and early thirties.

"I wasn't going to be any superstar. They would pay me about twelve hundred a year. I would have all those thirty-six-hour train rides, and I could be fired at the drop of a hat," he said. "Playing for Hoffman, Kensington, Morris, Hancock, places like that, I could be a local hero, and get enough money to trade Fords every year. All week I was a plumber, a profession that lasted me all my life, and Sunday I had my fun. And it was fun." He told me he remembered getting into a fight with Swede Nelson in Hancock, and Valli Ray, the town cop, street commissioner, schoolboard member and sometimes umpire had put Swede in jail because he seemed the most out of line. Lewis said he sometimes got as much as a hundred bucks for playing a double header in another town. He would catch or play third base the first game to look over the batters, and then pitch the second game.

I started my baseball research by asking Joe Wiese about his brother Frank Junior. I said I remember my friend Myron Benson saying that Junior was good enough to play in the big leagues. "No, he was too slow," Joe said. (Hope I haven't started a family fight.) Joe recommended Woodie Anderson for the local superstar. He played for Clontarf and DeGraff for years.

Local baseball was really big, and while Fargo, Duluth, and St. Cloud were pretty heavy into it, the interesting action was local, with people you knew, and little competition from the big leagues with all their promotion and big bucks. Personally, I dislike big cities, big crowds, and the big bucks that are necessary to maintain the big leagues now. The fun is still there, but a lot of it is hidden under the million-dollar salaries and the ambitions of the owners.

I decided that if I wanted to find out about old-time baseball in this area, I should ask Tib Kirwin. He's a genuine fan, and has some real memories. He was in Hardee's having coffee with Al Schmidt and Walt Ericson when I found him, and I knew all it would take is one question to get him started.

"Do you remember when you saw your first ball game, Tib?" I asked. "Lord, it must be thirty years ago," he said. "You mean you saw your first game when you were sixty? What are you talking about, Tib?" asked Walt.

"When you think about it, it must be longer ago than that, I'm 91 now," said Tib. "I remember I helped Ben Loher haul dirt building that grade by your place, Doug. I kept my horses in your dad's barn. He never charged me anything for it."

"You mean that old railroad grade?" asked Al. "I'm not that blame old, that was built in the 1870s. I'm talking about the road across Long Lake, " he said. "That was about the time the WPA was planting the trees in the Pomme De Terre Park," said Al. "My brother Fritz and I were just kids, and we were watching them, and they dug up a body. It was in a box, but the boards were all rotten and fell apart. They picked it up and took it someplace, but I found enough bones in the sand to make up one of the guy's hands. Don't know what happened to them though. One of the old timers thought he remembered the guy's name."

"You sure it wasn't an Indian?" asked Walt. "What kind of Indians were around here?" asked Tib. "Chippewas," said Al, "That's the ones they named the river after." "Yeah, but this is the Pomme De Terre. Never heard of no Indians by that name," said Walt.

I left then, as I was starting to have some doubts about my skill as an interviewer. I might have better luck talking to someone else about baseball in West Central Minnesota.

The next morning I was in The Owl's Nest in Hancock when Don Jepma came in. I asked him when he played with the Hancock Orphans. He said, "Right after the war Doc Apitz was still playing. He was good." Dean Leighton sat down at the table. "Say Don, I heard hogs were up four bucks this week, pretty good, huh?" "That's feeder pigs they are talking about. Doesn't do me any good," Don answers.

Ray Messner comes with a sheet of paper and the card deck. "I've got time for a game, anyone interested?" I lost fifty cents and didn't hear anything else about baseball.

Mutual Aid

Louise recently had cataract surgery on her left eye. It is healing and she expects to have the right one done in a month. Between us we are attempting to care for our ancient, deteriorating bodies. It gets more and more difficult to heal the wounds inflicted on us by the passage of time. Between going to funerals and going to the doctor our days are pretty well occupied.

We have lost count of how many close friends have died so far this winter. It is getting so I am running out of people old enough to ask when a date, name or details of an incident escape me. I suppose I will just have to wing it and use my imagination. If all the old timers are gone, who's to argue?

I was to the doctor lately and he removed a small basal cell carcinoma from my leg and patched the hole with a piece of skin from my arm. I have been dressing Louise's eye and putting drops in it for her, and now it is her turn to put ointment and dressings on my arm and leg, as the spots are in places difficult for me to reach. Who says the romance is gone after a long life together?

I suppose someone reading this epistle might get the impression that I am complaining. Actually I'm not; I'm just stating facts and giving excuses for not being a better citizen, a more productive member of the community. I have to do this, you see, because the only actual things I have accomplished so far this month are reading the electric and gas meters and carrying out the garbage.

The Sad Sack

When gambling, I mostly lose,
When buying cars, I always choose
The one that doesn't work quite right.
Some people say I'm not too bright.
But I'm just trying to get by,
So when I'm sad, I sometimes sigh
And go to rest beneath a tree.
But birds then come and poop on me.

The Winner

Everything with me is fine
When I want a thing it's mine.
I never made a big mistake,
Life is just a piece of cake.
I'm always moving very fast,
I'm always first, and never last.
I get things done, no ifs or buts,
'Course, everybody hates my guts.

Skinny Santas

As I get older, I become more and more of a traditionalist. Change is less and less appealing--even starts to bother me. I suppose it's healthier to be thin, and I suppose one looks better. But Santa Claus? Does he have to be thin too? I think these people like Richard Simmons and Susan Powter, the lady with no hair to speak of; both of these hyperactive diet missionaries are getting to be way too much of an influence on our civilization.

Here you see grown people, supposedly capable of offering good advice to the rest of us, leaping around and fidgeting, never still, constantly in motion and talking all the time. When my granddaughter acted like that it embarrassed us, and we blamed it on too much sugar, or drinking pop with caffeine in it. Of course, that was when she was nine years old.

Just pay attention, you are seeing more skinny Santas on television, and some of the little Santa dolls they are decorating the stores with are absolutely anorexic. They could never stand it up at the North Pole without that insulating layer of fat. Maybe they could get down a chimney more easily, but that isn't done much anymore. On these new furnaces, a rat would have a hard time getting down the little pipe and would end up in the firebox anyway.

But that's beside the point. I'm worried that fat is going out of style. I am not going to encourage obesity, but I see no need to be so thin and flexible. A little reserve for hard times, a cushion against adversity, it calms one down, keeps your feet firmly on the ground, and makes one more comfortable.

Sheep Dogs

I read that the American Kennel Club (AKC) has decided that those nice little Border Collies that specialize in herding sheep are popular enough now that they need to be recognized by that great institution. Some guidelines must be decided upon, like how big and what color they should be, and exactly how the perfect one should be shaped. Up to now, they were judged only on performance and intelligence.

They are interesting beasts, born with a powerful herding instinct so strong that if no sheep are available, they will herd chickens, ducks, children, and even attempt to herd automobiles, with sometimes fatal results. The name is from their native area, on the border between England and Scotland.

The AKC has done this to other breeds of dogs, forcing people to breed for conformation instead of intelligence. It has been the ruination of them, or so this fellow said in his article.

The St. Bernard, originally raised to live in the mountains and rescue people, is now so inbred that they have developed a mean streak, and while they look nice, many are stupid and disagreeable. With their large size, they can be dangerous.

The reason I am here writing this is because while looking for something halfway worthwhile on television, I must admit to becoming fascinated with a program called "Baywatch."

It was a story of no consequence, but with many beautiful people bouncing around briskly in skimpy swimsuits, in a place of eternal summer. I suppose this was the attraction for me.

The females outnumbered the men, and would seem to have better circulation or something, because they wore even less clothing than the men did. But both men and women were uniformly attractive. It gives me concern that perhaps we are doing the same thing as the dog raisers, breeding for conformation and nothing else.

We must look at our politicians. Is it more important that they are pretty or that they are smart?

The Silage Basket

To ensure our freedom and maintain good order in our society, we need a few rules. But too many rules and the wrong kind of rules will interfere with our freedom. Of course, if a lot of people don't follow the rules, we lose freedom then also.

The courts and the legal system should protect us and help formulate some of the rules, but sometimes I think maybe we are a little overprotected.

This lady from Eagan sued IBM because she felt that the design of the keyboard on the computer they built had caused her irreversible harm, a condition called Repetitive Motion Stress Syndrome. She and her attorney felt that the company should have warned her that doing things in the same way, time after time, would finally give her a hitch in her get-a-long. Her attorney said that a dangerous thing like a keyboard should have a warning label on it. She lost, but it is said that she did get a secret settlement from another computer company.

This makes me think I may have a case. Could be worth big bucks too, if I can figure out whom to sue.

You older farmers can remember silage baskets. They were in use before silage wagons, rototubes, automatic feed carts, that sort of stuff. After chopping it loose and pitching the silage out of the silo, you loaded it in a basket for delivery to the cows that would be waiting in the stanchions or in the knee-deep mud by the feed bunks outside.

The first baskets I remember held a bushel, were made of sheet iron, and had handles made of rope. Packed full and heaped up, they held about enough silage for breakfast for two cows. They would get another for supper, plus, of course, some grain and supplement each time, which was usually delivered in a smaller container, probably a five-gallon pail.

Then a big technical breakthrough. They began to make baskets out of aluminum, and as they were lighter, they put another ring around the top so that they held one and a half and sometimes even two bushels.

This was a way to make the farmers more efficient, so they could handle more cattle and could sell them for less. But if I remember correctly, there was no warning label on those baskets to explain how the constant lifting and carrying the heavy loads could affect your back in later life. All I have to do is find out who is responsible for making that dangerous basket and show them my x-rays. Be just like winning the lottery.

Manure Tour

When I hear people complain about odors out in the country, the word "fastidious" comes to mind, and if they complain a lot, words like "finicky" or "persnickety". When I was young, the toilet was not the best-smelling room in the house; in fact, it was not, in many cases, even in the house.

We have been sprayed with deodorizers, perfumed and sanitized until we regard a lot of natural things as unhealthy, when actually some of the things we use to make us smell better are harmful both to us and to the environment.

I went on the manure tour. This is a thing being studied, and rightly so, by various agencies. Some things stink. People complain, and we wonder what can and should be done about it.

Our first stop was at the Quackenbush hog farm, a fairly large family operation. They had built an outdoor pit that, together with the tanks under the floors of the buildings, could hold over a year's production of manure. This gives them flexibility on when and where they spread this valuable commodity and makes good management somewhat easier.

I could smell the contents while we were standing on the berm around the pit, and from my vast experience could tell that hogs were responsible for that smell. But I have smelled worse smells, much worse smells, while driving by the peanut butter factory in Minneapolis some years ago. I recall driving from Houston to Galveston in Texas, and wondering if we would die before we got far enough away from the refineries along that highway. These are things that really need some regulation.

When I stepped down off the bank around that pit and moved a few steps away, I could no longer smell pig. I imagine when they pump and haul the contents they will stir up a few evil spirits, but that too will pass, and quite soon if they inject the manure. There were a few flies, not many, and I did hope they wiped their feet before they lit on me.

We next visited Blackwelders, a dairy with a larger outdoor pit. Larger because cows are larger than pigs. On another site we saw an arrangement built to prevent run-off from a feedlot from polluting the Pomme De Terre River. Sensible, cost effective ways to make a healthy environment. With a little research, some government assistance and a little cooperation, most problems are solved. Not permanently, as conditions change, but good management will take this into account. It's up to us.

THE PRICE TO PAY FOR
LOOKING GLAMOROUS

Corsets and Girdles

I have heard it said that a civilization that does not record and study its history is doomed to repeat it. This makes me wonder why some lady or a group of ladies has not published a study of the history of girdles and corsets. I am not an expert in this field. What little I know is from looking at the corset ads in Montgomery Wards catalog and watching and listening to the complaints of my mother, aunts, and later my wife.

In those early days the ladies would occasionally get together to buy corsets. They would meet together at our house and I would sometimes see them walking around in their underwear, which of course by today's standards would be somewhat overdressed. This was so that the saleslady could measure them accurately.

Then these measurements would be sent to some sadists down in the cities who would construct these garments out of canvas, strong cord for lacing up the back and with spring steel stays to keep the devices from rolling. These things covered the women from just above the knees to the bottom of their ribs. You could buy the things over the counter, but they were more likely to fit better if they were custom built.

In later years women began to wear a cheaper, lighter thing called a girdle, and later still a thing called a panty girdle. This was kind of like a rubber pants with garters attached to hold up the stockings. I believe they only made one size, so for a while all women were shaped exactly the same in this critical area, from just above the knees to the bottom of the ribs. Larger ladies were just more firmly packed.

You had to be careful when going to dances. If a lady would bump you on the dance floor with her hip or butt, it could leave a bruise. I am not sure, but I think these things are no longer in use. This encourages me; it gives me hope that civilization may be improving the way people treat themselves. Now, if they can just get rid of high heels.

My Right Knee

I have one knee I do not trust
And if I'd fall, something might bust,
A thing that would be slow to heal
And of course it may not feel
So terribly good for quite some time.
And while I'm not still in my prime
I still have things I'd like to do.
Not a whole lot, only a few,
So I'll be careful when I walk.
It might be best we sit and talk.

Hearing Aids

A hearing aid is now for sale
That's very small but will not fail
To make your hearing very good
(At least the salesman says it should.)
So small no one will know it's there,
But tell me, just why should I care?

If folks refuse to talk real loud
Especially when we're in a crowd
That's not going to make me sore
Because I've heard it all before.

North Dakota, Still There?

Living where I do in West Central Minnesota, I am most times very aware of the existence of North Dakota. The northwest wind brings the very essence of Dakota to us. At least we blame Dakota any time dirt or snow is being carried on that wind. Louise is from North Dakota. I have worked and traveled extensively in the state, and have never for an instant doubted that it existed. A pickup truck has been named after it. The name of a popular kind of camera, the Kodak, is a corruption of Dakota, and if it weren't for North Dakota, we would be right next to Montana. I certainly wouldn't care for that.

Tom Isern, one of the regular columnists in T*he Walsh County* (ND) *Press* mentioned a few of the ways the state has been put down. Rand McNally forgot it in their atlas once back in the eighties and President Clinton once mentioned that perhaps the Dakotas are redundant.

This does not bother me and it should not bother any right thinking Dakotan with any sense of humor at all. I am Norwegian and have been exposed to jokes about my nationality for so long I am starting to enjoy these mindless, foolishly boring pieces of crap and am even starting to repeat a few of them.

But now in that same newspaper, Mr. John Rolczynski gives us proof that North Dakota does not exist. He wrote at some length of his research into the actions of the Territorial Legislature back in the early days and he is sure they screwed up. They did not follow the correct procedure. So since 1889 folks have been living in and paying taxes to an entity that is not there, never was there, and if something is not done soon, will never be there. So when we go west to Alexander to visit the brother-in-law and when we go to Park River to eat lutefisk, we are in never-never land, a nameless piece of real estate that may be in Canada, or possibly in France or Saudi Arabia.

21

John is evidently a detail person, one who is addicted to research, a person who insists on all I's being dotted and all T's crossed. I am not like that, and for that reason am frequently misunderstood. I am lacking in scholarship and have a tendency to jump to conclusions. While my leaps are somewhat shorter now that I am older, they are leaps nevertheless. When the weather gets a little warmer, I am going west to see for myself if North Dakota is really there. I know the cold northwest winds have been absent so far this winter, so maybe the state really did disappear.

Old Guys in Orbit

John Glenn, at the mature age of 77, volunteered to go back into space for a few days. He had been there before for a little while, and that made him famous enough so he could be elected to the senate. He has been a good senator, and when you think about it, that might be a good way to pick out the people who should be senators. To be an astronaut one has to pass various physical and mental tests and one must demonstrate that he or she has a certain amount of integrity. Not everyone qualifies. To be a senator, however, all you have to be is elected. Anyway, Glenn wanted to retire from politics and go back into space. He explained why.

When young people go into space and return, they act older for a while; they kind of limp around and forget things, repeat themselves and are very critical and hard to get along with. Then, after a while back on earth they get over it and act normal again.

Glenn wanted to find out what would happen when an old guy makes the trip. Would he be better or worse when he comes back down, and how would the old body stand the trip?

The research results may make all of us old folks nicer, healthier and easier to get along with. Glenn is in excellent health for an old guy, and did a great job.

If they want to send up another senator, and an old one, why not send Jesse Helms or maybe Strom Thurmond? If worst comes to worst, and heaven forbid we have an accident, we could get along pretty well without them. And if older is better, they are about as good as it gets.

In an interview I watched, the real reason for sending Glenn up finally came out. It is the same reason he stopped being an astronaut in the first place. He was a hero after the first trip, and President Kennedy let it be known that as there are dangers in space travel, he didn't want to lose a hero up there. It would damage the whole program if John Glenn were killed. John got tired of waiting for an assignment, resigned and went into politics.

Later, however, the program needed a little publicity. It is fairly safe, and sending a high-profile person into space seemed like a good move for all concerned, except possibly the taxpayers.

Raising Children

Our granddaughter stayed with us for a few days this week. One morning when I drove her down to the end of the driveway to catch the school bus, she asked me if I still was friends with my old schoolmates.

Now this was a long time ago, but after a little thought I had to admit that our relationship was pretty much the same. She asked me if they had changed much. I told her that they were older, grayer and some were dead, and yes, I suppose we all change to some extent.

I asked her what brought this up. She said she was wondering about her friends in school. She explained that the kids were kind of arranged in three categories: A, B, and C. I asked her where she thought she was, and she said about a B. She said she thought that this was good, because she had a few friends that were A's and a few that were C's even if most were B's like herself. I asked her if she wouldn't like to be an A. She said of course not, nobody likes the big shots, they don't even really like each other very much.

I was not this deep a thinker when I was twelve, but then I had not been in as many different school systems as she has. In elementary and high school there were so few of us we didn't have an opportunity to separate into cliques. When I think back, I suppose there were cliques in college, but I just wasn't conscious of them--wasn't even aware they existed. Sometimes it pays to be insensitive.

She didn't say anything that would make me think she had been exposed to any cruel treatment by this system, and I don't know if she would tell me. The trouble is, I can think of a few kids that I have thought perhaps it would be better she did not associate with. If I would tell her this, am I perpetuating this system she has identified? Is it true that it takes a village to raise a child? What are my responsibilities? I'm just an old person. What can I do?

Reader's Digest

I received a huge envelope from *Reader's Digest* the other day. It was very official looking and it said on the outside that the U.S Post Office would deal harshly with anyone who tampered with it before I got it. Mine arrived in good shape, so the post office people won't be disgruntled, and I was tickled about that.

A Mr. Anthony A. Aponte, who is evidently a big shot with Donnelley Marketing Company, wrote me a nice little note. It was enclosed in this huge envelope with a lot of other stuff I didn't get around to reading. I took it to mean that $25,000 had been set aside for me, and all I had to do was fill out a bunch of crap and send it back. Oh, and as long as I was doing this, why not order a cookbook or something that they had made available for me. He even enclosed a slip of paper indicating that my money had been transferred from someplace to someplace else so it would be handy for me when the time comes for me to get it. There was a slim chance, it says in the fine print, I may not win the money, but what the heck, life is a gamble anyway.

I am really getting sick of this stuff. I have subscribed to the *Reader's Digest* for years, but this is the end. It has been building slowly, more goofy mailings and prize contests, more dumb things they offer you. But this is it now. I am done, and will never again open an envelope if I suspect it comes from the *Reader's Digest*.

I am a little crabby, and the weather may have almost as much to do with it as does *Reader's Digest*. There is a little snow on the ground and more is falling. The wind is howling and the temperature with the wind chill is very uncomfortable. I knew there would be days like this. We all knew winter was on the way, but it still takes a little getting used to. The second episode like this we will just nonchalantly grab the snow shovel. The first one, however, is always a shock.

Plugging the Book

It has been quite a week. We finally got the books back from the printers, and of course we found that there were a few mistakes, but not any more than I can live with. I have to, as they were entirely my fault. It was an experience I will not soon forget.

I have long noticed the resemblance that Louise and her sister have to their mother. This is to be expected, as the old saying goes, "The apple falls not far from the tree." Now, however, I am starting to notice similarities to Ed, my father-in-law. As he grew older, he became less and less reluctant to express an opinion on any subject. I recall an incident when we visited them in Watford City, North Dakota. They had one of the apartments connected to the local old folks' home, and took their meals with the residents.

We were to join them for lunch one day. As we walked down the hall we had to wend our way carefully among the other old folks who really had nothing to do, so were waiting in the hall in their wheelchairs or with their walkers for the dinner bell to ring. As my father-in-law passed among this throng of the elderly, he said, loud enough for all to hear, "Have you ever seen under the canopy of heaven such a mass of human wreckage?"

His daughters are no longer young and are beginning to be quite frank and open with their opinions also. I have grown accustomed to this gradually, and would hardly have noticed it except for an incident related to the book.

Part of my ordeal was an interview with Glenn Zimmerman on KCCO-TV in Alexandria. We talked for about fifteen minutes; I gave him a lecture on the wonders of the Lake Region Arts Council and all the help my project had received from various others. The only part that appeared on the screen, however, was some dumb remark I made about toenail fungus. I can live with this however, as I guess it represents the real me as well as anything.

After the interview was accomplished, we were visiting in the newsroom when Jean showed us exactly who her father was. She looked Zimmerman in the face for a second, and then told him, "You are quite a bit better looking in person than you are on the television." He said, "Thank you." For what, I don't really know. We left.

A HAPPY CONTENTED PIG LIVING
IN ITS NATURAL ENVIRONMENT

Pigs

Few pigs are still being raised the old fashioned way. When I was young, most pigs had a birthday before they were large enough to butcher. When I was in 4-H, one of my projects was a ton litter. The idea was to get the product of one sow up to 2000 pounds in the least amount of time. They would take your word for the birthday, and then six months later your pigs were weighed and the heaviest litter won.

I picked out a sow with thirteen little ones, and put her in an old brooder house down in the pasture under some trees. She and her children lacked for nothing. They got all the skim milk that was produced on the farm, their oats were hulled, their corn was not moldy--the best was none too good for them. A sack of Occo mineral was for their personal use, and the little house they lived in was moved occasionally to cleaner places in the pasture.

With all that love and attention they prospered, at least as compared to our less pampered hogs, and in six months they averaged 200 pounds apiece. They won no prize, but they didn't care. I suspect that the litter that won was composed not of brothers and sisters like mine, but a batch of cousins picked from the family's hog population in general, and they may even have lied about their birthday. You can generally tell if a bunch of pigs are used to each other, and those winners seemed not to like one another as much as they should. Of course, maybe I was just a bad loser.

Now pigs are improved genetically, they are fed scientifically and they live in large communities--pig penitentiaries, if you please. I wonder if one would adopt a pig from one of these institutions and raise it with love and understanding if it would taste any better. Sort of a foster pig program. It seems to work with chickens. If they are left to their own devices and can chase grasshoppers and roost in trees, they seem to have a better flavor. But then, pigs have more personality than chickens, and it would be hard to eat a friend.

Senior Citizens

Louise and I attended the Midwest Senior Federation meeting this morning at the senior center in Morris. We were there because we were specifically invited and if you can believe this, we were to be the entertainment. We didn't know exactly what was expected of us. I was kind of hoping someone would tell us, so we just sat there, talked a little and had a nice dinner when it was over.

This was our first time, and it was interesting to hear some of the concerns that the group has about health care and the way government actions affect us old timers. Dick Honetslager, a regional coordinator for Senior Citizens, spoke to us concerning lobbying efforts being made in St. Paul and who needs to be made aware of our opinions. We old folks vote every chance we get, so the politicians do pay attention to us, and that is a comfort. Still, it is good to be vigilant.

Of course anytime an old farmer has something to say he will find it necessary to mention the weather. We haven't needed sunglasses much this winter, but neither have we needed a lot of heavy clothing and snow shoveling, so I guess we should be happy without a lot of sun. I have heard that low levels of light make one depressed, but of course this does not affect me as I am Norwegian and am always depressed, regardless of sun or clouds, cold or warm.

I have blown more stuff out of my nose this last week than I thought humanly possible, and it continues to come. I doubt it is the flu. I believe I am suffering from the same cold I caught back in 1941, and it was just a little more active than usual. I am sure it is the same cold--the one I caught while threshing sweet clover that fall long ago. It has never left me. It only goes into remission occasionally, leaving me with only a slight sniffle. Then it returns to remind me that it is still boss. I thought that when I quit smoking I had a chance for victory over it, but that was not to be. It is still with me.

Sex, Sex, Sex

I have discovered that I have something in common with Paula Jones, the lady from Arkansas. I too am suffering from physical and mental anguish and have acquired an aversion to sex. I imagine there is treatment for this, but doubt that Medicare will handle it. I don't know who exactly to blame, but have decided that perhaps the media is the primary cause of my discomfort.

Now that the ship has left the shore as far as I am concerned and my interest has waned, sex seems to be all the media wants to talk about. A teacher is mentioned as having a child with her fourteen-year-old student. Washington DC seems to be thinking about nothing else. Some people in Israel are buying and selling young Russian girls for immoral purposes. I wonder what we will hear about next.

I am an old and suspicious person, however, and have a theory. I imagine these things all have happened in the past, but they were not discussed in such detail. How much do I need to know? Is it important to me and mine to know what the circumstances were and whether or not the president had an affair while in the Oval Office? Do we need a poll to tell us how people feel about this, and how it has affected his popularity?

Here is my theory. Like any good magician, there are people in charge somewhere who want you to look here so you do not notice what they are doing there. Misdirection is their game. What is happening that they don't want us to find out about? Is a war going on somewhere? I remember the "Secret Bombing" in Cambodia during the Viet Nam era. Is something happening to our Social Security checks? Is Doctor Kevorkian going to qualify as a Medicare provider? I worry and I want to know.

Colonoscopy

I don't suppose we'll ever see
A pleasant colonoscopy.
I know I need one every year
And while it is a thing I fear
As it is by no means fun
I'm always happy when it's done.
It may prevent a thing that's worse,
An early ride in a big black hearse.

There's No Accounting for Taste

I've heard a lot of people say it. In fact I suppose I've said it myself once in a while, "There's no accounting for taste." It's a temptation to say that when you see somebody who obviously enjoys doing something you would not want to do, or eating something with gusto that you could not force yourself to swallow. You see something like that, and you say, "There's no accounting for taste."

I'm starting to wonder, however, just how true that is. I think in most cases we can account for the tastes people have. Mostly, they are learned from kids they admire in school, television, and maybe even once in a great while from church or parents. I see youngsters now wearing their underwear pulled way up high and their pants hanging somewhat lower. They have learned this by watching weird people on television, and now they are acting weird.

When one is young, the brain is soft and spongy, and absorbs stuff easily, which is nice if they are listening to wise old folks like me. But see what happens when they are allowed to look at television. They pull up their underwear and put their caps on backward. They would never learn this from me.

Now I like most everyone, but do not care for mimes. You know, those people who don't say anything, just paint their faces white and pretend to be trying to get out of an invisible box, or pulling on a imaginary rope, or maybe walking into a strong wind.

But suppose the only way I could get lutefisk was to have one of those strange people serve it to me. I'll bet in just a little while I would start to drool every time I saw one of those white faces. Put something everybody likes together with something nobody likes, and you force people to compromise.

I think there is something of value in this knowledge. There is profit to be made by knowing how easy it is to change people's tastes. If you make the other guy want it, and think that he or she really needs it, you could really do business. If I were only a little better at creating a need, maybe I could get rid of the old car I have sitting in the grove.

Teeth

I wonder what's causing it? Could it be from the fluoride in the water nowadays? People seem to have better teeth, which, on the face of it, would seem to be a good thing. I, for example, am old as the hills, and still have nearly all my original equipment in that part of my body.

The last time I was to the dentist, I needed only a couple of fillings and a cleaning. I can chew most anything. When I was young, there were a lot of smooth-mouthed people around, people whose chins came nearly to their noses when they closed their mouths.

Like I said, it seems nice on the face of it to be able to keep one's teeth, but that can be misused too. First it was the boxer Tyson biting off his opponent's ear, and then this Marv Albert, the basketball announcer chewing on his girl friend. I never heard of anything like that when I was young. Lord knows how many other incidents like this take place--people biting each other--but as the folks are not famous or on television we hear nothing about it.

Gun control has been mentioned a few times around the table of knowledge where I sometimes have my coffee. I myself am of the opinion that there are some folks that I do not want to have firearms. But tooth control has never been mentioned. I suppose it would be really difficult to write out a set of regulations for that. While teeth may inflict some damage, they would be less likely to be deadly than guns.

I don't know exactly how those folks could be picked out, those potential tooth criminals, but I am sure that if a method could be perfected society would be safer. I'm not an expert on this, as I have never been shot or bitten--not even a near miss.

This reminds me of another thing, the phrase "near miss". Exactly what does that mean? I hear it used, for example, when two airplanes have a close call, and they call it a near miss. That would seem to me to mean that they almost missed hitting each other, and that would be a hit, wouldn't it? Well, I am getting off the subject again. You get to a certain age and even if your teeth are good, your mind wanders.

Back in the Old Country

I know it's wrong, but I can't help but think of Norway as the Norway of my ancestors. The image I have of the place is the one that my grandparents put into my mind, and it is reinforced by the things they left behind--the old chests, books and other small articles that they brought from the old country. It doesn't help when people go there and bring back clothing just like what we would expect, things like grandma and grandpa had.

The pictures they come back with don't help. They are generally of the fjords and mountains, things that don't change much. The most photographed buildings are the old ones; very seldom do they take a picture of something modern. I know better. I know that they are at least as modern as the average American is, but it's hard to keep that in mind. I know they are probably a lot more cosmopolitan than the residents of Hodges

Township, Minnesota and I have to keep reminding myself of that.

Our daughter in Wisconsin hosted an exchange student from Stavanger, Norway. The girl has visited our house before, but this time she brought with her some things her mother sent her. This little care package contained two envelopes; those plastic and aluminum foil ones containing fast food, but this was Norwegian style.

One was Bergensk Fiskesuppe and the other was Risengrot. It said on the Risengrot package that it "med den gode smoken. Serveres med sukker, kanel og gjerne et lite smoroye." Some of the "Os" should have a line through them, but you get the idea. (I think I have just driven my spell checker insane.)

So we had fish soup and rice mush for supper last night. It was a white meal like all Norwegian food is supposed to be, but to have it come out of a package, just like Hamburger Helper--this is going to take some getting used to.

Titanic

I'm doing it again--writing about something I know very little about. I know I shouldn't do it, but I can't help it. Something comes over me and away I go.

I haven't been to the movie, and I have felt no great desire to see it. Let's face it, what can it be? Big ship hits iceberg, big ship sinks, screams, a lot of splashing around with millions of dollars worth of special affects and that's it.

I was surprised to read that the Titanic movie earned more money than any of the other big movies of the year, and set box office records. I realize that anything can be sold with enough promotion, but still, to set records it must have something in it that people like. Then I heard a review that explained it to me.

There is more to it than just gurgle-gurgle, splash-splash. I heard that the young hero, the star of the show is an artist. He steals this rich and beautiful girl away from her not-very-nice boyfriend, paints a picture of her in the nude, and then gets lucky with her in the back seat of an old car. One or both croak then, so it is very romantic, besides the special affects.

This is what it takes. Granted, I am an old person and this stuff does not jiggle my jollies around as much as when I was younger. I admit to still looking forward to summer when the young girls will start wearing shorts again, but I very seldom stare. And I am not going to pay big money for a movie with nudity in it unless it has a little something else going for it.

Water Skiing for Fitness

In the autumn of our lives, it seems we spend more time around and in places where medical services are provided. I was waiting for Louise in the doctor's office this week and to pass the time looked over the magazines. They were the kind you generally find in a place like that, magazines that hardly anyone subscribes to, and if they do, never read. They are strictly for people trapped by circumstance, people who are desperate and will read anything.

The one I picked up was about bodybuilding and the health and beauty that vigorous physical activity could give you. Every page had several ads for bicycles, skiing equipment, huge weights for one to lift, treadmills, that sort of thing. For some reason, none of this particularly appealed to me.

Mountain climbing was pointed out as a healthful activity, and marathon running was described as a good way to lose the blues. None of these things turned my crank either

Then I saw the picture of the water skier. The caption said that this skinny old guy was ninety-one years old. He was attired in one of those form-fitting rubber suits and was skiing on one bare foot while holding the towrope in his mouth. Talk about an ad for Super Poligrip.

Trying to be honest, I ask myself, "Self, if you were capable of doing a thing like that, would you do it?" My honest answer is, "If I were capable of that, there are probably other things I find vastly more interesting that I could do, and I certainly wouldn't waste any of my few remaining years on water skis."

Valentine's Day

I was listening to the radio when they were discussing some of the romantic places various people would like to be on Valentine's Day. One thought a nice supper in the African twilight out in the wilderness after a picture-taking safari, while listening to the calls of the animals. A couple thought it would be romantic to meet atop the Empire State building in New York City and repeat their wedding vows. Still another mentioned a trip to the Caribbean, lying in the sun with a cool drink and no worries.

What Louise and I did on Valentine's Day was not mentioned. We went to Hancock to The Owl's Nest. I had my oatmeal and she had a poached egg and we played two games of whist with Alma and Lila. Not exactly looking at elephants, but what the heck, it works for us.

I have never seemed to need a whole lot of adventure. We are more likely to be spectators than participants, and we like it that way. I suppose someone has to do the things that excite, stimulate and entertain, but for the most part, we sit and watch--perhaps make a comment or two occasionally, but that's about it.

Louise's sister told us of an incident early in her life that may have made her the more adventurous member of the family. The practice had evidently stopped by the time Louise started school, but in the early grades back in Rawson, North Dakota they would occasionally come to class with little bags of peanuts to throw at the teacher. One at a time, I believe she said. She said she seemed to remember that this was done with the approval of all concerned, both the throwers and the throwee were OK with it. The reasons this was done are lost in antiquity.

Whales and Asteroids

I wasn't too worried when the news came that an asteroid was approaching the earth at 17,000 miles an hour. They said it would take about thirty years to get here, and by that time I will be some over 100 years old and ready for a little excitement. But now I hear that it will miss us by at least 600,000 miles. That is close by the way astronomers measure distance, but plenty as far as I'm concerned.

I understand that the last really big one that hit our planet wiped out the dinosaurs. I can get along without those things pretty well, but then of course I never had occasion to get accustomed to having them around.

In 1906 a fairly large meteorite hit somewhere in Russia, and knocked down a lot of trees and dug a considerable hole in the ground. Now it is said that we have instruments that could detect the approach of something like that. We could shoot one of our surplus rockets at it and blow it to smithereens. Whether it is better to be hit by one big rock or a huge number of smaller ones is a question I will have to leave to the experts.

During WWII my cousin and her husband were living in New Jersey. At the time the United States was concerned about spies, Nazi submarines and other strange things along our eastern seaboard. Civilians with boats were enlisted to cruise around and aid the Coast Guard in protecting our shores. The government gave them fuel for their boats and on some of the larger ones mounted a fairly formidable gun. It happened that one of these amateur sailors mistook a whale for a submarine and shot it.

The beast floated up on to shore close to where my cousin lived, and all the neighbors came around to inspect it, take pictures of it, climb on it and generally amuse themselves. This was fine for a while, but it was summer and quite warm.

After a while the novelty wore off and the beast started to smell. The odor was stronger every day, and the folks knew something had to be done. Finally they got someone with a big boat to pull the whale back out into the ocean. The tide put it back on the beach in just about the exact same place, and so quickly that it nearly beat the boat back to shore.

Then the experts decided the animal should be pulled out and exploded into thousands of pieces with their cannon. They soon discovered that particles of whale are just as buoyant as whole whales and they smell at least as bad. For the balance of the summer that portion of the New Jersey shore was covered with oily rotten fragments. I hope the asteroid doesn't stink.

Signs of Spring

As spring approaches, for some reason one's thoughts turn toward income tax. While we have made little money of the taxable kind, Uncle Sam nevertheless expects to hear from us. I don't know why. There are others whose papers could be shuffled more profitably, but the IRS seems to want to know all the facts about our financial condition. I understand that the agency is supposed to be kinder and gentler than it was formerly, but we still do not wish to trifle with them. If they say "Jump!" we merely ask, "How high?"

I suppose we are being good citizens when we add things up and send in the papers with a little money. Whether we do this out of good citizenship or out of fear, you will have to decide. Perhaps it is a little of each. I only hope that the following generations continue to pay taxes so our Social Security checks continue to arrive. We are accustomed to this now. We have the habit, and would miss them. This brings up the subject of Medicare, supplemental insurance, and the vast number of mysterious letters those folks send us.

Louise and I, one or the other and sometimes both, have been to the doctor nearly every day for the last two weeks. Nothing serious or life threatening, just general maintenance. We are not alone in this because we see the same people there when we go, all about the same age, all getting patched together for a few more years on the planet. We all sit in the lobby and discuss modes of treatment, the various pills we are taking and the doctors who are attempting to repair the damage time has done to us. It's not exciting like mountain climbing or sky diving, but it is the best we have under the circumstances, and will have to do.

Frost Boils

The weather is cold and miserable; nothing new about that. But it's the fishing opener and that's the way the weather is supposed to be. Even the pelicans are shivering. We saw a few people in boats out on the lake, but they were too cold to even wave when we drove by. You really have to hate fish to want to kill them so bad that you would be out there in the northwest wind on a morning like this.

We have a frost boil in our yard that makes it hard to get out of the garage. One slip and we would never see the car again. I'm sure it's bottomless.

Makes me wonder if there aren't a lot of things we know about, things we endure in this great northern area that people in softer, gentler climates don't know about.

How would you explain a frost boil to someone from Arizona or Texas? Tell them that it is evil spirits? Or for that matter, try to explain, and then justify, lutefisk, or smelt feeds, all those things that make us Minnesotans what we are, able to endure anything and ask for more.

Maybe we don't exactly laugh in the face of adversity, but at least we can generally manage a sickly smile.

On Paying Attention

It's never too late to learn. Maybe learn is not the right word. Perhaps rediscover, or take more notice would be more accurate. What happened was I have been getting some help with this writing business, and am learning, or rediscovering, or whatever, that there is a difference between how people talk and how they write.

If this help has any effect on me, you should notice shorter sentences, fewer commas, and no, or hardly any, sentences starting with "and" or "but". And no sentence fragments. Oops, I'm backsliding already.

But about this difference between talking and writing, I'll give you an example. Suppose that Louise and I are watching television from our recliners, feet elevated, perfectly relaxed, and I click the remote to another station. Louise says, "You want to watch that." Depending how she says it, it can mean two or possibly three entirely different things. The inflection, volume, and pitch of her voice tell me what she means, not just the words. I am either supposed to go back to where we were, leave it alone at the new station, or perhaps she may just be critical of my taste in programs. I can tell exactly what is expected of me, but if she had just handed me a note, with those words on it, I would have no idea what she meant or what I should do.

I recall watching an exhibition of horsemanship at the State Fair in the Hippodrome. The riders got their horses to perform all sorts of tricks--kneeling down, prancing around using incredibly fancy footwork--and they communicated their instructions to the horses by unnoticeable movements of their hands and knees. Maybe someday Louise will not have to say anything at all.

Dear Ann

This is meant as a complaint for Ann Landers, but I suppose she will never see it, as the chances of her reading my local paper are pretty slim. Anyway, someone had written to Ann concerning the Doonesbury comic strip in the daily paper.

One of Garry Trudeau's regular characters, an elderly congresswoman, was going to resign, as she had been diagnosed with Alzheimer's. It was early enough in the course of the disease that she could recognize her limitations, so she had made her own decision to resign. A few little jokes were made about her increasing forgetfulness. This was what had upset the letter writer. This person had lost a close relative to the disease and resented any attempt to make jokes about it.

Ann agreed, and said Trudeau was off base on this. Well, I think Ann is all wet. I read this particular comic strip, and the humor was gentle, there was no meanness in it, and if one can't use a little humor to handle adversity, this is a terrible world.

I recall visiting a good friend a few days before he died. He had been receiving treatments for his cancer, and had lost most of his hair. The first thing he said when I entered the room was, "I suppose you want the name of my barber." It was not much of a joke, but it relieved the tension. It made me feel a little better, more relaxed, and I was able to talk to him with ease. I think I was even able to help him more because of this light approach to the situation.

Tears and sadness, joy and laughter are elements of this life. There has to be a balance between them. That balance may be different for different people, but as long as there is no meanness in the humor, I prefer it to grim, long-faced grief over things we can't control.

The Luddites

Remember the Ted somebody they caught out in Montana who turned out to be the Unibomber? They say he may be a Luddite, one of those people who is opposed to progress in any form. The name comes from a guy named Ned Lud, who smashed a weaving machine back in England in 1779. He was against progress because it would lower his wages. They say he was feeble minded, but nobody likes to be poor, even if you are not very bright.

Lud gathered quite a following, which goes to show that just because you are a little stupid, it doesn't mean you can't be a leader. Look at Pat Buchanan, all he has is a loud voice and one idea that he keeps beating on.

But I digress. I wanted to talk about throwing a little sand into the gears of technological advancement. This is not always a bad idea. I don't think one should bomb anybody or even bust up machinery, but there is nothing wrong about kind of hanging back a little, sticking with the old methods for a while, just to make sure that the new way isn't going to cause more pain than it delivers in progress.

I have heard of a group back in the old days known as the "Lead Pencil Luddites." They felt that the invention of the lead pencil was an OK thing, and they started to use them occasionally instead of the traditional pen and ink. This caused them to divide from the more orthodox group, but they felt that with pencils one had less to carry with you, and you could erase and correct your mistakes. Then if you wanted permanence, you could trace it over with ink.

I was comfortable when I was using a second-hand computer, a writing program copyrighted in 1985, and a dot matrix printer similar to the one Gutenberg used.

When I am convinced something newer would serve me better, I will think about changing. I hear of people with internal modems in their computer, and they hook up to the Internet, and begin surfing the world wide web, and never are heard from again. Lost in cyberspace.

The Summer Olympics

The 1996 Olympics took place in Atlanta, Georgia, the hottest place on the planet (if it is necessary for me to share this information with you). Have you ever in your natural life heard of an event that was promoted, advertised, and generally hyped up to such an extent?

Corporate sponsors are needed for these events, of course, and they are determined to get full value out of every cent that they contribute. Not give, invest is a better word.

Why should I be willing to pay more for a hamburger or a soft drink because it is in some way decorated by the intertwined circles, the symbols of the games? I think not.

Some new scientific discoveries were expected as a result of those '96 games. A new generation of performance-enhancing drugs has been discovered, things that cannot be found by the ordinary urine test, so new tests will have to be developed to find these chemicals in the blood of the contestants. New ways for athletes to kill themselves.

The Cat

It used to embarrass Louise and me when our children acted like our leaders in Washington are acting now. Remember when the entire federal government closed down? I understand that Newt had his feelings hurt, and the president was being resolute for a change, and as a result they had to close the Washington Monument and the National Parks. Social Security applications were not processed, one could not get a passport, and they could not buy gasoline to haul the next batch of new marines to the camp at Parris Island for training

I was confused. I did not understand what was going on, and I did not know what to do about it. But then I saw the cat, and was comforted.

I stopped to get a license for the car, and then went in to Delta Commodities to visit with Jan Asmus and get her assessment of things in general. She was watching the screen on her computer, watching grain and cattle being traded. On the chair next to her was a cat, staring intently at the screen. She explained that the cat belonged to some friends, and she was caring for it for a while. It was not in the best of health, not up to making it outside on its own, as most cats are expected to.

Now this cat did not understand commodity trading, but this fact did not worry it. It knew where the litter box was, and it had a warm, comfortable place to sleep, and did not worry about things that were beyond its comprehension. It did not know what I was doing; it did not know what Jan was doing, and as long as food and water were present, it could get along.

I have a warm place to sleep, food is plentiful, I do not need a passport, my Social Security application has long since been processed and I am not contemplating joining the marines, so I think I will quit worrying. Our country has survived worse.

BULLS GET MAD IN THE HEAD— COWS GET MAD IN THE FEET.

Mad Cow Disease

The panic is over now, but some time ago Europeans didn't want to eat any beef from England, as perhaps as many as six or eight people contracted a brain disease, maybe brain fever, from British beef. Six or eight people--so we condemned the beef. Still we sell cigarettes and whiskey. I suppose we all know quite a few people who have died from those things. Since I quit smoking, I am starting to have a sort of self-righteous attitude about tobacco.

It bothers me when the media gets hold of this kind of news. You remember the Alar scare, a substance that was sprayed on a small part of the apple crop some years ago. Harmless, but the *Sixty Minutes* TV news show got on it and ruined a lot of apple growers. Before that, rumors of a possible cancer-causing agent on cranberries caused a lot of trouble for that industry, with no basis in fact. Eggs were supposed to clog your arteries if you ate more than one or two a month, but now they have changed that recommendation. I'm getting to the point where I hardly believe anything any more.

But speaking of mad cows, we used to have some pretty angry cows on this farm. Occasionally we would eat one, and I suppose that accounts for a lot of my trouble.

When we went out of the cow business, Wally Feuchtenberger wanted to buy a few of our lady Charolais from us. We had been shipping them to South St. Paul, and the tame ones, the ones that were reasonable and calm, were already gone. I warned him that a few of the ones he was interested in had a bad attitude, but he said that that was no problem.

They were all mean, but I will never forget the last one to go into his trailer. We fastened a gate on the front of a tractor, and herded her in with that. She had made up her mind she was going to kill somebody, or else tear the barn down. Wally said she was a good mother, though, and healthy and athletic.

Eleven million British cows needed to be destroyed to prevent the spread of that disease. I have a possible solution. Eleven million land mines are still buried in Cambodia. Why not just turn those crazy cattle loose over there and solve both problems.

Checking Our Mail

We don't get a lot of mail. Ed McMahon and Dick Clark are the only people we hear from with any degree of regularity. And to tell the truth, I'm starting to doubt some of the stuff they tell me. Over the years, they have promised Louise and me millions of dollars. They said they would deliver the dough in person and would put us on TV, but so far we have not seen one red cent.

Oh, of course the people from Medicare send us stuff, but it's not very interesting; just says, "This is not a bill, it is an explanation of your benefits." Then a line recommending that we save these letters for our records. Now we have so many letters that we could never find the one we wanted anyway. So we have decided to throw them all away. I hope this isn't illegal.

We did get an interesting letter today. The State of Minnesota sent us a refund on our income tax, and it was just luck that we discovered it. They put the check in a kind of folder that doesn't look like a check. I suppose they are hoping that a good share of them will be thrown away and never cashed. We are retired and have time to horse around with these things, so we found the money. If we had been gainfully employed, busy people we would never have discovered it.

Which makes me wonder--if a person is elected to the Minnesota house or senate, do you have to go to St. Paul? Wouldn't they pay you if you stayed home, just called in once in a while to see how things are going, and vote over the phone? This Internet business should let you do everything at home that you could do in the cities. If I was a little smarter and had a modem, maybe I could run for office.

We hear from *Reader's Digest* and Publishers Clearinghouse regularly, but we have given up on any chance of winning anything and have quit wasting our stamps. Besides, the entries are getting too complicated to fill out. They ask you to "put this stamp here, scrape this off and see if the numbers match, read the rest of this letter for the secret clue." Too much work.

When I send a letter, it costs me thirty-three cents. I can live with that, but a lot of the people who send us mail seem to have made a deal with the post office. Like today, we got two letters from Sears. Up where a stamp is supposed to go, it said, "Bulk rate U.S. postage paid." I'll bet it didn't cost them thirty-three cents.

One Sears letter was addressed to Louise, the other to me. I wondered why they didn't put them in the same envelope. Louise opened hers, and it was a pre-approved line of credit for $2520. We discussed the odd number, wondered why the extra twenty bucks, and I handed her my envelope. Mine was the same deal, except my line of credit was for $3570.

She gave me a rather cold look, and left to play cards at the senior citizens center. Now, why should I be blamed for something that Sears does? Is she going to let a lousy $1050 extra credit come between us? After all these years?

Renewing Old Acquaintances

For some reason I was unable to take my customary nap one Sunday afternoon, so was thumbing through an alumni publication from my old school. I came across a phone number for a friend, a former roommate in the days when I was young and carefree.

I let my fingers do the walking, dialed the number, and then began to worry as I heard the phone ringing. I have had no contact with these people for about 35 years. Even if they are alive and rational, what in the world will we have to talk about, especially while I pay the phone bill? Before I could hang up, Beverly answered, and I identified myself. Darned if she didn't remember who I was and called her husband, my old roommate, to the other phone.

It was fun. We trashed the reputations of some mutual acquaintances, found out that neither of us had any children in prison, and that we all are in moderately good health. They were both working, not any harder than they wanted to, and sometimes traveled through this area to see children and may stop. I hope they do, and stay with us, because they live in Minot, North Dakota, and Louise and I would really like to have a place to stay if we ever get up the courage to go to that giant Norwegian and Swede convention they have there yearly. Motels are hard to come by when the Norse are swarming.

If this scheme of mine works out, it will be well worth a four-dollar phone call.

Taking the Heat

The misery index, that combination of high temperature and wet, steamy humidity that makes fat people like me uncomfortable, was at a ten-year high yesterday, according to the weatherman. I believe him. Went on a tour looking at various kinds of trees in the morning, stood around in the red-hot sun and listened to experts tell us what we were seeing

In the evening, went to a play at the Theatre L'Homme Dieu north of Alexandria. I remember living before air conditioning, but have no idea how we did it. The usher gave us each a fan before we went into the place, and the whole audience used them with vigor during the performance.

The play was *The Miracle Worker*, about Helen Keller's childhood with Annie Sullivan, the young girl who taught her to communicate with sign language. Louise and I were less than enthusiastic about seeing that particular play. I figured it was some of that uplifting crap that doesn't seem to work on me anymore--especially in this kind of weather. Being away from our air conditioner at times like this makes us homesick, an attitude shared by the couple who was with us.

We had advance tickets, so what can one do? We decided we would go to the play, and when the misery index approached an unacceptable level, we would quietly leave and go home.

Well, we stayed right to the end. We sweated, we fanned, we stuck to the seats and finally left, soaked with sweat but thinking about something besides our own comfort.

I've read about Helen Keller, but had never seen the play. I suppose everyone in the whole world has seen it except me. The performance by Ruth Christianson, the little girl who played Keller, and Ninoska Meyer, who played Sullivan, really brought the story home to me. If it was hot for us, I can imagine how it must have been for them in their 1890s costumes, having to exert considerable physical activity to do their parts.

A little humor and a happy ending for a bad situation are just what I like.

Art in the Hinterlands

This morning Louise and I stopped for coffee at Hardee's. We were waiting for our stuff at the counter when a lady drove up to the window that people in a hurry use. I noticed she had a lipstick in one hand, a hairbrush in the other, and a cellular phone stuck between her neck and shoulder so she could talk to someone while waiting for her order. My time has never been that valuable.

As everyone who knows me is aware, I am old and unemployable, so must serve on committees no one else wants to be on, and go to meetings that no one else wants to attend. So that is now my life. I mow my lawn, drink coffee, play a little cards, and go to meetings when called.

It is not all bad. The other night Ray Strand asked me to come to the Morris library and meet with a few people for some vague purpose, and I, of course, went. Mark Michaels, a student from the university was there, among others, and he showed us what he has been doing in the last few months. He had contacted about forty of the one hundred fifty visual artists (by his estimate) in Stevens and Pope Counties, and had pictures of the work and a little history of about twenty of them in a loose-leaf notebook he had prepared.

I know a lot of these people, and had no idea that they could do this--create things that I would like. Lots of painting, carving, weaving and ceramics, and I thought all that stuff was done in the cities.

The purpose of the meeting was, I gather, to find some way that more people can find out, like I did, the quality and quantity of things being made out here in the hinterlands. Just think, wouldn't it be nice if you could take down those plastic butterflies and artificial flowers you have hanging on your wall, and put up a picture that one of your neighbors painted?

Why should the products of these talented people be kept such a secret? I think the news should be out. Let's tell everyone.

Mountain Climbing

I don't get out of the county much. Everything I find out I either read about, hear it on the radio or television, or hear from somebody that gets around more than I do. I am a little naive, so I suppose I am sometimes misled when I have to take other people's word for things I don't see for myself.

We got to talking about mountain climbing, and how some people out here in the flatland are practicing on bridges and places like that, anywhere they can find a rock wall rough enough to get a grip on it and climb.

Dave Jungst tells me of one constructed just for that purpose down in the cities. But in Montana he says there is one built like a big motor-driven belt that goes down as you climb up. The hand and foot holds are movable so the degree of difficulty can be adjusted, and you can climb all day and never be more than a foot above the ground. Good for people who get dizzy. Isn't science wonderful? And I thought my exercise bike was the state of the art when it comes to getting exercise without going anyplace.

But climbing rocks isn't the main thing on my mind today. On the news from the Alexandria television station I hear this guy say that bread is going to get more expensive now because we are not going to let the Canadians sell their wheat in this country anymore.

Wheat might go up as much as fifty cents a bushel, he says, which would put the bread price out of reach of the average person. Boy, this statement is even more ridiculous than an automatic rock-climbing machine. When did the price of wheat have anything much to do with the price of bread? Why do people say things like this? I'm pretty sure the wrapper costs more than the flour.

Some Favorite Adages

These old sayings that people quote when they can't think of anything original really come in handy sometimes. Especially as one gets older and the brain slows down and you get so you don't much care what people think of you anyway. I remember one my grandfather used to say in connection with helping out a family member: "Nothing is lost that just runs from the nose to the mouth." Neither my mother or Louise appreciated that statement, but it has an element of truth in it.

Another saying I appreciate more as I grow older is one I heard to the effect that "A pessimist is an optimist who knows all the facts."

Mark Twain, when discussing human nature, said that if you took in a stray dog, fed him, gave him shelter and made him prosperous, he would not bite you. That, he said, is the difference between dogs and people. I don't know what it is in us that makes us that way, but I must acknowledge that it is in all of us.

We can be grateful for only a short time, and then we begin to resent our leaders, make fun of them, and Lord only knows we have shot a good number of our presidents, governors and other leaders. Maybe it's because they don't make us prosperous enough. Anyway I thought that was a nice statement on Mark Twain's part, a little too long for a bumper sticker, but accurate nevertheless.

Winter is Coming

One of the surest signs that winter will soon be upon us is the view from our bathroom window. When the leaves are no longer on the trees around the lake, we can see Erland's yard light from there. I realize it is bound to happen, but I still am disappointed when I go to the can in the middle of the night, look out the window, and realize that summer is history.

We are more or less ready for winter though. The new furnace is in and running, I have checked antifreeze in a couple of things and made arrangements for the final resting place for our machine shed that collapsed last winter. When its remains are buried, the place where it stood will be available to pile more snow and last winter we ran out of places for that.

Another sign is the renewed activity of the people who are planning on spending the winter months in the south. On the way to Hancock I see that Erv Reed has a hitch leaning against the back of his motor home, preparing to pull more of his stuff with him when they head south.

I guess that may be the reason we never got into the habit of spending time in warmer places. In order to go, you have to make a lot of decisions. You have to decide what to take along and what to leave behind, and how to care for the stuff in both categories. If we just stay here it eliminates a lot of planning and decision making, a thing we were never good at.

If we stay here, we get to see the harvest being completed and still not have to be very involved in it. Years ago I picked corn two rows at a time. If the corn was good, I could sometimes fill a fifteen-hundred-bushel crib in a day. Now with these outfits taking eight, ten, or maybe twelve rows at a time and the corn yielding much better, that would take just a few minutes. I am obsolete.

We didn't get to this stage of development in just one step, however. A friend told me about helping a neighbor pick corn when he was young, back in the early fifties.

The corn was dry, and the guy had it contracted at the elevator in town. So they set up the corn sheller on the end of the field and he hauled the loads to the sheller and dumped them into the drag. Another guy with two trucks hauled the stuff to town.

At first this went fine. They had those crank hoists on the wagons, and a self-starter on the tractor, so this was all state-of-the-art equipment for that time. But then, as the day went along, the cob pile grew so high that he would have to take time to shovel cobs away from the machine, and the corn would pile up in the trucks and need to be leveled out, so his activity became more and more frantic.

It got quite late, but the guy on the picker wanted to finish, and promised that they would all go to town for supper when they were done. This would be a big treat, something that he didn't want to miss. When they finally finished it was dark, but he went home, cleaned up and rode along into town.

As was the custom, they had to have a beer or two before eating. At his age and in his exhausted state, this was too much for him. He went to sleep in the car and didn't get his town supper.

Tough on Cars

This last year has been hard on our car fleet. We have, for the most part, old vehicles. In order to have one always available and running, we have to have several. This last winter the machine shed collapsed on one. Early this winter Louise hit a snow bank and then the ditch, resulting in another car biting the dust. It had well over two hundred thousand miles on it, so it may have committed suicide. It had seemed depressed lately. We have an ancient Datsun stored away that runs fairly well, but it is so rusty that we might fall through the floorboards. It is not what you would call classy transportation.

I am having trouble adjusting to today's prices. For some time now I have been shopping for a pickup. I have looked and looked, and am amazed at what they are asking for them. If they are fairly new and in reasonably good condition, they cost at least an arm and a leg. I can see possibly spending that kind of money for a life saving medical procedure or maybe a good education that would lead to a lifetime career, but for a pickup, they should get real. If there was a pickup shortage, I could understand, but wherever I go there are pickups for sale, all for more money than I am willing to part with.

I finally did buy one. It was the cheapest one I found, and it suits me. It is carrying quite a bit of age; it has traveled many, many miles and possesses a few hitches in its get-a-long. It should serve me, however, as I do not go far and never very fast. All I have to do now is get accustomed to it and remember what it looks like, so that I can find where I have parked it and do not get into someone else's vehicle. Life is a constant learning experience.

How Brains Work

I don't think anybody really knows how the human brain works. Oh, they come with a lot of explanations, they use a lot of big words, and once in a while they can even fix something in somebody's head that has quit working. That doesn't really mean anything though, because I have fooled around with stuff I didn't understand and got it to work. Don't know what I did, but I fixed it.

For instance, a few of us were seated around a table in the café having our usual coffee and conversation when another person walks by. One of the people at the table says "Hello" and gives the person's first name. Someone asks, "What was that person's last name?" and no one can think of it. Someone comes up with where the person works, another with the name of the spouse, another with where the person lives. What in the world is happening in these people's brains when this is going on? What kind of a little thing is roaming around in their heads, looking under stuff, digging through all sorts of memories? Everybody knows, we just can't think of it. Suddenly the answer comes, and we all feel a little foolish.

I thought at one time that this was a sign of old age, but sometimes the young can't come up with needed information either. They have had less of life's experiences though, and excuse themselves. They pretend that they never did know, weren't there when it happened or never heard about it before, and therefore can't be expected to know. This doesn't work for us old folks as we have experienced it all, heard it all, and are expected to know it all. We do, of course. We just can't remember offhand. But wait, it will come to us.

We were at our granddaughter's band performance last night. The violins were playing and doing, I thought, quite well when Louise asked me for my pencil. She wrote industriously for a minute of so on her program and then handed it to me. It was quite dark in the auditorium; the pencil writing didn't show up real well on the blue program, so I held it over in the aisle to read it. She had written, "We have to tell our kids about death benefits and funeral expenses if we are killed in a car accident. That's any car. It's in our policy."

Now, what caused that? Violin music, the tune that was being played, what? I couldn't control myself, I started to laugh and nearly fell out of my seat. I hope the kids playing didn't see me.

Good Old Formerly

Louise and I are only slightly saddened that we were unable to attend either of the concerts given by the Artist Formerly Known As Prince. He was at the Fargo Dome, followed by two nights at the Metrodome, and we missed the whole thing. I am not really sure what he does, but judging from the little promotional things I see on television, he dances around and sings.

He is the "Minnesota nice" version of the guy who walks backward while holding onto his crotch. Before he was Prince, I believe his name was Nelson, so his Norwegian fraction may account for some of the nice. This other guy has a normal name, however (I believe it's Jackson). Formerly is married, has children and is really quite respectable. Both these gentlemen are incredibly light on their feet. I have never heard either of them sing.

Formerly has a fixation with the color purple and an odd shaped guitar, and this shape, he says, is now his name. This is unusual, but he is doing well financially, and I would not hesitate to take a check signed with his peculiar mark. I think it is remarkable that anyone can get so popular that people will wait for hours for the chance to buy tickets to one of their performances.

An Elvis fixation I can almost, if not quite, understand. I am kind of fond of his music, and can see how a person who really likes Elvis could be carried away emotionally if in the company of a big bunch of others who shared this fascination. In fact, Elvis is so famous that my computer's spell checker knows how his name should be spelled. Now that's fame. Of course we all know what Elvis did, but I am not exactly sure what these other two gentlemen do.

I read someplace that one can judge a civilization by looking at its heroes. I don't know how this applies in these cases, however. Lots of people go to their performances and buy stuff that has their names on it. But if something should happen that the fans don't like, these same admirers are ready to do terrible things to them.

My List

Being with people that one loves,
Blue and sunny skies above,
Finding something you thought missing,
Seeing young folks busy kissing,
Watching old folks acting sappy,
These are things that make me happy.

Dogs that bark for no good reason,
People hunting out of season,
Approaching cars that do not dim,
Those exercises to make one slim,
Food that tends to constipate,
These are things I really hate.

Mystic Lake

I dreamt I was an Indian,
And worked at Mystic Lake.
Dealt blackjack 40 hours a week
And seldom took a break.

My bank account was growing
For our profits were alarming.
Another twenty years like this,
I'd be able to start farming.

Half a million bucks a year
Sounds like a lot of dough.
But think of what we Indians owned
Two hundred years ago.

Stuff

Louise and I took a trip to Wisconsin to see our daughter and son in law this last weekend. We have made the trip often enough so the route has become less than interesting, and while driving, I am forced to entertain myself. Louise is no help. When the route becomes dull, she goes to sleep or reads. I suppose if I had a more scintillating personality she might stay awake, but such is not the case. Nothing good was on the radio, so I began to study the only thing that was different, that constantly changes, the approaching traffic.

Trailers, campers and motorhomes are getting a lot more popular. And so big that I wouldn't be surprised if some of those bigger ones have basements in them. A lot of them have boats on trailers behind them, and some are pulling smaller cars on two-wheeled trailers or have motorcycles or bicycles strapped to the back or on top. Then I saw one approaching, big enough to hold church services in, and it was pulling a four-door Chevrolet Suburban, four-wheel drive, with a custom paint job that alone would cost as much as a beach front villa on the Mediterranean.

I think it all boils down to the fact that people want their stuff with them. They have worked for it, and they want it along, if not to use, to either show off or protect it. Now this is either overweening pride or else distrust of one's fellow man. These people take everything they value with them when they travel, kind of like the '49ers in their wagon train, heading for California.

Another thing I noticed--if a boat isn't moving, it's for sale. We passed signs for about twenty garage and yard sales in the 230 miles, and at least 10 times that many boats for sale along the road.

I like to travel light. I plan on coming home again, so I leave my stuff, for the most part, there. I have trouble figuring why these people must take it all along. A change of clothes, a tooth brush, a coat in case the weather could changes, and a credit card for the motel, if you can't bum a nights lodging from friends or relatives. Even a lot of the motorcycle people, the traditional light travelers, are pulling trailers now. As they acquire more, they find a need to take it with them.

Getting Dry

Science and modern technology have finally come up with an answer to a problem I have had for most of my life. I retain water. Not just inside me, but on the outside also.

I never noticed the inside water until I had my heart attack, and then the doctor prescribed a pill that would handle that problem. This pill causes other problems of course, but then that is neither here nor there, so we will not talk about that at this time.

But about this outside moisture. I had noticed for years that other folks could get dry after a bath quicker and with less effort than I. As a youngster, after football or basketball practice, we would emerge from the shower. Others would shake themselves a few times, wave a towel around themselves a little, and be dry. Not only that, but their towels would still be only a trifle damp. My towel, on the other hand, would be soaked and the water would still be running off me.

I admit to being hairier than most, but I have seen men still hairier who could dry themselves quickly. I have come to the conclusion that my flesh actually absorbs water. I noticed that when I went swimming, I would seem much heavier when I got out of the lake than when I went in. I suppose if I had stayed in there long enough, I would not have been able to get out at all.

Louise purchased some large, thick towels, but they do not seem to help. In fact, they do not fit into the various orifices in my body well enough to work as well as the old fashioned thinner towels.

The problem has been solved now. We bought a new furnace. It is one of the new highly efficient ones that get a larger percentage of the heat out of the fuel that it burns. One of the ways that it does this is that it blows a great deal more air out of the outlets at a lower temperature than the old one. In fact it blows so much air that I can get out of the bathtub now and stand over the register in the upstairs hall. It acts just like one of those electric hand dryers one sees in public rest rooms. The furnace runs a lot in this cold weather, so I generally only have to wait a little while before it starts up with this tremendous blast of air, and in just a little while I am dry as can be.

Some of the newer car washes have a deal like this. After the car has been soaked, soaped, scrubbed and waxed you drive ahead a little and a huge fan blows down on your auto to get it fairly dry. I wouldn't be surprised if someday most bathrooms will be provided with a device like this.

Haircuts

For many years I had what I believe is called a crew haircut. It was real short, so it stood up on top of my head. It was easy to clean, required no combing--it was what you could call a minimum maintenance haircut. It had one disadvantage. If you were out in the sun without a hat, you could get sunburned, but this didn't happen too often, and I liked my crewcut. Not everyone liked it, but I didn't care. I felt it suited me.

Then I got married. Louise pointed out that I had lumps on my head that showed, and more hair would cover them up. Of course, she said, if I wanted to look stupid, it was all right with her. Anyway, for some reason, I ended up with longer hair, and haircuts started to take on more importance. More hair makes more chance for variability.

The old timers here in Hancock are slowly getting used to each other again. We recognize each other, that is no problem, it is just that we all look just a little different than we did when Harold Austin was our barber. Now we have a new barber, with a slightly different technique, and we all look a little different. Not worse, not better, just different.

Snowflakes, fingerprints, and haircuts are all different, and haircuts are different because barbers are different. I have no idea why snowflakes and fingerprints have to be different.

So, until they make a machine like a giant pencil sharpener that you put your head in and someone turns the crank, haircuts will not be identical.

I have seen some people instruct the barber on how they want the haircut to proceed. They try to tell the barber his or her job. It may make them feel better, but it is a waste of time. Sit down, shut up, and take what you get. In a week or so no one will know the difference.

Having Faith

It's all right to have faith in someone that you've been with for years. In fact I guess you should, but I have decided that you still have to use a little common sense. For years I have had the habit of driving up to a stop sign, looking to my left while Louise in the other seat looks to the right. If she says, "Nothing coming," I drive on through. Now, however I am going to carefully check the situation out myself after what happened in church last Sunday.

We were seated in our usual place and the organist was just getting organized when Louise poked me. "Go light the candles" she said, "No one lit them last Wednesday at Lenten services and now they must have forgotten again today." Like a good husband, I lurched to my feet and went back into the office to get the instrument one uses to light candles. I thought it strange, as I could smell burned matches back there, but I lit the tool anyway and went out to do my duty.

As I approached the altar, I saw that the candles were lit, just burning kind of low, as they were low on fuel. (These are fake candles that run on kerosene or something.) I put the tool away and quickly slunk back to my seat.

It was a little embarrassing, but I can handle that. A car crashing into us from the right is another matter, however. Louise is scheduled to get new glasses in a couple of weeks, and that should help, but I think I will still check both ways for oncoming traffic.

Learning Life's Lessons

I never seem to learn. You would think that after over forty years of wedded bliss one would start to understand what is appropriate to say or not to say under all circumstances.

What brings this to mind are the events that took place this Monday. The weather was nasty; it snowed a little and blew a lot. The roads were icy in the morning and I had a meeting in Glenwood. Louise took her car and went to Hancock.

I came home from the meeting a little after noon and Louise's car was not in the garage, but I could hear the television going in the other room. I hollered at her, and asked, "What happened to the car?" Big mistake.

Louise was sitting in her recliner growing black and blue spots from running in the ditch and nearly tipping the car over, and this was the wrong, completely wrong, question. Thinking back, if I had said, "Where is the car?" I might have gotten by.

"How are you, are you all right?" would have been the best, but of course hindsight is always accurate.

Anyway, she got the impression that I was more concerned about the car than I was with her. I wasn't, of course, because the car had over two hundred thousand miles on it and had recently developed a new hitch in it's get-a-long. In all likelihood the poor old thing was sick of it all, and decided to commit suicide. Things are better around here now, but I was in the doghouse for most of a week.

It's a little like a friend of mine, who told me his wife was having some foot trouble and went to the doctor. The doc suggested she see the surgeon about fixing the problem, but the surgeon said an operation was not necessary. He advised, "Just buy bigger shoes and you will be fine."

The lady was pretty pleased with this diagnosis, but my friend had some second thoughts. She went to the store and bought three pairs of shoes at about eighty bucks a pop, and he has a feeling she is not done with her shopping yet. This is an out-of-pocket cost, while Medicare would probably have paid for the surgery. He is careful about what he says to her, of course, but then he has been married even longer than I have.

New Things

I shouldn't believe everything I read. It seems that I read something and it seems a little far-fetched, but then I start to think that maybe it's possible. Surely they wouldn't put it in the paper if it weren't a fact. Then I remember that a lot of my stuff gets printed in the paper, and I would be hard pressed to prove some of it. So you can see how it works--how it makes me wonder.

Lately I've been reading about some scientists who are studying about how people learn things. They hooked up the test people to machines that measured electrical impulses in the brain, and some way or other measured how much blood flowed to various parts of the brain while these test subjects were learning stuff. The scientists came to the conclusion that you could only learn one thing every six hours. If you crowded things together too much, nothing was gained. You just stayed dumb.

Now let's see. I'm a little over 70 years old. About a third of that time I was asleep, or doing something that would absolutely eliminate the possibility of learning anything, That leaves me with 560 of those 840 months that I could have been learning stuff. That's 16800 days, times 24; that's 403,200 hours; divided by 6 would be 67,200 things I should know how to do.

They were talking about acquired skills. Pitching hay in an artistic and joyful manner should qualify. I wonder if shocking barley would be an acquired skill. I had an uncle who could belch "The Star Spangled Banner". Did he have to practice more than six hours before he was ready to do this before an audience? I suppose I'll have to try to add up how many acquired skills I have, and figure out just how much of my life has been wasted.

Unmodern Math

Louise and I received our education, such as it was, before the invention of the pocket calculator. When we had something to figure out that we could not do in our heads, we had the option of either asking someone for the answer or taking a piece of paper and pencil and figuring it out.

I worked for the government for a few years, and our outfit had to do quite a few primitive calculations concerning the amount of water and mud that could be expected to fill the various dams that were being built out west. I had learned to use a slide rule and in the office we had some very slow, expensive and untrustworthy electric calculators that were continually either lying to us or breaking down. They cost about as much as a new car did at that time, and were nearly as large. Anyway, we had to depend on our heads a lot to come up with the right answer.

I thought about this when our granddaughter was here doing her arithmetic. It is not too often we are asked things like what $1/2 + 7/8 - 1/4 \times 3/16$ equals, but it happened last night. Answering questions like this is something that lends itself only partly to the pocket calculator. Paper and pencil and a little thought are required, but once you get into it, it is almost as much fun as playing cards.

We concentrated on teaching her our method, which is not new math by any means. It seemed to fit in with what she was learning in school, so I honestly think she benefited to some extent and Louise and I had the opportunity to enjoy a valuable refresher course.

Per Diem

I'm going to get per diem today. In my career as a retired person I have had, and continue to have, many jobs. This, however, is the one I get paid for doing. I don't get paid much, about enough to pay for the wear and tear on my socks and underwear. But then I don't have to do much either, just show up and speak up when no one else is talking. Some folks have told me that I'm getting more than I am worth, and that may be, but I don't care.

I attended these kinds of meetings even when I was still farming, but not quite so frequently. Now, however, I have no excuse, so I go when asked, and that is with monotonous regularity. I put all these jobs in the same category, whether it is on a city council, a township board, school board, anything like that. They all function pretty much the same.

I have made some observations on the people who attend these meetings and what they do when they get there. They are generally people with gray or missing hair, mostly male, elderly and underoccupied. They are patient folks for the most part, and have iron butts so they can stay seated for long periods of time with only a minimum of discomfort.

While some have deep interests in what is going on, others may have only an interest that comes and goes, according to the subject that is under discussion. Some, of course, are interested only in the free lunch, a ride to a different town, and a visit with a few old friends. It is not for me to say just what category I am in, as that may vary from time to time.

I recall once several years ago, at a meeting in Marshall, Minnesota, one old guy got carried away with a report he was giving and went into far too much detail. Some left the meeting for other places. Three in my group went for a cup of coffee, then went to their rooms for a nice long nap before returning to the assembly hall. The old guy was still at it, and at least half the audience was sound asleep. I'm not sure if this was the time that another old timer slept so soundly that he fell from his chair.

Be that as it may, not everyone goes to sleep, and an occasional good idea emerges from these people. When lots of people are involved, interest is stimulated and the system seems to work. About the time I decide that I have wasted another couple of hours, something good happens, something that might not have happened if our system were not in place.

Minutes of My Meetings

I go to meetings, some good, some not so good, and find myself taking my own minutes. Some examples:

Area II Executive Committee

Now the meeting's ending, and my leg has gone to sleep.
We talked about our spending, then made the mental leap
And spoke of moral issues, whether we need a code
To keep us fair and honest. Then we hit the road.

Area II General Meeting (A long one)

In nineteen hundred fifty-two
They came to us, out of the blue,
A set of bylaws, tried and true,

To guide us, and to see us through
The problems we'll encounter.

But now some things are causing pain,
The money shortage makes us strain
And some units sing that sad refrain,
"Your spending habits are insane
And we'll not pay our dues."

Jamie Whitten quit as head of Ag Appropriations,
It is said. He got us money from the Fed
In past--but now that source is dead.
What shall we do?

We study graphs and charts and maps,
We're tired, but we take no naps.
How much longer must elapse
Before we have our lunch?

The first choice motivational speaker couldn't make it.

I see this next gentleman taking the floor
And I'm thankful that I'm not very easy to bore,
But my head starts to nod, and my eyes start to blink.
He'll never get done, I'm beginning to think.

The stuff he is saying he told us last year,
So his speech should be better, his points really clear.
But I'm just as confused; I'm filled with self doubts.
Is mine the only mind wandering about?
But no, I see other eyes starting to close;
The hands on the wall clock seem to be froze.

Will this never end? Will I never be free?
Think I'll go to the can and have me a pee.
It might clear up my head, and if I don't hurry,
I'll be wide awake and won't have to worry
About falling asleep, and I can go home.
With any luck I will finish my poem.

What Do Names Mean?

It's funny about names. Most of them are words that don't really mean anything, but we are so used to them that we associate the word with the object, or the place, or the person. Now, we live near Hancock. I guess the town was named after some guy that had something to do with the railroad. But where did he get the name in the first place? What's a Hancock?

There are a lot of Smiths, Carpenters, Bakers, names like that, and maybe way back they had an ancestor that had one of those occupations, but how did they name the occupation in the first place?

82

My great grandfather on my father's side came from Norway. His name was Rasmus Larson Woxland. His son, my grandfather, was named Lars Rasmusson. The old guy was not just trying to be cute; they did things like that back in those days.

Lars was born in Norway, and as near as I can tell, the kids in the family born in the old country went by Rasmusson and the ones born here went by Vaagsland. Confusing. When we went to a family reunion one time down by Kenyon, Minnesota we met a big bunch of relatives who spelled the name Voxland, Waxland, and a couple of other variations that I don't recall. Some said that differences in the alphabets accounted for a part of the variations. And then maybe some of them couldn't spell. I think that Woxland was a place, so that makes a little sense. If you are going to discover who was related to whom in the old country, you really have to study the records.

We have a lot of new occupations now. As we have a lot more people, maybe we could use some of those new jobs to name some of these new people.

I know a family whose name, short and easy to pronounce and spell, does not indicate that they truly are of Norwegian ancestry. Then I found out why. I will not mention the name, to avoid embarrassing them. The old fellow homesteaded in North Dakota someplace, and in the process of cleaning up his property started a prairie fire that burned out a good part of the state. He moved quickly and quietly, and adopted the new name for safety reasons.

Mother Nature

I'm starting to think that Mother Nature is a lot more flexible than people think. I may have mentioned our wood ducks. While they may prefer hollow trees, they have no reservations about using a man-made house nailed to a tree if the hole is the right size and it is close enough to water. A friend tells me he saw a mallard raising a family in a hole in a tree. He just got new glasses, so I believe him. That's real flexibility.

I heard a biologist lecture once on the need for little water ponds in the fields, the kind that drive farmers to distraction. He said that we should not drain them, because if a pair of mallards is going to establish a meaningful relationship, they need a private place like that. Then, after the ceremony, they will take up housekeeping in a clump of grass somewhere and raise a family. Well, that may be the preferred method, but they are capable of doing things differently if they have to. I have seen them in Long Lake, an 800-acre body of water, not a bit embarrassed by the fact they were right out in public doing what comes naturally. In fact, as I write this, a pair of mourning doves is standing on the railing around the deck outside my window. The way they are rubbing their necks together and making funny noises would make me think that they are planning on a family, and that is about as artificial an environment as I can imagine.

We have a few pheasants around now, not many, but better than it has been for many years. When I was young, pheasants used to roost in trees. That way they were safe from many predators. Only raccoons and kids with flashlights and .22 rifles could get them. And we didn't have very many raccoons.

The weather change, starting with the November 11th, 1940 blizzard put pheasants on the endangered list. But they were never a native bird anyway. In my life I have seen only one prairie chicken on this farm. I seem to remember it was in 1938, shot by a city hunter who was camping on the lakeshore.

Coyotes, pelicans, deer, even leopard frogs were not around here when I was a kid. But a muskrat hide was worth about a day's wages and a mink was worth about a month's wages. Hard to figure.

Computer Complaints

I imagine you have heard me complain about computers before--that is, if you have been paying attention. The first one we had was very basic. We got used to it. It could do a few primitive things, but we got along.

Then we got a hard drive. It was a learning experience, which is not always pleasant for old Norwegians. But there were advantages. Then we got one that could do everything; at least that is what we were told. And if it didn't, it was our fault. The first job of a computer salesperson is to convince you that you are smart, and after they cash your check, demonstrate how stupid you really are, all without getting you angry. It takes a certain talent; not everyone can do this.

Call that first machine learning to walk. Most people do that at an early age without much trouble. The second computer could be compared to learning to do the two-step. Not an impossible feat for most folks, if the band is playing an appropriate tune.

Now with this new machine they are trying to make me do the ballet on a tight rope, and it's not working out too well.

Life Is Improving

It's remarkable how things have changed since I was young. I suppose that when a new thing appears and you get accustomed to it, and then something else comes along, you don't realize how many changes you have seen until you begin to add them all up.

Take dip, for instance. You know, the stuff you put on potato chips. It first appeared in my life about 1953, if I remember correctly, and of course that was here in a provincial backwater, so it may have surfaced in more sophisticated places before that. I think it was some people in Cyrus that fed me my first dip. I have never thought of Cyrus as an especially progressive place, but then I may be wrong.

Now you must realize that even electricity, at least here on the farm, was a relatively new thing to me. I was born and raised in the kerosene lamp era. I had adjusted to electric lights pretty well, though, by the time I was married.

This was about the time we got our first television. I was aware of it for a few years before this, had even watched it while staying at the YMCA in St. Paul. The picture was tiny and about a hundred fellows were crowded around the machine watching it with me, so it didn't impress me a whole lot at that time.

The equipment has improved a lot since then, but now the programs are composed mainly of car chases and explosions, and ads for machines to improve your abs, whatever abs are. I see these people on the ads, with their puny, wrinkled bellies, and I suppose this is the before example. When they are finished with the machine they will have nice, round smooth stomachs like I have.

By the early fifties women began wearing slacks to church, especially in the winter. Lightning did not strike them dead, so they have continued with that sensible practice.

Computers are new to my generation. Ours replaces a typewriter, which I needed, as my handwriting is illegible, even to me. It sometimes keeps books for us. For younger, more knowledgeable people, it will do many other exotic things, but for Louise and me, it will not.

I suppose belted tires and heart transplants, things like that, are important too, but those are things you don't just take for granted. It's this other stuff, like onion dip and computers, that sneak up on you.

New Year's Eve

In a few hours it will be another New Year. I thought about that this morning as I was waking up. And then I thought about how the guarantee on my car battery is one day closer to expiring, and the softener probably needs salt, and how I did not win the powerball last night, and that I am one day older, and all my parts are one day older, and thus closer to complete failure, and I wonder what is going to go next. I remember that I now know more dead people than I do live ones.

Then I go downstairs and turn on television, and there is an infomercial (did I spell this right?) on, and this guy tells his audience about this wonderful product. They all clap and cheer, and I wonder what would make people act like that. I realize that I am paying someone to send me this crap over the airways, so I turn it off and notice that the barometer must be dropping, as I can smell sewer gas from the vent by the washing machine. That must mean a storm is coming.

I hate to admit it, but I may need a hug. I am not a hugging person, I am Norwegian, and we do not hug each other; we make it a rule not to touch.

New Year's Day

It is bright out today, and while we can not actually see the sun, we are at least sure of its existence. The car started, there was salt in the softener, and had a phone call from the daughter. All is well, and the youngest son loaned me an electric implement to remove the hair from my nostrils. The sewer no longer smells, and it's a much better day.

Perhaps this malaise is brought on by darkness, combined with the need for a particular vitamin. Whatever it is, it was nearly cured by a good nightmare I had last night. You may ask, how can a nightmare be good? Well, let me explain. I dreamed that the silo was empty, the manure spreader was broken, it was 30 below, and the tractor wouldn't start. Then I woke up and remembered that I no longer have cattle. What a relief.

Palm Sunday

The old come early to church,
And I am one of the first.
I watch as the altar cloths are changed
To red for the season.
It will be stripped bare
Before Good Friday.

How long? Forty, fifty years,
This has been my place here,
Since this church was built,
And before that, in the old one,
Since I was born.

Over there, I know who will sit
There, and there, and there.
That, and something else
Comforts me. It warms me
And gives me peace.

Some ask me why I need this,
And I don't know.
But I say something.
I use words I have heard
For I can't explain the mystery,
That I have learned to accept.

Nose Hair and Baseball

A couple of things have been bothering me lately: nose hair and people getting paid for doing fun things and then not appreciating it.

The baseball players come to mind right away for the latter, of course. It was fun for them when they first started, and then when they started to get money for doing it, it became work, and they wanted more money.

But closer to home, we have snowplow operators. I have a little four-wheel drive with a blade in front. To drive it down the driveway and see the snow fly out of the way gives me a great deal of pleasure and satisfaction. So I can imagine how it must feel to operate one of the really big ones, seeing the snow fly way across the fields as you sit high, warm and secure in that powerful machine.

To be able to throw up huge drifts of snow across someone's driveway in town, or surround an illegally parked car with enough snow to immobilize it till summer, should give a person the chance to get rid of a lot of hostility and give others a lot of healthful exercise with a shovel.

I mentioned nose hair. I don't mean the kind that comes with age and grows on the outside of the nose; I mean the kind that grows in the nose. It has me confused. It must serve some purpose; we all have it. It's probably needed to filter and warm the air we breathe. But if that is the case, why does there seem to be a policy to discourage it? Style seems to have dictated that it is so unattractive that it must be eliminated completely. Just watch the people on television. When they lean their heads back, one can see way up into their sinuses.

Oatmeal

I have been an oatmeal person for most of my life. Oh, I like bacon and eggs. They are certainly fine for someone with a more active life style than mine, but with all the publicity that the low-fat diet is getting, and having had a heart attack, cereal in the morning seems like a good option for me.

The thing that really firms up my decision to eat oatmeal instead of flakes is the price of other stuff appropriate for breakfast. Most of it comes in boxes with pictures of famous people on the outside. For a couple of bucks I think you could buy enough oatmeal to feed Stevens County. But these flake people think they can take a couple cents worth of grain, process it, add some vitamins we don't need, put it in a box, (the most expensive part of the unit) and then charge more per pound for it than T-bone steak.

I've been watching the Special K ad that the Kellogg Company has been running on television lately, and I think I can see why they think they can charge so much for the stuff. They make a big fuss about the fact that it contains no fat, and then they show you the results of its use. You've probably seen the ad--it features a young lady wearing either a very tight Spandex suit or else an equally tight leather pants posing in different ways while admiring her butt in a mirror.

Louise tells me it is the same girl in both ads, but to tell the truth I've never noticed her face.

Thoughts on Aging

As most trees get older, they get strong and tall.
Ever more handsome,
Rising high above the stones around them.
Until we bring them down with ax and saw,
And build with them. They live with dignity.

Oh, fire, insects, sickness, may take its life,
But that is the exception. Life's a quiet thing, for trees,
Cold and heat are all the same to them; they feel no pain,
They're only a little different from the stones.

We're not like that.
We have our little time on earth,
A struggle for the most part,
A hurried growth and then a long descent
Into the grave.

Our bones, our ashes, what we leave behind, are worthless,
Not lumber, not firewood, certainly not fruit.
We become one with the earth.

But we are blessed, more than the tree or stone,
For we can make a mark, make a record of our thoughts,
That may persist, may in some infrequent instance
Have a value, for those who follow us.

This is the gift of life we have,
We think, we build, we use the tree and stone.

The Organ Transplant

My cousin Lillian, Mrs. Arnold Olson, passed away last May, and last week her personal property was auctioned off in Starbuck, where she had lived at the last. Louise and I went, hoping to get some article to help remember Lillian, and perhaps Rev. Olson and her parents, Mr. and Mrs. Carl Feigum.

There were three wagons of stuff besides the furniture. The weather was raw and cold, but the crowd was considerable. I looked through boxes of things for some article I would recognize and found a small pocketknife that I believe I remember Carl having. I was successful and got the right box after buying about thirty bucks worth of the wrong boxes. But that's OK, we can always use more duct tape, dead ballpoint pens, rusty paper clips, and small parts of things that were saved for some unknown reason.

Then the auctioneer took us inside the apartment to bid on the organ and davenport, and Louise and I went along. He had difficulty getting the bidding started on the organ, and Louise helpfully bid fifty bucks. Another guy bid sixty and I sighed with relief. But then, Louise couldn't get stopped. The auctioneer had explained that while the organ had functioned when it was in the apartment in Morris, some little thing must have happened to it during the move, and now it failed to toot. It looked heavy, another thing not in its favor. And then the other guy quit bidding, and Louise won.

So today I am sorting through my boxes of junk and throwing most of it away. We have the organ in our house, close to an electric outlet, in case it heals. We are not going to talk about the auction for a while.

A Warmer Spell

Well, I thought we outlasted the bad weather. In one week it went from 37 below to 37 above, and while I suppose we could have lasted a little longer, I'm glad we didn't have to. In fact it got so nice that I even starting to think of a few things I should do outside, but then I took a little nap and the feeling passed. It's surprising how many things you think you should do that don't really need doing because maybe somebody else will do them.

Then on Friday we had a little wind. I went down to the mailbox about three o'clock and the wind actually blew my car into the ditch. Thank goodness it was mainly from the north--it blew me back up to the house.

Went down to look at the car Sunday. It was completely full of snow under the hood, and I think it will stay right where it is until spring. This was my summer car, anyway, because the air conditioning works really well in it, and a rear-wheel drive is not the best for snow and ice.

If it sounds like I'm complaining, you're right, I am. I have lived here all my life, and have a right to complain. Of course, 1936-37 was much worse, but I was too young to leave then, and now I am too old. Since we can do nothing about the weather, let us complain away.

Louise told me to construct a hot dish of some kind for supper tonight. She is still in her recliner with her busted leg in the air, so I tried to follow her instructions as best I could, and we ate some of it. She was polite, and said it wasn't bad, but I notice that she didn't say it was good. At least she didn't request seconds. I made a lot, so we will see how it goes tomorrow and the next day.

The last experiment of mine in the kitchen went out to the dog this morning, and she seemed to enjoy it. In fact my son's dog came visiting, and they both had a good meal out of it.

Finding a Mate

Groundhog Day is past and Valentine's Day is nearing. If I remember right, this is the time a young person's fancy gently turns to thoughts of love.

Back when our kids were young and we had a herd of cows, we would turn the bulls out in the pasture with them about the end of June. We were in the process of doing this one summer, when one of the youngsters asked me why exactly we were doing this.

Louise didn't offer to answer their questions, so I told them that it was the bull's job to teach the calves to eat grass. I thought it saved a lot of explanation. They know better now, and give me a hard time about it.

I don't know if it is the weather causing it, but I noticed an ad in the local paper, people looking for companionship of the opposite sex. The guys went for an ad alone, but four women got together to advertise for soul mates. I'm wondering what will happen if the four of them get only one answer. How will they divide the guy up? Or if they get a few extras, how are these poor souls, the losers, going to handle the rejection? Well, that's not my problem.

I do wonder what the circumstances are that would cause someone to advertise for a partner, so I am in the process of doing a little research. I went right to the source; I answered a bunch of these ads that I saw in a magazine. I told them that I was old, married and completely unsuited as a mate for them. I only wanted to know what circumstances would cause them to advertise. They all say in the ads that they are smart and good-looking. It must be that they are too busy to put in the required search time. I suppose that means they will be too busy to answer my letters.

My Chicken Dream

We went to Wisconsin to visit our daughter and son-in-law. I had a cold, the weather was frightful, it rained, turning finally to sleet until the ice was an inch thick on the front of the car by the time we had covered the 260 miles.

The first night I coughed all night. Well, I could not have because I would have had to have been asleep enough to dream this weird dream.

I dreamed that I was visiting with a chicken. Telepathically, of course. Even in my dreams I do not talk face to face with chickens. You see, I had been reading Stephen Hawking's book, *A Short History of Time*, and that, together with my weak, feverish condition, sleeping in a strange bed, and the long, unending winter must have been responsible for the dream.

Anyway, the chicken and I were visiting, and I mentioned the book to the chicken. I told her how I understood maybe one or two percent of the book, and how it is about time, and how time relates to gravity, and how the universe is either expanding or getting ready to collapse, I forget which. This is important stuff to the physics industry. If they could figure out just a few more things, they could have a unified theory that would solve all our problems.

The chicken, a very bright chicken, by the way, said that she was familiar with the book and had been giving it a lot of thought. Didn't have much else to do, she said, in her cage. As long as she laid her daily egg, feed came by automatically and water was always available. Her roommate was not much of a conversationalist as she had been debeaked and had a terrible lisp.

So this smart chicken had spent long hours thinking. She had come to a number of conclusions and could verify her theories mathematically. Then she explained how space is curved, and how a clock on top of a tall building will run just a little slower than one on the ground, and elaborated on a number of other things that had bothered me in the book. I went to get a pencil so I could write down her equations, but when I got back, she was gone. Then a little while later, I received a few weak signals from her. She said that she had missed delivering an egg three days in a row and had been sent to the soup factory, just a little out of range for good communication.

I was hoping to get together with her the following night, but was feeling much better, had a good night's sleep, and now will probably never enjoy chicken soup again.

Louise read this, and was critical. But I told her that anyone who can handle Hawking's book would have no trouble at all with the concept of talking, telepathic chickens.

Use It All Up

Not so much anymore, but it used be a universal rule that nothing should be wasted. "Clean your plate. So what, you don't like your gruel (or your cold fried egg sandwich, or whatever). Somewhere a child is starving and would give anything for that bowl of slop."

All us old folks heard that when we were growing up. "Use it up, wear it out, or learn to get along without." That's another one I heard quite a bit.

Suppose you were going to 4-H camp or going to stay overnight at friends, you had to find some socks and underwear that had no patches or darned spots. Sometimes that was not easy to do. I don't know why we did this; others were in about the same shape as we were.

I think the worst summer I ever put in was the year my Uncle Ross died. I inherited his shoes, and had to wear them out. This was all right in the spring, but it was the summer I did most of my growing. So for the last part of that summer I limped or went barefoot until school started and I was entitled to a new pair.

Cleanliness may be next to godliness, but when I was young it was also next to impossible. My folks talked about how nice it was back when our lake had water in it. They said they would go for a swim every night in the summer time and wash off the dirt they had accumulated walking behind the horses all day. By the time I came along, the lake was as dry as banished hope. It didn't fill up again until I was married, but by this time we had a bathtub, and didn't really need the lake.

But getting back to this using up thing, a friend of mine told me about a conversation he had had with his thirteen-year-old grandson. They had been working together getting the kid's dad's harvest completed, and the young guy said, "If you can hold out for another four of five years, grandpa, dad and I will have it made." Wear out the old first.

The National Endowment for the Arts

Is it true that NEA is dead?
Will get no more money from the Fed?
How will poor poets buy their bread?

No one will pay to hear a poet.
They're free, like air, and we all know it.
They must have grants; we must not blow it.

A breeding herd must be maintained.
They must be cared for, must be trained,
Even if budgets feel constrained.

For if their numbers get too low,
Like whooping cranes or the dodo,
Well, you see what happens to quality.

A New Suit of Clothes

Louise took me to the clothing store to buy a suit so I could look nice at our daughter's wedding. It's a long time since I had a new suit. The one I was married in will not do, as my dimensions have changed considerably since then. Oh, I have other suits purchased since that one, but they are neither adequate nor recent enough, according to the women folks.

The suit we ordered has a feature I was unfamiliar with, a "double reverse pleat" in the front of the pants to conceal my stomach. It worked to some extent, and I was pleasantly surprised.

I wonder about this. If my problem were less, could I get by with a single reverse pleat? Would some cases require a triple or quadruple reverse pleat? How about a forward pleat? Some are afflicted with large rear ends, would a pleat serve any good purpose in that case? I discussed this with Louise, and she showed me a picture of an "inverted pleat" in a catalog. There is a lot I do not know about style.

My overalls look about the same as the ones my grandfather wore, and I guess the new suit is very little different from the one he wore.

Take shirts, for instance. For years I wore work shirts made of cotton chambray, simple blue things that you pulled over your head. They had a short zipper in the front and no buttons that catch on things and tear off. I liked them, and many of my neighbors shared my affection for these things.

Then they began to make them out of some man-made fabric, and they became hard and scratchy, and would stink when one sweat in them, much more than the cotton ones. We found another supply of cotton shirts, striped ones, with zippers. They were hard to find, so when we had a chance, Louise ordered a couple of dozen. Then we thought they might stop making these too, so we bought another two dozen.

Since I retired, I am not hard on shirts, so have plenty on hand, and mentioned that to a friend. He was amazed that one of my great age and physical condition would buy anything in such large quantities, even if they wouldn't go out of style. He said he was younger than I am, but still wouldn't even buy green bananas. No confidence.

Women's clothing, on the other hand, changes. I think it changes from minute to minute. Oh, some men's clothing may change; clothing for special occasions, but the suit that one is married or buried in never changes. Except you need a back in the one you are married in.

Riding the Waves

Our lake was green, about the consistency of thin green paint, so our granddaughter requested we take her to Page Lake to swim. Nature will change the condition of our lake somehow, sometime, but we do not have to wait, as we generally have alternative lakes here in Minnesota.

The wind was light from the south, and while not clear, the water at Page Lake was much better--odorless and warm. Louise's nephew has a thing to ride fast upon the water, a cross between a boat and a snowmobile. He goes about on the lake getting wonderfully wet and enjoying himself. The beach was well occupied; a water skier was putting a boat in as we were leaving. The weather was pleasant, and all was well with the world.

I remember that long ago Alan McArthur, young Francis Hiland, Wilbur Page and his sister Marion and I attempted to swim in Page Lake. A raft made of large cottonwood logs was on the beach on the south; so we pushed it out and jumped on to have a ride. Our weight made it sink until it stuck in the mud, so we would get off and push it a little further, looking for a deeper place. We pushed it all the way across the lake and back again, and the water was never deeper than up to our waists. We were shorter then, although much more physically active.

Of course, this was over fifty years ago. I remember going swimming at Starbuck, at about this time. Ernest Charles had hauled the Hodges 4-H club over one Sunday in his Terraplane to give us a treat. We changed into our suits in a building about where the bathhouse on the beach is now and then got in the car and drove a considerable distance east to find water. Moisture was a scarce commodity then, even in Lake Minnewaska. While too much is a curse, we are much better off now than when we had too little.

Speed

I was listening to a talk radio show the other day and the moderator was asking callers to express an opinion on the speed limit laws. I guess that there are a few in Washington who are interested in removing the federal 55 or 65 mph speed limits, and this fellow thinks that it is a good idea. He figures it's just big government interfering with our God-given right to crash into each other at high speed. If our cars will go 80 or 90 mph, there is no reason we shouldn't have that privilege.

He said that the reason we aren't killing as many on the highways as we were some time ago is that now we have air bags and seat belts and 55 and 65 on the highways is just too slow. I've got a different idea. Not that anybody pays much attention to the speed limits if they think they can get away with going at least as fast, and maybe a little faster, than they are capable of controlling their car.

I think that the speed limit should be 25 miles an hour. Cars could have tiny motors, tires would last practically forever, and we would get fantastic gas mileage. Two hundred miles would be a big day's travel, but we would have time to look at what we were driving by. We could enjoy ourselves. Our time just isn't as valuable as we sometimes think.

Besides, we have good radios now in the cars. We have books on tape we could listen to while riding, and with laptop computers and car phones we could be in contact with the world, and have time to enjoy the scenery. At 25mph we could even read our mail. No more white-knuckle rides through the traffic near the big cities, where the cars are so thick that the police can't stop anyone, so they all go about 80.

I will have to let someone else decide how we can enforce this new law. I had planned on having cars made so that they would explode at about 26 miles an hour, but then if one had to take someone to the hospital, it would be nice to go a little faster. Fire engines and ambulances could be excused I suppose.

How to Gather a Crowd

There are a lot of ways to get a crowd of people together. A free lunch is always good. Anything free, for that matter, will draw people to some extent.

The Pohlad family is trying to draw crowds to the Twins games, but are not having much luck. Their latest solution is to have us taxpayers build a new stadium for the Twins to play in. This new place will have a roof that can be opened and closed. It will be more exciting to watch than any old ball game. Then everyone will come to see the new facility, and Carl will make enough money so he can pay even larger salaries, thus getting better players, so a larger, newer stadium will be needed, and so on endlessly.

Back in the old days, a hanging generally drew a crowd. Of course, that was before television, and now I suppose most folks would just stay home and watch the rerun on TV. We are more sophisticated now, and it takes more to generate excitement in us.

I am finding out that it is never too late to learn. Yesterday I discovered the very, very best way to accumulate a crowd of people. It's so simple, I should have known. Cheap gas.

The Hancock Co-op celebrated the grand opening of its new facility by selling gas for ninety-nine cents. That's not quite accurate, the pumps were set at .999 dollars--that is about as close to a buck as you can get. It really drew a crowd. Let's see, .001 dollars less than a buck, that would be 0.1 cents, so if you bought 1000 gallons you would have purchased it for a whole dollar less than if you had paid a buck a gallon in the first place. Still, everyone I talked to said they were going to buy that 99-cent gas. Louise and I were right in line with everybody else.

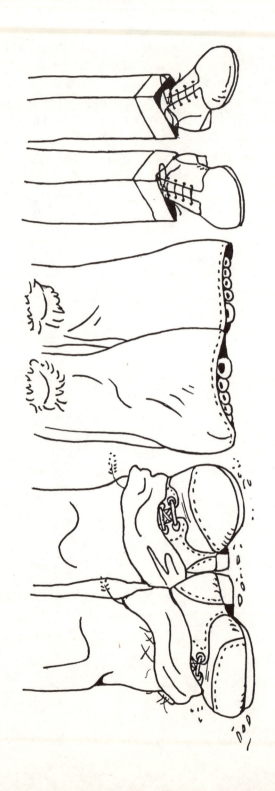

Pant Legs

I believe there is a relationship between one's prosperity and the bottom of one's legs. Saw a guy this morning with cuffs on his pant legs and little tassels on his shoelaces. I think he was either quite rich or else had a good line of credit as he was driving an expensive car, had a big gold ring on his finger and a watch set with valuable looking stones of some kind. I am going to make a point of paying more attention to pant legs and shoes in the future, to see if this theory holds up.

I remember the doctor, the main one that told everyone what to do down at Abbot Hospital when I had my heart attack. He had cuffs on his pant legs, and if he had more than four or five patients like me, he is bound to be rich. I could hardly lift the bill, much less pay it. Thank goodness for insurance. Or maybe, if no one had insurance, things would be cheaper.

But getting back to pant cuffs. When I was young everyone had cuffs on their dress pants, and as they became shiny at the seat and disreputable, no longer fit for church, they were used for work pants. Then the cuffs would fill with straw and manure, and would finally be cut off. I got the impression that cuffs were for people who never had to go to the barn.

Now, of course, a lot of people feel they can dress nicely, but in a more casual manner. One can buy denim clothes now that are priced so high that when you get them on, you feel well dressed, even if you are dressed like your grandfather's hired man. Not that there is anything wrong with this, I'm for anything that is comfortable.

The last pair of overalls I purchased had 34-inch legs. I had to get longer legs in order to get the diameter I needed to accommodate my stomach. You see, I have short legs and a long back. So now I have cuffs, and I am feeling a little more prosperous.

Paul Harvey

When Paul Harvey talks, people listen. He has a voice that inspires confidence and makes you believe whatever he says.

I have no argument with the stuff he advertises on the radio. I am sure that it is all fine stuff; I just never had any use for any of it. That is, until lately. I didn't actually hear him say it, I got the information second hand, but he was quoted as recommending soaking two pounds of golden raisins in a pint of gin for a while, then taking a spoonful of the mixture every night at bedtime for arthritis. For medicine, it doesn't taste bad at all. And I think it helps a little.

But now I hear him promoting a supersonic toothbrush. The machine emits a high-pitched sound, he says, that shatters the plaque below the gum line on your teeth, so you can just wash it away with water. I know what the sound of a fingernail on the blackboard does to my teeth, and want nothing to do with this machine in spite of Paul Harvey.

Peace at Last

I worry sometimes about the way my mind works because I am not normally a bloodthirsty person. Maybe it only shows the brokenness of the human spirit, or perhaps it's only a protection against the feelings of horror at what I see on television and in the papers, about the killing and starvation in the Muslim parts of Bosnia.

I am reminded of an old story about some raccoon hunters whose flashlight battery went dead just as the dogs had something treed. One of the hunters volunteered to climb the tree and shake the coon loose from the branch, as it was no use to try to shoot it in the dark. When he grabbed what he thought was a coon, he found to his surprise that it wasn't. The hunters on the ground heard a lot of screaming and crashing about in the tree and then heard the guy in the tree holler "Shoot, Shoot, it's a wildcat." The guys on the ground said "We can't, we might hit you." The guy in the tree said, "It don't make no difference, one of us has to have some relief."

What brings this to mind is the fact that the French have these atom bombs they want to test in the South Pacific. The Greenpeace people and a lot of the natives down there aren't too crazy about this and would like them to go someplace else, or not do it at all. Maybe they could test them in Bosnia, or maybe Belgrade, or wherever that Serb big shot hangs his hat, and give relief to everyone concerned, and let the Good Lord sort out the right from the wrong.

I'll bet you are all glad I don't make a lot of big government decisions.

Governor Perpich

It was quite a few years ago, an election year, I suppose, when Rudy visited Hancock. I was standing on the street visiting with old Herb Ericson when the whole entourage drove up.

Governor Rudy was in fine form. He leapt out of the car and headed for the Senior Citizens center with his helpers, the county commissioners and all the other movers and shakers following along.

He was in there for only a few minutes, as the crowd was a little light, and then raced across the street to shake hands with the card players in Bob Sax's place. His followers trotted right along behind him.

Now Herb was not in Bob's place playing cards as he usually did because he and Bob had had a little disagreement a few days before, and Herb did not feel welcome there. Bob had accused him of drinking coffee over at the Senior Citizens Center, where it was a little cheaper, and then using the toilet at Bob's, and Bob felt he should use the facilities where he bought the coffee, as that was what paid the water bill. Anyway, Herb sees the Governor going into Bob's, and says to me, "I hope he doesn't try to use the toilet, that would really make Bob mad."

Rudy, Herb and Bob are all three gone now, and this is the kind of thing that comes to mind for me. I suppose I should be thinking about Rudy's record length of service as our chief executive, or his efforts at bringing prosperity to the state he loved so much, something important like that. But that is not the way my mind works. I am always reminded of the unimportant, and there is nothing I can do about it.

Second Guesses

It is said that you must be at least fifty miles from home to be an expert, so I am not one in Herman, as I live near Hancock. What I am is an overweight, bewhiskered, retired farmer who has been taught by his wife to use a word processor. It is a thing that can be done sitting down, a big advantage for me at this time in my life. So now I can waste other people's time, as well as my own. An example follows.

It seems as though people will never leave well enough alone. In Washington they are going over the Whitewater land deal the Clintons either were or were not involved with. Then they are investigating the people that were at Waco, trying to see whose fault that mess was, and then finding out why the FBI shot a tax protester out west someplace.

Now they have dug up Jesse James, and are going to test the remains to find out if it really was Jesse. How they expect to tell is beyond me. Something with DNA and people who are related to him. This is to quash a rumor that he died in Texas at the age of 107 and never got to serve his time in jail. Personally I think it's a little late to be worrying about that now.

But then this morning Fritz Schmidt told me that they were excavating in the Holy Land, over where the Philistines and the Israelites had that big battle, and dug up Goliath's skull. It had not one, but two holes in it. That pretty much proves that there was a second slingshot on the grassy knoll. Never too late for a little second guessing.

Stranger in Town

I was having coffee in The Owl's Nest the other day when a stranger came in. This happens seldom enough that the regulars kind of sit up a little straighter and stare, but of course they don't say anything. We could tell right away that he was a stranger because he just went and sat down--didn't help himself to coffee first. He was a young fellow, I doubt if he was 60, and had long, nicely combed hair and a beard. He looked a little like some of the pictures we see of Jesus.

Pat went over to the booth where he sat to take his order, and I hollered at Pat to find out who he was. After all, it doesn't cost anything to be friendly. She just gave me a dirty look and the guy said something to Pat I didn't catch. I don't hear that well anymore.

I did, however, hear her tell the new guy that some crazy old guy at the round table wants to know who you are. He got up and came over and introduced himself. Said his name was Kolstad, if I remember correctly. He said he lived down by the twin cities of Hagen and Big Bend north of Montevideo. He had property north of here, and it was convenient to travel through Hancock to get there.

He would probably have preferred to eat his macaroni salad and beef sandwich in peace, but we invited him to sit with us and continued to question him; in fact, Jim Swenson was still at it when I left.

We found out a few things. He mentioned having to go to Colorado to get his dogs that his daughter was caring for, so we know he has at least one child. He didn't mention a wife, so if he comes back, somebody should ask about that, and maybe find out just how prosperous he is, so we know exactly how nice we need to be to him.

Tough Luck

You people who have heard all you want to about that old lady in France, supposed to be the oldest living human being, can go do something else, because that's what I want to talk about. Saw a picture of her on television the other day, and she was moving, but to tell the truth, she really looked her age.

I suppose it's only natural for me to be interested, because when you get old, you think about old things, and she is really old. Anyway, she has lived in the same apartment in Paris for many years, and as it is in a rent-controlled building, the rent is very cheap compared to the rest of the city. Paris has only so much room, and housing of any kind is scarce and expensive, and a new lease on her place would bring big bucks.

About 30 years ago, when she was a youthful 90, a young man of 47 said he would pay the rent for her, about 500 bucks a month, until she croaked, if he could have the place when she no longer needed it. It looked like a good deal for him, and it would spare her the problem of paying rent.

He passed away now, at the ripe old age of 77. She is still going, not strong, but what do you expect at 120 plus? This is what I call really bad luck. Can you imagine that guy checking up on the old girl every so often, watching his investment get bigger and bigger? I understand she quit smoking a little while ago, and I suppose that was a big disappointment for him. I suppose he was loading her down with gifts of high cholesterol candy and trying to get her back on Camels with no filter. But it was hopeless; she was too tough for him.

Pickup

The pickup has huge tires
And a kennel in the back,
And in the rear window is
A three-passenger gun rack.

The dog is riding up in front
With his head out in the breeze
The way his ears are flapping,
You'd think his brain would freeze.

Prairie Pioneer Days

'Tis four score and some odd years ago
Since first was made an arch of hay
Across a street in Morris town to show
A new crop, alfalfa, which would pay.
No more would farmers feed their cows
On only things the buffalo had eaten.
As the prairie yielded to the plow
The native vegetation's yield was beaten.
No more the prairie needles from the grass
Would stick in horse's tongue and farmers butt.
And if the proper weather came to pass
A second crop of hay could then be cut.
So now a good excuse we feel is made,
We can now justify a big parade.

The Predestinarian

Now
is just a point
on that crooked line of time
that wanders behind us,
as far as we can see.
But we've been there, it's of no consequence.
Just look ahead and hope.

Planning's no good
because
we're pushed by circumstances, this way and that,
and led by needs and urges we do not understand.
Like Johnny Cash, we walk the line.

Problems

It seems as if all I have been hearing lately are complaints. Oh, the weather accounts for a lot of it and that can be expected. A fairly fierce winter after a couple of wet, cold summers gives an agricultural community the right to complain. Some say it doesn't do any good to complain, and when one does it, it shows a weakness of character. Some of those self-righteous people who don't believe in complaining complain about the complainers. How do you account for that?

So I have started to look for complaints that are a little different, not about weather, or crop prices, or any of that ordinary stuff that we can do nothing about except complain. And some of them are a little frightening.

Jack Brown has a complaint, or maybe you could call it a worry, that fate means for him to starve. Not that he seems to be in any great danger yet, but he always thinks ahead, and he doesn't like what he sees in the future.

When he first left home, he ate at the Red Dot until it closed. He moved to the Shell Cafe--now it's gone. Then he moved his allegiance over to the Pool Hall until that also vanished. Some of you may remember Ada's; he closed that one up. Then for some time he could be found at mealtime at the Holiday Cafe, but that was bulldozed out of existence. Now Mitch's is closing, and he is worried. If I were he, I think I would learn to cook. When I talked to him he was in Hardee's. I wonder if he will manage to drive the whole chain into bankruptcy, as this one has now turned into a Burger King.

Prozacville, USA

Psychology Today is one of those magazines I am sometimes exposed to and can't resist reading, although it confuses and sometimes even frightens me a little.

The other day I was killing time in the library and read an article about 47-year old Jim Goodwin, Ph.D. He was from Wenatchee, Washington, a small, conservative farming community. The writer said that the town had the reputation of being "Prozacville, U.S.A., a happy town." In a place with a little over 17,000 people, the doctor had 700 patients on Prozac. He said that there was a lot of undiagnosed depression going around, and he was going to fix it.

The state health department investigated him and disagreed. They decided that maybe he had taken a little too much of the stuff himself, and he should quit the practice of medicine. The patients interviewed were divided, some saying he had hurt them, others saying that it was the greatest thing since sliced bread.

Then the Eli Lilly Company, which makes Prozac, says that actually the per capita consumption of Prozac in Wenatchee was a little below the national average.

The magazine article said that since the story broke, Wenatchee was the scene of some hard-to-explain forest fires and a few strange murders. Doesn't sound happy to me.

My knowledge of mind-altering chemicals is limited. But I do know that the one I'm familiar with doesn't act the same with everyone. Had a friend once who was the happiest drunk you ever did see, but turned into a real grouch when he sobered up. Then again, some people want to fight as soon as they get a few drinks under their belts.

Years ago, when I was attempting to raise cattle, I had a cow that developed an emotional problem. This cow had a calf, and she decided motherhood was not for her. She tried to kill the calf, and failing that, tried to kill me.

Doc Christianson, our local vet, was at my place for another purpose, and said that he thought he had some stuff that would calm the cow down. He said that it was new, and while it sometimes had side effects, it had a good chance of helping. We roped the cow and he gave her the shot. When we turned her loose, she went out through the window of the barn, taking a good part of the barn with her, over the fence and away. "Like I said," Doc explained, "It doesn't work the same all the time."

Symmetry

It's a good thing people aren't judged like livestock. People are, for the most part, not built symmetrically. It's not just that the feet and hands are not quite perfect mirror images of each other, with the two big toes and the thumbs on the inside, I mean other stuff, stuff you think should be the same on both sides, but are different.

And it's not just that people are either left handed or right handed, although a very few can use either hand with equal dexterity. The hands and feet are not mirror images of each other. One eye is generally stronger than the other. I have one bad ear, but that may be an acquired weakness. When I was young, I did not notice this so much, but now, as I grow older, I am forced to pay attention.

My legs are not equal. In spite of what the chiropractor says, I believe they are very close to the same length, but they do not act the same. The right one was my bad leg for years. Then I broke the left one, and now I have to remember to use my bad leg as my good leg when I climb onto a tractor or step up on something high.

This is the wisdom of old age, learning to live more or less comfortably with various weaknesses. Little efficiencies you learn make you able to keep up, or at least not fall too far behind.

Powerball

If I should win the Powerball,
I think I'd buy new overalls
And four new tires for the car
And take a trip, but not too far
Cause traveling far and spending money
Would make me feel a little funny.

See, I've been farming in tough luck,
I know it's hard to make a buck.
So we've learned to economize,
We'd starved if we'd done otherwise.

But should we win the real big one,
We might decide it would be fun
To do some things we've never done.

At these new places where we'd go
Our new-found wealth would start to show.
We'd find new friends with lots of dough
Then pretty soon we would not care
For people that we used to share
Our life with. But that isn't fair!

So it may be best if we don't win.
We just don't have the discipline.
But still, it really would be fun
If we could win a little one.

Eat More Geese

Some of the larger towns around here are filling up with geese. I suppose all the short grass for them to eat and the fact that no predators or dogs are running loose makes it pretty nice for them. It's nice for them, but I wonder about how nice it is for the people.

The geese seem to know when they are safe. I was in Fergus Falls the other day and the geese were strolling around on the boulevard just as unconcerned as could be. I am sure that all you need to bag one would be a golf club or maybe one of those weed whackers. Just walk up to them casually and then knock them alongside the head. I suppose using a gun in town would be frowned on.

I think eating them is the answer. I suppose that is why they were put on this earth. We humans are meat eaters and geese are mostly meat after the feathers are removed. I have eaten some that are not half bad—almost as good as lutefisk

It is easier, however, to get a goose than it is to get it ready for the table. Katie told me that her family received a gift goose, and after three and a half hours in the oven it was still entirely too tough to chew. I suppose this was not one of those tender, lazy local geese, but a traveling goose, one that had made many trips to the south and was old and muscle- bound. She said it just seemed to tighten up in the oven and get harder and harder. I understand they sometimes live to a great age and that would tend to make them tough.

I don't understand why the goose population has exploded so. Ducks I could understand, as they have large families. With geese you seldom see more than four or five goslings. Still I see few ducks and geese by the thousands.

People will eat most anything if they think it is stylish. It does not even have to taste good; all it needs is to have a famous person advertise it. I guess we will have to get a basketball player to give a few testimonials for goose. Julia Child could help with some recipes too.

Prunes

Louise cooks me up a big bowl of prunes every so often, and puts them in the refrigerator. Then, whenever I feel the need, or rather slightly before I think I may feel the need, I have a bowl of them.

She has always said that I have inherited from my mother's side of the family an unhealthy preoccupation with my regularity. But rather than put up with my whining, she cooks prunes.

This problem has always been with me, but as I grow older, and am less physically active, I find that everything slows down even more, and I feel that the prunes are a healthy, economical way to speed up at least that one important function.

It took Louise a long time to get used to my family's habit of attaching so much significance to one's bowel function. She seemed to think that it was a little indelicate to discuss the subject unless it was a real crisis situation. It was hard, I suppose, for people to sympathize when they have never had the problem themselves.

Radio

I learned something the other day--that Alberta used to have a radio station. And not only that, one that is presently in Fergus Falls started out in Barrett. I suppose I could have gotten along without knowing this, but I still find it interesting.

When I was young, we would listen to a station in Del Rio, Texas. That was before they put a limit on how much power a station could have, and this one must have been supercharged, because it came in here much louder than the ones in Fargo or Minneapolis.

I remember hearing a little cowboy music on that Texas outfit, and then a lot of advertising for a clinic of some kind run by Dr. Brinckley, who owned the station. He claimed to be able to cure most any ailment by installing monkey glands into the sick person. Where in the invalid he would place these things, and exactly how he would do this was his secret, and you would have to come to Del Rio with money in hand if you wanted to find out.

I was a little curious about what happened to the monkeys. Were the parts he removed from them really essential for their well being, or was it just stuff like maybe the monkey's tonsils or appendix he transplanted? And if you were really sick, would it take a whole monkey?

I remember hearing that the government got after him, and he moved across the line into Mexico for a while. Finally international agreements limited the power of radio stations, and he was out of business.

WDAY in Fargo was one of the ones I listened to in my youth. The Fairmont Old-timers, a musical group that told some jokes and advertised a creamery in the Red River Valley was one of the really big shows at the time. They talked with strong Norsk accents, and one of the stars was Axel, with his snow-white violin. Another performer was called the trick one-armed piano player.

In 1944 when I started college, a friend and I went over to the Black Building in Fargo to see the Fairmont Old Timers. Was I ever disappointed. Axel's violin was not white, the piano player had two arms, and the whole outfit wore suits and ties and looked just like the guys in the bank or a store.

Respect

If you were to ask what the biggest change has been in my lifetime, I would have to say it does not have anything to do with technical or scientific advances or that sort of thing. The big change has been in human nature.

The young no longer give us old people the respect and attention we deserve. It was not like that when I was young. I would stand and listen to those old buggers for hours while they repeated themselves and criticized the things I was doing. Never once would I tell them they were full of crap. I was too polite. I had too much respect.

The youth of today no longer seem to value all the experience that we have had and wish to share with them. This is dangerous. It means civilization is deteriorating. We have been there, and know.

Reunion

Louise and I recently had lunch with three of my remaining cousins from my mother's side of the family and their husbands. I have other cousins from this branch, but they are older and less adventurous. It's good to see these people, to see them smart and looking good, dealing with what fate hands them. That makes me happy too.

It's been family time; I'm planning on a reunion with my father's side of the family at Gully, Minnesota. I have cousins there too, but am not sure of their physical condition, and I suppose they may have some doubts about me.

I have not been to Gully in many years. It is not far from Fosston or Oklee, famous as the home of Coya Knutson. If you are old enough, you will remember the "Coya, come home" appeal by her husband that cost her a congressional election many years ago.

The last time we were up there a sign advertising the Gully Mall astonished us. It turns out that they had built a school too big for the population, joined another school district, and then moved most of the town's businesses into the schoolhouse.

I hope to find the place where my aunt lived when I was about eight years old to see how well my memory serves me. I visited her later, when I was about twenty, but that was at the farm to which they retired and was less impressive, or maybe I was worldlier by this time.

This second farm was known as Rabbit Louie's place, as the previous owner had heard that rabbits were bringing a dollar a piece in Fosston, so set about snaring as many as he could that winter. Unfortunately, he had misunderstood. It was jackrabbits they wanted, and he had only cottontails. So in the spring when he brought his wagonload of rabbits to Fosston, they wouldn't buy them. As he had no use for them, he dumped them in the road ditch on the way home, and the town board made him pick them up and bury them. Now, why do I remember stuff like that when I can't remember my Social Security number?

It is well that I write about it before I go to the reunion, in case it is too big a disappointment. This first place was a long, low old house with woods all around it. I remember walking through the pasture, around a small lake to a place inhabited by a relative of my grandmother's. I remember picking wild strawberries on the way, and seeing a lot of machinery and junked cars. They were big cars, not the Fords and Chevies we were accustomed to.

So I hope I find a relative up north as lucid as the ones I mentioned at the beginning of this tale to tell me if my memory is failing me.

Roosevelt and Hoover

I'm a little discouraged when I see the actions of our politicians in Washington. I would like to go back to a happier time, when people could come to a conclusion, when people could sit down and talk things over, and maybe compromise enough to keep the government running.

I think it was in the early 1930s that I had my first political discussion. I was just a little kid, and was riding into Cyrus with my Uncle Ross and a wagonload of hogs. A trip like this took a good two hours, maybe more if you were leading an old cow along behind. Anyway, you had a chance for a good long conversation.

I don't have to be too careful of my facts in this story, as most of the people are dead and can't contradict me. As I recall, the stockyard we went to was located on the west end of Cyrus, and Julius Halvorson was the shipping agent.

There was another shipping association located east along the Northern Pacific tracks that ran from Morris to Little Falls but we never went there. I asked my uncle why, and he explained that the east one was the Democrat stockyards, and the western one was the Republican one, so that was where we had to go.

In my later years I decided that he was kidding me, but recently an old neighbor, Herb Tonn, told me that was a fact. I believe that Cyrus even had two Lutheran Churches, one for the Republicans and one for the Democrats.

I remember that on the way home I asked my uncle if we were Republicans. He said we were. I then asked him whom he had voted for in the last election, and he said that I should not tell anyone, but he had voted for Roosevelt, and he hadn't talked about it with my dad and mother, but he suspected that they might have also. They had had it with Hoover.

I suppose there is a message in there someplace for these modern politicians.

The Routine

The remnants of this branch of the Rasmusson clan gathered at our house. Louise and I had been looking forward to this for some time. There is a lot of pleasure in seeing and hearing from the kids, especially as they are no longer children, not by a long shot, and they have ideas, accomplishments and interests that we enjoy hearing about.

Now it is Sunday, and soon they will all be leaving, going back to their homes and jobs, and Louise and I will be alone again. I'm a little ashamed to say it, but I am kind of glad that they are leaving so that we can get back to our familiar routine again. It's funny, I can't remember that they were that much trouble, that they interfered with any of our plans when they were young and lived here full time. Actually they are pretty easy to have around even now. They know where everything is and we don't have to do any major thing very differently when they are here.

But it seems now that Louise and I have acquired the habit of going there, and the kids feel they need to go somewhere else. We always do this, they have started doing that, well, and you get the idea. We have grown apart. Not very far apart, just a little bit, but it is noticeable. It takes more than one weekend to get used to each other again.

It could be that we are the ones that are changing. We must be getting more rigid, less capable of making any adjustment in our lives to accommodate others. I wonder, will Medicare pay for the pills necessary to make us more flexible in our daily lives?

Next weekend we are going to our daughter's home in Wisconsin. We are sure that her husband and she are looking forward to our coming and will be disappointed if circumstances prevent us from getting there. But they, too, have a routine, and when we leave we are sure they will smile, wave goodbye and sink happily back into their own comfortable rut.

To Spring

The sun doth shine a little longer now,
The snow has melted, spring appears at last.
The farmer hooks his tractor to the plow.
We're finally free of winter's icy blast.
On trees, the tiny leaves now show.
The pastures, while still brown, are greening fast.
The ice is gone; we see the river flow.
The air is warm; the cold is in the past.
This changing of the season that we know
Is coming, we should be able to forecast.
But still when soft, warm winds do finally blow
We have a feeling of relief at the contrast.
Now, if I can get these last two lines to rhyme,
I've made a sonnet, like in Shakespeare's time.

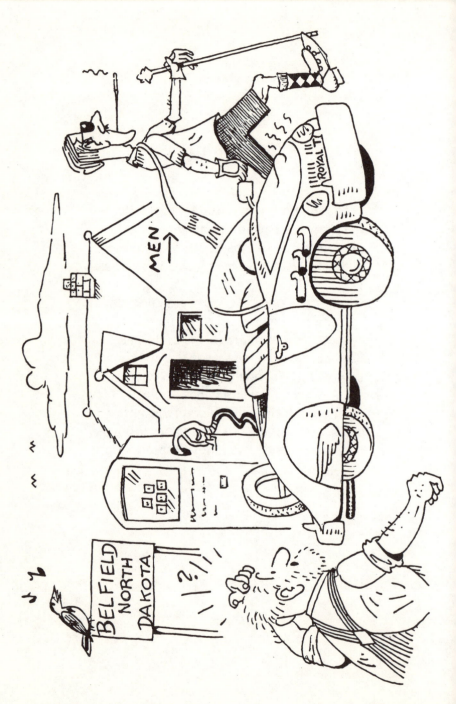

My Brush with Royalty

Nobody believes me when I tell this story. I've been telling it for years, and while a few listen politely, most give me to understand in no uncertain terms that they think I'm making it up. So I thought that if I printed it in this book it would give the story a little credibility. Everything printed is true, isn't it?

It happened in the summer of 1951; I was working for the US Geological Survey measuring rivers in western North Dakota, South Dakota and a little in Montana. The Government was getting ready to build Garrison Dam and a bunch of smaller dams on the Heart, Grand, Moreau, and maybe the Cannonball rivers too. Several of us worked out of an office in Dickinson, North Dakota to collect information on these rivers for the Army Corp of Engineers and the Bureau of Reclamation, the people that were going to superintend the building of these dams.

Anyway, in the course of these activities I found myself one day filling gas into my Government truck at a gas station in Belfield, North Dakota. This was before the interstate was built, and old US highway 10, soon to be replaced by the interstate and north-south highway 85 crossed right by the town.

As I recall, it was in the afternoon, and a little sports car, a convertible, pulls up to the next pump. It has no top. It is not a convertible in the usual sense of the word, but it is a nice day, so no top is needed.

The guy who gets out of the car is not dressed like one expects at this time and at this place. He has a scarf wrapped around his neck, is wearing gloves with no backs in them, and has a short-sleeved shirt. I think you would call it a polo shirt. His shoes have flaps covering the laces, and his socks are a very bright plaid. He stretches, points languidly at the gas cap for the attendant, and strolls toward the can.

Just about then this really big car pulls up behind him. A guy in a dark suit gets out and walks around the sports car, kicks the tires, opens the hood and checks the oil or something. He monkeys around with it and then closes the hood.

The other guy comes out of the can, climbs into the sports car and drives off without a word to anyone. The attendant barely gets the gas cap back on. The guy in the dark suit fills his big black car, pays for all the gas, and takes off too.

I asked the attendant who it was. He said he had no idea, but thought the big car was a Bentley. Now I could tell right away that this was no cattle buyer or rodeo cowboy.

The guy at the filling station and I talked about it and decided we thought it might have been a movie star or something, but we didn't think he looked familiar. But of course we were not too familiar with movie stars either. One doesn't run into many around Belfield, North Dakota.

About once a month I would buy a Minneapolis Sunday paper to read while eating my evening meal in Binek's Cafe in Dickinson. Shortly after this encounter, I read about Elizabeth and her fairly new husband, Phillip, taking a tour of Canada, and Phillip taking a little side trip to Denver or maybe the Black Hills.

I decided that I had seen him and the guy that his wife had sent along to see that he didn't fool around. Even in those times the royals needed watching. To think I was that close and didn't even try to strike up a conversation.

I don't get that many chances to talk to famous people. I once shared a urinal with Halsey Hall, but we didn't speak. Once I shook hands with Bob Bergland when he mistook me for someone else. Another time Arne Carlson waved at me, but he may have been waving at the guy standing behind me. So you see I have a habit of blowing my chances.

Iowa Stories

I started to read *Moo*, by Smiley, and got about half way through when too many other things interfered and I had to take it back to the library. I mean to give it another shot, though, a little later.

I had better luck with *A Thousand Acres*, an earlier book of hers. I finished it, and quickly. Quite a story. It is about a farm family, working on this very good land. The final generation falls apart and loses it. It seems to me the people had questionable values, and I think the old man was either a mental case in his later years or a bona fide jerk. It is a retelling of Shakespeare's King Lear, set on a farm in Iowa. Instead of a crazy king, we have a nutty old farmer.

Mainly it's about the three sisters, two of whom stay on the farm with their husbands, and a third, the youngest, who becomes a lawyer and marries a Rasmusson. This got my attention, of course, but in spite of this good fortune, she turns out to be a jerk also. Anyway, you should read it.

The author teaches at the University of Iowa, and I gathered from the book she has spent time listening to farmers in cafes, sales barns, at church and in feed stores, but should maybe have spent a wee bit more. At least, that is my opinion, or maybe authentic Iowa farm talk is slightly different from authentic Minnesota farm talk.

That will be three books set in Iowa I have read lately, and I am starting to see a pattern here. *The Bridges of Madison County* movie is in video stores now. Louise brought it home and we watched it, so it is fresh in my mind. *A Thousand Acres* is not by the same author, but the two stories seem to have a lot in common--about reasonably young Iowa farm wives and male vegetarians with fine looking rear ends in their tight jeans. Especially the wives of hog farmers, as this particular herbivore

137

got involved with both of the older sisters and then left. Did twice as well as old Clint Eastwood.

This, of course, is not the main tragedy, just something I noticed and worry about. But *A Thousand Acres* is a good book.

Our Things

I was watching the CBS morning show on television while putting on my shoes. Harry Smith was interviewing a fellow named Peter Menzel. He had traveled around to many different places and talked people into taking all the stuff out of their houses so he could photograph and videotape it. He must have been very persuasive.

I'm glad he didn't stop at our house. Four generations of Rasmussons have accumulated a lot of junk. It would have taken two weeks to get it all out in the yard, and then Louise would have made me throw most of it away.

But this guy had made quite a statement with the videos he had collected. He had been in Africa, to Ethiopia and Mali, to various places in Europe, Japan, the Near East and in the United States.

The Kuwaiti household was champion for most possessions. Four big Mercedes were lined up in front of the house along with a 45-foot-long sofa and everything else to match. The Americans and the Japanese shared second place for having the most stuff, and the Ethiopian household was the smallest.

Albania, the poorest country in Europe, still managed to have satellite dishes in some of the houses, picking up a signal from Italy. No running water, but they could watch reruns of "I love Lucy."

"The Material World" is the name of the production. I would like to see the whole program sometime. I imagine it says something about the quality of life in various places.

I don't suppose it is really scientific. It can't speak for the country as a whole, but it must give a kind of snapshot of the differences around the world. Harry Smith asked Menzel to make some judgement about quality of life for these various people, but he wasn't willing to give an opinion.

I suppose you can be poor and happy, but I would have trouble adjusting to life in Ethiopia. Of course, if I lived there, I wouldn't have seen the Kuwaiti household on television.

This House

The house was built in 1918, nine years before I was born. Born
in a bedroom in the southeast corner,
Downstairs, where my sister had been born some time before.
She was born with only a whisper of life,
To be baptized by my aunt and then buried,
Not named, a little way from where
Our parents now rest in a cemetery some miles to the east.

The house was square then,
To be added on to later by three generations.
Back then, when you came to the door on the south,
You saw a few feet inside, a stairway leading up,
And to the right of that door,
The double doors opening into the cellar.

There was, still is, a chimney in the center,
But then it was fed by a tall stove in the sitting room
On one side, and a kitchen range, a Monarch, on the other.
A sink was by the range, with a pump
Sucking water from a cistern beside the house,
To fill the reservoir on the range.

There is a door on the east.
Then it was used only on hot days,
For the breeze, and once, I remember,
To take out my grandfather's body when he died.

The house was sheltered first by cottonwoods, tall and straight.
They all died in the drought, except one, near the house, Whose
roots reached through the bricks and into the cistern, And
shared our water.
The lesser trees, the box elders, the plum and chokecherry,
Didn't mind the drought, and grew thick over the ground.

We lived in the house then,
My parents, my grandfather, and a bachelor uncle.
And people came and stayed with us.
I have talked to some of those people now that they are old,
And they tell why they did this
The circumstances that put us all together,
And some of what it was like.

But that is not important,
For the house could shelter us all.
Grandfather died in 1933, my old uncle in 1938,
Three deaths and two births then.

Only my parents remained till I returned with a wife.
We raised three children.

My parents and her parents have died, but not while here.
Others came and stayed with us, and now they have all left. The
house shelters only the two of us most times.
Added onto by three generations,
It is larger by twice what it was at first,
And now only us, and some things they have left here.

Toy Show

Everyone should get his or her name on the list as soon
as possible to take a trip with Lyle Swenson like I did this last
weekend. We went to a toy show held in a motel by the airport
in Williston, North Dakota. A gun show was taking place in the
next room, so I was able to see two different types of collectors
doing their thing.

Getting all his stuff out of the van and onto five tables,
(two of them triple decked) went surprisingly fast, and we were

able to get all the boxes back into the van when it was over. If I hadn't seen this, I wouldn't have believed it possible.

Lots of people from Canada and Montana were there, and it was interesting to talk to them. A Canadian bachelor explained that he remained single because women were like parking places--the good ones were all taken, leaving only the handicapped. The ages varied widely; a group of Future Farmers of America kids were as interested as some old retired people. They were not exclusively farmers, but I suppose they all had roots in agriculture.

Of course, I had my usual insecurity dream that I have when I am experiencing something new. I dreamt that I was at a Farm Bureau dinner and nobody would talk to me for some reason. Everyone was dressed quite nicely, but then I noticed that all I had on was my beige, knee-length support stockings and my jockey shorts. I got into my car somewhat quickly, turned on the heater, and went home. I don't know what this dream means, but I have had it before.

The weather was not the best. The snow Saturday night and cold weather may have cut down on the size of the crowd, but the interest that grown people have in toys fascinated me. They take their fun seriously.

Lyle and I are both somewhat elderly and need our rest, so we were generally in bed early. If anyone is interested, he snores moderately, does not talk in his sleep, and would disturb only the lightest sleeper.

Bicycles Across Minnesota

I enjoy kidding people who ride bikes. I tell them that we have cars now, enclosed cars, where one can ride in comfort, protected from the weather, and arrive at one's destination rested and relaxed and not soaked with sweat.

I hate to admit it, but I think I do this because I envy them. I envy their dedication, their ambition, and their commitment to healthful living. So I made a point of visiting with a few of the bikers that were in Morris recently.

A little before ten in the morning a couple of them came into the cafe where I was having coffee. Young fellows dressed in the appropriate clothing--tight pants and shirt, funny cap, and one even had shoes with knobs on the bottom that clipped onto the pedals. I asked him what would happen if he should fall off. He said this was undesirable, as it required a certain amount of agility to get loose from the pedals quickly. He was from Texas and was riding here in Minnesota to take advantage of our cooler weather.

Later, about two in the afternoon, I saw another biker coming into one of our eating establishments. On this one, the bloom of youth had definitely left his cheeks. He was gray and somewhat creased with the lines of time and experience. He was not dressed in the rubber pants and shirt of the more youthful ones, and was not walking with nearly as much pep as the others. I assume that it had been a struggle for him to make the forty-some mile distance from Ortonville, so I joined him in the booth to visit with him and verify my assumptions.

Boy, was I wrong. He said the reason he was so late getting in to eat is that he makes a point of getting over a hundred miles every day, so had gotten to Morris early, rode back part way, and this was the second time he had been in town.

He is nearly my age, within five years, and does this mainly as a conditioning thing for his favorite occupation, mountain climbing. He has climbed Mt. McKinley in Alaska, been up over 22,000 feet in the Andes and on top of Kilimanjaro in Africa. In between mountains he has biked over New Zealand, across Alaska, and covered most of Europe and the United States. I believed him and was impressed.

And here is the good part. The two young fellows and the older gentleman both enjoyed West Central Minnesota; they were doing something here that was not possible, or at least difficult, in Texas because of the heat in the one case, and in the Twin Cities because of the traffic for the older man.

They are reinforcing an idea I have had for some time, that this is a good place. Here we have room to live. We can breathe the good air and drink the water. It's pleasant here, even if you don't ride bicycles.

Hope for the Future

Tuesday of this week Louise and I had occasion to go to the Twin Cities. We're used to it as we have to do it several times a year, we can stand it, but we still don't like it. Every time we discover another service, previously available only in the cities, that can be obtained out here in the hinterlands, we cheer.

Computers and modems, these mysterious things people speak of, I suspect may some day eliminate the need for large cities altogether. This will certainly be a wonderful thing. They already make it possible to file one's income tax over the phone lines, the doctor can diagnose some ailments the same way, and so progress is being made. If only a way can be discovered to do something pleasant on the Internet.

We listened to the radio on the way, and heard a great deal of complaining about the coming road construction season and how it was going to make life even more difficult for Twin Citians. A bridge on highway ninety-four over the Mississippi is going to be under construction for the next two years, and that, together with the completion of the paving of the rest of the seven-county metropolitan area is going to make life there completely intolerable.

Well, they know what they can do about it. Our oldest son has his shop by the university near that bridge and has only recently moved to St. Paul, so will not have to endure that particular hardship, but I do not expect to see him again until the road is repaired. We can speak on the phone and write, so that will have to suffice.

For me, driving up to a stop sign, looking to the right and the left, and not seeing another car clear to the horizon is one of the things that makes life worth living. It's not that I don't like people, it's just that really big concentrations of anything tend to make things unpleasant. All we really need is a big enough group so that a good conversation can be carried on, or enough for two or three tables of bridge, that's plenty of people in one place. The rest of the stuff we can do over the phone.

Broken Leg

It's been a long week. Cold, way colder than it would need to be, just to remind us that we are here in Minnesota, and then Louise decides to break her leg. Oh, she probably didn't do it on purpose, because it makes things very inconvenient for both of us.

Louise has had to miss quite a bit of bridge already this week, and I have had to miss several games of smear and have had to wash dishes, clothes, all that kind of stuff that I ordinarily do so poorly that she does not let me do it at all.

I can make coffee. I fry an adequate egg. Toast is no problem, and I can boil spaghetti. That, together with what our friends bring in, will stave off hunger. Better yet, two or three weeks without food might be good for both of us. So now she sits in her recliner, much like I did when I had my prostate surgery, except that with her it is her leg that needs to be elevated because it is swollen and sore.

One thing I do not do and have no intention of learning how to do, is how to fold clothes. After she sorts them (I have trouble telling which are dark and which are light), I can wash and dry them, but then I place them on Louise's lap for folding. Then I put them on the bed in a spare bedroom so that Louise can put them away when she gets well. That way I can find what we need and will not screw up her system of what goes in which drawer.

Actually, I shouldn't complain. When I broke my leg I sat and she waited on me. When I had that other surgery, she waited on me. So I suppose she has the right to get even.

Two Love Poems to Warren Buffet

Haiku

Warren Buffet says:
Give me all your money now
I can make you rich.

Sonnet

Confounding Wall Street, out of Omaha he brings,
New mutual funds that don't obey the rules.
Old customers his praises loudly sing.
They're making money fast, and they're not fools.
They bring him more; the fund just grows and grows,
The pessimists wait sullenly for the crash
But Warren never waivers, for he knows
He can protect these people's hard won cash.
If only back in 1960 I had known,
Or had a hunch, and put a few bucks down
My poems would have a much more cheerful tone,
And I would smile, and hardly ever frown.
But then, if we had gotten filthy rich
I'd maybe be a real mean son of a bitch.

COBS FOR
COOK STOVE

HAND
CRANK

EAR CORN

SHELLED
CORN

148

Pigs and Cornshellers

On his way to work my son passes Punk DeGier's place and evidently had noticed the hogs by Punk's hog house. They belong to Pete Joos and are approaching market weight. The price is low right now, and he thought it might be a good time to stock up, so he called and asked me to make the deal for him.

He said it like this, "Tell Punk to ask Pete to put a pig away for me. I'm out of pork, and the price is poor, so let's put a pig in the freezer."

Repeat those two sentences fast a few times. You could almost put it to music, and if I could sing, I would do that.

But that's not really what is on my mind today. Years ago, when Mrs. John Edwards had her sale, I bought a pile of scrap iron. I invested in this particular pile because amongst the stuff were the remains of an old two-hole cornsheller, with a wooden frame and bearings made out of round cast-iron pieces with rawhide wrapped around the wearing surface. For its time I think it was pretty much state of the art. It even had a little elevator to take the cobs out the end, and a fan to blow the bee's wings away. I'm pretty sure that it belonged to Mrs. Edwards's father. His last name was Freeman, but I forget the first name. The sheller must be very old.

When I bought the thing, I was younger and had the idea that I would fix it up so the youthful people could see how things were done in the old days. I gathered the pieces together, squirted a little WD-40 in the appropriate places, and even went so far as to have some oak sawed for the frame.

But this was a heart attack and an operation ago, and I lost interest. Not in getting it done, just in doing it myself. So if someone out there has the time, ambition, and craftsmanship, I would appreciate it if they would take over the project. I have no idea what that person should do with it once it is functioning; maybe we should just look at it and be thankful for progress.

The Turkey

I don't remember the year it happened, only the weather. Winter must have come early that year, because although it was not yet Thanksgiving, the snow was hip deep on the average Norwegian.

Harold and I thought it would be nice to give our friend Myron a little something to remind him of his agricultural roots, as he had sold the farm and moved to town. He hadn't distanced himself from the soil too much. He was working at the experiment station, but we thought he needed a reminder anyway.

After a little discussion and out of respect for the season, we decided on a turkey. We wanted one of the old fashioned kind, dark colored, not one of those newfangled white ones. We searched, but were unsuccessful. Had to settle for a white one. One of the Smiths out in the western part of the county said he had a gobbler he was willing to part with, so Harold and I drove out to his place to make a deal.

I remember the snow being so deep Smith had dug a tunnel down to the little shed where he kept the turkeys. It was a struggle getting the big bird out into the light of day. He was large, quite elderly, and looked like he would be a real challenge to defeather.

We got a nice card, hung it with a ribbon around the turkey's neck, and Thanksgiving morning tethered him to Myron's garage door. We gave him a little corn to nibble on, and he seemed quite content to wait on top of the snow bank in Myron's driveway for the Bensons to wake up.

150

It didn't turn out exactly as we planned; our knot must have slipped. We heard later that the paperboy came by and rang Doris' doorbell. "Mrs. Benson, I think your turkey has gotten loose," he said. Doris said he acted like turkeys in people's driveways were an everyday event.

The twine had slipped off the garage door handle, but the turkey wasn't aware of his freedom, just stood there and gobbled at the people. Doris was able to grab the end of the twine after a minute or two in the snow in her bathrobe and slippers. I think at about that same time she was complaining about her husband's choice of friends.

Doris refreshed my recollection of the incident the other day. She said it happened in 1977, and they were invited out that day, but had to dress the turkey in their basement before leaving. Had no other place to leave him except in the freezer. Had him for Christmas. She even had a picture of him.

If the turkey had been eaten that day, I am pretty sure the company would have had to pick out quite a few pinfeathers. Like I said, it was not a young and tender beast.

Growing Older

I was listening to public radio the other night, and some lady gave a long and sorrowful soliloquy on how terrible it is to turn forty. Please, spare me.

From my point of view there is little if any difference between being 10, 20, 30, or 40. Up to 50 and maybe even a little beyond, things are pretty much the same, at least from my prospective. When you get far enough away from a group of things, they all start to look alike.

There is nothing wrong with growing old. I feel that it beats the alternative by a country mile. This is what I am doing, and I plan to continue doing it as long as I can.

Granted, some people seem to do it differently than I, with fewer ailments, but then they are not having all the experiences that I am having, so I don't believe that they are really getting all the benefits of their golden years. You can listen to someone describe a hemorrhoidectomy for hours, but will not really know what it is like until you enjoy one yourself.

While a lot of my parts function poorly or not at all, I accept that. They have had over 70 years of fairly hard use, and one must expect a certain amount of deterioration. There is a certain amount of pain associated with growing older, but that merely gets one's attention.

I see people who are trying to delay the onset of old age with vigorous physical exercise. But look at their faces as they run by, contorted with pain and exhaustion. They are just getting the pain and suffering sooner than they would need to have it. All the distance runners I knew when I was young are dead now. That tells me something. Face it, aging is an interesting process.

For example, I do not have hairy toes. In fact, my legs are hairless half way to the knee. This, my doctor tells me, is a result of poor circulation, as it requires blood to fertilize the hair. I used to have hairy toes. Evidently I have good circulation in my ears and nose, as they have an abundant crop of hair.

The nurse called with the results of some blood tests I had a while back. Sugar is a little high, better watch the diet. See how interesting it is?

Solutions

It was some years ago, I had hauled a load of grain into town and was waiting for my turn to unload by the elevator. An old neighbor was visiting with me, and spoke at great length about some of the problems he was currently having in his family. "How much does that truck of yours weigh?" he asked. I told him that I thought about 38,000 pounds. "Tell you what," he said, "I'll give you twenty-five bucks if you run over my son-in-law."

It wouldn't have solved his problem. It's a failing we all have; we try for the simple solution, the first thing that comes to mind. Oh, I suppose in some instances the first easy answer is the right one, but it wouldn't have worked in this case. The truck was too slow, and even if we could have done the deed, we would have been arrested. So I guess a little careful deliberation is called for in most cases, taking the many different things into consideration that may have a bearing on what the results may be.

I have thought about this particular thing a long time, so I must be right. We need to completely overhaul the way we organize our communities. This is not a new pulpit I am speaking from, but a slightly different approach.

All towns must be small enough that when a resident is walking down the street, that person will recognize at least a third of the people he or she meets, and will be able to call at least a fourth of them by name.

Each teacher in the school shall know and have visited with the parents of each of the children that teacher has to interact with. A teacher shall know the name and disposition of all the kids that he or she is likely to encounter in the course of the year.

The parents shall know the teachers of their children, and talk to them, and be close enough to them so that they understand them, and can talk out the mutual problems they may have. If they could arrange to like each other, so much the better.

Mainly, I want everyone to know everyone else. I could go on, with the business community, the law enforcement people, the churches, but you get the idea. We have to be extremely careful and not grow too large, too impersonal, and too coldly efficient.

That was one of the problems with the dinosaur. They got too big, ate too much, and had tiny brains. I have seen reproductions of some of these animals in museums, and they do not look like thoughtful beasts. It is said by some that a climate change is what did them in, but I think it was just the size.

Sweet Corn Time

We got to discussing sweet corn around the table of knowledge the other morning. Eddie mentioned he had a good meal of it the night before, and described in great detail how he had carefully cut it from the cob, put butter on it and a little sugar, and eaten it with much enjoyment.

I was critical of his technique and told him so. "Why," I asked, "as long as you have teeth, would you cut the corn from the cob when you can have corn like that from a can or frozen anytime, and only now, in August, do we have the privilege of eating it fresh from the field, and gnawing it off the cob like it was meant to be eaten?" I didn't even mention that one shouldn't put sugar on it, salt is more appropriate.

He explained that he did it this way because if he tried to gnaw it off his lips got sore, swelled up and turned blue. I doubted this, and said so. Harry was listening, and agreed with Ed, said he had the same problem with his lips, and cut his corn that way too.

I think I know the reason. When I eat sweet corn, I spatter. My shirt pockets get full of corn, and the floor around me is pretty well covered. This is because I keep my lips well away from the action, so there is clearance all around for corn to escape.

Eddie and Harry, on the other hand, are so obsessed with neatness that they press their lips tightly around the cob while chewing, and while no corn leaks out, this tight puckering causes bruising of the lips. These people have to learn to relax.

Rover

Bill is looking for a new hunting dog. He says he'll settle for one that isn't quite as birdy as his last one. That big Chesapeake was a good one, but I guess there is such a thing as being too eager.

What happened was the geese started moving into town. Like all Minnesota towns, ours has its lake, and while it was not much of a lake, it was good goose pasture.

They were smart, too. They would land on the lake, coming nearly straight down, and when they took off again, they would circle over the business district until they were high enough to be out of gunshot. Then, in the evening they would come back, have a good crap on the local lawns, and rest safe and secure out on the lake until the next morning.

One day Bill was working on the top of the leg at the Harvest States elevator by the lake. It was morning, and the geese flew by so close he could smell their breath. He decided that that would be a good place to put his blind, up on the big flat roofs of the concrete silos.

He figured that rushes and weeds, that kind of stuff wouldn't work for camouflage up there amongst the machinery on the roof, so he fixed up a little hiding place out of sheet iron, and early the next morning rode the lift to the top and then took the two flights of stairs to the roof of the big silos.

If Bill went anyplace with his shotgun, old Rover was right there with him. Turns out that was a big mistake.

It was broad daylight before the geese started moving. The weather was bright and clear, a high flying day. The first two or three bunches went off the lake to the south, but then the light breeze shifted and about a hundred came right for Bill's blind. He jumped up and started blazing away. He got one with his second shot. Old Rover was out of the blind like a bullet and nailed that goose before it hit the ground. A long, long time before it hit the ground, it turns out, because they were both over the edge and about one hundred twenty feet in the air.

You've got to give the old dog credit; he hung on to that goose. That is until they hit the ground, and the forced landing put his teeth on through. Bit a chunk right out.

Bill says another thing about his next dog; it should have a little softer mouth.

I hope nobody believes this story.

Temptation

I don't get around much. Most of the information I get about far away exotic places comes from others or the media. When I travel it is mostly at someone else's behest because I feel that everything I need is fairly close to where I live. If I lived in Mexico or Greenland, I would probably travel more, but as I now reside in the center of the universe, travel is mostly not necessary.

But temptation is always present. There is a certain prestige that one can gain by visiting certain places. Climbing Mt. Everest, for example, or going to the Mall of America. While going to these places is difficult and dangerous, not to mention very expensive, many people do and act like they are glad they have done it.

I had promised myself I would never go to a casino, but when our son-in-law promised us a free meal at Turtle Lake, I relented, and it cost me a roll of quarters. Then, as I had failed once, it was easy the second time to stop at the Four Bears Casino in North Dakota, on the way home from my brother-in-law's place. I had to go to the can anyway.

But they tempt you. Putting an amusement park in the Mall of America, and now a huge aquarium, things out of place in a store, just to tempt more customers. It must work, and I wonder if that same technique could be applied to other things.

For example, in church, replace the pews with hot tubs, maybe not all of them, just the front few rows. In the doctor's office, arrange it so you could watch when others were being examined, and having things pushed into various places on their bodies, so you would feel more connected to the procedure when your turn came. Well, it's just an idea.

A Fair Tax
(One somebody else pays)

We received an envelope from the county treasurer the other day telling us how much the first half-year of our real estate taxes is going to cost. After the shock wore off to the extent that I was able to breathe normally, I got to thinking about how we could do it a little better.

Nobody really likes to pay taxes. You always figure that you are paying more than your fair share. But we have to pay them, so that the government can continue to live in the style in which it has became accustomed.

Some taxes are less painful than others are. Like the tax on cigarettes. It bothered me when I was smoking two or three packs a day, but now that I've quit, I say sock it to them. I figure that the ideal tax is one that someone else pays. And I think I have it mostly figured out.

Tax neckties. They are uncomfortable, unnecessary, and in some cases extravagant, so I say tax them. I'm not exactly sure just how we would do it; maybe they could issue a necktie license, like a driver's license--renewable every year on the holder's birthday. It would be class A, B, or C depending on the average cost of the person's neckties or how many hours a week the tie was worn. Maybe special really expensive one-time permits for those neckties that look like a fish, or have a naked lady on them. They should be discouraged. And maybe a special stamp for bow ties, like a duck stamp.

Or maybe a tag, like a little license plate that one could hang right on each necktie. It would have to be stapled on pretty good, so it couldn't be moved from one tie to another. And maybe a two-day special permit for weddings and funerals. I suppose it wouldn't hurt to exempt the corpse.

Of course this is never going to happen. Just think where you see the biggest collection of neckties. In Congress, of course. There are a lot down at the state capitol, but nothing like Washington. And you know politicians are not going to do anything that might cost them money.

Party Line Telephones

We got a new thing on our phone the other day. Makes me think about the first phone I remember when I was a kid. It was oak, hung on the wall by the stove, so you could rest on the wood box if the conversation got too long.

Our telephone number was 16f11, that's a long and a short. We would call the people on our line, about ten or fifteen neighbors, by just cranking the phone the appropriate number of times. If we had to call somebody in town, or on one of the other country lines, we would ring one long and the operator would plug us in.

There was a general call, if I remember, about five or six shorts, in case of a fire or something, and then everybody would pick up their receivers, and it would get very hard to hear anything, especially if a few on the line had weak batteries.

Of course, we rubbered a lot on calls that weren't any of our business too, we didn't have television to entertain us, and we could hear some interesting things once in a while. The Germans would speak German. The Norwegians would use their language--anything to try to keep a little privacy. Long distance was something else. It generally didn't work; at least that is what my folks told me. Maybe they just thought it was too expensive.

The Hubble Space Telescope

(I quote "they" a lot)

From its vantage point, high above the dust and fog of earth,
It sends us pictures. Things we've seen before but dimly
Now are clear, and new things are discovered.
Now they see a dust cloud so big its dimensions are measured in
light years,
And the tiny glowing spots on its periphery,
Occlusions of its dust, they say, are bigger than our galaxy.
Think of a thing so big that light from its left side you may see
Years before you see the right. Or, of course, the opposite.
But closer to home and more important,
We ordered a new mattress pad from Lands End,
It's quilted in soft little squares of some new material.
Space age, they said, and it makes our bed seem like sleeping
on a cloud.

Term Limits

I hear lots of politicians talking about quitting lately. They say they have been in there fighting the good fight long enough and are not going to run again. Go home, do something different for a while, they say, or spend more time with their families. And then, of course, some figure they won't make it, anyway. The voters are onto them.

They're kidding, of course. They may not run, but they will never leave Washington. They will only change their job description. A law firm or some lobbying outfit will hire them at twice the money they have been making, as suddenly the connections they have made while in office have become very valuable. They may go back home for weddings and funerals, but their livelihood will remain in our nation's capitol. This is not good for us.

They talk about term limits, but that is only while campaigning. Once they are elected, they become strangely silent on this subject. But I think I have an answer. I think senators, representatives, and the president should all be entitled to one ten-year term.

The terms would be staggered, so we could have an election every other year or so. While serving they would live in barracks, be issued uniforms, and eat in a free government-operated mess hall. They would receive free health care, like they do now, but they would be permitted to talk only to bona fide voters from their respective districts, and to each other. No experts in this or that and no consultants with their own agenda would be allowed near them.

At the end of their ten-year term, we would hang them. I know this sounds a little drastic, but it would serve two purposes. Only really dedicated people would run for office, and they would not be around to screw things up after their years of service. A firing squad would not be acceptable to the gun control advocates, and I think hanging would be a little nicer than either electrocution or lethal injection. I think it lends itself to more of a ceremony. It could be outdoors, the candidates for the soon-to-be unoccupied job could do a little campaigning, there would be speeches extolling the virtues of the condemned and bands playing, and then we would put up a nice statue of the guy. He could even get to see it before he hit the end of the rope.

I believe I heard once that the Hawaiians used to throw an occasional virgin into a volcano to satisfy the angry spirits, and we have a lot more politicians than virgins.

Uncle Adolph

Adolph was my father-in-law's uncle. Ed told me many stories about Adolph but always gave me the impression that he was a little ashamed of him.

Ed's bachelor brother Albert on the other hand seemed proud to have Adolph in the family. Louise and her sister and brother had occasion to meet this man when they were very young as he would pass through North Dakota occasionally and would stay with the family. Louise's mother looked forward to his coming with some trepidation as he generally had some visitors with him that he had picked up in his travels. They would have to dose the mattress and bedding with kerosene and Black Flag bug killer after he left.

Louise's older cousin Lloyd Dysland traveled later in his life to Europe and Australia and commented in his letters that he was "Taking after Uncle Adolph," so you can see that he had a reputation, at least in the family.

Adolph had somehow gotten the idea that the Bank of Canada was after him. He had homesteaded there once and left under circumstances that seemed to give him a very guilty conscience. He had the idea that as long as he kept moving nothing much bad could happen to him. He once walked clear across Russia on his way back to Norway where he figured he would be safe. He then had second thoughts about that and came back to America. I believe he is buried in Wisconsin somewhere, so if the bank still wants him, that is where they should look.

The inclination to travel seems to have skipped most of the people in Louise's family; at least I thought so until lately. Now, however I am starting to wonder. Louise's sister Jean started slowly, first with a trip to Norway and Scotland to look up relatives and so forth. This I could understand. Then a trip to Tanzania in East Africa to look at missionaries, which I imagine is an acceptable trip for a good Lutheran Church Lady. But this last expedition of hers has me thinking she surely has some of old Adolph's genes. She has taken a trip to Rio de Janeiro for the Carnival. This I understand is revelry with partial nudity and much carrying on that is seldom if ever seen here in Minnesota. This is not a Lutheran Church Lady type of trip.

Additional copies of this book may be purchased from

Asgard Publishing
P.O. Box 454
Hancock, MN 56244

Phone: (320)392-5634

e-mail: drasm@info-link.net

Round Table at the Seniors Center

Round Table at The Owl's Nest

SAVIOR ON THE SILVER SCREEN

Savior on the Silver Screen

Richard C. Stern
Clayton N. Jefford
Guerric DeBona, O.S.B.

PAULIST PRESS
New York/ Mahwah, N.J.

All scriptural citations are taken from the Revised Standard Version of the Bible unless otherwise noted.

The Publisher gratefully acknowledges use of the following: Photo from *The King of Kings* courtesy of the Academy of Motion Picture Arts & Sciences. Copyright Modern Sound Pictures, Inc. Used with permission. Photo from *King of Kings* courtesy of the Academy of Motion Picture Arts & Sciences. Copyright 1961 Turner Entertainment Co. Used with permission. Photo from *The Gospel According to Saint Matthew* courtesy of the Academy of Motion Picture Arts & Sciences. Copyright Cifex. Used with permission. Photo from *The Greatest Story Ever Told* courtesy of the Academy of Motion Picture Arts & Sciences. Copyright 1965 Metro-Goldwyn-Mayer, Inc. All rights reserved. Used with permission. Photo from *Jesus of Nazareth* courtesy of the Academy of Motion Picture Arts & Sciences. Used with permission of Photofest. Photo from *Monty Python's Life of Brian* courtesy of the Academy of Motion Picture Arts & Sciences. Copyright Python Productions. Used with permission. Photo from *Jesus of Montreal* courtesy of Academy of Motion Picture Arts & Sciences. Copyright 1990 Orion Pictures Corporation and Max Films, Inc. All rights reserved. Used with permission. Excerpt from "Howl" from *Selected Poems 1947–1995* by Allen Ginsberg. Copyright 1955 by Allen Ginsberg. Used by permission of HarperCollins Publishers.

Cover design by Cindy Dunne

Book design by Theresa M. Sparacio with assistance by Gary Nardozza

Library of Congress Cataloging-in-Publication Data

Stern, Richard C., 1948-
    Savior on the silver screen / by Richard C. Stern, Clayton Jefford, Guerric DeBona.
      p.   cm.
    Includes bibliographical references (p.   ).
    ISBN 0-8091-3855-7 (alk. paper)
    1. Jesus Christ—In motion pictures. I. Jefford, Clayton N. II. DeBona, Guerric, 1955- .
III. Title.
PN1995.9.J4S74   1999
791.43´651—DC21   99–14057
                                                            CIP

Published by Paulist Press
997 Macarthur Boulevard
Mahwah, New Jersey 07430

www.paulistpress.com

Printed and bound in the
United States of America

Contents

How to Use This Book   1

Preview of Coming Attractions   7

First Feature: *The King of Kings* (1927)   29

Second Feature: *King of Kings* (1961)   61

Third Feature: *The Gospel According to Saint Matthew* (1964)   95

Fourth Feature: *The Greatest Story Ever Told* (1965)   129

Fifth Feature: *Jesus Christ Superstar* (1973)   161

Sixth Feature: *Jesus of Nazareth* (1977)   197

Seventh Feature: *Monty Python's Life of Brian* (1979)   233

Eighth Feature: *The Last Temptation of Christ* (1988)   265

Ninth Feature: *Jesus of Montreal* (1989)   299

Appendix   337

Reading List   360

96542

But who do you say that I am?

Matthew 16:15 and parallels

Acknowledgements

The authors would like to acknowledge the role of Father Mark O'Keefe, O.S.B., President-Rector of Saint Meinrad School of Theology, who administers the school in which we all teach. We have received generous sabbatical and leave time to work on this project. We have been encouraged by Father Mark, as well as by our students and colleagues, to take this book from its origins as an elective course into a form that could be used by those outside the Saint Meinrad community.

We also acknowledge Father Archabbot Lambert Reilly, O.S.B., who manages to sustain a vital interest in all that goes on at Saint Meinrad Archabbey and provides the energy and vision to keep a complex community up and running.

Thanks, of course, also must go to the students who took the original Savior on the Silver Screen course and provided many helpful ideas for shaping the enclosed material.

We are grateful to our editor, Kathleen Walsh, for her good editorial sense and for her enthusiasm for this book. Thanks are also expressed to Father Richard Sparks, C.S.P., former editor at Paulist Press and alumnus of our school, who set us in a productive direction with some formative suggestions in the early stages of writing.

Father Damian Dietlein, O.S.B., our colleague, performed his frequent service as fearless and relentless proofreader. To him, we offer our thanks, not only for his eye for detail, but for his faithful work as our colleague.

About the Authors

Richard C. Stern received both a master's degree and a doctorate in education at Northern Illinois University, where he also taught speech and media production courses. Author of numerous articles and essays, he is currently serving as associate professor of homiletics at Saint Meinrad School of Theology in Indiana.

Clayton N. Jefford received his Ph.D. from The Claremont Graduate School of Southern California and has served for the past decade as associate professor of sacred scripture at Saint Meinrad School of Theology in Indiana. An archaeologist and biblical researcher, he is the author and editor of several books, including *The Sayings of Jesus in the Teaching of the Twelve Apostles, The Didache in Context,* and *Reading the Apostolic Fathers.*

Father Guerric DeBona, O.S.B. is a monk of Saint Meinrad Archabbey and teaches in the homiletics department at Saint Meinrad School of Theology in Indiana. He studied at the State University of New York at Stony Brook and received his Ph.D. from Indiana University. He has published widely on film and cultural history, including contributions to *Literature/Film Quarterly, Cinema Journal,* and *The Journal of Film and Video.*

How to Use This Book

First, a few comments on the format of this book. Apart from the introduction and concluding chapter, there is a chapter for each of the nine films examined. The films/chapters are arranged chronologically. Each chapter addresses a single film, yet all have a common format. The chapter begins with a general introduction of the film with some basic information about who wrote, produced, and directed the film. Then come comments intended to help establish a context for viewing the film. The attempt is not to answer any of the major issues about the film or the questions it might raise, but to prepare the viewer for watching the film. Next comes a set of pre-viewing questions to help guide the watching of the film. The second set of post-viewing questions is, obviously enough, a list for leading discussion after you have watched the film. Here, too, you may well come up with additional questions and observations. Then comes the discussion of some of the major issues or features of each film in the three interpretative lenses. The appendix at the end will be a helpful tool for assessing how the film makes use of Scripture passages. The reader should keep in mind, however, that this is just one read on how the film employs the listed passages. We have tried to be rigorous in determining which passages are quoted, referenced, or alluded to, but this is not a foolproof process. Nevertheless, the appendix should be a valuable reference for both

the students of Scripture and of film who wish to see how Scripture has been employed in service to film!

It is the suggestion of the authors that anyone preparing to view some or all of these films, whether as an individual project or in a group setting, first carefully read at least the canonical gospels: Matthew, Mark, Luke, and John. Read them individually, from beginning to end, as you might read a novel. What image or images of Jesus are prevalent? How are the images created and reinforced? What is the author seeking in each gospel? What is the opening scene? The closing scene?

After an initial reading, read through the gospels again, noting particular differences in them, how the character of Jesus is portrayed and what techniques the author used to create the image of Jesus in that gospel. A synopsis of the gospels would be helpful for this task, such as Kurt Aland's *Synopsis of the Four Gospels*. What events are included in all four gospels? in the synoptic gospels alone? in only one of the gospels?

Further, we suggest that the leader of any group planning to watch these (or any other) films be sure to watch them carefully before screening them for the group. The leader should not be caught by surprise concerning any scenes, comments, portrayals, or references made in the movies. The leader should be familiar with the films before screening them for the group.

We offer then some initial suggestions on the use of this book. These suggestions are based on our own use of this material. You may have some additional ideas on how to use the book and the movies. We have used all of these movies within a single course, which has been taught several times with success. In other courses, we have used the movies or clips, either singly or in groups, to illustrate various points about film, Scripture, and theology. We use these (and other) movies a lot! Watching movies or parts of them can make concrete what is often abstract in an academic setting. They can help people to think, relate, process information, and draw conclusions. In preaching and in writing, the maxim holds that it is better to show than to tell. This is to say, a picture is worth a thousand words, which is to say....You get the picture.

These movies are cultural responses to the person and the image of Jesus. Moreover, our interrogation of the figure of Jesus could hardly be more timely and urgent. The United States Catholic bishops met in Kansas

City, Missouri, in 1997, unanimously adopting a pastoral plan for church communication. Among several goals enumerated at their meeting was an examination of how the media "influence the values, judgments, and actions of U.S. society."[1] Uncovering the ways in which Jesus himself has been reproduced in the age of technology can only enrich the faith community's understanding of the Word himself, God's definitive and eternal communication to humankind. This book only examines feature films about Jesus, but we suggest that print media, radio, cable, and broadcast television images of Jesus be investigated as well. The weekly appearance of Jesus as a cartoon character in the Comedy Channel's *South Park* once again presents the Christian community with a challenge: Why *this* Jesus at *this* time, the end of the second millennium?

The process of viewing these movies should not be perceived or conducted as a test of orthodoxy, however one defines that term. A fearless dialogue of faith and culture helps us to understand how various cultural responses to the historical Jesus came to be. The films may also help us to understand our own image of Jesus, either as that image agrees or disagrees with those of the several films. Yet one need not, indeed one should not, watch these movies initially with the primary goal of finding their heresies or theological failings and inadequacies. First, let the movie be a movie. See how it works as a movie before delving into deeper analysis of the theology implicit in the movie as a text.

We recognize that not everyone will be able to show every film. We have chosen nine films because nine films seem to work well in the time available during either a quarter or a semester. A semester would allow a little more time to explore associated topics. One could show, before moving to the feature films, the video entitled, *The Portrait of Jesus: A Shade of Difference,* which examines how the image of Jesus has developed in the medium of painting.[2] A semester might also allow for greater comparison of films, for example, editing together a sequence of parallel scenes of several movies, for example, the annunciation, the crucifixion, the resurrection, Peter's betrayal, Jesus' trial, and so forth. One might also create a sequence comparing how different movies portray the same character, Judas, Mary Magdalene, or Peter, for example.

Prior to watching the Jesus films, we have played examples of television commercials for a single product or by a single producer to approach the matter of characterization and visual style, also known as media literacy. The commercials are obviously much shorter than entire movies, yet they do manage to develop short story lines, develop character (especially if a series of commercials uses the same characters), and reveal various camera techniques. A recent series by Nissan, for example, features an interesting, almost godlike character, an Asian man who seems to be overseeing, even manipulating, events portrayed in the commercials.

Because of the time available, or for various other reasons, some selection from among the movies may need to be done. Indeed, as we have offered courses and workshops prior to and during the preparation of this book, we have faced the same situation. We have chosen to arrange our movies in the order in which they were produced in order to provide a chronological rendering of the portrayal of Jesus in cinema. But one might also group them according to Hollywood and non-Hollywood films. One could compare the two groups after assessing their commonalties within groups.

It has been our experience that many audiences respond very positively to *The King of Kings* (1927). Perhaps this is because it represents their own view of Christ; it has not seemed as alien as it might seem purely on an objective cinematic basis. Perhaps because the film is black and white, "silent," and rather primitive according to the standards set by current computer-enhanced movies where one's imagination is the only limit of what one can portray on film: bodies "morphing" from one shape into another, bodies with holes in them walking around, tricks of all sorts. But the Christological perspective of the movie is not dissimilar from that of many contemporary Christians, with a distinct emphasis on the divinity, not the humanity, of Christ. Jesus is very piously portrayed; his comforting paternal style might be very appealing to many Christians in this demanding, complex postmodern world in which every traditional authority seems to be battered or destroyed.

When the number of films viewed must be whittled down, we suggest showing either *King of Kings* (1961) or *The Greatest Story Ever Told* if a choice must be made there. They are certainly not identical, not redundant. But they do both represent examples of epic Hollywood portrayals of the life of Jesus. One could also make a choice between *Monty Python's The Life of Brian* and *The Last Temptation of Christ* if one wanted to show only one controversial film about Jesus' life, although, strictly speaking, *Life of Brian* is not about Jesus, of course. They are quite different films with vastly different styles and characterizations. *Jesus of Nazareth* is extremely long, yet it has become something of a standard fare on television around Eastertime. Many have seen it time and time again, but may not have viewed it with an analytical eye. Perhaps instead of showing the whole film, the instructor could select certain scenes or segments in order to compare/contrast with other films, rather than show the entire six hours.

We suggest that participants, in any group presentation of the full or partial series, commit themselves to the whole series, however it might be structured. This is, admittedly, extremely hard, especially in a parish setting. But if participants come hit and miss, they will miss the flow of the portrayals from early to recent. In addition, there is the tendency to miss the movies that have an element of controversy or that people do not like aesthetically. This matter of sporadic attendance has an effect on the group discussion that should go with the movies. The group dynamic is inhibited significantly when the composition of the group is always changing, especially when new members come in. There is little common basis of experience, little history with the group or with the previously viewed films.

If the movies are to be presented to a group, someone needs to take some modest responsibility for guiding the discussion prior to and following the viewing. As part of guiding the discussion, it should be made clear that one's contributions to discussion do not constitute some sort of theological truth-test. People should be free to make contributions. Not everyone will agree with every comment of course, but it should be made clear that people's orthodoxy is not being measured.

Viewers can simply watch the movies as movies, noting strengths and weaknesses in plot, characterization, camerawork, and such. Further, one can look at them as theological texts with implicit and explicit statements about God and about Jesus of Nazareth. Last, viewers can see them as cultural artifacts that provide insight into both the people and the times connected with the films' productions. Above all, however, enjoy the movies, even the ones you don't especially like. Each time we watch them we see something new that we had not noticed in the previous viewings. It is not all that different from reading and rereading novels, poems, even the Bible, and finding new meanings, new insights, new passages that had been overlooked in previous readings.

One logistical concern is where to find all of these movies. We purchased all of them (plus others not reviewed in the book) from Facets Multi-Media, Inc. at 1517 West Fullerton Avenue in Chicago, Illinois 60614 (1-800-331-6197). Films may be rented or purchased through Facets. Most of the films purchased were about twenty dollars, with a few costing more than this. Distributors of Christian books and films and national and local video rental stores may carry some of the movies, but we have found that most do not carry all of them.

NOTES

1. *The Pastoral Plan for Church Communication,* NCCB/USCC, Copyright 1977, USCC, Washington, DC.
2. Distributed by Manhattan Center Studios, 311 West Thirty-fourth Street, New York, NY 10001.

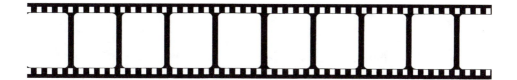

Preview of Coming Attractions

There is something about the medium itself which makes it difficult for a cinematographer to approach the image of Christ directly.[1]

Introduction

The curtains part, the house lights dim, and after endless previews of coming attractions, the house lights go down, the picture fades up, and you settle in as the film finally begins. Or, in a variation on this scenario, with pop and popcorn cradled in hand, you walk from the kitchen into the living room and plop down on the sofa or recliner. With the remote control poised like a futuristic weapon in the other hand, a deft flick of the thumb sets another evening's entertainment in motion. After fast-forwarding through the promotions...the film finally begins. Either way, you have settled in for two hours (more or less) of entertainment, distraction, excitement, suspense, terror, a bit of cultural exploitation, and possibly even religious education.

Films are big: big screen, big money, big business, big influence. Films influence the way we think, believe, and behave. It seems to some that the influence of film may be decreasing. Attendance has declined over the last few years. According to Michael Medved, audience numbers in 1992 were at a sixteen-year low in terms of gross attendance and at the "lowest level ever

in terms of percentage of our population."[2] Yet the number of tickets sold is still in the hundreds of millions (960 million in 1991) and the money spent is staggering, money spent on talent, promotion, production, and so forth.[3] But movies are more than just entertainment. Medved proposes, as one of three arguments in his book, that movies and other media "influence real-life behavior."[4] "Every commitment to produce a movie, TV show, or popular song involves an element of conscious or unconscious value judgment."[5] It seems obvious then that media also have the potential to influence the basic values of those who watch and listen, with the further potential to influence the direction and shape even of our religious faith and our understanding of the person of Jesus of Nazareth, a person who lived two thousand years *before* moving pictures were even invented.

If it seems preposterous that contemporary media (specifically television and film) could influence our Christian faith, one need only examine how images of Christ portrayed over the centuries in other media—painting and stained glass as examples—have influenced and been influenced by theological understandings of Jesus: who Jesus was, what he did. If you were asked to picture Jesus, the image that commonly comes to mind is likely that of Jesus as a thin-faced, brown-haired, bearded, blue-eyed slightly effeminate, and gaunt northern European. So pervasive is this image of Jesus as a European that much of the world pictures Jesus in this same fashion. Yet early paintings of Jesus did not picture him as any of these things but as more Semitic and without a beard.

With the advent of the printing press and the ability to replicate images of Jesus over and over and over, it became both easier to control and to popularize the images of Jesus that were disseminated. But, as Bernard Brandon Scott has noted, "Interpretation, like reading, now became the private and individual, not public and common."[6] Those producing the image had control over the original production, but subsequently lost some of that control because of the lack of control of access to the image itself.

We should note here that the influence of any medium on the image of Jesus is not necessarily a *negative* influence. Each of the authors of this book would claim that his image of Jesus has changed through this project of watching and rewatching these and other films and from discussing their impact and their perspectives. This is not at all to say that any one film represents the definition of orthodox dogma about the person of Jesus or even that we "liked" every film that we include here. Quite the contrary. Some perspectives clash dramatically with our own. Some of the cinematic views of the church were hard to swallow. The movies, however, became vehicles for clarifying and expanding our own experience, of conversing explicitly with students and implicitly with the film itself.

Jim McDermott has claimed that cinema is a "post-Christian invention" and as such it lacks "the roots in faith the other arts enjoy"; it lacks a "mainstream spiritual tradition to lend guidance to film makers."[7] One wonders what makes a medium Christian or at least compatible with Christian beliefs? What influence does the medium have on the message? This is a question Marshall McLuhan wrestled with thirty years ago when he wrote about the medium as the message (or massage) and hot versus cool media. Nevertheless, if the claim by McDermott that opened this chapter has merit, filmmakers have nevertheless not been hindered from making one cinematic life of Jesus after another.

Filmmakers have attempted to portray some vision, or some version, of the life of Jesus since at least 1898, when *The Passion Play of Oberammergau,* written by Salmi Morse, was produced by Richard G. Hollaman; it was all of nineteen minutes in length.[8] It should be noted, if only in passing, that *The Passion Play of Oberammergau* was not filmed in Oberammergau—a foretaste of things to come, when the life of Jesus would be filmed from Tunisia to Utah to Tuscany in the search for a locale that was more real than the real thing. Oftentimes, reality is just not quite real enough in the world of cinema.

In addition to films explicitly about Jesus, there is another category of film that we might label as secular or, at least not self-consciously religious, but which does employ a Christlike figure as its key character or hero. Bernard Brandon Scott has explored this phenomenon in *Hollywood Dreams and Biblical Stories.* We refer the reader to this book as an excellent exploration of American culture and its myths as employed and exploited in Hollywood cinema.

If films (and television) both reflect and influence our fundamental cultural values, it is not a long stretch to assume that they also influence our religious and theological values as well. As Christians, each of us has an image of Jesus that is important to us, an image we appeal to when sorrow or danger threatens to unravel our world, when no one else seems to care, when it becomes clear that there is no salvation in human enterprises, when we are awed at either the depth of joy or sadness. This image is made up of more than a visual image, a picture; it consists of the qualities of the Christ that we value, ways of describing the importance the Christ has for our living. This image, although there may be more than one, is not to be taken lightly or dismissed too readily. It should not be tampered with except with great devotion and careful attention. What is *your* image of Jesus? When and where did you come by this image of Jesus? Through the words and lessons of Sunday school teachers? Through careful study of Scripture? Through paintings on the walls of your childhood Sunday school rooms? Through stories of the legendary exploits of church heroes? In what way has your image of Jesus become an important lens for the way you view the church, the secular world, yourself?

One faithful but slightly misinformed person lamented to his pastor, "We need to teach our children more about the Bible and what it means to be a Christian, like when the Queen of Sheba handed over John the Baptist to be killed." Indeed. If not quite historically accurate, he was right to suggest that we must and do teach others about Jesus through many media. In so many ways and through so many media, we develop our understanding of the person of Jesus.

This book will introduce you to just a few of the films about Jesus of Nazareth. We hope viewing the films and working through the chapters will encourage you to be reflective or analytical about the role that film and other media (including books!) have played in shaping your religious life and values. We also have several additional goals in mind. Most obviously, we want to examine nine films about the life of Jesus, using three "lenses," which will be described later in this introduction. The movies are arranged chronologically to give a sort of historical sweep of how Jesus has been portrayed via the movies. Each movie, however, also has some other quality that makes it of interest: characterization, use of color, parabolic quality, controversial elements, and so on. Four of the movies are Hollywood productions, big budget films with certain standardized characteristics in common that mark the movies as "Hollywood." The others are varied in source and style: Italy, Montreal, Great Britain; parody, parable, musical, fiction.

A second objective is to examine the implications, if any, these films might have for the content of our faith. How did they "work" in you? Did you gain any insights into the person and work of Jesus by watching and discussing these movies? What in the movies resonated positively or negatively with your sense of things?

There is not just one image of Jesus, of course, to which we all look. Even in Scripture, quite a collection of titles, each of which has its own associated meanings, is employed to describe who Jesus "is" to the ones who worship him. The titles are rarely used in an exclusive way, that is, as though that one title captures Jesus completely. The list of titles includes references to Jesus as King, the suffering Servant, Christ or Messiah, Son of God, Son of man, Lord, Word, and Savior. In the Gospel of John, Jesus speaks of his work using a collection of metaphors including vine, bread, good shepherd, life, and others. So both Jesus himself and others who sought to describe him employed many images to try to create a sense of Jesus and his work. These images communicate something to us about Jesus, but they also give us some insight into the person who employed the images, even into ourselves. Homilies and hymns have been added to the attempts to explain and inspire. Whatever medium comes along is available to be used for good or ill. But it will be used; that you can count on.

One goal of this book, then, is to create a more analytical eye when viewing "Jesus films" in particular. While these films add little to the storehouse of scholarly information about the person of Jesus, they do say a great deal about the people who produced the films and about the times in which the films were produced. They are not neutral presentations free of subjective agendas and values. The more influence they have, the more we should attend to the message(s) they are communicating. Is it a message we can support, that is consistent with our own beliefs? Or does the movie seek to destroy the image of Jesus? In either case, movies are, in part, cultural responses to some prevalent image of Jesus. In few cases is this image totally consistent with the Jesus of any *one* gospel. It may be consistent with the larger catalog of images of Jesus in the gospels from which we gain most of our information about the person of Jesus. Yet, it is evident that even the gospels, which we affirm as God's Word, are also literary constructions with plots and characters interacting with one another. The gospel authors and editors had personal beliefs, as do you and I, and tried to shape the text to reflect and promote those beliefs. Their handiwork is evident the more one studies the language, images, and issues of each book in the Bible and in the Bible as a whole.

The gospel authors had very powerful perspectives at work when they described and recorded the events of Jesus' life. Indeed, John, near the end of his gospel, professes that the events of Jesus' life he has chosen to record were written for a very particular purpose: "...these are written so that you may come to believe that Jesus is the Messiah, the Son of God, and that through believing you may have life in his name" (Jn 20:31 NRSV). This is John's purpose for writing, and it certainly influenced what he recorded from the inventory of events and sayings of Jesus, and it shaped how he developed and arranged his material. So, perspectives are not somehow evil per se; everyone has one. Indeed, having a perspective, an opinion, or a viewpoint is natural and inevitable. Uncritical and uninformed perspectives can, however, turn to prejudice.

As Robert Muffoletto has observed, "Representations...are social and historical objects that have been assigned meanings, values, and functions through already established and maintained codes of discourse and meaning."[9] That is, no representation is neutral. It has had to select certain qualities of the original to be represented. All representations fall within some social, political, and historical landscape.

After viewing and discussing nine film versions of the person or image of Jesus, we hope you will be willing to look at your own image of Jesus and explore its origins and its present influences, not as something you must destroy, but as something of value that is worth examining more closely. We hope you will examine your faith, your collection of beliefs, to determine how you may have come by some elements of that faith, particularly those pieces related to your image or vision of Jesus the Christ. The goal is not to lead you away from your present image of Jesus nor to any particular theological outcome. The goal is to encourage a willingness to examine your own understanding, checking it for consistency and seeing if it can be enriched by examining a few films, which hopefully will get you thinking not only about movies but about the complex of values and elements that constitute your faith.

While the Scriptures are more than just another literary medium to those of us who are Christian, they are nevertheless a medium, a vehicle, by which we gain understanding of Jesus. Thus the Scriptures share some of the qualities of all media. While we certainly do not equate these cinematic presentations of the life of Jesus with the Word of God contained in the canonical gospels, there is a very real sense that both the individual gospels and the various films work to present different images of Jesus. Matthew emphasizes different *qualities* of Jesus than Mark or Luke or John. Some *events* are of greater importance to one gospel author than to another. For example, the Gospel of Mark contains no birth narrative and no postresurrection appearances. This is very different from Matthew and Luke. Matthew and Luke record different genealogies of Jesus.

What is each gospel author trying to accomplish? What techniques did the author use to achieve the intended effect? As we apply certain skills of reading and understanding to the films, perhaps you, the reader, will want to engage the gospel writers and other scriptural authors in such a way that individual differences can be detected, authorial intent discovered and explored, and a sort of open conversation can ensue that does not seek to limit or destroy scriptural authority, but which, on the contrary, seeks to honor it with a respectful and knowledgeable dialogue.

Finally, we hope you will become a more savvy viewer of any film you watch, noting the techniques used to communicate the film's message and reflecting on that message and what the message says not only about the producer but about the intended audience. What are the values inherent in the film? What do we learn about ourselves by watching films? The more one is alert to the process and stages of perception, the less one is likely to be controlled by unexamined notions and less-than-noble intentions of some communication messages of whatever medium. It may be something like living in Indiana, as all the present authors do, but knowing nothing about basketball, which is the case with at least one of us. Knowing the game—the plays, the players, the moves, the scoring, the officiating—makes enjoyment that much greater. Knowing little or nothing may mean you can still enjoy the game, but it does limit the range of enjoyment and the insight into what makes for a good game of basketball...or a good movie, for that matter.

The Three Lenses

In order to provide some organized, relatively simple way of analyzing these movies about the life of Jesus, we have adopted three "lenses" to use when viewing the movies. The lenses are not comprehensive, that is, there are probably additional insights, influences, factors, or elements that will be left unobserved, or unmentioned about the movies. These may come to you in your own viewing and/or in discussions about the movies. At the same time, there is probably some overlap among the lenses. Observations that come into view with one lens may be just as "visible" or appropriate when viewed with another of the three lenses.

The lenses, then, are really key questions that we bring to the viewing and discussion of each of the films. They are meant to focus discussion but not to limit it.

Lens One. *How does the film compare to the historical record?* Actually we know extremely little about the day-to-day life of Jesus. Albert Schweitzer observed some decades ago that the results of attempts to determine or set down the historical life of Jesus inevitably seem to resemble the ideal human virtues of the author and the time in which the biographical material was written. It is not any different today. Karen Armstrong, in *A History of God,* has noted that each generation has to create the image of God that works for it, adding "that religion [in general] is highly pragmatic....it is far more important for a particular idea of God to *work* than for it to be logically or scientifically sound."[10]

Within the Christian realm, a rash of recent biographies of Jesus of Nazareth reveal distinctively different images or descriptions of Jesus, yet are products of the same era and the same church. Obviously, then, one can interpret the data differently, coming with different results and arriving at vastly different conclusions. So, at best, what we can do in this book is compare the images of Jesus portrayed in the films with the images of Jesus portrayed in historical documents, canonical and noncanonical, that were recorded closer to the time of Jesus' life and death. What sources did the film's writers use to reconstruct their picture of the Jesus of history, and how did they use them? The Gospels of Matthew, Mark, Luke, and John will be important, but other material is also available, such as various noncanonical gospels, early church authorities, and writings by contemporary observers and historians.

In the appendix, a table of the texts and textual allusions is provided for each film. Examination of those passages of Scripture the director or screenwriter has used provides important insights into the beliefs about Scripture that informed those choices. Even when it is clear that the film is using events recorded in the canonical gospels, which events from which gospels are chosen or left out? There are, for example, few miracles portrayed in these movies and few parables, but lots of Jesus' sayings. Has the biblical narrative been supplemented or altered to make a better story? In *The King of Kings* (1927), for example, a young boy is healed by Jesus. The boy is introduced as Mark, who would later write the Gospel of Mark. There is no record of this event in the gospel itself. In this same movie, much is made early on of the relationship between Judas and Mary Magdalene. What purposes do these additions serve?

Babington and Evans have observed that the Hollywood versions of Jesus' life tend to be rather conservative, even unimaginative, deriving from "eighteenth- and nineteenth-century lives of Christ....Inevitably, in the popular cinema of a culture, where since the mid-nineteenth century a huge gap has existed between advanced theology and mass belief, the devotional and consolatory rather than the critical traditions of such lives have exerted the greatest influence...."[11] Smaller and more recent productions have not been so inhibited by traditional standards and views. Whereas Hollywood productions are "characterized by an absolute directness of presentation," movies like *The Gospel According to Saint Matthew* and *Jesus of Montreal* have ventured into more radical portrayals, more stark in some cases, more metaphoric in others.[12]

Lens Two. *How does the film's producer create and communicate the content of the film?* Once the author of the screenplay and/or the director of the film has conceptualized an image of Jesus complete with characteristics, personal qualities, physical qualities, values, virtues, series of actions, and supporting characters, there remains a monumental task. How shall this image be communicated to the viewer?

In written work, there is a verbal grammar and vocabulary on which to draw. So in film, there is an audiovisual grammar and vocabulary employed to communicate the character of the figures being portrayed, the level of the action being recorded, mood, and so on. Unfortunately, we are not usually so conscious of this grammar/vocabulary, that is, we are not so self-consciously "literate" in audiovisual communication. Texts and subtexts often slide right by us unnoticed, at least unexamined. A few of us can become downright annoying when watching movies or television with others who have not been initiated into a more analytical way of watching television and movies. "Did you see the way they edited that sequence?" "Did you notice the use of the color red in that movie?" Visualization has powerful effects and broad influence, but we are not so likely to be critical or aware of how it works to create the image and the meaning in our consciousness.

Helping the reader to become more visually literate is a goal of this book. The discussion of this lens is somewhat longer here than it will be in the "feature" chapters. For now, the intent is to bring categories to the mind of the viewer/reader for the eventual viewing of the films. Once you get into the swing of it, you will notice much more than you had ever "seen" before. The discussion with the feature chapters is mostly intended as a prod or starter to help sharpen rather than create your visual acumen for watching these and other films.

In "Making Meaning from Visuals," from their book *Visual Literacy,* Couch, Caropreso, and Miller have made some observations about creative thinking. Their references are not limited to creativity in the sense of creating artworks such as poetry, painting, or music, but to the everyday processing of information. They first ask, how many of us really "try to interpret a visual message with the kind of openness that allows us first to develop the relevant knowledge base needed to make meaningful interpretations?" The next step is to "seek alternative solutions always remaining open to possibilities, not jumping to the solution of a problem which may be superficial or may not even exist."[13] A third step in creative thinking is to seek an alternative angle from which to view the problem or question. For example, if I were the director, how would I communicate my image of Jesus?

This is closely related to the process of perception itself. Perception has three steps: selection, organization, and interpretation. Each of us is constantly bombarded by stimuli, some of which have to be ignored or overlooked. We cannot possibly attend to all the stimuli that are around us, so we select out certain stimuli that we pay attention to. Certain physiological, psychological, and/or experiential factors suggest what stimuli may be more attention-getting. In a realm of familiar stimuli, the new or different stimulus will stand out. In a situation where most everything is new, a party of newcomers for example, we may be more likely to notice the familiar face in a sea of otherwise unknown faces. A more colorful stimulus may stand out against an otherwise bland background. We *select* stimuli to attend to.

Once the stimuli are selected, we try to organize them or place them in some meaningful relationship or configuration in regard to what is also going on at that moment or to what we have perceived in the past. But we can hardly help but try to organize the selected stimuli into some pattern or context based, for example, on proximity, similarity, notions of proper form, and so forth.

Once stimuli are selected and organized, we then try to place meaning on the occurrence or try to interpret the stimuli. Here again, certain principles apply. A person's prior experience will influence interpretation, recent experience often carrying more weight. Present feelings influence how one interprets an event as do expectations one may bring to the situation. But then the process begins again through selection, organization, and interpretation. More than a series of steps, perception is a cycle out of which we can never really step.[14]

Mise-en-scène. Much of what is to be considered under Lens Two can be captured under the term *mise-en-scène,* which refers to everything in the frame or view that is under the control of the director. Bordwell and Thompson, in chapter 5 of *Film Art: An Introduction,* have broken this into several subcategories.[15] **Setting** includes the locale of the film and any aspect of the setting that is constructed for use in the film. For example, the locale is not the same for all the movies treated in this book, even though we know quite well where Jesus lived and the places he visited. The movie locales vary from Utah to Tunisia, each providing a slightly or dramatically different look. Also part of the setting, however, are the sets. Compare, for example, the sets in several of the movies used for the trial scenes or Jesus' encounter with Pilate. The entire set for *Jesus Christ Superstar,* for example, is contrived or artificial, lacking verisimilitude. How does this influence your viewing and interpretation of the film? Each setting communicates something beyond merely a neutral place for action to take place. There is a subtext being communicated by the director and set designer.

A second element of mise-en-scène, according to Bordwell and Thompson, is the area of **costume** and **makeup.** Again, one only needs to compare how Jesus is garbed in the several films to see that this is not a haphazard choice. As you watch the several films, note how different characters are costumed: Jesus, most obviously, but also note Mary, Herod, Pilate, Mary Magdalene, Judas, and other key characters. Note how Mary is costumed in *The King of Kings* (1927), simulating the habit of a nun, or how Mary Magdalene's costume goes from erotic to monastic to signal her conversion. Note the red robe of Jesus in *King of Kings* (1961) or the always white robe of Jesus in *The King of Kings* (1927) when everyone else wears shades of grey; the film is black and white, of course. Costume does more than merely clothe the character; it identifies and qualifies him or her as well, and signals changes in status or place.

Lighting is a third category. Lighting includes its own subcategories of quality, direction, source, and color. The quality of light refers to whether it is soft or harsh. Direction indicates the source of the light, whether it is from above, below, or from the side. Pasolini's *The Gospel According to Saint Matthew* makes an especially good study in the use of lighting. Light and dark also play roles in *The Greatest Story Ever Told,* as when Pilate exhorts Jesus, "If you are the Messiah, say so plainly." At that moment Jesus steps out from the darkness behind some netting and into the light, both physically and verbally making his statement. Another example in this same movie is Jesus' encounter with the devil in a wilderness cave. The devil is lurking in the shadows while Jesus is out in the open in the mouth of the cave, looking out at the world. Finally, the Roman armies seem often to be pictured in the dark. This, one must remember, is all very deliberate on the part of the director. Whether the viewer is conscious of it or not, there is, at least, a subtle effect.

Camera work includes the angle at which the camera shoots the subjects as well as how the subjects are framed in the viewfinder. Camera angles affect one's view of the action in a scene: Is the point of view an intimate one in which the viewer feels a part of the action, or is the point of view that of a distant, uninvolved, or omniscient viewer? Is the camera placed above, below, or level with the character or action being photographed? A camera above the character places the viewer in a superior, even omniscient position in relation to the action, as in several scenes from *The Greatest Story Ever Told*. Within each scene, how are the characters framed, that is, placed in relationship to one another; who is in the foreground? the background?

Editing—how the many shots and scenes are arranged—is another important element in creating a visual effect. Editing really creates the movie by establishing the flow of the movie, the pace of the action, what scenes follow other scenes, the sense of the relationship of the characters. Is the pace smooth or rough? Jumpy or seamless? Fast or slow? For example, compare the flow of *The Gospel According to Saint Matthew* with that of *Jesus of Nazareth*. The former is intentionally rough and jumpy; the latter is smoother and more evenly paced. Does the editing call attention to itself as in *The Gospel According to Saint Matthew,* or does it seek to be invisible or seamless, as is customary in most Hollywood films? Is there continuity in the editing or discontinuity? Again, with reference to Pasolini's *The Gospel According to Saint Matthew,* by means of editing and changes in lighting, Jesus recites the Lord's Prayer over what seems to be an extended but undetermined amount of time. We cannot tell how long it took, however, the clear implication being that the recitation took place over a very long time, and not merely the "real time" that it takes during the movie—a couple of minutes.

In addition to the visual portion of the film vocabulary, **sound** or audio is also used to communicate the message of the film. This includes, for example, vocal qualities of the characters. It is of some mild interest that the character of Jesus in many of these films has a British accent, especially *out of character* in *Jesus of Nazareth,* where the actor (Robert Powell) has what seems to be an inappropriately upper-crust British accent. What is the subtext here, that is, why did the director want *that* accent? Now, of course one might respond that this might be the actor's natural accent, but actors can and often do assume other accents. The choice of that accent must have been intentional on someone's part.

In addition to vocal qualities, sound effects and music contribute powerfully to shaping the message of the scene. As an example, the choice of music in Pasolini's *The Gospel According to Saint Matthew* is very unusual and certainly very intentional. Music is an important element, as is suggested by the many soundtrack recordings that sell so extremely well, sometimes better than the movie itself.

A few checkpoints should be included in every discussion of these films. First, what is going on in the opening scene? The opening scene serves to establish place, mood, tone, and other qualities as well. Who is featured in the opening scene? Compare the opening scene of *The King of Kings,* which contains an extended scene with Mary Magdalene and her consorts, with *The Greatest Story Ever Told,* which begins with a slow pan of a fresco on the apse of a cathedral and finally settles on an ascetic-looking figure of Christ. This visual is accompanied by Orson Welles reciting (over soft violin instrumentation) from the prologue to the Gospel of John.

If the opening shots set the scene and tone of the film, the closing scene gathers the whole work together to provide you with some "take-home" image such as the shadow of a cross on a beach in *King of Kings* or, in *Jesus of Montreal,* two women reprising the opening song, which took place on a church balcony in the opening scene but in a deserted subway in the closing scene. What are you left with at the end of the movie? What is the parting image the director wants you to take away? While the rest of the film ought to move toward this closing scene, it may also add some new interpretation, some new piece to the puzzle, or a final message that contains the "meaning" or represents the "heart" of the movie. Does the closing scene resolve the fundamental tension in the movie, or leave it for the viewer to resolve? For each film that you watch, note carefully the opening and closing scenes.

These are just a few elements of the vocabulary available to filmmakers to create the images they present to us. As you watch more and more films and as you watch them more and more analytically, your "visual literacy" will increase, and you will tune more quickly and deeply into how the filmmaker manipulates the vocabulary to achieve the purpose(s) of the film. Lens Two will provide some examples of notable audiovisual elements, but will certainly not exhaustively discuss the possibilities. Let the readers take it upon themselves to develop their skills at becoming visually more media literate!

Lens Three. The filmmakers create an image of Jesus they wish to portray, then select and arrange various elements from the audiovisual vocabulary to communicate this image. The process is then turned over to the viewer. One can simply just watch the movie for the immediate experience. One can also process the experience more deliberately, assessing not only the movie, but looking for clues into the filmmaker's motives and meanings.

The observant viewer may begin to get some insights into not only the specific content of the film and the character of the Jesus portrayed in the film, but also into the author or producer of the film and into the time in which the film was produced. It is almost as though one could look backward through the camera lens to see who was behind the camera making the film, through the eye of the camera operator into the mind of the director. What questions does this film raise? What answers does it propose? What was going on in society at the time the film was first distributed? Is this film consistent with or in contrast to the prevailing mood of that day? How does the film "play" today? Does it seem dated? What does each of the films reveal about the creator of the film? If the producer has made other films, how is this film consistent with the others? Or is it distinctly different in style?

One can follow particular issues through the sweep of the movies. For example, how are women portrayed in the several movies? Follow Mary Magdalene or Mary the mother of Jesus. How are they portrayed in a particular film and how do their portrayals compare to other movies? The same could be done with other characters or types as well. To what extent are these portrayals consistent with or in contrast to the cultural mood of the day in which the movies were produced? How about a comparison with the mood of today?

We can never forget, of course, that each of these films was a commercial enterprise intended to make money for those involved. Yet, a broader set of values is also implicit in the film: a vision or characterization of humanity, the world, the church, and Jesus that is discernible despite or because of the profit motive that was involved in the preparation of the film.

The films may also say something about us, the viewers. Each of these films was produced with some sense of audience in mind. What in the film appeals to you? What do you find troubling, even distasteful, or irreverent? What does the film evoke in you that causes you not necessarily to reject but to examine the vast inventory of your beliefs about God, Jesus the Christ, the church, and the life of a Christian disciple? What *do* you reject in these films, or at least find problematic? What do you find especially confronting, moving, challenging? While the films about Jesus may not tell us much that is new or even accurate about Jesus' life, for the observant viewer the films may help reveal some of the characteristics of our own image of Jesus and how it may need reinforcement, revision, or possible replacement. As we interpret the film, it also interprets us by what it evokes and arouses in us. This is known as the hermeneutic circle.

Viewer Discretion

When a film is created, after filming the many sequences, one of the last steps is to choose among all the shots that have been taken and assemble or edit them into a hopefully coherent whole. The editorial process requires a holistic vision of what the film should look like and what it should communicate. Editing a film is what really creates the pieces into a whole. On occasion, films have to be reedited because the pace, message, or look was judged to be off-target.

Likewise, the viewer has an editorial role to play. The viewer has certain choices to make. Even the viewer can apply or remove certain "filters" while watching these movies. As you watch these various movies, we hope you will practice a certain "willing suspension of disbelief." This phrase refers to the decision to suspend final judgment about the movie—its value, point, theology, historical accuracy—until after the movie is over. One cannot view a movie with total objectivity, of course. Only a robot could do such a thing. We come to the movie with values in place. The point here is to acknowledge that each viewer *does* have a personal point of view, but so does the movie. Suspension of disbelief is the willingness to evaluate the film initially on its own terms. What does the film seek to do? Was it successful in accomplishing its goals? According to the values implicit within the film, is the message effectively presented?

After the film is over, you are certainly entitled to take whatever supportive or contrary viewpoint you desire. As in conversation, however, we are more likely to understand what a person has to say if we "hear them out." We hope you will hear each of these movies out on its own terms. Suspend any final judgments, pre-viewing opinions you may have developed about a movie until after the movie has had a chance to "speak" for itself. Do not discard your values, beliefs, and opinions! Instead, place them on the back burner for retrieval at the end of the movie. Doing this completely, of course, is impossible. Yet it is important, at least, to be aware of our systems of belief, values, faith, and behavior so that we control them and not they us.

Another editorial function to put in place is to remember that while the experience of watching a big-screen film and watching the same film on a television screen are somewhat different experiences, they are close enough for our purposes. Do keep in mind, however, that these films were intended for theaters with big screens and different aspect ratios than video, that is, that the ratio of height to width is greater in theaters for that panoramic look. In transferring the films to video, unless the letterbox format is used, some part of the scene has had to be cut off. Television is closer to square and is obviously much smaller in overall size. The difference between film and video is not insurmountable but is something to keep in mind.

In addition to availability, several other criteria went into selecting the films included in this book. One criterion was to choose some of the major Hollywood productions over time: *The King of Kings* (1927), *King of Kings* (1961), *The Greatest Story Ever Told* (1965), and, in a somewhat different fashion, *Jesus of Nazareth* (1977). We then sought to compare these with some of the smaller productions that seemed to come virtually in response to the Hollywood productions. These other productions include: *The Gospel*

According to Saint Matthew (1964), *Jesus Christ Superstar* (1973), *Monty Python's Life of Brian* (1979), *The Last Temptation of Christ* (1988), and *Jesus of Montreal* (1989). The result is a selected film chronology of the cinematic portrayal of Jesus. There are many, many other films on Jesus' life or that contain references or allusions to Jesus' life, but we believe this is a representative and workable list.

Certainly, by the end of the book, we trust you will have developed a critical viewing skill that you can readily adapt to other "Jesus films" as they become available.

Happy viewing.

QUESTIONS FOR DISCUSSION

1. What are some important components of your faith about the person and work of Jesus?

2. What are some of your favorite Scripture passages about Jesus? When you watch the films, try to notice which of these favorite passages are portrayed in the film. If they are not there, why do you suppose they were omitted?

3. What has been your favorite "Jesus film" up to this point? What is there about it that makes it your favorite?

4. Prior to viewing, what is your impression of each movie? Have you watched it or only heard about it? Are you willing to watch it? If not, why not?

5. Who seems to be the intended audience for each of the films? Who is being addressed by the content of the film?

6. What expectations do you bring to this study of films portraying the life of Jesus? What do you hope to learn?

NOTES

1. Jim McDermott, "Is It Possible to Portray Christ in Film?" *Christianity and the Arts* 1 (1994): 20.

2. Michael Medved, *Hollywood vs. America* (New York: HarperPerennial, 1992), xvi–xvii.

3. Ibid., 8.

4. Ibid., 14.

5. Ibid., 33.

6. Bernard Brandon Scott, *Hollywood Dreams and Biblical Stories* (Minneapolis: Fortress Press, 1994), 30.

7. McDermott, "Is It Possible to Portray Christ in Film?" 20–22.

8. Roy Kinnard and Tim Davis, *Divine Images* (New York: Citadel Press, 1992), 19.

9. Robert Muffoletto, "Representations: You, Me, and Them," in *Visual Literacy: A Spectrum of Visual Learning*, ed. David M. Moore and Francis M. Dwyer (Englewood Cliffs, NJ: Educational Technology Publications, 1994), 295.

10. Karen Armstrong, *A History of God* (New York: Ballantine Books, 1993), xx–xxi.

11. Bruce Babington and Peter William Evans, *Biblical Epics: Sacred Narrative in the Hollywood Cinema* (Manchester: Manchester University Press, 1993), 99.

12. Ibid., 98.

13. Richard A. Couch, Edward J. Caropreso, with Helen B. Miller, "Making Meaning in Visuals: Creative Thinking and Interpretation of Visual Information," in *Visual Literacy: A Spectrum of Visual Learning*, ed. David M. Moore and Francis M. Dwyer (Englewood Cliffs, NJ: Educational Technology Publications, 1994), 288–89.

14. See Richard Stern and Rhonda Robinson, "Perception and Its Role in Visual Learning," in *Visual Literacy: A Spectrum of Visual Learning*, ed. David M. Moore and Francis M. Dwyer (Englewood Cliffs, NJ: Educational Technology Publications, 1994), 31–52.

15. David Bordwell and Kristin Thompson, "The Shot: Mise-en-Scène," *Film Art: An Introduction*, 4th ed. (New York: McGraw-Hill, 1993), 145–84.

melancholy that mutes both the joy he seems to have in the presence of children and the anger he expresses at the cleansing of the Temple. The challenge in any film portrayal of Jesus is finding the proper balance between the divinity and humanity of the Christ. It will be interesting to see how this is played out in the eight films viewed in the remaining chapters.

Second, already suggested, is the importance of children to this telling of the story of Jesus. We first see Jesus through the eyes of a blind girl healed by Jesus. She is brought to Jesus by another one of Jesus' healed little ones, a child named Mark, the eventual author of the Gospel of Mark. Jesus gathers with children on several other occasions throughout the movie. In no other movie do children play so central a role.

Third, the role of women in the movie is important. Indeed, the first twenty minutes of the movie deal with Mary Magdalene's opulent but depraved life prior to her meeting with Jesus. Mary Magdalene is an important study by herself but especially so in comparison to the characterizations of other men and women characters in the story: Jesus' mother, for example, or the paunchy, slobbering Roman officials who are in her presence (and power) at the movie's start.

Clearly, in this movie (and all the others we shall view) critical decisions were made about the characterization of Jesus that become visible in the people with whom Jesus associates and in the way he relates to them. These decisions say something important about the image of Jesus presented in the movie, but they say as much about the people behind the camera.

How was the movie rated in its day? A *Variety* review of the time describes the movie as a "stupendous outworking in celluloid of an inspired thought," although the reviewer also added, "It is still a jumble to one who little knows the Bible and [is] perhaps but little more familiar of his own faith."[3] This comment suggests something about the intended audience of this movie. If we think we are alone in assessing our age as a time of singular moral decline, this same *Variety* review from 1927 saw the movie as "providentially presented at a moment when the North American side of the universe appears concededly to have about gone crazy in its ideas and opinions or movements and notions or morals."

Even though this is clearly a *motion* picture, there still is a sense that the movie's creators were working out of a developing notion of how to use the medium. There is no real narrative plot that holds the movie together. While there is a certain amount of action, Jesus does very little of it, even though he is often at the center of the action. There are a great many poses struck throughout the film, with characters, chiefly Jesus, looking regal or paternal or consoling or, in the case of Judas, shameful. Indeed, some claim to have identified 276 representations of paintings in the scenes of the movie, paintings that might have been present in many homes or were at least familiar to viewers and art lovers at the time the movie debuted and are probably still evident today.[4] The result is a rolling history of religious art.

While clearly dated cinematically, the movie still resonates well with many Christians today. What is there about this portrayal of the life of Jesus that makes it still appealing?

Movie Preview: Questions and Suggestions

1. *What do you know about this movie? What expectations do you have?*

2. *What is your image of Jesus? How does he look in your mind's eye? How does he walk? What about Mary, Jesus' mother. Or Mary Magdalene?*

3. *Note how the Bible is employed in this movie. What texts are primary? What key events are present and which are missing? Where in the biblical narrative does the film begin? Who are the chief characters?*

4. *Watch for any stylistic techniques in lighting, music, sound effects, and such. Some things have been suggested already.*

5. *What are the views of women, children, Romans, Jews in this film?*

6. *Watch for visual symbols or motifs that recur throughout the film.*

Movie Viewing

Movie Review: Questions and Responses

1. *With what/whom does the opening of the movie deal? What do you think the purpose was for this directorial choice?*

2. Did the image of Jesus in the film match yours? Describe Jesus, his physical characteristics, his overall mood. How old does Jesus look in the film? How did you respond to the image of Jesus in this film?

3. Is there a primary gospel used here? What key passages and events are portrayed on film; which are missing? Are there any liberties? How is Scripture used?

4. What questions do you have of the film?

5. Who is the audience for this movie?

6. What do you think this film asks of you? How does it seem to define faith? Is there a social message in this film?

LENS ONE

Again, the basic question here is how does this film employ the historical record, particularly Scripture, to create the character of Jesus? The
beginning of the twentieth century was a time when American perspectives
on Jesus could be generally divided into two distinct camps. In the first
camp, many biblical scholars had raised a banner of victory on behalf of
Jesus, the man of Nazareth, the so-called "historical Jesus." They had come
to claim that the Jesus of Christian tradition was every bit as human as are
we. He had walked as a man, shared an inspired vision of what it meant to
dwell in the world of God's kingdom on earth, and had struggled to live in
obedience to that particular vision. Whoever Jesus of Nazareth was as a first-
century Jew from Galilee, he had not descended to earth from the clouds in
order to perform awesome miracles in the name of a God who remained distant from humanity. There was little wonder for scholarship, therefore, that
so many of Jesus' contemporaries had rejected him as the glorious apocalyptic Messiah who had been promised by Israel's prophets as the means to
the ultimate salvation of Judaism.

In the other camp were the majority of modern Christians, the "persons
in the pew," who continued to focus on a vision of the divine Jesus that had
been influenced by a long tradition of theological development within the
institutional church. Jesus was and is the Christ, the Messiah of God! Unlike
any limited mortal, he was a being with special powers of perception who
could perform miraculous feats of wonder that had no equal. Though human,
he was more than mere mortal—he was and is divine! All who met him as he
walked through the hills of Galilee and Judea were moved by his presence
and either drawn to or repelled by his special charisma, by his ability to

change lives and to shape the mind-set of human error and weakness to God's holy will. In the light of this vision, how scandalous it seemed that so many Jews in first-century Palestine had chosen to reject Jesus as the Christ and even called for his death on the cross. How scandalous, that is, to those American Christians who, some two thousand years later, had come to accept Jesus' status as the incarnation of God.

In which of these two camps does *The King of Kings* rest? Cecil B. DeMille is well known as a producer of epic movies, of course. No doubt, he was well aware that his intended audience would be the average people in the pews (the contemporary Christians of the time), rather than biblical scholars who made the academic study of religion their profession. As a result, DeMille's vision of Jesus is shaped by carefully chosen gospel texts from the New Testament Scriptures that would have been easily recognized within popular culture—likely even by the unchurched—and that tapped into the common imagery of broad Christian traditions. Although the scenes in his movie are depicted in multiple tones of gray, the portrait of the first-century Jesus that DeMille paints in these settings is clearly "black and white," that is, created with little subtlety or nuance. DeMille's episodes from the life of the Savior are black and white with respect to his vision of the person of Jesus Christ as Son of God, which theologians, priests, and pastors have fervently proclaimed for almost two thousand years. Moreover, his scenes offer a series of black-and-white, right/wrong ethical choices—either follow Jesus "in his steps" to a moral lifestyle (coincidentally consistent with the Western values of democracy and capitalism) *or* doom oneself to a world of darkness in opposition to the clear plan of God for human salvation.

DeMille is careful to make use of two primary tools in his presentation of the figure of Jesus. On the one hand, he makes a conscious effort to appeal to the most easily recognizable images of Jesus drawn from gospel texts in the Bible. At the same time, traditions from popular Christian piety commingle with Scripture in a way that reinforces the status of these pious traditions as valid and authoritative.

Scripture Texts. First, with respect to the Bible, for example, DeMille's only real choice of biblical translations during his time (the early twentieth century) was the King James Version of Scripture, an English rendering that today, some seventy years later, seems stiff, awkward, and perhaps excessively pious to many. This is especially true in the wake of the numerous translations of the Bible that have been published since the 1950s, versions such as the Jerusalem Bible, the Revised Standard Version, the New Revised Standard Version, Today's English Version, and The New English Bible. Curiously, however, DeMille manages to make the King James text sound even more holy and reverential in approach than the original translators did. For example, where the written text reads "you" and "ye," DeMille often provides "thee" and "thou." In all cases where a pronoun is used in reference to Jesus, it is capitalized (even when Jesus refers to himself). Throughout the movie, DeMille exercises a certain license to nuance and paraphrase Scripture passages when they are spoken by secondary characters. When Jesus himself speaks, however, DeMille follows the text strictly. One might conclude that DeMille works from his own "red-letter edition" of the King James text, since the red words of Jesus appear to be off-limits to editorial alteration. By means of this approach DeMille makes a subtle appeal to the popular piety of his audience and gains sympathy for his own vision of Jesus as the Christ.

Such a humble and reverent invitation to simple piety is enhanced even further through those passages of Scripture that DeMille chooses to include in his film. He skips freely through the New Testament materials and chooses an episode first from one gospel and then from another. There is no apparent effort to tell the story of Jesus from the perspective of any single evangelist—rather he creates a homogenized gospel, blending passages, stories, and themes. This freestyle selection of materials is very typical of what one might expect to hear from an average Christian who, if asked to tell the story of the life of Jesus in brief, probably would assemble a running narrative from bits and pieces of that old, old story that would come to mind—regardless of the particular source. DeMille thus has tapped into the mind of his audience. His is not a concern for the historical story of Jesus as presented in the flowing narrative of the New Testament Gospels, but for the life of Jesus as it has become synthesized into the faith memory of the modern believing Christian. This sense of Jesus as fully formed, unchanging, immutable, is further reinforced by the choice *not* to include portrayals of either Jesus' birth or his baptism by John. We see no hint of Jesus' developing role as the Christ or Messiah. Jesus arrives on the scene complete, even middle-aged.

It remains true that in any retelling of the life of a famous individual the hearer (or viewer, in this case) can discern distinct elements that offer a clear perception of the subject as viewed by the person telling the story. Such elements are clearly observed in the work of DeMille, as is illustrated by his bold use of several facets from common Christian tradition, and, as suggested above, by what is not used.

By way of example, the stories of the New Testament Gospels that appear in our film are blended as a pastiche, as though all of the gospels tell the same tale without any difference or nuance. Undoubtedly, however, the reason that the early church originally decided to include *four* gospels into the New Testament was to provide evidence of a fuller, more complete account of the life and teachings of Jesus than was contained in any one gospel. Yet, at the same time, each gospel reveals its story from the vantage point of its own author and with its own special insights. Of course, neither DeMille nor the average modern Christian would necessarily be expected to recognize the need to emphasize the differences among these gospel accounts. While there is a real value in multiple approaches to any single issue, to be sure, the natural human tendency is to overlook inconvenient differences and to focus only on those places where the texts agree or where the text agrees with the reader's sense of things. This, in effect, is what the film does—it "harmonizes" the Scriptures.

Popular Tradition. DeMille has also incorporated popular tradition, which is indiscriminately intermingled with the actual gospel accounts. These elements of tradition often bubble upward from the witness of later church historians who attempted to explain the forgotten origins of each New Testament Gospel or to understand the history behind the transmission of the texts. By way of illustration, since there is some limited historical evidence that the Gospel of Mark was dictated to the disciple John Mark by the apostle Peter, DeMille portrays John Mark as an apparently homeless young boy who accompanies the apostles as they travel about Galilee with Jesus. This image had already circulated in the vague memory of the early Christian tradition, but was more clearly formulated by later church speculation.

As further illustration, some of what appears here is only pious imagination with roots in historical and theological speculation during the medieval period. Peter is portrayed as the "Giant Disciple," perhaps because of his reputation as a great fisherman, but more likely because he was recognized within the medieval church as a theological giant among the other disciples. Peter's character is more the product of a morality play than of historical fact. This exaggeration of a single personality trait is evidenced in the limited characters of the other apostles as well, most of whom are named with some particular attribute (such as John *the beloved,* Thomas *the doubter,* Andrew *the fisherman*), though none of these characters has any real role in the plot of the movie (which is true as well in the gospels themselves).

In addition, those few women who surround Jesus throughout the film are draped with clothing that suggests their participation in the sacred and celibate activities of a religious order. The sweet and kind nature of Jesus' mother is secured by her trappings as a nun. Mary Magdalene is introduced at the beginning of the movie as a scantily clad and loose woman, but eventually covers herself from head to toe in dark and simple garments after she is cleansed of her seven devils. She has been "purified" into Jesus' vision of what is correct behavior for women.

Finally, DeMille engages in a certain popular, if naive, speculation about the nature of Jesus himself, as well as of those with whom Jesus came in contact. There is much psychological interpretation throughout that has no special basis in historical fact. For example, though no connection is ever made between Mary Magdalene and Judas Iscariot in the gospels, DeMille portrays them as lovers. Theirs is a relationship of frivolity, excess, and petty jealousy. Indeed, the defiant attitude that Judas first assumes toward Jesus is spawned by his apparent jealousy over Mary's newfound interest in the Messiah as a rival love interest!

In a similar fashion, DeMille soon examines the close association that develops between Jesus and Judas. The connection between these two men and, ultimately, the ability of a disciple to betray his master, received little satisfactory answer within the early church. If Judas was to betray Jesus, why did Jesus choose him as an apostle to begin with? Did Judas act on his own accord? under the influence of Satan? as an agent of God's divine plan for salvation? Was there more to the connection between Jesus and Judas than has been preserved in the New Testament accounts; in other words, what emotional struggle is inherent in the decision to betray the intention of God's own work by a person who has been selected by God's own Son? DeMille unmasks a gnawing issue that continued as a focus of concern in later movies about the life of Jesus. Judas agonizes over his decision to betray Jesus. As DeMille explains, Judas acted because he was "bitter, panic-stricken...desperate...all hope of earthly kingdom gone."

Perhaps DeMille's most poignant example of early modern, psychological explanation comes with the figure of the high priest Caiaphas, whom DeMille depicts as a greedy religious demagogue. The primary concern of Caiaphas is for his vocation as a professional priest. He seeks to maintain the religious status quo and his role as Israel's supreme religious authority. His deeper interests, however, are not so much in sympathy with the will of God as with his own personal gain.

In many respects, DeMille has drawn the first-century religious character of Caiaphas with the bold strokes of a medieval and Reformation caricature of the greedy Jew. Caiaphas stands at the heart of the Jesus story, the prime antagonist. He represents all things evil about the unwavering hardness of first-century Judaism as it was portrayed by the later church.

DeMille has looked at the gospels and found an unyielding, corrupt beacon of legalism against which the faithful (and religiously pure) Jesus offers the flexible mercy of the loving Father God. The contrast is stark and clear. The characters are in obvious conflict. Caiaphas is a practical man; Jesus is an idealist. Caiaphas is a business realist; Jesus is an ethical visionary. Caiaphas views only the false goals of tangible rewards; Jesus perceives the deep realities of God's work within the world. Caiaphas accepts what he falsely believes to be true in the temporal world; Jesus anticipates the divine truth that God will soon introduce from the eternal world! These two characters represent the consistent cycle of the human predicament: the struggle between falsehood and truth.

The "Modern" Christian. Into all of this (DeMille's choice of biblical texts and his use of popular faith traditions) yet a third element has been added to the film's historical presentation of Jesus. This element is the appeal to the normative religious experience of the "modern" American Christian, which we refer to as "the comfort factor." DeMille's presentation of Jesus is consistently assembled around the broadly accepted Western standards of common decency and traditional Christian ethics. We are limited to a vision of Jesus that is "constitutive" (or supportive) of the mainline church, never "prophetic" (or challenging) to middle-class American standards of faith.

Jesus heals a blind girl and chats with children; he is kind to the helpless and weak. Jesus transforms the life of the wanton Mary Magdalene and the woman who is caught in adultery; he defeats the powers of a sinful lifestyle and brings order into the world. Jesus defies first the effusive Judas, who wishes to turn the Messiah into an earthly king, and then the evil corruption of the high priest, who wishes to protect a deviant Temple lifestyle; he condemns misguided zeal and the false faith of other religious perspectives. The Messiah Jesus is and does what twentieth-century American Christianity wants him to be and do. He is charitable and tolerant of the poor and helpless. He brings order and safety to a world of disorder and moral danger. He endorses a single view of salvation, which rejects other approaches to God as deviant and misguided.

When the late twentieth-century Christian looks at DeMille's use of Scripture (those passages that are employed and those that are ignored) and popular tradition, as well as at his inclusion of "the comfort factor" behind the traditional Christian understanding of Jesus as the church's champion, several questions should immediately come to mind:

1. *Where are the teachings of Jesus?* Most scholars now believe that the original message of Jesus can be best discovered in the parables that are preserved in the gospels. None of these is employed in our film. This can perhaps be explained by the awkward approach that silent movies must take toward the presentation of long passages of material. The viewer wants to see action, not read successive paragraphs of text. Since many parables are rather long, they are not conveniently presented by the workings of the silent screen. But their omission is the viewer's loss. Not only are the parables missing, but most of the sayings of Jesus (whether long or short) are absent as

well. What about the teachings on divorce, on the reign of God, on not resist-ing violence, on the future coming of the Son of Man? The viewer ultimately is presented with a Jesus who stands as the presence of God in the midst of common humanity, yet who is stripped of most of the very words of instruc-tion and enlightenment that characterize him in the New Testament Gospels.

2. *Where is the challenge to the church itself?* DeMille's Jesus spends most of his time correcting false belief, moral disorder, the chaos of errant lifestyle choices, and the pursuit of human gain that is couched in the guise of religious fervor. Such activities and beliefs presumably fall outside of the realm of the pure faith of the church, of course. These deeds and thoughts are the possession of the unfaithful, the unchurched. One looks in vain for the challenges of Jesus to those who exist within the congregation of God and those who would call down condemnation upon sinners and unbelievers (see Lk 9:52–56) or who wish to be called followers of Jesus yet refuse to for-feit their economic gains (see Mt 19:23–30). Where do we hear Jesus say that the faithful Christian must break ties with the biological family (see Lk 14:26) or must abandon traditional values of the local culture (see Mt 8:18–22)? There is nothing in DeMille's choice of text and tradition that speaks prophetically to the very institution that Christianity claims was established by Jesus himself—the church. The "harsh words" of Jesus are applied only in a literal sense to those who rejected him as the Messiah (that is, the unbelieving Jews). Never do we see these words offered as a challenge to the developing ethic of the Christian enterprise, or as a concern to the twentieth-century church, which in many ways has become fat with its wealth and satisfied with its religious smugness.

In this same line, it must be noted that there is no reference or allusion to Peter's betrayal of Jesus, which might sully, humble, or diminish the viewer's self-image. Babington and Evans observe that all of the texts used are "enormously familiar...[and] become almost talismanic, the source of comfort alone, with no sense about the discomfort of renewal and the shak-ing of the foundations."[5]

3. *Where are the miracles that defy reason?* The power of Jesus' authority and charisma is made evident in three specific scenes: the cure of

the blind girl (that scene in which Jesus is first seen by the viewer), the raising of Lazarus, and the resurrection of Jesus. Each of these "miracles" is achieved through the power of God, of course, and never through any human physical contact. They are dramatic moments that both inspire faith in the believer and require the seed of faith in order to be accepted by those who have witnessed the event. But DeMille does not focus upon gospel episodes in which the laws of nature are defied or in which the logical, modern understanding of how the world works on a daily basis is challenged, such as the walking on the water, the feeding of the five thousand, the expulsion of demons from possessed peoples, the curing of the lame, or the stilling of the storms. This may be DeMille's tip-of-the-hat to early twentieth-century New Testament scholars who explained such "miracles" as the fantasy reports of faithful Christians who wished to portray Jesus as a "God man," a Messiah who was bigger than life. At the same time, however, DeMille has managed to avoid the uncomfortable position of having confronted the Christian viewer with endless healings and nature miracles that continue to defy the logic of modern reason, and thus can serve as a challenge to pious faith.

There is little question that DeMille has crafted a film based upon carefully selected Bible texts and common faith traditions as a means to nurture modern Christian belief and endorse contemporary religious standards. The characters are little more than caricatures. Here is the obvious choice between good and evil, between what is religiously pure and patently corrupt, between the true power of God and the false frailties of humanity. Here the pre–World War II Christian is congratulated for his or her faith, and receives assurance that this peculiarly Western form of Christian confession about Jesus as the Christ of God is good and true. There is every reason for hope and optimism. No presentation of difficult teachings from the New Testament Gospel accounts, no challenge to the comfortable faith of the church pew, no reversal of the logical course of nature and history are thrown at the viewer as means by which to stimulate speculative thought about the Jesus of theology and history. We are reassured by the authority of our Scriptures and tradition that the modern American mainline Christian is just fine in the eyes of God. "All is well! All is well!"

LENS TWO

With this character of Jesus and Christianity in mind, along with some speculation about the issues DeMille wanted to address and perhaps avoid, how then did DeMille translate his inner sense of Jesus into the cinematic vocabulary? "Sir, we would *see* Jesus!"

Observations in "Lens One" have already alluded to some of the ways this image took shape on celluloid. Opening scenes, for example, are significant. As suggested in the introductory chapter, they set place and tone for the entire movie. In this case the opening scene and the next approximately twenty minutes deal with Mary Magdalene's lascivious life and her illicit relationship with the power brokers of Jerusalem and with Judas and her ultimate conversion. As noted above, little of this part of the narrative has any specific biblical referent. But this opening scene does, as Peter Malone notes, "set expectations of how the movies would handle the Bible: sex, sin, and reverence for Jesus."[6]

If DeMille is taking rather liberal license with the gospel narrative, what might his purpose be in opening with such extended emphasis on Mary Magdalene? The opening seems to establish a contrast between two extremes: the worldly lifestyle of Mary Magdalene and the selfless, noble lifestyle of Jesus and other peasants. The film opens with a scene of sophisticated, self-interested, and self-indulgent opulence and then moves immediately to a scene of the selfless, humble poverty of the common folk, where the viewer encounters the young Mark in a street scene and, several scenes later, Jesus himself.

Also of obvious and important note is the use of black-and-white filmstock—until near the end, with the resurrection scene. The resurrection scene in Technicolor is startling and impressive. This is original and not a modern, computerized colorization. Indeed, this mixing of color and black-and-white film stocks anticipates a style that is in vogue in contemporary television advertising. One might wonder why the whole movie was not done in color, but that would certainly have diminished the effect of the resurrection scene. The resurrection is an event beyond comparison, and its visualization must stand out and stand alone. Following the scene at the empty tomb the film narrative returns to the human, the mundane, signified by the return to black and white.

In the black-and-white segments, several rather obvious lighting techniques or stylistic devices have been employed. One is to place Jesus in a seemingly different light throughout the movie, apparently to set him apart visually from the other elements and characters in each scene. He often appears to be slightly overexposed, that is, there is less contrast and shadow on him. He is also in "soft focus" much of the time. The edges, while not fuzzy, are not quite sharp either. This type of lens is often used in portrait photography to soften wrinkles in the subject's face. Here the purpose seems more to demarcate Jesus as "other." This soft focus gives him an ethereal aura that none of the other characters has. This aura is created, in part, by having a backlight illuminate Jesus from above and behind, creating a glow that traces his head and shoulders. Again, the effect is to set Jesus apart from his environment, both physically and metaphorically. Another technique to note Jesus' otherness is used at the stoning scene. Jesus is dressed in a white robe while everyone else is in various shades of grey. The white obviously signifies Jesus' purity, but it also makes him stand out visually in the scene. One last example of the desire to develop Jesus' otherness is in the crucifixion scene. Note how only Jesus is hanging on the cross in the way most of us grew up assuming he died. The two thieves appear not to be even nailed. They appear to be suffering much less and are tortured less by their manner of crucifixion.

Another use of light to draw our attention to important meanings occurs in the setting of the Upper Room, where the Last Supper has just concluded. Jesus and the apostles have all left. The chalice remains on the table, however, spotlighted. A dove flies from the window to the glowing chalice. The monumental and sacramental aspect of the scene is highlighted lest anyone miss the point that this is no mere cup of wine and no ordinary bird.

Keeping in mind the relative prohibition from even picturing Jesus on-screen, the number of close-ups in this movie must have been startling. Despite the pedestrian theology behind the image of Jesus that has been visualized, the *means* of visualizing Jesus are startling, if not revolutionary. Throughout the film, close-ups force the viewer to see that which is of singular importance in the scene, for example, eyes and hands. One cannot help but notice, for example, those hands counting out the thirty pieces of silver for Judas.

Significantly, our first vision of Jesus is another close-up, this time through the eyes of a blind girl whom Jesus heals. The camera looks up, dissolving into a close-up of Jesus' face as he is revealed through a radiant light, his kindly face coming to greater and greater clarity in the girl's eyes. It is as though we are seeing Jesus through the young girl's eyes. This is an obvious but effective allusion to the often used biblical metaphor for our own childlike dependence on Jesus, who alone can open our eyes to the realization that he is the Christ, the Savior, and he alone can heal us of our blindness. Several scenes later we see Jesus repairing the broken wooden toy soldier of the girl. The toy appears to be a toy Roman soldier. Was this irony intentional? A Jewish peasant girl playing with a toy representation of her Roman oppressor?

Much of the action in this film is rather close-in. There are few panoramic vistas as in later movies, particularly *King of Kings,* the 1961 remake of the movie now being considered. The exception to this fairly small scale of action comes during the crucifixion, which is pictured from a distance to capture and imply the widespread devastation that is occurring.

While we label *The King of Kings* a "silent film," there is no lack of sound accompanying this film. It is true that sound effects are used in very particular places for specific effect, unlike current movies, which keep the audience awash in high-power sound throughout the entire movie: music *and* effects. *The King of Kings* certainly does not overpower the viewer's ear in wave after wave of Dolby stereo surround sound.

One use of sound in any movie is the sound effect. In *The King of Kings,* these effects were, of course, added later (as they often are in contemporary films as well) and do not present a seamless interface with the ongoing visuals; there is no pretense of verisimilitude here, only dramatic effect. There is no ongoing dialogue, no background noise to provide a sense of environment and so forth. When sounds occur, they jump out. One thinks here, for example, of the clanging of the gong when Mary Magdalene summons her servants prior to her departure in order to confront Jesus as her competition for Judas's attention. What is the significance of this sound effect? Why not others? Another notable sound effect, already mentioned, is the heavy, clear clinking of the silver pieces that Judas receives for betraying Jesus to his enemies. Finally, the thunder and lightening at the crucifixion come to mind. Someone had to decide which few sound effects to include. It is interesting to speculate about the choices that were made.

In addition to the occasional sound effect in *The King of Kings,* there is nearly constant music underlying the visual action. Indeed, music precedes the visual at the opening of the movie with a majestic, hymnic score orchestrated to prepare the viewer for the initial screen (not the opening scene yet), which reads: "The events portrayed by this narrative occurred in Palestine nineteen centuries ago when the Jews were under the complete subjection of Rome—even their own High Priest being appointed by the Roman procurator. [signed] Cecil B. DeMille." If many of the visuals in this film are reminiscent of familiar paintings, familiarity would also be the hallmark of this movie's musical score—a nostalgic aural pastiche of popular hymns set to moving orchestral arrangements, "music with inevitable communal, and especially nostalgic childhood Church and Sunday School-attending, resonances of recollected security, momentarily converting the secular dark of the cinema into a dim simulacrum of Church or chapel."[7] All of this reinforces the comfortable predispositions of the faithful viewer. There is no discord present to challenge the viewer's ear or faith.

Given then the screenwriter's or the director's sense of Jesus and the subsequent translation of this image into the aural/visual cinematic vocabulary, what does *The King of Kings* reveal about the producer/director, DeMille, about the times in which the film was made, and about the audience who was to view the film?

LENS THREE

If we could look backward through the camera lens, what would we see of the times and people who made this film? Few films underline the importance of the "culture text" more than *The King of Kings*. Some estimates reckon that *The King of Kings* was the most popular of the movies about Jesus' life and, amazingly, played faithfully to as many as five hundred million people until its remake in 1961. By all accounts, the picture was an epic event: children were given the day off to view the film and numerous special showings were held for religious groups, including a special exhibition for about one thousand religious sisters at Grauman's Chinese Theater on August 16, 1927. Ultimately, *The King of Kings* became the third most popular movie of 1927, behind *The Jazz Singer* and *Wings*.

With countless production values, such as newly developed Technicolor sequences of the resurrection, elaborate art direction by Mitchell Leisen and Anton Grot, and even a priest (Daniel Lord, S.J., who would later become an architect of the Production Code in 1934) as technical advisor, *The King of Kings* exceeded all expectations by upstaging even the famous Passion Plays themselves. The Reverend John A. Marquis, head of the Board of National Missions, said that although he had been to the Oberammergau Passion Plays, they did not reach the heights attained by *The King of Kings*. Opening on Good Friday, *The King of Kings* received the endorsement of several religious organizations and a commendation by the administrative committee of the Federal Council of the Church of Christ in America. Even prominent Jewish rabbis found *The King of Kings* "inspiring." *The King of Kings* was not only hailed by critics, but it was also the most expensive, talked about film of its kind in the late 1920s. More importantly though, *The*

King of Kings' technical and commercial success helped to bestow moral and religious credibility on the film industry.

Strangely, though, if we were to show *The King of Kings* today to a group of contemporary, media-savvy undergraduates, chances are that there would be more laughter than applause. But that very dissonance is educative: to move away from the culture that helped to inscribe the distinctive Jesus fashioned by DeMille in the late 1920s is to distance ourselves from what we ourselves have currently fashioned as "Jesus." If every age guarantees its own *Imago Dei* (image of God), it is the destiny of future generations to try to make sense of those images. In a certain sense, "Jesus" is only completely legible to the culture that makes him over in its own image.

So, to see *The King of Kings* from the point of view of late twentieth-century spectatorship is to recognize divergent aspects of American cultural politics. It reminds us of the complex, contemporary ideological networks—often obscured, but deeply embedded—in our society. In reading *The King of Kings* as a movie, what we are suggesting as a critical tool is nothing less than a historicizing of this and other films into a politics of *redeployment* in which "Jesus" is reproduced amid the fluctuating industrial and cultural influences of its day. A director such as DeMille, then, adapts his reading of the gospel text, not strictly as a "matching" context from book to screen. The image of "Jesus Christ" is resurrected, created anew from age to age for multiple purposes.

A Sign of the Times. *The King of Kings* occurred at one of the most fascinating and complex times in our nation's history. After a devastating war, the 1920s were guided by conservative presidents Harding, Coolidge, and Hoover, who promised to return the country to "normalcy." In the closing moments of his moody novel about lost dreams, F. Scott Fitzgerald wrote in *This Side of Paradise* (1920) that the generation after World War I was unalterably changed, "grown up to find all Gods dead, all wars fought, all faiths in man shaken." Indeed, writing by Hemingway, Stein, and others has helped to shape a new kind of American writing that portrayed their contemporaries as "a lost generation." Frederick Lewis Allen's *Only Yesterday: An Informal History of the 1920s* read the ten or so years following World War I in America as "spiritually tired." At the same time, however, the United States was enjoying an unprecedented national cohesion, an "Americanism" that had freed itself from Europe and found itself in the midst of a new emergent order, or what French author André Siegfried called in *America Comes of Age,* "an entirely original social structure."[8]

Spiritually bankrupt? A new social order? The conflicted historical discourse or conversations about the 1920s mirrors the age itself. The decade was fashioned, above all, by high energy, a consumer revolution, or what Paul Johnson in *Modern Times* calls a "prosperity on an unprecedented and monumental scale," which transformed luxuries into necessities.[9] This cultural transformation made it possible for over eleven million families to own their own homes by 1924 and saw the growth of a salaried middle class, as well as the beginning of a distribution of governmental power to women. Yet, for some, the shift in power in American culture during the 1920s meant the vulgarization of fine sensibility, even the erosion of moral values. "Commonplace prosperity" meant a loss of spirituality and the growth of wanton materialism. Similarly, T. S. Eliot wrote about the "wasteland" of the 1920s in his monumental poem as, at least in part, a somber elegy to highbrow enlightenment, now replaced by a massified culture of automobiles, radios, and, yes, movies. In short, a middle-class liberation was occurring very rapidly in America and a massified culture, enabled by technology, was making the dream of many come true.

With its enviable ability to draw in and expand a diverse audience, project a utopian space of dreams, and gather a galaxy of immortal stars, Hollywood film culture would be destined to play an important role in democratizing American culture during the 1920s and beyond. As is well known, the movie audience at the turn of the century was largely composed of immigrants or the children of immigrants who adored the movies. Film historians reckon that by 1908 as many as eighty million people (out of a population of one hundred million) frequented the nickelodeon. Yet despite what was certainly the overwhelming popularity of the moving pictures in 1908, there were other (chiefly moral) interests and demands at work that threatened the very existence of the movies. One short episode even led to the nickelodeons being closed in New York City on Christmas day in the same year. The tug-of-war in the emerging film culture between spectacle and censorship would introduce major reforms that would attempt to guarantee an audience and determine the very nature of production for years to come.

But who would regulate these films, which were viewed by conservative religious groups and those suspicious of mass culture as detrimental to America's well-being? Before standardized regulations were introduced by the Motion Picture Producers and Distributors of America (MPPDA), and later, the Production Code in 1934, it was often the individual director who maintained the power to shrewdly and artfully crusade the thin line between market and artistic interests. In the early days of the silent feature, the country was poised and ready for directors who would bolster the film industry by its own very puritanical prohibitions, but also bring it to a new level of artistic achievement. D. W. Griffith, a brilliant, pious Methodist working as a director for Biograph Pictures, went independent and initiated what cultural historian Lary May has called "the aesthetics of reform."[10] Although he is often reckoned as one of the ten "pantheon" directors by Andrew Sarris, Griffith would claim that the major reason he directed films was not because of art, but because of his compelling interest in reforming the moral behavior of America.

Griffith is an example of a major director negotiating and transforming the perception of popular culture for a moral majority. He did this by reconciling two seemingly bifurcating values: a puritan moral code that loathed and mistrusted theatrical spectacle on the one hand, and a rising immigrant American consumer who could not get enough of it. Griffith was not alone in those early days of Hollywood, however. Close on Griffith's heels was a director whose business savvy and recycling of biblical narrative made him a household name. On the way, he turned the most reproduced face in the history of the West into a movie star and would make millions—and a dignified reputation for himself and the film industry. His name was Cecil B. DeMille.

Some directors were very good at negotiating art and politics. As Griffith knew early on, the movies needed an untarnished image and might even accomplish the work of evangelization, but old-fashioned morality plays would never bring an audience to feature films. Griffith's *Judith of Bethulia* became perhaps the first in a long series of biblical stories recycled in American cinema. DeMille learned a lot from Griffith. The question DeMille faced throughout his career was how best to guarantee middle-class respectability for the Hollywood industry while still enticing viewers to the theater.

The son of an Episcopalian lay minister, DeMille began his meteoric rise in the film business as a copartner in the Lasky Company in 1913 which, by the time of the release of *The Kings of Kings* in 1927, became Paramount Famous Lasky Corporation and one of Hollywood's five major studios. After a somewhat grandiose production of *The Squaw Man* (1916), which was both critically and commercially successful, DeMille enjoyed almost unprecedented control over his productions; this powerful axis allowed DeMille to shape an industry around public taste, particularly in the areas of spectacle and star power, during the emerging years of the Hollywood film business. There are at least three ways in which DeMille redeployed the story of Jesus of Nazareth in order to garner the widest possible audience, from urban Catholics to Bible-Belt fundamentalists—spectacle, point of view, and special effects. In so doing, DeMille would secure prestige for the industry and himself.

It is not coincidental that DeMille's important breakthrough films, such as *Male and Female* (1919) were often sexual teasers. *Photoplay* announced, somewhat notoriously, that Lady Mary (Gloria Swanson) was photographed in her bathtub nude. But cleverly, after a sensuous dream sequence in Babylon, *Male and Female* leaves us with a kind of puritan allegory on fidelity in marriage. Even though the stern moralists were shaken by the shocking sexual content of his early films, DeMille would subdue many would-be detractors by including a moral appendage. Always walking the cunning line between desire and moral correctness, DeMille's instinct for changing postwar middle-class values brought movie audiences to theaters by the millions. Having participated in their guilty cinematic pleasure, theatergoers left the sexual exploits of adulterers absolved: the plot neatly punished the offenders.

The King of Kings, then, becomes exemplary of DeMille's ability to charm us with spectacle but, also paradoxically, to educate us about its fatal attraction. Undoubtedly, the story of Jesus and Mary Magdalene was made to order. Although DeMille photographed one of the most glamorous Hollywood actresses as something of an erotic spectacle, he insisted that the fifty-year-old H. B. Warner lead a very Spartan lifestyle off the set. Further, the famous opening sequence of the film begins as a fairly eroticized scene in the emperor's palace, only to be displaced by an allegory about sexual mischief. Mary Magdalene (Jacqueline Logan, a former Ziegfeld girl at the peak of her film career), who, as the subtitle reads, "laughed alike at God and Man," is surrounded by a carnival atmosphere of the court, replete with the emperor's flatterers, exotic animals, and scantily clad servants.

Reclining on the emperor's couch, the bare-shouldered Mary summons her pet leopard and begins to embrace it lovingly, after which the emperor says, "Mary, if thou will give thy kisses to a beast, why not to me?" Mary's passions are further aroused when she suspects her lover, Judas, of unfaithfulness. After learning about "the carpenter" she then departs to look for Jesus and Judas, driving a chariot driven by wild zebras. She arrives at Jesus' house and asks Judas where she can find the one who keeps him from her embraces. When she encounters Jesus, Mary is visibly transfixed by his glance and, in a series of interesting double exposures, the seven deadly sins are cast out of her. Embarrassed by her bare midriff and head, the repentant Magdalene covers herself and then sits at Christ's feet. Finally, the sequence closes with the soundtrack playing an instrumental version of the classic hymn, "Franconia" ("Blessed Are the Pure of Heart").

It is easy to see that the Magdalene sequence is double-edged. On the one hand, the camera photographs Mary lovingly from the beginning: she is reclined, bare-shouldered, and seductive. Additionally, from the beginning, she is associated with wild animals, with whom she shares a certain kinship. We are provoked by the suggestion of sexual misbehavior not only with the emperor, whom she scorns, or with Judas, who is her lover, but with kisses for the leopard. On the other hand, running through all of these actions is talk of Jesus of Nazareth, who ultimately purges Mary from her seven sins. And it is the Savior who ultimately subdues Magdalene's sexual energy as well. If Mary was associated with wild beasts, bold action, and aggressive conversation before she met Christ, her encounter with him has left her utterly domesticated: she has been tamed by Jesus. Like the mother of Jesus, whom we also glimpse in the home at Nazareth and who is associated with peaceful doves, Mary Magdalene becomes a veiled and docile matron, submissive and speechless (as she will remain throughout the film). Any previous sexual past has not only been cleansed but erased.

Thus, Jesus figures here into DeMille's narrative as one whose gaze has de-eroticized and domesticated the spectacle of the woman into a silent, regularized space. It is easy to see, however, DeMille having it both ways. We have already been enticed by the sumptuousness of the more prurient aspects of the cinema, only to have ourselves, like Mary, cleansed in the process. All this should not surprise us after the numerous orgies in *Manslaughter* (1922) or *The Ten Commandments* (1923), in which such debaucheries are typically followed by retribution. Such a narrative might remind us of 1920s America as a conflicted space of temperance reformers, cultural conservatives, or the "lost generation," which represented itself as spiritually tired and bankrupt, while, paradoxically, the middle-class world became prosperous and eager for pleasurable consumption. DeMille was able to tap into these class and cultural conflicts and bring them together into a narrative.

Point of View. *The King of Kings* also presents us with interesting issues concerning point of view. As noted above, Jesus is introduced into the story from the point of view of a little child, a blind girl (Muriel McCormack) who appeals to him for help. As the girl begins to see, so do we begin to make out the outlines of Jesus' face. Some interesting details here are worth noting. The shift to the child's point of view engages us in something quite unique for films about Jesus. First of all, of course, the point-of-view shot here is quite unlike standard Hollywood close-ups, which are traditionally photographed from an oblique position. Moreover, having Jesus gradually fade into view as he stares directly at us is a departure not only from Hollywood productions, but reminds us of the myriad of representations of Jesus in Christian art, in which the viewer stares directly into Christ's face.

DeMille's fade-in of Jesus is a personalized portrait, allowing the spectator a privatized, religious encounter with his or her own Jesus. Moreover, consider the way in which Jesus' face is portrayed: soft-featured, bathed in light, welcoming. With the invisible "fourth wall" of the stage removed, the face of Jesus is not the Jesus of the Passion Plays, distant and suffering, but the Jesus of our most intimate thoughts, who walks into our lives: a vision granted to us through a child's innocence and our personal encounter with the Savior. Like devotional paintings, depicted in endless Christian churches in the West, and even postcards, DeMille's opening shot of Jesus convinces us that the Savior only has eyes for us.

When seen from the lens of the 1920s—with the numerous subjective literary experimentations of James Joyce and Virginia Woolf, for example—a first-person perspective in the late silent era is not as innovative as it might seem. DeMille deployed much the same effect in *Why Change Your Wife* (1920), in which Beth's face gradually fades into close-up. The films supply motivation for an arty technique. Moreover, the subjective point-of-view shots were enabled in *The King of Kings* by the newly developed Eyemo, a small camera manufactured by Bell and Howell in 1925 and used for aerial documentary footage or in areas difficult for a large camera to shoot. Some of the more elaborate camera sequences in late silent films—especially those influenced by German expressionism—were made possible by lighter and more sophisticated camera equipment.

Although smaller cameras like the Eyemo and the DeVry were not used on a regular basis (Hollywood preferred the larger Bell and Howell or Mitchell), DeMille used an Eyemo to shoot *The King of Kings* in order to get the hand-held shot he required for the healing of the blind girl. In fact, Bell and Howell promoted the Eyemo by showing DeMille using the camera in the January 1927 issue of *American Cinematographer*. There is, to be sure, a certain agility to the shot of the little girl in her wandering through the crowd. All at once, the story becomes her story (and ours as well): personal and subjective. Jesus no longer becomes someone seen on a distant proscenium stage, but close up. Certainly appealing to the evangelical section of America, we might even say that DeMille managed also to give us one of the first really *cinematic* portraits of Jesus.

DeMille became famous for making stars of his actors. With advanced Hollywood photography and lighting, Jesus takes on the aura of a movie star in *The King of Kings*. Indeed, the shots of Jesus from the viewpoint of the opening glances of the child, newly restored to sight, are glamour shots. In fact, the three-point lighting—which was by now standard in Hollywood cinematography—works very well with Warner's somewhat ascetic features. Here DeMille has made Jesus himself a kind of movie star.

Amazingly, DeMille has neatly bridged the world of the sacred and the secular, or rather, blurred their distinction for audiences of the late 1920s, who were by now used to seeing stars in their pantheon of gods, and eagerly moved into lush, huge movie palaces like the Roxy or Radio City Music Hall in New York City, which more than one critic has described as resembling "cathedrals." This discussion of the representation of Jesus in *The King of Kings* still raises questions today about the difference between piety and adulation, or, for that matter, between Jesus and celebrity culture. DeMille has given Jesus an aura, that is, in secular terms, star power.

Technology's Contribution. It would be hard to underestimate the contributions of technology to the evolution of DeMille's epic films and, in particular, to *The King of Kings*. The film was made to be spectacular and the video reproduction hardly does justice to its original exhibitions at huge movie palaces with orchestras. Certainly, *The Ten Commandments* set the blueprint for what the audience could expect from a biblical adaptation and, indeed, much of the success of rendering the Bible into film, as we have suggested, comes from recalling the common tradition of Western painting. And DeMille was able to recall sacred history, then, as a *vivant tableaux*, gleaned from famous paintings, such as the work of Gustave Dore. Indeed, the improved lighting techniques in the late silent era helped to bestow an almost magical, sacred glow on Jesus' face and actions, including the already noted scene of the Last Supper. As contemporary movie reviewer Mordaunt Hall wrote in *The Screen* magazine in the late summer of 1927, *The King of Kings,* traces the past masters, now animated by film technology. After seeing The *King of Kings* he said that "one of the most beautiful scenes in this production is that of the Last Supper. It is strikingly like the old paintings of this subject, but here the figures come to life."

Rendering the story of Jesus realistically and in "natural colors" is nowhere more apparent in *The King of Kings* than in the resurrection color sequence. DeMille had already experimented with color in *The Ten Commandments,* but these were inserts that used a "process two" technique, which was not terribly lifelike and, additionally, often caused the chemically toned film footage to warp when projected. While more advanced than hand-tinted frames (occasionally used from the earliest films), the process-two system was not considered natural enough. But in 1926, Technicolor invented a "process-three" system, which not only did not warp when projected, but also produced a more even color palette and warmer tones. A full, three-strip Technicolor system would not be used in Hollywood until the mid-1930s, so audiences were truly dazzled by this albeit brief sequence, in the most spectacular of places—following Jesus' death.

In a way, the transformation from black and white to color in *The King of Kings* anticipates a kind of dream landscape such as we might expect from Victor Fleming's *The Wizard of Oz* (1939). And there is, in fact, a surreal quality to DeMille's narrative of Jesus: the mundane world of everyday black and white replaced by the more transcendent, idyllic fantasy space of color, only to return to the everyday again. This is not to suggest that DeMille was an avant-garde surrealist (he was far from that), but he was almost certainly tapping into the audience's fascination with color as a code for the unknown, the unexpected, the fantastic. Furthermore, Jesus' resurrection depicted as a dreamscape reminds us of the wider cultural interest in dreams, psychic phenomena, and Freudianism, especially common after shell-shocked soldiers returned from World War I. At the same time, however, the "natural colors" of the resurrection suggest a more realistic representation.

Undoubtedly, Hollywood as a dream factory was in familiar territory here, as it delivered us from the gritty world of first-century Palestine, what DeMille called a "manly" Jesus, and, in its stead, promised us a kind of apocalyptic vision of the Savior in "natural" Technicolor. In a curious way, *The King of Kings* has managed to bring together the world of psychology and religion: the unconscious is disclosed as a vision of the Savior. DeMille has once again managed to evoke a religious sentiment with codes that remain entirely secular, naturalizing the resurrected world that the heart and faith alone may know. No wonder DeMille managed to appeal not only to so wide a segment of the American population but to reach so deeply into the human person as well.

NOTES

1. Babington and Evans, *Biblical Epics*, 101.

2. McDermott, "Is It Possible to Portray Christ in Film?" 20.

3. 20 April 1927.

4. Babington and Evans, *Biblical Epics*, 118.

5. Ibid., 120.

6. Peter Malone, "Jesus on Our Screens," in *New Image of Religious Film*, ed. John R. May (Kansas City, MO: Sheed & Ward, 1997), 58.

7. Babington and Evans, *Biblical Epics*, 125.

8. Quoted in Paul Johnson, *Modern Times: The World from the Twenties to the Eighties* (New York: Harper & Row, 1983), 227.

9. Ibid., 224.

10. Larry May, "Apocalyptic Cinema: D. W. Griffith and the Aesthetics of Reform," in *Movies and Mass Culture*, ed. John Belton (New Brunswick, N.J.: Rutgers University Press, 1996), 26.

Photo courtesy of the Academy of Motion Picture Arts & Sciences. © 1961 Turner Entertainment Co. Used with permission.

SECOND FEATURE

King of Kings (1961)

"The Kingdom of God is within you."

Directed by: Nicholas Ray

Produced by: Samuel Bronston

Screenplay by: Philip Yordan

Actors Include: Jeffrey Hunter (Jesus), Siobhan McKenna (Mary), Carmen Sevilla (Mary Magdalene), Ron Randell (Lucius), Harry Guardino (Barabbas), Robert Ryan (John the Baptist), Hurd Hatfield (Pontius Pilate)

Running Time: 170 minutes

Introduction

The King of Kings (1927) proved so popular and enduring that it was some time, literally decades, before anyone had the courage or the reason to attempt another cinematic version of the life of Jesus. H. B. Warner's portrayal had come to define the cinematic image of Jesus: the gentle, consoling, fatherly savior figure. To be sure, there were other films that had been produced in the meantime that incorporated or made reference to elements of Jesus' life or that portrayed Christlike figures. Some of these movies include *Jesus of Nazareth* (1928), *Destination Unknown* (1933), *The Last Days of Pompeii* (1935), *Strange Cargo* (1940), *The Lawton Story* (1949), *Quo Vadis?* (1951), *The Robe* (1953), and others produced both in the United States and in Europe. (The fine overview, *Divine Images,* listed in the Readings List, contains a fuller listing.)

King of Kings, however, was the first of the modern major "Hollywood" productions dedicated to a direct portrayal of the life of Jesus. It reflects a style that has come to characterize the productions of that time. Peter Hasenberg describes some of the qualities of films of this era. He observes that the "new filmmaking was noted for (1) a dominance of the subjective point of view, (2) a critical view of society, sometimes even with a strong political motive, and (3) a conscious and critical use of conventional narrative and genre structures."[1] Especially characteristic of *Hollywood* films of this time, according to Hasenberg, were the strong influence of youth culture and the growing influence of technology on filmmaking.[2] These elements are present in *King of Kings;* the movie reflects very clearly the cinematic times in which it was produced. Some of the features will be explored in the lenses below.

One must assume that *King of Kings* was perceived by its creative staff as an updated retelling of *The King of Kings.* One could hardly entitle a movie so similarly (although apparently with just a bit less pretension, dropping *The*) without inviting comparisons to the predecessor. This comparison is inevitable, and one should not shy away from the task. The obvious question, which is unavoidable, is *why?* Why that title? Why the revision? Why the remake? Why the reconstruction, and why the deconstruction? Was it because the old telling was somehow inaccurate? Had audiences appreciably changed during the intervening years? Was it because the characterizations, emphases, or fundamental assumptions about Jesus had changed; was there new research that provided provocative insights into the history and person of Jesus? Or perhaps the reason was related to changes in society and society's perceptions of Jesus and of itself. What had changed? What needed to be changed?

Between the 1927 *The King of Kings* and the 1961 *King of Kings,* several key differences should be noted now, although they will be treated more fully in the Movie Review. First and foremost is the matter of characterization. There is a significant difference in the portrayal of Jesus from *The King of Kings.* This will become immediately apparent when viewing the movie. But how might one characterize these differences; what are the clues or techniques used to visualize the differences? While Warner's portrayal surely leans toward emphasizing Jesus' unchanging divine nature, Hunter surely plays up Jesus' humanity.[3] The film falls into the three-step pattern of self-recognition, ordeal, and triumph or tragedy of the Hollywood "biopic" hero or heroine.[4]

Certainly, the Ray film permits Jesus to experience and to express a far greater range of emotions than its predecessor from 1927. It will not spoil the film for the viewer to be tipped off to this before viewing the movie. Hopefully, to the contrary, the viewer will be better tuned-in to spot differences in the images of Jesus being portrayed in these two movies, as well as in all the others that follow.

One should keep in mind, there is no neutral portrayal, no objective view of Jesus in any of these "Jesus" films. This is not to imply that the people who crafted these films were being criminally manipulative or fraudulent, or even that they were misusing the person of Jesus for their own evil ends. It is only to say that the image of Jesus is always filtered through the eyes of the people who make the films and then again through the eyes of those who watch the films. It is much the same observation that Albert Schweitzer made of the images of Jesus developed in the scholarly quest for the historical Jesus. In analyzing images of Jesus developed by various eras and various scholars, the images all seem to reflect the ideal of humanity of the time and/or of the author. We all bring our preconceptions to the viewing. It may not be profound to observe that there are differences in the images of Jesus in each movie, but to note and assess the changes in these images serve to form an analytical step that is not often enough taken. In *King of Kings,* assessment of characterization forms the backbone of the analysis of the film. It becomes the doorway of opportunity to explore the many other ways in which this film differs from its predecessor(s) and which mark it as a product and reflection of its time.

How was the film evaluated in its time? A *Variety* review of 11 October 1961 claims the film has "[c]arefully and beautifully made this retelling of the ministry and agony of Jesus Christ...." The review notes that "Hunter's blue orbs and auburn bob (wig, of course) are strikingly pictorial." The review concludes by claiming that *King of Kings* "succeeds in touching the heart." Subsequent judgments have not been nearly so favorable, however. Lloyd Baugh, for example, believes that the movie falls short in a variety of ways, including its use of the gospels (both adding unhistorical events and omitting key events in the gospel accounts of Jesus' life), failures in the movie as a whole with the complexion of subplots and strained editing, and ultimately in the film's portrait of Jesus as "expressionless and almost inarticulate."[5] "The film does everything to limit the scope and range of Jesus' messianic identity and role."[6] Kinnard and Davis label it "strangely uninvolving."[7] They quote from a review by Moira Walsh in *America:* "There is not the slightest possibility that anyone will derive from the film any meaningful insight into what Christ's life and sufferings signify for us...."[8] These are the poles in the spectrum of judgments about this film.

A few other points of comparison with *The King of Kings* should be noted. Locale would be one obvious one. Whereas *The King of Kings* had a rather limited sense of locale, *King of Kings* has a much more open feel, made even more obvious by the use of the wider 70mm filmstock. This latter film is shot in the wide open spaces. What would these differences do to the impact of the film and the message of the film? Those are important considerations as we take the next step in determining just who is the Savior on the silver screen.

Movie Preview: Questions and Suggestions

1. *Why do you think someone would produce another movie with almost the identical title as its predecessor?*

2. *How would you describe the late 1950s and early 1960s in the United States? What was the mood of the country? What sort of portrayal of Jesus would you expect in a remake made at this time? What characteristics would be evident in a late-1965 Jesus?*

3. *What other movies were produced by Nicholas Ray about this time? How do they compare and/or contrast to* King of Kings?

4. *Note the difference in overall locale between these first two films. What is the view of the city versus the countryside in the movie? Where do the important revelations take place?*

5. *Watch for the use of visual rhetoric, that is, repetitive motifs, symbols, or devices that recur in order to provide the viewer with subtle hints about interpretation of the action, scene, plot twist, and so forth.*

6. *Note the role of Lucius in the film. Watch for his presence in the several subplots.*

Movie Viewing

Movie Review: Questions and Responses

1. *Describe the opening and closing scenes. What context and tone were established in the opening scene? What are you left with at the closing scene? What do you believe the closing scene was intended to communicate to the viewer? What do you think is the point of the way that this film portrays the resurrection of Jesus and the post-resurrection influence of Jesus?*

2. *Describe the character of Jesus in* King of Kings. *What are Jesus' qualities, characteristics? What are the clues or the techniques used to create this image?*

3. *Relatedly, how does Jeffrey Hunter's portrayal differ from that of H. B. Warner? Why the difference? What was the difference in the cultural situation between 1927 and 1961?*

4. *What are the key biblical passages employed in the movie? What key passages are left out?*

5. *How does this film "play" today? Compare the societal situation of the late 1950s with that of the late 1990s. What changes might need to be made for a remake of* King of Kings *for today?*

LENS ONE

The 1960s was a decade in which the American public awakened to a new hope for the potential achievements of the human spirit. This was a period in which national politics claimed the former glory of Camelot, in which a postwar unification of the West generated broad economic development, and in which a new wave of spiritual realization surfaced throughout all facets of society, especially on college campuses. It is an awareness of these same three elements—politics, economy, spirituality—which also seems to have shaped the background of Nicholas Ray's vision of the historical Jesus. His portrayal of the "man from Nazareth" remains consistently focused upon the political issues of first-century Palestine, the economic situation of the region and times, and the deep spiritual consciousness of the teachings of the rabbi from Galilee.

Ray's depiction of Jesus of Nazareth, at least as it is viewed from the perspective of biblical and historical considerations, deserves comment in four specific areas. First, the viewer finds a new concern for the historical background of first-century Palestine. Unlike the caricatures offered by DeMille, the land and the people come into consideration in a more meaningful way. Second, there is a conscious effort to define Jesus' role as a teacher, a communicator of wisdom and eternal truths, a real person with a genuine message for society. Next, there is some liberty taken in the development of the theological intentions of Jesus and the interpretation of his activities by those who met and heard him. Sometimes these views are boldly declared, but often they are more subtly revealed. Finally, there is a new attempt to offer some psychological explanation for the motivations of those persons who are featured within the gospel narrative. This exceeds

DeMille's investigations of Mary Magdalene and Judas Iscariot, though it certainly continues in the same vein. Each of these calls for further discussion.

Historical Background. After World War II, New Testament scholarship developed a renewed interest in accurately reconstructing the historical worldview of first-century Palestine. It is apparently under this same influence that Ray seeks to pay specific attention to the historical details that lie behind the subjects of his film. Gone are many of the anachronisms of the first *(The King of Kings)* production, including DeMille's use of a late medieval lamp by the Temple guards who come to arrest Jesus in the garden of Gethsemane. Gone are the whimsical costumes of DeMille's characters, some of which reflect the clothing styles of a much later period (for example, the "monastic" Mary, mother of Jesus); some are simply fanciful products of DeMille's own imagination! With more evidence from ancient literature and modern archeology at his disposal, Ray constructs his scenes with an elevated sense of historical accuracy. This is a key turn in the development of the epic Jesus-films.

The viewer must also consider that this new film about the life of Jesus moves away from a mere pastiche of disjointed scenes that have been freely and randomly selected from gospel texts. It attempts to provide a more continuous movement in the developing plot of Jesus' experiences and teachings. Unlike DeMille, Ray seeks to include imagery from the birth and early youth of Jesus' life, episodes from the gathering of the disciples and the ministry around the region of Galilee, and scenes from the events in Jerusalem that led to the crucifixion and the ultimate disappointment that befell Jesus' earliest followers. This is perhaps the most fundamental shift within the development of the great Jesus movie epics—the continuing quest to offer an ever more complete picture of the life and teachings of the Christian Messiah.

Most significant of all is Ray's attempt to place the story of Jesus within a fixed, defined historical moment. While it is true that the movie uses a wide selection of texts from each of the New Testament Gospels, there appears to be a conscious effort to follow the Gospel of Luke's focus on the importance of history. The story of Jesus is told much in the same approach as that of a typical court recorder. Events are revealed within a particular setting and time. Characters are portrayed against the backdrop of a broader Mediterranean worldview. The story gradually unfolds during the reigns of particular Caesars and during the administrations of specific local rulers, illustrated by the scene where Joseph and Mary travel to Bethlehem in order to be enrolled for the taxation while Quirinius is governor (see Lk 2). This historical narrative style—often called "historiography" by modern scholars—is a strict concern of the author of the Gospel of Luke and Acts, but not of the other gospel authors. Ray has chosen to incorporate this Lukan concern within the development of his film, and it gives the work a much more historical feel than what is found in DeMille's portrayal.

Add to this historical concern the contribution of an additional ancient author from *outside* of the Bible, specifically, the first-century, Jewish historian, Flavius Josephus of Rome. It is through the specific vision of Josephus that we see the arrival of Pompey in Jerusalem at the beginning of the movie, as is recorded in Josephus's *The Antiquities of the Jews* (see 14.4.1–5). This is true again with the later uprising against the Romans, which leads to the imprisonment of John the Baptist (see 18.3.1). So too, at the beginning of the Passover in act 2 of the film, the zealous Jews raise further trouble, and the revolt becomes a breaking point for Roman patience. Josephus depicted similar struggles in his *Wars of the Jews* (see 2.9.4), providing some historical background for the period that was omitted by the authors of the New Testament. The inclusion of the perspective of Josephus is certainly a new attempt to make the story of Jesus appear more like a modern biography rather than a loose collection of popular stories about the life of the Savior. It is an effort that will continue throughout all subsequent traditional Jesus movies, as will be seen below.

Jesus the Teacher. The modern Western mind-set has a strong tendency to be concerned about the development of history and the role of historical figures within the movement of time. While such figures have been preserved for the American public in almost mythic proportions (for example, consider the glory often associated with George Washington and Abraham Lincoln), there is a prominent desire to recover what is most human about such persons. Perhaps the most telling evidence of this same concern within our film is captured in Ray's decision to focus upon Jesus as a teacher rather than to emphasize his role as a miracle worker, healer, or divine revealer. This focus on teaching and wisdom undoubtedly reflects the rising effort within twentieth-century scholarship to rediscover the historical Jesus. In Ray's approach, three distinct features are worthy of note:

1. Our Jesus of the 1960s is primarily a speaker of sayings, not a worker of miracles. He appeals to logic as he speaks. This logic is based upon a firm belief in the good intentions of God, as is illustrated by the Old Testament, and in the basic goodness of humanity. So it is that the Roman centurion Lucius, who serves as a guide and narrator throughout the film, reports that Jesus speaks of "peace, love, and the brotherhood of man." Likewise, Judas Iscariot must make a choice between his devotion to Barabbas (a man of war) and his attraction to Jesus (a man of peace). Finally, when Pontius Pilate asks "What is truth?" (Jn 19:38) at the trial of Jesus, Jesus responds, "There is only one truth, and it is written in the commandments: Be true to God." Each of these illustrations indicates Ray's focus on Jesus as a teacher of conventional religious wisdom and on a logic rooted in the spirituality of first-century Palestine. It is a truly pious and serious view of God and humanity. It is a focus that is similar to much that came to typify the thinking of later Christian spirituality in the 1960s, a devotion to God and a belief in human goodness.

2. Our Jesus is a "rebel with a cause." His concern is with the limited restoration of the people of Israel, not in a political or economic sense, but in a religious sense of renewed spirituality. This is not to be confused with later Christian claims that Jesus intended ultimately to find his way to the cross and there to die as a saving act of the will of God. Though Ray does not discount such an idea, it certainly receives no emphasis in this film. Jesus is very much a human champion! He is the epitome of the Greek tragic hero, a unique man of God (almost more of a prophet than a messiah) who became enmeshed in the complex and conflicting currents of history. Jesus' message is one of love, truth, and a sincere devotion to God. He is a man of peaceful ways. During Passover week, however, his message runs headlong into the zealous and violent revolt of Barabbas and his comrades, a juncture at which Roman patience reaches its breaking point (see Josephus's *Wars of the Jews* 2.9.4). It is at this very intersection that the man Jesus and his message of peace are swept away in the struggles between Rome and the

Jewish zealots. At first this might appear to be a mistake in the flow of time, until one realizes that the apparent struggle and pain of external human events are ultimately undermined by the glory and victory of God at work among Jesus' followers.

3. Our Jesus is not an apocalyptic visionary who spends most of his time in the performance of healings and miracles. In most respects, this Jesus is a person who is like any modern human. While a few limited healings are included as a sidelight of the story, these are by no means a primary feature of Jesus' work. They do not remain outside the sphere of modern medical explanation, but can be rationally explained as the ability to cure psychosomatic illnesses or mental deficiencies.

Furthermore, this Jesus is not a seer of the future. His concern is not with the final coming of the Son of Man upon the clouds so much as with the present Son of Man at work upon the earth. There are no dire predictions about the advent of future destruction, the resurrection of the dead, or the supernatural transformation of the old world into a new reign of eternal glory. Instead, Jesus prods those who follow him to undertake God's work as they find it around them and to share this reality with those whom they encounter. That element of divine power and omniscience that is true of Jesus in the theology of the Gospel of John and that characterized so much of later Christian speculation about the nature of the Christ simply is not present in Ray's depiction of the historical figure of the man of Galilee.

Theological Speculation. In many respects the theological development that appears in this film lies parallel to Ray's view of Jesus as a teacher of religious wisdom. Ray's Jesus is considerably more human in dimension than is the Jesus of DeMille. Jesus is steeped both in the tradition of wisdom and in the need for devotion to God. He is not characterized by the miraculous deeds that he performs but by his insight into the power of God that lies within humanity.

Early in the film, both Mary the mother of Jesus and John the Baptist come to recognize the traditional Christian affirmation that Jesus is without sin. The average viewer may choose to bring any one of several traditional lines of interpretation to this statement. In the mind of Ray, this confession of sinlessness is best defined as the understanding that Jesus is fully consumed with the vision of what God truly is—there is no sense in which Jesus falls short of this beatific vision. It is from this vision that Jesus eventually informs his followers in the Sermon on the Mount that the kingdom of God is to be found within each person. Salvation does not come from outside, but from the power of God at work within each individual who knows how and where to find it.

There remains within this film a curious blending of theological confession from the Christian tradition with the exploration of human potential from the modern mind-set. On the one hand, the baby Jesus is honored by wise men from the East (Mt 2) and shepherds from their fields (Lk 2) in a careful, symbolic portrayal of the traditional confession that Jesus came as a king and shepherd under the will of God. We have already seen that Mary and John the Baptist recognize the essential nature of Jesus. Later, Mary is even asked to "intercede" with Jesus in his work. Thus the roles of Mary and John as intercessor and prophet respectively are confirmed from within the tradition. In one additional example, the crucifixion of Jesus is undertaken during the slaughter of the Passover lambs in sympathy with the view of the Gospel of John that Christ was killed for those who would believe in him.

Such elements of traditional Christian theology are unabashedly preserved throughout the film. At the same time, new twists are introduced. Jesus does not seem bent upon any particular desire to challenge Rome or the authorities of Palestine with his message of salvation. As the narrator states after Jesus has chosen the twelve disciples who will follow him most faithfully: "This then was Jesus' task, to keep his disciples from the doubting cities and to give them fresh wisdom wherewith to cleanse themselves as with water to make them men of God. Peace and love he taught them with many tongues." Unlike the depiction of Jesus that DeMille has already provided for us—a holy Savior created with a pastiche of scenes in which the glory of Jesus is revealed through his actions—Ray's primary depiction of Jesus comes through the message of the Sermon on the Mount, which is actually a compilation of numerous sayings and answers to pointed questions both from disciples and opponents. There is little of the miraculous here; however, there is much of the reasonable and rational.

Ultimately, despite the theological speculation that Ray finds within Christian tradition regarding Jesus as the divine presence of God on earth, we find within this particular film a view of Jesus as an extremely charismatic spokesman of God's divine will. His tools are rhetoric and persuasion, not raw power and miracles. His power is revealed in a subtle interplay among other people, not in a bold refutation of supernatural challenges from the world of evil.

Psychological Development. In a very real sense Ray asks a basic question of his gospel sources: "What makes this Jesus of Nazareth tick?" The answer to this question is not so clearly illustrated with the notation that Jesus could do such and such a task or was unable to achieve this or that goal. Yet certain keys are offered for the viewer throughout the film.

First, we see a Jesus whose claim to be the Son of Man is confirmed primarily by other people, but rarely by himself. It is his clarity of vision, concern for others, and devotion to God that must inductively lead the viewer to this same conclusion. His insight into the divine will is clear; his ability to confront major questions of spirituality and the meaning of life is without doubt; his influence upon those who surround him is amazing. Certainly these are the characteristics that Christians would expect to see portrayed by the Christ of God. Yet, there are no clues to suggest where the source of Jesus' motivation lies. Perhaps this motivation derives from his compassion for others, or from his devotion to a true spirituality, or even from his desire to persuade the Roman government to have mercy and compassion for its Jewish subjects. Ray never provides a clear answer.

The authors of the New Testament Gospels offer their own interpretation of this source of motivation. Jesus is the Son of God, someone whose purpose for living was to die for others. As we read in the gospel texts, Jesus comes to the world in order to anticipate the cross and to call others to take up their own crosses and follow in his path. But Ray does not wade through this speculation. For him, the story of Jesus is the tragedy of a good will that appears to have been crushed by the whim of the flow of history.

The passion of Jesus is the product of a collision of events that involves the more clearly stated aims of two zealots, Judas Iscariot and Barabbas. Their intentions for Israel against Rome are clear, while those of Jesus are not. One may add to this the rampant speculation that has already developed with regard to Jesus among the crowds prior to the crucifixion. We hear "rumors" of his ability to walk on water and to feed the masses. But none of these so-called miracles is confirmed; they remain the speculation of willing believers and thirdhand reports. Those who would put Jesus to the test, such as Herod Antipas for example (see Lk 23:9–12), receive no satisfaction of their demand to see a miracle. Indeed, their encounters with Jesus confirm for them that he is a person much like themselves. All the same, such meetings confirm for the viewer that the depth of Jesus' insight into the human situation and his association with the will of God indicate that he is a person unlike the rest of us.

So it is that Nicholas Ray has combined four very special elements into a new vision of who Jesus was as a first-century teacher in Palestine. His concern for historical facts is refreshing to the modern student; his depiction of Jesus as a wisdom teacher is convincing for postwar humanists; his speculation about theological issues associated with Jesus as the Christ is intriguing to free-thinking theologians; his exploration into the psychological motivations of the Jesus story has a disturbing appeal for nontraditionalist Christians.

Ray has combined these elements through a careful interweaving of factual data with the historical novel genre. He realizes that the text of Scripture tells the story, but that reconstructions of missing conversations between the characters of that story are necessary in order to historically "fill in" what is missing from the theological picture. DeMille has already attempted this same approach in more limited instances, as with his depiction of the conversion of Mary Magdalene from a shameless harlot to a chaste disciple. A parallel example exists in the turmoil that Judas Iscariot undergoes as he attempts to decipher the goals and desires of Jesus' ministry. Yet Ray provides so much more in this regard with his careful utilization of numerous characters and their witness to the man Jesus and his nature. One recalls the obeisance of the wise men from the East, the testimony of Jesus' mother Mary, the witness of the forerunner John the Baptist, the continual bewilderment of the centurion Lucius, the considerations of the tentative follower Nicodemus, the realization of the released Barabbas. For Ray, the essence of the major story is in the movement of the minor subplots that the gospel authors have too often been constrained to omit.

Ray appeals to the Jewish historian Josephus and to the author of the Gospel of Luke to provide the historical scenario. This is carefully undertaken and supplemented with an appeal to geographic details and the findings of archeological discovery. There is a focus upon dates, times, and specific locations. The multitudes are fed at the foot of Mount Tabor near Galilee. The eastern end of the hill country near Jerusalem is dotted with a "honeycomb of cellars" where the zealots of Barabbas hide. Jesus is neither crucified alone nor with only a few others, but is raised in the midst of numerous crosses in a virtual killing field. All of these details and trivial concerns would appear to be true to an actual first-century Palestinian world and serve as a witness to the late twentieth-century fascination with an "accurate" reconstruction of history.

Through it all, however, Ray remains true to his gospel texts! He often turns to the Gospel of John to provide the symbolism behind his vision of the Messiah. Curiously, the symbolism of John is eagerly employed (the good shepherd, the light in the midst of darkness, the reality of truth, the slain lamb of God). Yet the theological impact of this symbolism is translated into the common realities of everyday life, much like the vision of Jesus contained in the Gospels of Matthew and Luke. We see this illustrated in Ray's extrahistorical character of the centurion Lucius, who provides a walking witness to the development of the plot of the life of Jesus. It is a plot that makes no obvious association between the will of God and the death of the man Jesus as a Savior who has been crucified for the sins of humanity. Indeed, Lucius's witness to the life of Jesus is that of an outsider. In the eyes of the righteous outsider, which Lucius is portrayed to be, our Jesus is perhaps best defined as that figure who is preserved in the Gospel of Mark—God's best and most complete person, chosen to reveal the divine will for humanity, until the sinful world puts an end to that unbearable witness!

The question remains for Ray, much as it does for DeMille: "What does all of this mean for the twentieth-century believer?" And the challenge that both directors offer to their respective audiences is the same, each film having come to an end with the same text of Scripture from Matthew 28:20: "Teach them to obey everything that I have commanded you. And remember, I am with you always, to the end of the age." Much like the respective endings of the New Testament Gospels themselves, however, this leaves much room for interpretation for those who consider the historical facts and theological ramifications of the story of Jesus of Nazareth.

LENS TWO

Any discussion of the use of the cinematic vocabulary in *King of Kings* must begin with the conclusion of the 1961 *Variety* review of this movie: it is "a big picture." It reportedly cost eight million dollars to produce. Jeffrey Hunter, the actor portraying Jesus, was selected from the stable of major stars of the time. The film was shot on 70mm film, which resulted in screen images with a greater width-to-height ratio, that is, the screen image was much wider than was previously possible. Technicolor film processing resulted in more vivid colors. Imagine those extreme close-ups of Hunter's "blue orbs" in vivid 70mm Technicolor on the big screen at movie theaters of the day. It was surely impressive, if not a bit frightening. The effect both of the Technicolor and of the 70mm filmstock is unfortunately lost by watching it on videotape. Television/video reproduces film's resolution and color very poorly and the width of the movie picture has been sacrificed to make it fit the narrower video screen.

Even on video, however, one still can sense the grand scale on which this film was shot, for example, the marching legions of Roman soldiers in their red cloaks in the opening segment, or the wide open spaces and endless blue sky in the Sermon on the Mount scene. Yet, even compared to *The King of Kings,* there is little in the way of special effects, at least not of the type that call attention to themselves. Indeed, this would have been antithetical to Hollywood's aim of that time, which was to create "large" images on a grand scale, yet to place the emphasis on the story or narrative structure rather than on the technology. How things change over time! Lens One discussed how this concern for narrative played out in the movie's use of the historical record. This concern is also evident in production of the movie's visuals. Concerning the audio influence, the viewer should note that the use of a narrator also seems intended to contribute to the sense of story. The narrator (Orson Welles), however, is mostly relating what is visible on-screen, so he provides very little additional information for the background and movement of the story.

Think back to the opening scene of *The King of Kings* in Mary Magdalene's apartment, where she is teasing and entertaining and manipulating the power brokers of Jerusalem. Opulent, extravagant, intimate, behind-the-scenes sorts of activities are going on. How different in this 1961 "remake." No Mary Magdalene, no apartment, no opulence. Instead we see legions of Roman soldiers marching to Jerusalem to inhabit it as conquerors, oppressors. The scene set for the movie is clearly and radically different. The foundation for the succeeding activity has changed from personal to national, from Mary of Magdala to the Roman Pompey, from personal conversion to political machination, from small scale to vast scale—all suggested by this opening scene. The scene, as they say, has been set.

As mentioned in the introduction of this chapter, characterization is an important factor in describing and analyzing this or any film. Some elements of the "new and improved" Jesus have been suggested already, but the comparisons must also extend to the other characters. The role of Barabbas has been expanded to that of a major character. Jesus' mother Mary has developed significantly. She has become a foreground figure, nearly omniscient in her predictions about the turns Jesus' life would take as he grew up. Finally, Judas becomes much less the swarthy and unsavory character he was in *The King of Kings*. If Lucius, the Roman centurion, is the discerning, noble, just, loyal figure we would all like to be, Judas is the indecisive person that we often are: caught between two conflicting sets of values, doomed to inaction or wrong decisions. It is curious that the thirty pieces of silver that were featured so prominently in *The King of Kings* are absent as a motivating factor in this movie.

We could, of course, follow each of the characters, but the viewer would do well to create an ongoing comparison of the various characters in these first two movies to observe how they have changed and how the changes affect the viewer's enjoyment of the film and one's identification with the characters, as well as the film's narrative structure and message. Follow the characters through the remaining movies as well to see how they evolve or change over time.

There are numerous visual elements that contribute to the development of the narrative structure. They serve as hints or symbols for the observant viewer. The use of color in this movie is of interest. In *The King of Kings,* color was employed in a singular and spectacular way by reserving it exclusively for the resurrection sequence. The use of color is both more subtle and more pervasive in the present film, even though the colors themselves are certainly vivid! Jesus' (Jeffrey Hunter's) intense blue eyes have already been mentioned. Jesus' blue eyes will become something of a fixed feature in this genre of movie.

Another example in *King of Kings* is the use of red as a symbol of power. In the opening scene, the Roman legions are all garbed in red cloaks, as are various other authority figures throughout the movie. Perhaps significantly, Jesus is wearing a red cloak for the first time only after John the Baptist's execution and during the Sermon on the Mount scene, the scene where Jesus portrays his most powerful and representative role. In other settings then, he is in red when speaking authoritatively. He is wearing white when he seems to be more in the role of victim, as in the temptation, in the Garden of Gethsemane, and at his trial. In more mundane settings he is in brown. But Herod then places a red cloak on Jesus in the trial sequence.[9]

Perhaps only slightly less symbolic, and a very nice visual touch, is the scene in which Pompey (with red cloak!) invades the Temple on his horse, and eventually exits to look out over a sea of worshipers gathered in a courtyard. We see all the worshipers wearing white shawls over their heads facing away from the camera and then turning en masse to look at Pompey, still on his horse, after his defilement of the Temple. Elsewhere white is symbolic of purity and innocence. Likely here as well. Note how Mary often wears a strikingly white shawl on her head.

One can certainly become overly zealous about interpreting the meaning of colors, but there are obvious and key places where color does provide clues to the narrative action that is going on in the scene. This is one more element that makes watching films interesting and entertaining on a level beyond the basic story line. It also makes multiple viewings of the same film possible, educational, and even enjoyable.

The viewer may also want to watch for the use of cruciforms at various points throughout the movie. The first is at Herod's death, when he is lying on the floor in roughly the shape of a cross. As if to reinforce the visual image, the narrator tells us that Herod has "crucified himself." Just before John the Baptist's execution, we hear Jesus preaching outside John's cell. As John looks up to the barred window, clearly the bars form a model of Jesus on the cross, head hanging down. The last and most obvious cruciform is in the final scene of the movie, where the disciples encounter the resurrected Jesus at the beach. His figure casts an elongated vertical shadow on the sand. The crosspiece is formed by the fishing nets laid out on the beach. From the camera angle, Jesus would have needed to be extremely tall to form such a shadow, but perhaps that is the very point.

Torn curtains also occur several times in the movie. The first instance is during Pompey's violation of the Temple, when he cuts open the veil setting off the Holy of Holies. The torn curtain occurs again at Herod's death, when he himself, in falling to the floor, pulls it down. Strangely, it is absent from the portrayal of the crucifixion, where, according to the gospel accounts, the Temple curtain was torn in two. Is this symbolic of something in particular? That is left to the viewer to decide in this case. It is noted here to suggest that the more one watches, the more one sees, that is, the more "literate" one becomes in the cinematic vocabulary. This is no different than rereading poems and novels, or viewing artworks over and over. One approaches the works not totally new, but from a different angle, with a different perspective, with a different "eye," and in the process sees more and more with each encounter.

The use and placement of the camera in *King of Kings* are worth noting as well. One goal of Hollywood cinema of the time was to try to make the viewer feel a part of the action. Many of the camera shots therefore are taken from a "subjective" point of view. This is to imply that we, the viewers, see the action from the point of view of the subject or the characters themselves. When Jesus goes to see John the Baptist in his cell and converses with Lucius, we look up at Jesus and down at the seated Lucius. We could just as easily have looked straight on at the whole scene, taking more the role of observer than participant. With the subjective point of view, however, we are *in* the scene and not remote, above, or superior to the scene, as a passive or disinterested bystander would be. We look, for example, directly into the eyes of Jesus and John the Baptist just as they would have seen one another's eyes. Throughout this film we look up and down at the action rather than straight on.

At a few points, the camera seems to take an omniscient or godlike vantage point. For example, at Herod's death the camera is high above, indeed directly above, the action. Then at Jesus' death, the camera seems to be mounted on top of the cross. These stylistic techniques stand out significantly and beg for some sort of interpretative stance. They are unusual partly because of the unusual perspective they provide but also because they are exceptional in light of the general desire that camera work not be made obvious. If this is another example of the subjective point of view, the subject can seemingly only be God.

Film editing not only creates the pace of the movie—how quickly the shots come one after another—but it can also play a creative role in building or enhancing the narrative. For instance, in an early scene in *King of Kings,* the focus is on the building of analogies. Shots of Jewish peasants and sheep are quickly alternated, both being herded and moved about by the Roman soldiers. Clearly the analogy is that the people are being treated as sheep.

Sometimes visuals that are absent are as suggestive or important to understanding the movie as those one actually sees. It may be of some interest that in *King of Kings* we do not see Satan during Jesus' temptation in the desert; we only hear the voice. In *The King of Kings,* Satan was a rather suave-looking figure, but here we have only a voice. This leaves the viewer in some doubt about who the devil is in this film—a person? an inner voice that only Jesus hears? In the few miracles Jesus performs, we only see his shadow hovering over the scene and his blue eyes in extreme close-up, without actually seeing Jesus perform anything tangible. What does this suggest about the film's view of miracles, or about the maladies of which people were healed? Similarly, we only see Jesus' shadow and hear his voice in the final scene of the movie at the beach. His postresurrection appearances are only reported by the narrator. In what sense then does Jesus live on—only in the disciples' hearts, or as an inner voice that guides them? Or is Jesus physically resurrected and standing there at the beach with the disciples? Again, what is not visualized is as meaningful sometimes as what is.

It would seem that the only noteworthy element concerning the audio in this film is the omnipresent music that comes up at every significant moment. The emphasis in this film is clearly on the visuals, employing the new technologies that made "big" pictures possible. But for what purpose and to what end? That is the subject of Lens Three.

LENS THREE

Although they both directed a movie about Jesus with nearly the same title, few directors were as different as Cecil B. DeMille and Nicholas Ray. DeMille was an early film pioneer and businessman; he was notable for the absolute control and supervision he had over his productions. Those skills helped to create an industry and, in the process, he invented himself as a famous director of epics. On the other hand, Ray had his roots in the radical Federal Theater of the 1930s and was something of a maverick in Hollywood. DeMille was a political conservative, a producer of grand spectacles at a time in which Hollywood required an image of respectability in order to guarantee an undifferentiated, homogeneous audience. By contrast, Ray was a liberal whose professional career was shaped by the New Deal ideology. He worked for several different studios, all of which faced a financial crisis and instability brought on by reorganization, the baby boom, and other forms of post–World War II media, such as the radio and television. DeMille even managed to recycle his own work, remaking his *The Ten Commandments* (1956), which, once again, articulated the epic's moralistic edge and restated traditional values in a conservative age. Ray tended to make small, even off- beat "social problem" films, such as *They Live by Night* (1949), *Knock on Any Door* (1949), and *Rebel Without a Cause* (1955), which dealt with a generation of underdogs and loners. Far from DeMille's preeminent supervision over his films, Ray lost control over *King of Kings* and the picture was eventually edited by MGM.

It should not surprise us, then, that the only similarity between Ray's 1961 "remake" and the earlier production of *The King of Kings* began as something of a joke in Hollywood. Apparently, Ray had inherited what he described as a "hopeless script" *(Son of Man)* from another director and decided to change the title to *King of Kings*. But after negotiating with DeMille's estate for 10 percent of the distributor's gross, Ray took a whimsical gamble instead, registering the title with the MPAA. As it turned out, even with all his legendary business savvy, DeMille had failed to do one thing—register his title! So Ray got the title he wanted for six cents, the price of a first-class stamp. But for many critics and moviegoers, MGM's lavish production of *King of Kings*—with a screenplay by Philip Yordan, billed as "the most exciting human drama the screen has ever told," and shot in 70 mm Super Technorama at the cost of eight million dollars— the joke was really on Ray who, according to *Time,* had made one of the "corniest" and "ickiest" biblical films ever.

The End of an Era. The difference between the two productions of Jesus' life (more or less at either end of the Classical Studio era) educates us about the dramatic shift that occurred in American cultural politics after World War II. Indeed, we might say that the years before and after World War II are like the difference between night and day. Like a soldier returning home after a long absence, DeMille's savior would find the silver screen and its audience in the late 1950s and early 1960s not only unrecognizable, but perhaps unredeemable by earlier twentieth-century standards.

After a long and arduous communal investment in the war effort and the taste of victorious moments all too short-lived, the years after World War II became shrouded in the dark knowledge of the Holocaust, the Armageddon-like destruction of Hiroshima and Nagasaki by the atom bomb, and the Red Army's domination of the Balkans, Poland, and elsewhere in Eastern Europe. Domestically, the future appeared to have a brighter economy than ever before: the market was exploding with new, more affordable suburban housing and newly created jobs. Between 1947 and 1961 the number of families grew 28 percent, the national income increased over 60 percent, money spent on household goods and appliances rose almost 250 percent, and income for leisure and luxury items doubled.

The conservative establishment, with economic investments in postwar America, maintained and articulated a picture of domestic stability, but the homestead was far from a Norman Rockwell illustration. The Congress of 1946 was perhaps the most belligerent on record, characterized particularly by its targeted accusations revolving around its fear of the spread of Communism and "Red lies." Hollywood began to suggest the deep disturbance that lay under the surface of economic progress and global expansion: that some veterans, like Homer Parrish or Fred Derry in *Best Years of Our Lives* (1946), returned severely disabled or found that their former jobs in manufacturing had disappeared. Even some strong, healthy marines came back from combat as disabled veterans to lead lives with handicaps like the blind Al Schmid in *Pride of the Marines* (1945). The men in such homecoming films are more typical of a kind of widespread alienation and even a mistrust of the family and traditional commitment after the war. Indeed, the dark existentialism of film noir culture reflects the human subject's profound loneliness in the face of a more industrialized future. For individuals such as Walter Neff in *Double Indemnity* (1944) or Jeff Bailey in *Out of the Past* (1947), there is no possibility for escape into traditional courtship and marriage.

The noir culture suggests, in fact, that there is no escape, not even from the past. Despite how we may now think of the 1950s as "Happy Days," and even as an era of steadfast family values—characterized by naive children and adults with all the answers—these conditions never really existed except as an imaginary, comfortable space in the collective mind of the American society. Ideal visions of suburban utopia were first projected on the pages of *Life* and *Better Homes and Gardens* in the late 1940s and early 1950s as part of an ad campaign for appliance makers and building-material manufacturers. According to Clifford E. Clark, Jr., the ideal ranch house in suburbia was "the focus for family, fun, and relaxation."[10] Thus, some experienced the years after 1945 as the fruition of an American dream, the myth of American autonomy.

But far from the unified World-War-II culture, America after the war was a world filled with diversity, out of which David Riesman in *The Lonely Crowd* (1949) says a "new middle class" began to emerge and "a more autonomous type of social character" developed. As everyone knows, America had always been a culture skewed toward individualism (or what Emerson called "self-reliance"). But now, perhaps for the first time in history, the economic and social conditions existed to make the American dream a reality—from owning a home to cruising the countryside in a convertible. In a word, America was now being populated by a new social character of a remarkably different sort, one in which New-Deal values and World-War-II sacrifice were seen, at least in part, as an element of an older world that, to some Americans, even smacked of socialism.

With America's urgent move toward autonomy, much of the specter of Communism in the 1950s is a kind of cultural hysteria that by today's standards borders on the absurd. Indeed, the decade is occasionally referred to as the days of the "McCarthy witch-hunts," and much of popular culture in those days helped to vitiate fears and construct meaning for the cinematic audience. Science-fiction narrative spectacles such as *The Fly* (1958), *The Day the Earth Stood Still* (1951), and *The Invasion of the Body Snatchers* (1956) focused audience attention to fear the mutant, the foreign, the threat to human freedom and identity. Meanwhile, popular television shows such as *The Donna Reed Show* (1958–66) and *Leave it to Beaver* (1957–63) underscored and galvanized the hegemony of utopian autonomy, the illusion that the years after the war fashioned a landscape for the pursuit of happiness. Thus, for the status quo, the family functioned as the site of containment and domesticity. As is well known, such family dramas often involved a youngster misbehaving only so that the patriarch could solve the problem and return the house to stability: after all, "Father knows best."

Nicholas Ray is an example of a director who came out of these post–World War II years. He was particularly proficient at both dramatizing and problematizing precisely how *little* "Father" knows. Ray arrived in Hollywood in 1944 and worked with Elia Kazan, a director also interested in the "social problem" film who was currently directing *A Tree Grows in Brooklyn* for Twentieth Century-Fox. The association with the noir-ish side of filmmaking, his deep roots in the Federal Theater Project and his ability to reinvent scripts through an imaginative, highly visual perspective gave Ray a long-standing reputation as a Hollywood auteur.

By exploring Ray's work as a whole, it is possible to see his films as investigations into the nefarious underside of the post–World War II years, where the human subject and the possibility for happiness are placed in a perilous, hopeless situation: the "awounded" protagonists in *They Live by Night* (1949), *In a Lonely Place* (1950), and *On Dangerous Ground* (1952) all seem to run on the edge of unhappiness and loss. Even the stable, long-standing genre of the American western is up for grabs in *Johnny Guitar* (1954), with its shrill gender politics and allegorization of bigotry during the Cold War and the years of racial unrest. No wonder that in *Cahiers du Cinema* (1955), Jacques Rivette wrote: "...Nicholas Ray has always offered us the story of a moral dilemma where man emerges as either victor or vanquished, but ultimately lucid: the futility of violence, of all that is not happiness and which diverts man from his innermost purposes."[11] In delineating Ray's auteurist characteristics, or mapping a certain tendency of a given director's body of works, we are also suggesting his political agenda: that Ray was able to critique his time while still evincing his own unique style. Thus, Ray redeploys the biblical narrative as a cultural commentary in *King of Kings* by using at least three important methods: history, genre, and allegory.

The Influence of History. Like the social problem film, *King of Kings* reminds us at once that we are in the grip of history. Thus the narrative about Jesus is immediately historicized not only with the great attention to historical mise-en-scène (or the film's visual setting) and through Orson Welles's voice-over, but with a fierce parallel and inference between past and present as well. The opening frames, for example, show General Pompey's legions attacking the "only living part of the city"—the Temple in Jerusalem. As the Roman soldiers massacre the high priests, Pompey defiles the sanctuary in the hopes of finding gold, only to discover a "covenant with the one God." After threatening to burn the Torah itself, Pompey disdainfully gives the scroll back to the high priest. "Thus for more than fifty years after Pompey's invasion," the narrator tells us, "the history of Judea could be read by the light of burning towns."

From the first moments of the film, therefore, the Romans become an oppressive force, cruelly and systematically slaughtering Jews without mercy or explanation. What is also in jeopardy, of course, is history itself—the Torah that is almost destroyed by fire. To view the first sequence of the film (in which a soldier also throws the body of a Jew into a bonfire) as well as a later one (in which hundreds of Jews are entrapped behind a wall and massacred by soldiers) is especially poignant after the Nazi exterminations of the Jews and the devastations at Dachau, Buchenwald, Auschwitz, and other camps. How can we *but* see such sequences from the point of view of historical memory, now brought into consciousness by *King of Kings?*

On the other hand, those opening sequences of *King of Kings* remind us that history can be redeemed, the Torah preserved even in the face of genocide. The scene in which the high priests form a mighty Super-Techni-rama 70 mm wall does indeed suggest that the Temple is "living." Despite the destruction of towns, their fire becomes the light of history. Furthermore, although the Romans are clearly represented as despicable, an army without a conscience, there remains one of their number, Lucius the centurion, who evolves in the film into a righteous Gentile and even a believer. The course of the narrative, then, takes us through the process of a conversion, as a redemption through history.

Lucius becomes the audience's entry into *King of Kings,* one who is acquainted with Jesus even as a child. Here we are outside of DeMille's narrative strategy, in which our window into the film was through the subjective witness of Jesus from the point of view of a cured blind child. That sequence is striking in the way it gathers the already converted into a single vision of the Savior. But with Ray, it is history, not evangelical witness, that plays the most significant role for the audience.

Additionally, Lucius reminds us that Ray is highly aware of an extremely diversified, post–World War II audience. Lucius would perhaps never have found a place among the 1920s immigrants: he is educated, worldly, and doubtful. In short, Lucius is a kind of secular humanist, much like Ray himself and a whole generation of Americans after the war. He is the soldier who has seen enough of battle and, like many Americans, is disdainful of politics and ambivalent about God. Lucius is, above all, independent of government and religion, both of which seem to have corrupted the world around him. An example of Emerson's self-reliance in an existential world, Lucius brings to bear his doubts and witnesses to the Jesus event.

Moreover, it is Claudia, Pilate's wife, who also finds herself among free-thinking, independent pagans and moves toward Jesus and his teaching. She is like Ray's depiction of Mary Magdalene insofar as she is redeemed not by Jesus' controlling gaze (a la DeMille), but by his loving example of forgiveness. Not coincidentally, these women exemplify a world independent of men in which they have held significant jobs and made important decisions. They are new women, a growing population in post–World War II America.

Ray hints at a political allegory as well, similar to the radical theater in the 1930s, where he found his roots. Indeed, like the expectation of transformation effected by the risen Lord, youthful and transformed, the hope of many in the late 1950s came with the election in 1960 of a young senator from Massachusetts. As is well known, Kennedy was for many the chance to resurrect pre–World War II socially conscious America, particularly through a new awareness of social justice issues. We are not drawing an absolute parallel between Jesus and Kennedy in *King of Kings,* but we are suggesting that for Ray sacred history becomes the occasion to comment on the conservative politics of the 1950s: to expose existing social problems through allegorizing a sacred narrative and, in so doing, to potentially rediscover communitarian values.

Ray, then, politicizes his Jesus to the left, a marked contrast from DeMille's trick camera shots, with an emphasis on highly spiritualized, personal point of view and the aura of spectacle. But like DeMille, the reconstructed "Jesus" would play an important purpose to the emergent pre-1960s culture. Ray had considered casting all youthful actors with charismatic looks: Christopher Plummer, Peter Cushing, and even the young Max von Sydow (who would appear as Jesus a few years later in George Stevens's *The Greatest Story Ever Told*). Ray, who had done endless amounts of historical research himself on the project (he cowrote the script and even did art direction), was particularly captivated by von Sydow's eyes; but he eventually cast another actor with equally striking features Jeffrey Hunter, who had played Frank James in his early film, *The True Story of Jesse James* (1957). Where DeMille made much of Warner's masculine sobriety and age, Ray could deploy Hunter's good looks to attract a youthful audience and stress Jesus' magnetism as a leader. DeMille's savior tames and domesticates; Ray's Messiah inspires and brings reconciliation. Ray's Jesus becomes the prototype of the 1960s messiah, or, as Bruce Babington and Peter William Evans put it in *Biblical Epics,* a "rebel with a cause."[12]

Ray clearly uses Jeffrey Hunter to his advantage. The curing of the man possessed by a demon shows him to be unusual, certainly unafraid to hold another man and look at him with compassion and love. Ray also makes his savior stand out in a crowd. The sequence shot on the Sermon on the Mount is particularly impressive insofar as it paints a beautiful vista of the disciples swarming to Jesus, who also stands apart. As if the scene were anticipating a kind of grass-roots political meeting, or teach-in, common in the 1960s, the Sermon on the Mount in *King of Kings* also functions as an important reminder of the political Jesus as teacher. Jesus recites the beatitudes, using the Lukan version, which is more socially related than the spiritualized version in Matthew's Gospel. In any case, those who come to this Jesus must be convinced; they are not just captivated by his mysterious gaze.

It is true that Jesus' youth and good looks undoubtedly had exhibition value for MGM, which counted on the commercial and cultural legibility of Hunter to attract a young audience. We know that with the flight to the suburbs and the increasing number of people being lost to television, Hollywood attempted to draw in the young viewer—specifically the teenager. Numerous "teenpics" flooded the market during the 1950s in an effort to lure the young into movie theaters. It seems obvious that the youthful Jesus will play a significant role in attracting a young crowd because he himself appears to be affected by society's malaise. Ray's Jesus is like a redeemed James Dean, justifiably moody in the face of political and cultural hypocrisy. Moreover, the depiction of Jesus as an ascetic who must flee the world into the desert is a nice bridge between the contemporary cultural representation of adolescence and the gospel itself.

The Impact of Melodrama. The genre of family melodrama, quite prevalent in the 1950s, was a useful strategy for both the Right and the Left: the Right could recapitulate patriarchal culture within a father-centered drama; the Left might hint at social unrest, positioning the family as the site of instability and profound dysfunction. Ray's use of melodrama becomes an occasion for a larger commentary on the fragility of society at large, an exploration of 1950s cultural anxiety.

Perhaps the most obvious instance in Ray's work of a family in jeopardy is *Rebel Without a Cause* (1955), in which James Dean famously throws his father (who, at one point, even wears a frilly apron) across the room for not answering him about what it means to be a man. Certainly,

Ray makes the most of vulnerability throughout the film in a style of acting that suggests an entire era of moody, Brando-like men smoldering with rage about the establishment. While the traditional family is often up for grabs in *Rebel,* even the remote possibility of establishing a new kind of nuclear family is left dubious by Jim and Judy's failed attempt to "adopt" the doomed Plato and save him from the hostile, violent world. Further, *Bigger Than Life* (1956) concerns a father's obsession with medication and the sadistic, violent assault he visits on his family. The brilliant, torturous staircase sequence (nine minutes long), in which the father dismantles part of the house, nicely symbolizes the broken backbone of the family, a fracture of domestic space.

It is easy to see how 1950s melodrama, with its emphasis on family crisis, would be valuable to Ray in a production about the life of Jesus the Rebel. And, in fact, Ray has deployed the exploits of Herod as a story within a story in *King of Kings* in order to reveal the problems of a postwar generation where stable values have been decentered, particularly in the area of sexuality. The Kinsey Reports *(Sexual Behavior in the Human Male [1948] and Sexual Behavior in the Human Female* [1953]) detailed the hidden world of American sexual preferences, habits, and practices, which were often at odds with the general perception and hegemony of heterosexual monogamy and stability. The more dominant view continued to endorse the importance of the reproductive, nuclear family (in part for ideological and economic reasons) and helps explain why, according to studio archival records, the Production Code had some concerns about the "orgies" at Herod's palace. And, indeed, Ray pays a great deal of attention to Herod and his family, as if to say that the origins of social evil begin in a familial space. Although the sequences at the palace appear much less erotic than the ones DeMille shot decades earlier, the leading players in Herod's palace are neither punished nor tamed by Jesus. Instead, the film suggests that there are some who have illicit sexual intrigues with impunity. Herod's incestuous behavior, the extreme youth of Salome, with whom he is obviously obsessed, and the general demeanor of violence at Herod's palace seem to be, if not normative, at least easily explained and understood in the age of Freud and Kinsey.

Far from the family in which "father" has all the answers, Ray has used the narrative to position a weak ruler and father amidst a collapsing patriarchy. Herodias, Herod's wife, is clearly shown to be the stronger of the couple and hints at the changing (dominant) construction of passive female desire already present in the Kinsey Report. With family representations that are clearly at odds with the Production Code, Ray has quietly decentered the notion of a patriarchal family structure. He shows himself, once again, attentive to the submerged undercurrent present in a conflicted society.

Ultimately, the energy of Ray's direction and visual composition reminds us of the potential humanist redemption lurking just under the surface in so many of his films. Indeed, one of the more compelling aspects of *Bigger Than Life* is its theological statement about hope, which ultimately begins to suggest *King of Kings*. The entire story in *Bigger Than Life* occurs during Easter vacation, and Ed Avery's attempt to kill his son is something like Abraham run amok: Ray's characters here and elsewhere appear to be thwarted by a post-Holocaust Yahweh who brings people to the brink of their own humanity. It is not the God of Sartre, however, but of the angry post–World War II generation like Ray, for whom so many things had gone wrong, and whose attitude resembles the cry of the crucified Jesus: My God, my God, why have you forsaken us? And yet Ray still maintains the radical vestiges of rebirth; this from a director who, by his own reckoning, went at night to the set of Gethsemane and sprayed the trees silver in order "to give them life."

For the most part, Ray created a lifelong reputation for picturing an alienated America. On the other hand, Ray's films are poignant, humanist records of admirable failures with a glimmer of hope. The closing sequences of *King of Kings* are, like the Sermon on the Mount, rooted in Jesus' proclamation and not his spectacle. After appealing briefly to Mary Magdalene, the voice of Jesus tells the puzzled disciples fishing on the sea to preach the gospel "to all who hunger." If they appear bewildered at the call to respond only in faith, then the apostles resemble the gamut of a stunned postwar generation. With nothing like the aura of DeMille's resurrected Jesus in color to guide them, Ray's risen Savior is literally invisible (with a haunting shadow) to the disciples and finally to us. Together we set out into the 1960s, which, after years of doubt and uncertainty, would ultimately declare God dead.

NOTES

1. Peter Hasenberg, "The 'Religious' in Film: From *The King of Kings* to *The Fisher King*," in *New Image of Religious Film*, ed. John R. May (Kansas City, MO: Sheed & Ward, 1997), 43.

2. Ibid., 44.

3. Babington and Evans, *Biblical Epics*, 127.

4. Ibid., 128–29.

5. Lloyd Baugh, *Imaging the Divine: Jesus and Christ-Figures in Film* (Kansas City, MO: Sheed & Ward, 1997), 22.

6. Ibid., 23.

7. Roy Kinnard and Tim Davis, *Divine Images: A History of Jesus on the Screen* (New York: Citadel Press, 1992), 131.

8. Ibid., 132.

9. Babington and Evans, *Biblical Epics*, 136–37.

10. Clifford E. Clark Jr., "Ranch-House Suburbia: Ideals and Realities," in *Recasting America: Culture and Politics in the Age of Cold War* (Chicago: University of Chicago Press, 1988), 182.

11. Jacques Rivette, "On Imagination," in *Cahiers du Cinema: The 1950s: Neo-Realism, Hollywood, New Wave* (Cambridge MA: Harvard University Press, 1985), 105.

12. Babington and Evans, *Biblical Epics*, 133.

Photo courtesy of the Academy of Motion Picture Arts & Sciences. © Cifex. Used with permission.

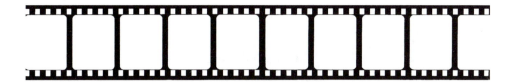

THIRD FEATURE

The Gospel According to Saint Matthew (1964)

*"What went ye into the wilderness to see...a reed?
A man clothed in soft raiment?"*

Directed by: Pier Paolo Pasolini

Produced by: Alfredo Bini

Screenplay by: Pier Paolo Pasolini

Actors Include: Enrique Irazoqui (Jesus), Margherita Caruso (Mary as young woman), Susanna Pasolini (Mary as older woman), Mario Socrate (John the Baptist), Marcello Morante (Joseph)

Running Time: 142 minutes

Introduction

The Gospel According to Saint Matthew (in Italian, *Il Vangelo Secondo Matteo*) is clearly not a film constructed on the Hollywood model. It is shot on grainy, black-and-white filmstock. It does not have the grand, polished, evenly lit, seamless look that is so indicative of Hollywood productions in general, including the cinematic lives of Jesus we have viewed so far. Its primitive look marks an intentional move away from the antiseptic look of the Hollywood renditions. A review in the 16 September 1964 *Variety* labeled the movie "rough-hewn." Other critics have labeled it one of the greatest cinematic lives of Jesus.

None of the actors is a professional. Pasolini even manages to include his own mother as the aged mother of Jesus. The film has the feel of a self-conscious reenactment of the passion story, something a small town might produce as part of a local festival. The lines of the actors seem more to be recited than acted out. (The English translation is provided in subtitles.) There are certainly some elements to the feel of the production that one might label as amateurish, much as paintings by Grandma Moses seem primitive in style. Others have characterized this film as an example of "neorealism."

The film was produced primarily in rural southern Italy by an Italian Marxist named Pier Paolo Pasolini and dedicated, perhaps ironically, to Pope John XXIII. Church leaders were initially critical of the film because of the political connections of the director but later embraced it wholeheartedly. Millicent Marcus has claimed that "Pasolini manages to pull off an atheistic retelling of the Christ story without yielding to the twin temptations built into his project: those of a hypocritical assumption of Christian sympathies in the interests of poetic coherence, or of a scientific analysis of the Christ phenomenon in dialectical-materialist terms."[1]

The rough, primitive quality does nothing to diminish the power of the production nor the strict adherence to its textual source, the Gospel of Matthew; the dialog is drawn directly out of Matthew's Gospel. Even so, the viewer should be sure to note what is included from the Gospel and what has been excluded, since not every word, nor every scene, from the Gospel has been included in the movie. The viewer will gain important insight into the values of the film's creator by analyzing what is included and what is left out.

There are certain features of this movie that need to be noted, and questions that need to be asked (without necessarily proposing answers!). First, why would a Marxist produce a film about the life of Jesus? What would a Marxist's Jesus look like, act like, sound like? What would such a Jesus seek to accomplish? What events or qualities in the life of Jesus might be attractive to a Marxist or socialist? Jesus clearly motivates more of the action in the movie than in previously viewed films, although frankly, there is very little action. He is also more emotionally expressive than in previous films. This remains one of the more interesting aspects of this film. Many of the participants in our school classes have been put off by this Jesus, who seems so "angry" in this film compared to others they have watched—angrier than their personal conceptions had permitted. But one must ask nevertheless, who might be attracted to the proclamations of an angry, expressive Jesus?

Another question noted above is how does this film work as a story? That is, if you did not know the basic outline of Jesus' life as presented in the gospels, the Gospel of Matthew in particular, would this film provide you with enough information to make sense of the story of Jesus of Nazareth? The answer is clearly no. There are many largely unexplained actions in the film, such as the deaths of Herod and John the Baptist. Pasolini seems to have depended on having an audience that knew the basic plot of Jesus' later life. The movie has less of a narrative plot even than the gospels themselves.

What might Pasolini's motivation have been for making this movie? What did he hope to add that was not present in other films about the life of Jesus? Keep in mind that this is not a harmonization of the gospels as all of the other movies being considered have been. Rather it is a film interpretation of the Gospel of Matthew. Viewers would be well advised to read carefully the Gospel of Matthew before viewing this film in order to get a sense (that is, form their own interpretation) of who Matthew thought Jesus was—the primary themes and motifs as well as the qualities of Jesus—before seeing Pasolini's interpretation of Matthew.

Perhaps one way of describing the differences between Pasolini's film and those we have already treated is to suggest that the Hollywood films seek to recreate the *look* of the time of Jesus, whereas Pasolini seems to be trying to recreate the *feel* of the peasant life of first-century Palestine, filtered, of course, through his own vision and ideology. Hollywood films are very lush visually: vast landscapes, subtle use of color, wide-screen images, smooth camera work, often an omniscient as opposed to a subjective point of view, and so forth. There is typically an attempt at recreating some degree of visual verisimilitude in order to create an appropriate sense of time and place and make one forget that one is actually watching a film. Yet the characters in the Hollywood productions often seem very contemporary and urban, even urbane. Rarely does Jesus ever appear or act as a peasant carpenter. Pasolini seems more interested in creating a sense of the people with whom Jesus likely would have interacted: mostly rough-hewn peasants and a few civil and religious authorities. Perhaps the difference in intent might be likened to the difference between a docudrama and a poem. The docudrama is longer, provides more detail, attempts to be historically accurate, and has a look of reality, but is largely a fictional re-creation, while the poem is more interested in meaning behind events, in recreating an experience rather than portraying history. The poem is interested in effects and residues of the events less than the events themselves.

Because *The Gospel According to Saint Matthew* stands out so distinctly from the other Jesus films, the viewer must ask both how and why. Author Jane Resh Thomas noted in a 1997 lecture at the University of Minnesota (Duluth) that while not all writing is autobiography, most writing is *autobiographic,* that is, it reveals much about the author. In a similar sense, the vision of Jesus created by a director probably says more about the director (or screenwriter) than it does about the historic personage of Jesus of Nazareth. The same could be said of our own faith constructs of Jesus. In what sense, then, might *The Gospel According to Saint Matthew* be autobiographic, that is, what elements of Pasolini's Jesus might reflect his image of himself and/or what he hoped Jesus was like?

Movie Preview: Questions and Suggestions

1. *Read through the Gospel of Matthew to determine the characteristics of Jesus that seem most important to Matthew. What are they? Who is Jesus for Matthew?*

2. *What elements would you speculate would be included in a Marxist vision of Jesus?*

3. *Summarize your impressions of the Jesus films you have viewed this far.*

4. *Write a short summary of the plotline of Jesus' life. What events did you include; which did you leave out in your summary? Be ready to compare your list with Pasolini's.*

Movie Viewing

Movie Review: Questions and Responses

1. *Describe the image of Jesus in this film.*

2. *How does it compare to your image? What are the points of comparison and/or contrast?*

3. *What elements from the biblical Gospel of Matthew have been included and which excluded? Which characters are included/excluded from the biblical text?*

4. *Why do you think Pasolini chose this neorealistic approach for the look of his film: seemingly rough camera work, harsh lighting, amateurish costuming, and nonprofessional actors?*

5. *Why do you think Pasolini used so many close-ups of faces? What is the effect?*

6. *What is the effect of the mix of musical styles and sources?*

LENS ONE

Pasolini's depiction of Jesus of Nazareth is unique in that it paints a picture that is largely unfamiliar to the American viewer: the harsh and barren countryside of Italy; the sun-chiseled features of the southern European farmer; the dilapidated surroundings of stone buildings that have been built and rebuilt over the course of millennia. To this picture Pasolini adds certain theological tones that reflect a decidedly European vision: a respect for the promise of Communism; a suspicion of those institutions that are symbols of the decadent power of an ancient regime; a recognition of God's presence in the daily life of the common person. All of this is clear as one reviews the film. But beyond these elements, there is something nevertheless that looks quite familiar at a fundamental level. It is Pasolini's understanding of Scripture and early Christian history, both of which seem to peer through the same type of lens that Nicholas Ray already employed in 1961. Consider three examples.

The Characteristics of Jesus. For Pasolini, as for Ray (in broad distinction to DeMille), this latest Jesus of Nazareth is the most human in every respect. Although he possesses a timeless beauty in the flawless features of his Mediterranean face, his lifestyle is that of any other person with whom he associates. He eats the meager meal of the lower classes, he dresses in the simple clothing style of his contemporaries, and he stumbles over the rough and dusty roads that serve all who live in the back country of the Roman empire. His steady, unflinching gaze reveals a man who has beheld the living face of God. Yet it is a look which invites the viewer to believe that any person may view God in the same way. It is by no means a vision intended to suggest that Jesus has transcended the turmoils of daily living in any physical sense. Indeed, it is a vision that thrusts him squarely into the midst of his fellow strugglers. At the same time, it is a vision that drives Jesus to lead his followers through the cares of their common existence in pursuit of a higher life of righteousness within God's glory. As with the vision of Ray, our Jesus is a solitary man, and yet, he is a man.

Secondly, we once again find Jesus portrayed primarily as a teacher. Pasolini has done well to choose the Gospel of Matthew as the foundation for this understanding, since it is in this particular Gospel that we find so many early Christian sayings from the historical Jesus. At every turn in the story of Jesus' life he is teaching those who gather around him. It is a teaching of unification: all things are possible for those who will rally around the cause of God. Power will soon pass from those who hold the trappings of religious authority in the name of God, but who stand as hypocrites with respect to God's desire for human justice. Jesus teaches about faithful devotion to the will of God, about treating one's neighbors with dignity and respect, about recognizing one's weaknesses before criticizing other people. His teaching is focused on personal dignity and responsibility and about the dangers of institutional abuse.

Pasolini's Jesus transcends Ray's Jesus with respect to the pedagogical role. Pasolini sees Jesus also as a miracle worker, and includes a scattered collection of miracles that Matthew has attributed to Jesus. Several of these are healings of the lame, the lepers, and the suffering (Mt 12). One is the cursing of the fig tree (Mt 21). Others include the feeding of the multitudes and walking upon the water (Mt 14). Pasolini also portrays Jesus as a prophet who speaks of his coming crucifixion and the eventual end of his days. Yet, there is no question that Jesus' primary role is that of instructor. He teaches a divine wisdom and seeks to lead others to a new vision of the presence of God in their world.

Finally, Pasolini recognizes the political reality of first-century Palestine. It is a reality that operates on two levels. In a broad way Judaism is in conflict with the Romans. There is an ever present feeling of oppression and struggle among the common Jewish populace. Their world is a place of harshness under Roman domination. One never detects any trace of hope that Israel may one day arise and cast off the yoke of Rome's oppression. To suggest such a thought is as unrealistic as to suggest that the disciples of Jesus will one day wear silk clothing and crowns of gold. The harsh realities of servitude under a foreign government shape one's hopes and fears.

At the same time that we feel the Jewish people under the weight of Rome, there is yet a second level at which the political reality of ancient Palestine operates in Pasolini's vision. Here begin the explicit ways in which Pasolini differs from Ray's depiction of the life of Jesus. On this second level the viewer finds Jesus in conflict with formal Judaism—the individual in struggle with the institution. With Matthew's Gospel firmly in hand, Pasolini portrays both John the Baptizer and Jesus as enemies of the Pharisees and Sadducees, those vipers who await at every corner to trap, condemn, and kill our heroes in a web of lies and deceit. John, of course, is eventually caught and beheaded by King Herod, whose fondness for his wife's daughter soon surpasses his respect for Jewish law and the norms of common decency. Jesus jousts with his opponents for a longer period, returning verbal jabs as the Temple authorities attempt to catch him in disputes over the laws of the Jewish tradition. His end on the cross is inevitable, of course. But it is less an end to one man's struggle than the beginning of his followers' own preaching about the kingdom of God.

This leads to a second way in which Pasolini differs from Ray in his view of Jesus. Though Jesus, as seen by Pasolini, unites his followers with a message of deliverance from institutional abuse, Jesus also divides people. He leaves mother and home to pursue his ministry; he takes James and John from their father's fishing business; he accepts the praise of the crowds in Jerusalem in defiance of the religious authorities and of those who support the ancient worship of the Temple.

While Ray's Jesus certainly runs afoul of his antagonists, this is primarily because the latter do not understand or cannot accept the peaceful, person-oriented teachings that Jesus espouses. Pasolini's Jesus, however, seems bent on the alienation of his opponents. He rarely speaks a word softly, but shouts his message of defiance against the scribes and Pharisees. His voice is like that of the ancient prophets of Israel, persons who spoke the words of God with confidence and who appear to have cared little about how others received those words. For Jesus, the truth of the message is in the words, regardless of whether or not people chose to hear them.

Finally, Pasolini's Jesus is eschatological to the core—a teacher and preacher whose message and motivation are driven by a vision of what is yet to be. The viewer finds little of Ray's hero here, a man whose primary concern is for authentic human life in the present as a living embodiment of the kingdom of God. Perhaps Pasolini's vision is best illustrated by his own words, which spring forward at the beginning of part 2, a virtual creed that incorporates the language of the Old Testament into the prophetic voice of Jesus' message: "Howl, O gate, cry out, O city; suffer, Palestine, for a river is coming and every man will gird himself with sacks for his way; and all will howl on the rooftops and the squares dissolved in tears." This language is highly reminiscent of the apocalyptic language of Matthew 25, but is not drawn from that material. It is a recasting of the message of the prophet Isaiah (Is 15:3) into Pasolini's cry of woe against the haughty attitude of the Temple authorities, here placed upon the lips of Jesus. It is perhaps the essence of how Pasolini understands Jesus as the apocalyptic prophet of God and tragic teacher of Israel.

Source Materials. Turning to the primary source material for Pasolini's work, the Gospel of Matthew, it is perhaps here that one can best see the director's own interpretative framework. On the one hand, it is relatively easy to track Pasolini's use of the Gospel, since he begins approximately with the opening of Matthew's own account (minus the genealogy of Jesus at 1:2–17) and ends with the resurrection instructions (28:18–20). Pasolini's approach is not particularly sophisticated when compared with that of Ray. For example, Ray is somewhat concerned to depict the life and teachings of Jesus within a broadly defined historical context. He wishes to give this significant moment in time the feel of a historical novel, a story in motion. Such an approach is appropriate for the modern cinema, but is in few respects faithful to the New Testament's own presentation. Instead, it is Pasolini who more accurately presents the gospel story as it stands in literature. Pasolini's story is not so much a modern, historical epic, but is a literalistic and episodic presentation of the events in the ministry of Jesus. This is just how Matthew (as well as the other New Testament evangelists) offers the recollection of Jesus of Nazareth. The story of Jesus is a pastiche of episodes, not a cinematic biography.

At the same time, Pasolini makes certain telling additions to his wooden presentation of the Matthean plot. Throughout the film one can easily detect the vestiges of later Christian iconography and pietistic symbols. Women in the story are consistently depicted in a certain Renaissance vision of light and shadows, of purity in the midst of desolation. The baptism of John at the Jordan River is undertaken through a ritual of sprinkling, followed by the classic devotional response of the baptized with folded hands and eyes turned heavenward in prayer. Otherwise, throughout the movie, those persons who pray do so on their knees with palms turned forward in quest of the power of the Holy Spirit. One finds this both in the scene where Jesus fasts in the wilderness before the temptation and again as the disciples pray prior to the arrest of Jesus at Gethsemane.

Apart from these anachronistic interpretations of the Matthean story, Pasolini also offers some minor alterations to the presentation of the text itself. These changes are most often made for specific reasons of economy. As stated above, the genealogy of Jesus is missing. But this material essentially serves no real purpose for the viewer, and its inclusion would greatly detract from Joseph's shocking discovery of Mary's pregnancy at the beginning of the story. So harsh a beginning to a phenomenal tale about the coming of God's Messiah is too often glossed over by those who interpret Matthew's Gospel. Its biting reality is clearly on Joseph's face, a look needing no words to explain his emotional turmoil, a feeling that no words can adequately explain or demystify.

Pasolini omits certain other materials throughout, though these omissions are mostly minor with respect to the plot. The biblical student might quickly observe, for example, that despite Pasolini's concern to follow the Matthean story with precision, he has chosen to omit the transfiguration scene of chapter 17. Curiously, this episode (which is difficult to explain or to understand in any case) is routinely ignored by most directors. In the case of Pasolini, it would certainly detract from his vision of the human Jesus. This omission is thus not surprising.

The diligent scholar might further note that the extensive materials about the coming endtimes that occur in chapter 25 are also missing. But recall that Pasolini has made some nod to this aspect of Jesus' teaching in the opening proclamation of part 2, which incorporates an element of Isaiah's prophecy. The flavor of apocalyptic thought is most certainly present, even if it does not draw specifically from Matthew's own materials.

For some viewers there may be a measure of discomfort with the fact that the famous Sermon on the Mount (Mt 5–7) appears to be a summation of the extended teachings of Jesus as delivered upon numerous occasions (notice the change in weather conditions as Jesus speaks), which only later are combined by Matthew into a single setting. Curiously, Pasolini is quite astute in his reading of the text, since it is this very understanding of the Sermon that had become common among New Testament scholars by the early 1960s and is widely held today.

Finally, there is something to be said for the fact that throughout our film Pasolini has chosen to interpret Matthew's "angel" as a messenger who appears in person and in a most unremarkable fashion. These appearances are never in dreams as such, but seem to be very much within the movement of conscious reality. Those times when angels in a divine sense would be demanded by the text are tactfully avoided, occasions such as ministering to Jesus after the wilderness temptation or when Elijah and Moses stand with Jesus at the transfiguration.

Perspectives on Judaism. Perhaps what is most disturbing about Pasolini's presentation of Matthew's story is the way in which institutional Judaism is treated. This is most often undertaken with a subtle manipulation of the text itself. But it is a manipulation that occurs at several levels and with respect to numerous scenes. This suggests that Pasolini has made a conscious decision in his presentation of the materials.

The case is as follows: The Gospel of Matthew is well known among students of Scripture as a text that seeks to present Jesus and his message within the light of early Jewish traditions and beliefs. The Gospel of Luke, in contrast, depicts a Jesus whose primary message and concerns are ultimately for the broader world of hearers and the salvation of humanity in general. The Gospel of Matthew contains an explicit concern for the salvation of Israel and the heritage of Judaism. This is not to exclude a broader mission to the nations, but it certainly seeks to avoid underemphasizing the mother faith from which early Christianity sprang. Matthew's Jesus speaks often with a Jewish flavor—he preaches about the "kingdom of Heaven" to avoid any use of the name of God; he offers a characteristically Jewish ethic based upon almsgiving, prayer, and fasting (6:1–18); he specifically states that he "was sent only to the lost sheep of the house of Israel" (see the episode of the Canaanite woman at 15:21–28). At the same time, of course, Jesus finds himself in constant conflict with the Jewish religious authorities and their "human philosophies." While he himself teaches a familiar Jewish ethic and devotional piety, it is in stark contrast to the particular spin that the Pharisees and Sadducees have given to Jewish theology and tradition in the light of their own understanding of the Temple as God's house.

For many modern Christians there tends to be a sense in which Jesus becomes a pious, lone voice for God's truth who finds himself in conflict with a self-seeking collection of Judaism's religious authorities. To the extent that the author of the Gospel of Matthew found the early church in struggle with the first-century synagogue, this is most likely true to the Matthean vision. The vision itself is likely to have been a broad caricature of the actual historical circumstances, since much of what Jesus teaches actually would have been satisfactory to Pharisaic theology and beliefs. But our author is concerned to offer early Christianity some foundation upon which to differentiate itself from Judaism, while at the same time offering some understanding of how Jesus himself was a Jew and respected Jewish tradition. The early church accepted this message readily, since it evolved directly from Judaism. Proof of this acceptance is demonstrated in the fact that the Gospel of Matthew was the most widely used New Testament Gospel among the numerous churches of the Roman empire.

The sad reality for subsequent Christianity is that it was institutional Judaism that ultimately became the target of anti-Semitic attacks as the result of such a vision. It is something of this vision that Pasolini adopts. The dialectic of truth versus falsehood, of pious faith in conflict with gross hypocrisy, of individual belief in competition with an aberrant religious institution tends to attract his interests. He sees the dialectic—the struggle of a genuine, personal devotion against false, institutional hypocrisy—within the Matthean story. His use of the text tends to exploit this motif, as can be readily demonstrated by specific examples.

In the first instance, we can look at Jesus' call of the twelve disciples. There are two texts about the call in Matthew, which Pasolini has combined (see 4:18–22 and 10:1–4). Each of these "call texts" is followed by certain words of instruction—in 4:18–22 it is the famous Sermon on the Mount in chapters 5–7, and for 10:1–4 there are sayings on the cost of discipleship in 10:16–39. These words of instruction are preserved by Pasolini. But something very important is omitted, the context of the great missionary journey that is associated with the call in chapter 10 (see 10:5–15, 40–42). This is especially unfortunate, since this context provides a vision of mission directed to the house of Israel and to the Jews specifically. Pasolini's omission serves effectively to remove the Jews from their right as valid recipients of the teachings of Jesus and thus absolves Christianity (as well as Pasolini) from any need to focus upon the inclusion of Judaism as an integral aspect of Jesus' original message.

Secondly, in the Matthean text many of the sayings that Jesus speaks and the miracles that he performs occur in or around local synagogues. Yet nowhere does Pasolini provide the context of a synagogue for these scenes! This is an obvious omission implying that Jesus works from a perspective of personal devotion and piety that has no need of traditional Jewish structures of community and worship. While the Gospel of Matthew is extremely concerned with the role of the community in the life of the believer, Pasolini has considered the Jewish roots of this community experience but then chooses to weed out such foundational networks. The resulting problem is that when the roots are removed, the stem dies and the fruit along with it. In other words, all the influences of Judaism on early Christianity are neglected. This is most unfaithful to the Matthean perspective; at the very least, it is a serious distortion of Matthew's reading of Judaism. Even though Matthew's Jesus finds himself in conflict with the hostile representatives of institutional Judaism, it is not with Judaism itself that Jesus is distraught. He is in opposition to its leaders. So too, it is not Judaism per se that the author of the Gospel of Matthew attacks. Indeed, Matthew wrote at the end of the first century, when the early church found itself in struggle with Judaism, a religious tradition that could find no room for the growing faith of Jewish Christians.

Yet it is not Judaism itself that Matthew rejected, but only those intolerant elements residing within the tradition.

For Pasolini, however, it is indeed with respect to institutional Judaism that the struggle of "individual versus system" becomes best symbolized. Of course, one assumes that Pasolini intends for the viewer to transfer this element of struggle, this tension between individual and system, to the modern situation of the individual Christian in conflict with the institution (whether religious or secular). But in this process there is the potential for a misleading result. Namely, all that is wholesome about community and tradition, about structure and common values, can be rejected by the viewer (and perhaps by Pasolini) because of its association with Jewish roots.

In the final analysis it is curious, and perhaps ironic, that Pasolini ends his film with the same text of Scripture that was previously employed by both DeMille and Ray, that is, Matthew 28:20: "...remember, I am with you always." Though the three directors approach the life of Jesus from different contours (DeMille from an ahistorical perspective; Ray with a humanistic touch; and Pasolini out of a pietistic bias), each chooses to conclude with the same words from Matthew—a promise of presence. One gets the impression that something different must be inferred from each director's use of this promise.

For Pasolini, one wonders if the promise is to be played out in the embodiment of the present, living worker of common society, a person who is in touch with traditional piety and devotion to the reality of a divine vision. Much like the Jesus of Nazareth who is known from Matthew's account, the eternal living presence of Christ radiates through any disciple who chooses to struggle against the injustices of the institution—whether religious, economic, or political. If Pasolini's interpretation of Matthew's ancient story can be accepted, then we can say that the theme of a struggle for divine justice in the face of religious, institutional hypocrisy may be acceptable. At the same time, however, the abandonment of a Jewish religious heritage as the foundation for the development of the authentic, Christian experience can hardly be substantiated. Indeed, the acceptance of such a perspective is both dangerous to the Christian vision and a denial of the very spirit of what the Gospel of Matthew intends.

LENS TWO

From a production standpoint, there are numerous noteworthy features in this film. First and most obvious, the film was shot in black and white, which gives the film its stark and grainy look. This was certainly a deliberate choice, a movement against the flow of film trends of the time, which used color as lavishly and evocatively as possible. What was behind this choice? Why use an "old" technology? What was the hoped-for effect of such a choice?

Even in current, very hi-tech commercials, black and white is still used to create certain effects. Typically, the effect is to give the photographed subject a remote look—not necessarily old-fashioned, but classic, timeless. It also conveys a certain flat look because there is less visual information (no color!)—only shades of black, white, and grey. The viewer has to supply more information to interpret the scene.

Marshall McLuhan coined the terms *hot* and *cool* in reference to the media. A *hot* medium provides more visual (or audio) information, which then leaves less for the viewer to supply imaginatively. A *cool* medium, on the other hand, provides less information, and so requires the viewer to supply more data, to be more active in the information-processing/meaning-creating task.[2] Black-and-white photography, then, is more likely to draw the viewer into an active role as viewer, rather than just be passively washed by the awesome display of color and technology.

Jim McDermott makes a related point about the difficulty of portraying Jesus on film because, in his case, the actor (not the filmstock) provides the information about the written gospel. "It's not that the actor brings too little to the screen, but that he brings too much."[3] Similarly, the scenery recedes in importance as the characters become greater foci of interest.

In a related way, the scene and setting of the film go against the trend as well. The film is shot in rural Italy, in various bleak, harsh, and rocky locales. There is no attempt to create the look of first-century Palestine, although one certainly gets the feel of an arid, desolate, even hostile environment where life would be difficult. The costumes are contrived. The intent is clearly not historical accuracy. What, then, is the effect? For many, this almost self-conscious approach brings a fresh naiveté to the viewing. The characters are not polished, although they are sincere and genuine. The camera work is not elegant and smooth, but it is powerful. The musical mix is unusual, to say the least, but it does create a mood and shapes the working of the scene. There is an overall earnestness about this production that gives it power.

However one describes the affect of the locale, that it is further reinforced by the lighting, which contributes to the harsh, unsophisticated, stark, and rugged look of the film. Was this a matter of primitive equipment, limited options, low budget, and/or limited experience by Pasolini, or was it a deliberate move to create a certain feel in this film? The latter is most certainly the answer.

Lighting is not only used to create the mood of the scene but also to indicate the passage of time as well. There is an extended section in the movie in which Jesus recites a long series of sayings. As suggested above in Lens One, this could have been shot as though he said all of these words at one time in one place, which would be possibly inaccurate and monumentally uninteresting. If one's eyes were closed during this section, it would be hard to tell otherwise. Watching the film, however, the viewer can hardly escape noticing the lighting changes, intended to suggest the passage of time. The light changes from light to dark to stormy, even though Jesus continues resolutely to face the camera. The basic shot does not change; only the lighting communicates the passing of time. It is a well-done affect.

In several shots there is a high-contrast lighting ratio, that is, the range from bright to dark is very great. Sometimes the effect of this is, for some of the very darkest elements of the picture, the loss of detail. For example, Pasolini periodically uses shots with extremely bright backgrounds. Initially, the characters walk out of this nearly blinding background toward the camera, with their faces in shadow. As they get closer to the camera, the details of their individual faces become clearer and we see who they are. This is a nice detail but might simply be misperceived as poor camera work, such as when you posed Mom and Dad in front of the picture window on Christmas Day. The window light was probably so bright that it dominated the readings of the camera's light meter and turned your parents' faces into mere shadows. In your case, it was an accident. For Pasolini, it becomes a nifty technique intended to cause a more gradual revelation of the identity of the figures in the picture. (We should add parenthetically that some of this effect is exaggerated in the translation of the movie from film to videotape. Videotape cannot handle large significant contrasts in lighting nearly as well as film; some of the subtle gradations from black to white are lost on videotape.)

Other features of camera technique should be mentioned as well. Much of the film is shot with a subjective point of view, that is, as though the camera/viewer is in the midst of the crowd or at the scene. Most Hollywood films choose an objective perspective, as though one were a dispassionate observer watching the scene through a window, or from an omniscient but distant viewpoint. The viewer is far above the scene and privy to more information than anyone involved in the scene. Pasolini, however, often places the viewer right in the midst of the action, turning quickly here and there, staring right into the faces of the other characters, or up to the Temple top during the Christ's temptation. We are in the scene, a part of the action. In some sense, the camera creates much of the action by panning and tilting in what would otherwise be a static scene.

The viewer gets a hint of this in the opening shot with the long close-up of Mary's face. She is centered in the picture, which provides a sense of a "static" shot, almost that of a still camera. This is followed by an equally long and static shot of Joseph. A little eye movement is about all the action that takes place here. Indeed, with a few important exceptions, there is little action in this film. There are, however, endless portraits of characters: shots of faces, singly or in small groups, panning from side-to-side over the group to record their reactions.

The camera angles also add to the impact. Many of the scenes, especially those in which Jesus is the central character, or when Jesus is speaking, are shot straight on. The camera is directly in front of the actor's face—literally "in your face." On many other occasions, the camera, as already noted, remains an agonizingly long time on faces of some of the characters. This, at times, seems to stretch the notion of "motion" picture. Those few times where there is action are significant, such as during the slaughter of the innocents. There the action seems frenetic, especially in contrast to the nearly static nature of the rest of the film.

This brings to mind another noteworthy feature of this film—the cast that is so carefully pictured within those portraits. Nearly all of the characters are portrayed by local people, selected from the area in Italy where the film was shot. No well-manicured figures here; no soft-focus lenses to erase minor skin flaws. Deep wrinkles are evident in nearly every leathery face; no pretty faces here; no smooth, subtle, sublime performances. These are *real* people. Indeed, at times the film has the feel of an extended passion play being enacted with great devotion by townspeople who have tremendous desire and enthusiasm but little acting experience. One can almost hear the director telling them from off-camera to smile, to look this way or that, to begin walking, and so forth. The actors respond with great sincerity and devotion.

As noted earlier in this section, a difficulty in portraying Jesus in movies is that there is often too much "information" in the portrayals as compared to the canonical, printed version of the gospel story. The actor provides interpretive content that should be in the realm of the reader or hearer. In Pasolini's movie, Jesus is played by someone with no prior acting experience, Enrique Irazoqui. His lack of experience, however, should not lead one to infer a lack of power or screen presence. In many ways, he commands more screen presence through the force of his acting than any of the previous renditions.

Still another notable feature of this film is the audio complex: sound effects, music, vocal qualities, and such. First, there is no "live" or environmental sound. This results in a certain remoteness from the action, nearly like that of a silent movie such as *The King of Kings,* to which sound was later added. Remember the clinking coins? This audio remoteness creates an odd juxtaposition to the camera's frequent subjective point of view. The audio does not provide the viewer with the sense of being there, while the camera work does just that.

Calling so much attention to the work of the camera and the audio complex is very "un-Hollywood." As with so many other facets of this film, the director seems to have chosen a contrarian direction. There is quite a variety of music used, including a blues song, "Sometimes I Feel Like a Motherless Child," which is heard on several occasions throughout the film. The movie viewer may wish to note those places where this song is used and try to determine what the song is intended to do at those points: what subtext is being proposed? There are also examples of African liturgical music and powerful Russian choral pieces. What did Pasolini hope to communicate with these music choices; how does the music shape the "reading" of the scene? Is there some subtle or not-so-subtle subtext being related? Certainly the music represents music of "the people" on the one hand: the blues of African Americans lamenting their enslavement and longing for better days, or the Russian folk songs, which again glorify the people and their struggles to reach freedom, albeit in a very different setting and with a very different outcome.

The various tools available to any film director have all been employed by Pasolini but to very different effects from those of the Hollywood films viewed so far. Hollywood movies typically try to create a seamless pretense with their use of visual and audio elements. Pasolini has chosen the opposite direction, calling great and obvious attention to the presence of the camera, placing unusual music in places where it creates odd juxtapositions to the visuals. There is a pervasive sense of cognitive dissonance throughout the film as Pasolini challenges Hollywood cinematic traditions with his use of the audiovisual toolbox to create his image of Jesus of Nazareth. He has used the popular and traditional text of the Gospel of Matthew, but there is no pretense at an "objective" reprise of this ancient text. His image of Jesus, his reading of the Matthean text, is no less shaped by his values, attitudes, and beliefs than are our own.

LENS THREE

As mentioned, we have thus far limited our discussion to Hollywood films. Any discussion of Pasolini's *The Gospel According to Saint Matthew,* however, takes us quickly away from conventional Hollywood notions of the Savior to one that is politically radical, eccentric, and distinctly European. In fact, the contrast between Pasolini's individualistic, poetic, and Marxist sensibility could hardly be more alien to the Hollywood studio system. Pasolini's film approaches a documentary style, and, like Sergei Eisenstein, the great Soviet director of *Potemkin* (1925), uses nonprofessional actors. A new Jesus emerges in the controversial mid-1960s—one very different from the Jesus of the Hollywood dream factory.

A Market for Art Films. As we have already seen from our analysis of DeMille's production of *The King of Kings,* the Jesus film was made for an era and an industry with a strong moral imperative and a Production Code endorsed by an American middle-class audience. With the introduction of foreign films into the United States by the 1950s, Americans considerably broadened their taste in film and their moral sensibility. The 1960s American film culture was remarkably influenced by the influx of foreign films like *The Gospel According to Saint Matthew,* together with a more global appetite in arty, international cinema. European directors became notorious—stars in their own right. Roberto Rossellini ran off with Ingrid Bergman and made headlines; Pasolini was a homosexual with articulate defenses about his lifestyle and his Marxist vision. From the point of view of culture, the arrival of Pasolini's film in the United States in 1966 (two years after its European release) to great acclaim among college campuses and art houses throughout the country, signaled a change in the American audience. In a certain sense, *The Gospel*

According to Saint Matthew would anticipate not only the new Hollywood of the late 1960s, but the changing face of American culture during that turbulent decade and beyond. As the culture in America began to shift during the 1960s, the collapse of the studio system and the stale state of the film industry gave way to the rise of another Hollywood, partially shaped by the economics of changing consumer interests in foreign media.

With the advent of seemingly endless ploys intended to lure audiences back into theaters, movie critics like Pauline Kael had already been complaining about the sad state of Hollywood movies in the mid-1950s. By the 1950s, the classic Hollywood studio system was on the wane, mostly due to the Supreme Court's 1948 Paramount decision, which forced the vertically integrated industry to dismantle its exhibition strategies from its production and distribution operations. The social implications of this realignment are impossible to exaggerate, especially in regard to the way the Paramount decision influenced American taste in film away from a massified, factory-driven studio product toward alternative forms of entertainment. Television is the most often cited reason for Hollywood's decline, but foreign films offered a new, emerging audience in the post–World War II years something different from a fantasy space. If Hollywood had dominated the foreign market before World War II, the divesting of its monopoly allowed foreign markets to infiltrate American culture.

At first glance it appears that the American film industry in 1966 represented a culture content with its domestic market. America produced artifacts that displayed few signs of radicalism. Of course, mass culture traditionally serves as a stabilizing force, not one that moves toward action, especially when that action involves changing the status quo. There were, for example, two successful westerns *(Stagecoach* and *Return of the Seven)* and a run of Disney films, even a top-grossing one, *That Darned Cat.* But when we probe a bit deeper, we might notice the enormous run of James Bond films still popular in 1966. Those films were British and so was the huge epic released the previous year, David Lean's *Doctor Zhivago.* Many Americans were not much interested in contemporary domestic issues in 1966, but were increasingly turning toward global interests and a concern for other cultures. After all, it was a playboy spy with a working-class British accent that captured most of the decade.

Even Americans were investing big money in films from other countries, the content of which challenged conventional American ideology and morality. For example, American studios financed 80 percent of British films in 1965. Considerable money was poured into Italy, France, and elsewhere. To complicate the issue further, we know the British film industry was experiencing a renaissance in the 1960s, promoting working-class politics. The "British invasion" typically refers to the influence of English rock and roll on 1960s American culture, particularly the Beatles' astonishing rise to fame in this country. But the Fab Four owe some of their meteoric rise in the United States to their two successful feature films, *A Hard Day's Night* (1964) and *Help!* (1965). Moreover, the British invasion did not stop with the Beatles, but helped to bring provocative material to 1960s Americana, which had grown up on (the now stodgy) studio practices, continuity editing, and the Production Code. *Georgy Girl* was released in October 1966 and was the first film to be "suggested for mature audiences." *Alfie,* starring Michael Caine, used the word *abortion,* and was okayed by the censors in the United States.

Other foreign imports became notorious for their sexually provocative material and their defiance of the Production Code. Michelangelo Antonioni's *Blowup* (1966) was never approved by the board, but its American distributor exhibited the film anyway. *Blowup* went on to win the Cannes film festival award the following year. In a sense, the revision of the Production Code in 1966 was due to the changing attitudes of the American taste, influenced, in part, by competition from foreign film markets. Foreign films avoided the problem of the Hollywood Production Code for an American public that was becoming more informed about and interested in sexual matters, especially after the Kinsey Reports in the late 1940s and early 1950s. In 1966 the Code replaced some "prohibitions" with admonitions (e.g. the "Mature Audiences" warning).

Over the years, Hollywood had helped to stabilize and negotiate middle-class aesthetics and socioeconomic interests. But European cinema exposed Americans to other options. Those who were used to a Hollywood factory system now encountered a global, art-house industry, glamorous stars, and inventive, challenging auteurs. The interest in foreign films helped to carve another audience out of the American public, although there had long been "art houses" in the United States for exhibiting foreign films like *The Cabinet of Dr. Caligari* (1919) since the 1920s. They were small venues in comparison to the movie palaces of the 1920s and 1930s, but so were the audiences of the time.

Shortly after the war, however, there was an active promotion of certain foreign films, beginning with the Italian neorealist Vittoria De Sica's *The Bicycle Thief* (1947), which won an Academy Award. By the 1950s, Hollywood exhibitors were told to create a specialized, nondomestic market and to begin actively "popularizing" foreign films in the United States. With production, exhibition, and distribution galvanizing around the foreign film industry, it was time for the American public to indulge in a taste for foreign films.

That increasing appetite for foreign films within the American public, especially in urban areas, would not have been hard to predict. After all, Americans had seen the map of Europe torn open during World War II; they were traveling more than ever before and had become increasingly globalized in outlook since the 1940s. But Italian neorealism, the French New Wave, and a newly forming working-class British cinema focused American attention on personal issues, even existential ones. Additionally, in a curious way, foreign films, with their less glossy look, tapped into a certain domestic unrest in America. In 1966, for instance, there were race riots in seven major cities. By 1968, the "war" at home would be almost as incendiary as the one in southeast Asia.

In the early 1960s, Hollywood took few risks and the "social problem film" common in the late 1940s and in the 1950s was no longer a popular genre. It would have been hard to guess that there was such turmoil in the United States from a glance at the the top five rentals for 1965 according to *Variety:* three musicals *(Mary Poppins, The Sound of Music,* and *My Fair Lady),* another Bond fantasy *(Goldfinger),* and a zany comedy *(What's New, Pussycat?).* Further, the division between foreign, and domestic markets (always present to some degree) was now widening. The foreign film market craved portraits of bohemian life and, in a certain sense, represented a legacy of film noir culture and the social problem film. But Hollywood narratives like *The Dirty Dozen,* which were being produced in the mid-1960s, only galvanized a hawkish politics that articulated the conservative American position.

Who was the audience for foreign films in the United States? Film was slowly growing into a serious discipline in academic circles. Before too long there evolved a "canon" of the writings of early European auteur directors such as Sergei Eisenstein. Often it was college students who took the lead in establishing on-campus art houses that showcased the latest Fellini or Antonioni film. An increasingly educated, politicized American public, with a more or less liberal worldview, was searching for an art form that might speak to its sensibilities. Foreign films helped college-educated Americans— those who, perhaps, read Herbert Marcuse's *One-Dimensional Man* or Marshall McLuhan's *Understanding Media* (both published in 1964) in college—to tap into the radical undercurrent of the 1960s. Fellini, Godard, and other foreign directors became popular with an American audience who could discuss films like *La Dolce Vita* (1960) as a record of the decadent West; or, again, *Breathless* (1959) as an example of *l'amour fou*. The Swedish director Ingmar Bergman, who made deeply symbolic, often tragic and existential motion pictures, holds a special place in this discourse insofar as he is responsible for a major success in America for foreign films (especially with *Wild Strawberries* [1957]).

This new foreign film connoisseur was a consumer of cafe culture, a European chic that was a worldwide phenomenon during the late 1950s and 1960s—especially conspicuous in the haute couture of the Paris fashion industry. Foreign film consumers clearly had at least the potential for elitist tastes. A taste for neomodernist literary cinema was to be found in this cafe culture, with its fondness for the sophistications of Europe: heavily symbolic, philosophical, stylized. Like early modernist movements, this neomodernism of European cinema had an air of "defamiliarization" about it, for a Hollywood-educated audience. That radical style was a key selling tool to an American audience bored with the predictable Hollywood technique. As is well known, much of this neomodernist cinema eschewed middle-class values—a disdain that would become a banner for the radicalized late 1960s.

Until its eventual modification into a Hollywood style, art house cinema disdained the Hollywood bourgeois film associated with vulgar pop culture. This film genre was *art cinema*—not vulgar "entertainment"; it was meant for the modernist literati who, like art critic Clement Greenberg many years before, frowned on commercial art, tap dancing, Hollywood movies, and mass culture as ersatz culture or "kitsch." Serious European cinema, then, is high art, designed for a cultivated spectator or the kind of reader that Susan Sontag had in mind when she wrote her famous essays on Bresson and Godard.

It is easy to see that the stylistic experiments in the 1950s New Wave in France and early 1960s Italian cinema were destined for a 1960s America—conflict-ridden, divisive, and filled with ambiguities. Alain Resnais's *Last Year at Marienbad* (1961), for example, is a deliberately puzzling narrative, with its labyrinth of rooms set in an elaborate French villa, in and out of which a confused group of bourgeoisie wander aimlessly. With the background of Freudian modernism, *Last Year at Marienbad* functioned also as a psychodrama, an interior journey, a mental quest. Once again, the use of a non-plot-driven narrative would have been alien to Hollywood, but was made to order for the connoisseur of art films and the New Left of the 1960s.

Perhaps only the most obvious stylistic feature to note here is the use of the abrupt "jump cut" by film makers such as Jean-Luc Godard or the enigmatic discontinuity of Michelangelo Antonioni. Where the Hollywood studio system was built on seamless continuity—a system that orders and orients the spectator into a predictable space—these European auteurs broke up space and time and thereby frustrated audience expectations.

That more radical style, which tends to place the audience on the edge of ambiguity, would find a modified place in 1960s America and become mainstreamed. Teenage audiences loved *A Hard Day's Night,* director Richard Lester's innovative, surrealistic comedy, deploying cinema verité style, which showcased a range of possibilities drawn from television aesthetics and the experience of European cinema. Hollywood directors such as Don Siegel appropriated a more European style in a film like *The Hanged Man* (1964). By the time another generation of young directors would use cinema verité techniques, improvisational acting, and modified jump cuts in their movies in the late 1960s, the American audience would have been familiar with a spectrum of imported, European cinema.

The issue of arty European cinema and its place in American culture is an important one to tackle, since we must consider how "religious" aura is imbued on a cinematic art that is shot through with cultural capital and artistic value. In other words, if European cinema, like the films of Bergman, appears less mass oriented and more "poetic," does this give these movies a "religious" significance with which we would not ordinarily endow Hollywood film? Do we call *The Gospel According to Saint Matthew* a "masterpiece" simply because of its difference from Hollywood cinema, that is, its antibourgeois look and documentary, gritty feel? More importantly for us here: Is Jesus more "authentic" because he seems more "radical" or "simple," or, in a word, less "Hollywood"?

Let us now consider Pasolini's film about Jesus, then, in the context of this emerging interest in foreign film culture in America and explore its implications for us, especially in regard to visual language, Marxist ideology, and the representation of Jesus. Among the most poetically inclined and articulate of European directors, Pasolini wrote extensively on a wide number of issues. He was intensely interested in articulating another kind of language—one that had not been co-opted by bourgeois culture. In the October (1965) issue of the French journal *Cahiers du Cinema,* for instance, Pasolini suggests that the language of cinema was "the language of poetry." Here and elsewhere, Pasolini wants to claim a priority for film in the realm of radical images that evoke the world of the unconscious. His use of the unconscious places Pasolini as a prophet at the margins of traditional culture and conventional interpretations of the gospel as well.

Visual Poetry. Note well the opening sequence of *The Gospel According to Saint Matthew,* especially the extended close-ups of the Virgin Mary and Joseph. The shots repeat. Then the camera provides a medium long shot of the pregnant Mary. Throughout the opening sequence the shock is the silence of the scene: no dialogue, no environmental sound. The images alone speak. In the subsequent long shot of Mary, she is framed by a grotto. The image alone accomplishes more than any dialogue could do. "Mary in the grotto" calls up a whole host of associated images about Mary that would be informed by the tradition and by Catholic iconography.

The first portions of the film express a remote, dreamlike quality by virtue of its silence. Pasolini wants us to place considerable freight on the dream and on the unconscious. When Joseph sees that Mary is with child, he runs off to the outskirts of town and falls asleep near some children. He wakes to find an angel talking directly to him: "Joseph take unto you Mary as your wife for that which is conceived in her is of the Holy Ghost." The dream itself becomes the instrument of the plot and soon a tracking shot follows Joseph on a bumpy road back to Mary.

In *The Gospel According to Saint Matthew,* communication by signs is the film's first (and last) project, establishing a kind of vocabulary for our own journey into the narrative. Indeed, plot motivation is rooted in the interpretation of dreams. Joseph, then, becomes a kind of paradigm for our entry into the film: the world of images glimpsed by him is simultaneously seen by us from the start. His dream becomes the way he makes sense of the mysterious event and so gives the audience a way to interpret their own experience of the gospel. For Pasolini, "semiotics," or a system of signs in language, becomes a vehicle for communication. The angel also helps the wise men make sense of their journey from Bethlehem, and tells Joseph to take Mary and the child into Egypt and then leads them back out. It should be obvious that this technique could not be more distant from Hollywood's system of continuity, shot/countershot, and highly motivated plot narrative. Where Pasolini's project is intended to *disorient* us (together with Joseph) in the beginning and then leave us with a way to discover the importance of dreamlike images in the rest of the film, Hollywood's system orientates the spectator immediately and precisely toward *familiarization*.

The overall look of *The Gospel According to Saint Matthew* has a remote, dreamlike quality. The style of the film certainly suggests a subjective quality. There are very erratic editing patterns, some of which appear discontinuous, with no motivation in or relationship to either time or space. Like dreams, people simply show up and disappear. The camera directs its attention first to this and then to that, occasionally by free association, as if Pasolini were making a home movie.

This experience of seemingly random photography is heightened by the use of nonprofessional actors. The actors are frequently captured as unposed, in a state of vulnerability, as if they were caught unawares by the camera; they seem more than a bit uncomfortable with what they are doing. Like the wise men, who are agrarian people with rough features, the film simply has no gloss, but succeeds through a succession of raw, primal images. When Jesus goes into the desert, Pasolini intercuts sparse landscapes, extreme close-ups, and chaotic whip pans of a cathedral. It is a dreamy sequence, and Jesus himself must learn to deal with it. Satan in the desert bears a striking resemblance to Judas, once again suggesting the dreamlike aspect of repetition and replacement, and showing us the way in which images form a symbol system all their own.

With intense close-ups, jump cuts, and handheld cameras affecting the ongoing psychodrama of the narration, *The Gospel According to Saint Matthew* presents us with an emotional, interior reading of the gospel. Finally, and most importantly, it is the language of the visual, carefully inter-cut with the gospel text, that creates meaning. Pasolini has created a dialogi-cal film in which two primary sources of information are continually in counterpoint. In fact, the interplay between the established text and its inter-polated, free-associated superstructure is one of the film's most interesting and controversial features. We are left unsettled by virtue of a narration that is itself deliberately unsettling. The dreamlike subjectivism of the film per-mits a commentary outside history, which, for Pasolini, has itself been con-taminated by capitalism and bourgeois ideology. Ultimately, we might imagine Pasolini's film as a kind of fugue, deploying the most disseminated text in the West. The clash between the visual images and the literal gospel perspectives creates a dynamic text. From a political point of view, tradi-tional images are cut free from what Pasolini would call "bourgeois history" and are recreated anew by a dialectical, Marxist aesthetic that forces the audience to think and act within a field of tension.

That *The Gospel According to Saint Matthew* would deploy a dreamy and dialogic system as a primary conduit of information within its narrative structure reminds us of the associative quality of the film. The movie intends not simply to portray but to evoke, drawing the viewer into the role of cocreator of meaning. We are not engaged in a "realistic" reconstruction of Jesus' life and times; rather, the gospel is being used for other, parallel purposes—in this case, political. The apostles have a peripheral role, Mary Magdalene is elimi-nated, and on and on. The associative quality that permeates the film grants Pasolini the impressionistic edge he needs to make current political statements while using a stable, well-known precursor text. Thus transforming the gospel of the middle class, the familiar becomes the vehicle for the radical.

The effect of the formal aspects of *The Gospel According to Saint Matthew* drives home the political agenda of the film. The polarity that exists between the hierarchical establishment and the agrarian peasants could not be more obvious, not only by their stiff manner and opaque speech of the former, but by their dress as well. The representatives of religious institutions appear silly in their ridiculous headgear and flowing robes. Pasolini calls our attention to the pretentious hypocrisy he sees in organized religion (those crazy hats look suspiciously like miters), but there may be other contemporary associations as well. For example, Italy has long faced a struggle between the agrarian South and the more industrial North, the dynamics of which often play out in the textile and fashion industry: it is often said that the Milan clothing industry exploits the land and the labor of the rural South. We are not saying that *The Gospel According to Saint Matthew* is a strict allegory about the Milanese textile industry; just that the narrative hints at a wide range of political references, some of which may implicate the Italian economic system.

It would be hard to exaggerate the role of politics in *The Gospel According to Saint Matthew,* the function of which seems largely to bring the middle-class audience out of its comfortable complacency into the world of action. The relatively long sequence of the slaughter of the innocents, one of the few action scenes in the movie, with its poised look at the faces of the military and their sweeping action as they invade the little town, suggests a post-anti-Fascist perspective in the film, that might be compared to Ray's allegorical portrait of (Fascist) Romans and the Jews. Despite Pasolini's efforts at freeing the spectator for a new system of signs or a refunding of old signs, the film contains its share of images often associated with Communism. These include Russian revolutionary songs and contented agrarian "folk" together with John the Baptist and Jesus himself.

The character of Jesus plays a vital role in shaping the politics of *The Gospel According to Saint Matthew.* In fact, Pasolini derived the adaptation of the gospel on what might be seen as one of Jesus' own political statements. Pasolini was giving a lecture in Assisi hosted by a religious group at which time he was moved by one of Jesus' least consoling statements: "Do not suppose that I have come to bring peace on the earth. I have not come to bring peace but a sword. For I have come to bring division, a man against his father, a daughter against her mother" (Mt 10:34). When this line is used in the film, it occurs after a long tracking shot of Jesus (the handheld cameras once again add to the uneasy quality) intercut with reaction shots of the apostles. All at once, Jesus turns his face toward the camera and makes his claim that "a man's foes shall be his own household." Then he departs and leaves the apostles before we cut to another scene. Rarely has any image of Jesus been so angry in an artistic portrait of him. The overall depiction of him is tireless action, a revolutionary momentum stirring up the countryside. Typically, people react as if they are emerging from sleep. Yet, despite the less comforting aspects of Jesus in Pasolini's movie, the function of this portrait of the Savior as an angry witness to injustice and middle-class complacency is to unlock our own grip on comfortable bourgeois living. It is as if Pasolini's portrait of Jesus is God's angel sent to wake us up from the nightmare of twentieth-century living.

What is the effect of this more politicized Jesus? This depiction of Jesus would certainly appeal to the rising political left in 1960s America. But we must also note that despite Pasolini's attempt to deglamorize Jesus—right through his death—he has bestowed on the Savior another kind of aura, a political one certainly admired by art-house audiences in the United States. That political presence of Jesus operates like so much of Pasolini's vision for film: that a new kind of language might dislodge the old and bring into consciousness the new. It is not an accident that *The Gospel According to Saint Matthew* is dedicated to Pope John XXIII. As is well known, John himself not only sought a relaxation between Marxism and the church, but also wanted to "open the windows" on a church that had become a bit stuffy. The goal was to articulate values in a contemporary idiom. There was to be new language that would bring everyday people into a new understanding, not so much of the absolute, but of the world in which men and women work and love. Pasolini's Jesus is like Pope John: he shakes the dust from an old world order.

Jesus could become an icon of the counterculture in the 1960s and *The Gospel According to Saint Matthew* might have served as a blueprint for an American society growing more and more radicalized. For the time being, Pasolini's Jesus gave the cafe culture a God to discuss, ironically, even when the "death of God" movement itself was at the threshold. The Jesus of the gospel (if not the gospel of Jesus) had been transformed by an Italian Marxist and by American culture.

NOTES

1. Millicent Marcus, *Filmmaking by the Book* (Baltimore: John Hopkins University Press, 1993),112.

2. Read Marshall McLuhan, *Understanding Media: The Extensions of Man* (New York: New American Library, 1964).

3. McDermott, "Is It Possible to Portray Christ in Film?" 20.

FOURTH FEATURE

The Greatest Story Ever Told (1965)

"I say unto you, the prophecy is now fulfilled. The Spirit of the Lord is upon me, because he has anointed me to announce good news to the poor, to give recovery of sight to the blind, justice and delivery to the afflicted."

Produced and Directed by: George Stevens

Screenplay by: James Lee Barrett and George Stevens

Actors Include: Max von Sydow (Jesus), Pat Boone, Jose Ferrer, Charlton Heston, Angela Lansbury, Sal Mineo, Sidney Poitier, Telly Savalas, Joseph Schildkraut, John Wayne, and more, more, more

Running Time: 199 minutes

Introduction

The first question one might ask of this, or any movie of course, is, "Why was this film made?" Who was in on the discussions? What were the factors under consideration? The question comes at various levels: developing a concept, securing studio approval, casting, site location, editing, afterviewing, and so forth. There are always commercial considerations that influence decisions about which films can and will be produced: investors want to make money. In the case of *The Greatest Story Ever Told,* in addition to the omnipresent financial factors in commercial film production, one needs to speculate about what might have changed from the time of *King of Kings,* which had been produced only several years earlier, to warrant another film of Jesus' life. One can understand a remake after thirty-four years, from 1927 to 1961, in the case of the "Kings" movies. But in just a few years, from 1961 to 1965, had the times changed so much that a new film was called for to reflect new discoveries or beliefs about Jesus of Nazareth? Had the culture (audience) made a significant shift and needed, therefore, a Jesus who would reflect those changes? What did the director want to say through this movie that was left unsaid in *King of Kings* or that needed to be corrected somehow by means of a major new movie about the life of Jesus? Perhaps the technology of film production warranted a new treatment.

In the first place, the viewer should note carefully the title of the film, *The Greatest Story Ever Told,* because this is, indeed, a story that is a fictionalized account of the life of Jesus based on a 1949 novel by Fulton Ousler.[1] To be sure, the story is based on the gospel accounts, especially the Gospel of John, but moves beyond the confines of gospel material and gospel structure, though not as much as *King of Kings.*[2] Yet, the viewer may also discover that *Greatest Story* is less a story than *King of Kings,* because it contains less narrative structure, less plot, and less character interaction intended to move Jesus along the road of self-discovery and mission.

In *Greatest Story* this is all more clearly settled, set in place, before the movie begins. There is a clear sense that this drama is playing out a grand scheme put in place by internal or perhaps transcendent forces beyond those discernible by an historical, earthbound Jesus such as in *King of Kings,* where we see Jesus' struggles played out in 70mm Technicolor, and whose mother seemed to have more insight into her son's mission than did the son himself. Larger forces are at work in *Greatest Story,* if only in the director's sense of how Christ should be portrayed. What we see as viewers is an extended denouement with all the major factors decided and resolved before the movie even begins; hence the opening shot of the Christ figure on the ceiling of the cathedral. Of course, in a sense, this is true of all movies about Jesus' life; we know the ending before the story begins. Only here it is made a formal part of the design, the plot, the narration. With no disrespect, perhaps the title would more accurately have been *The Greatest Revelation Ever Unveiled.*

"Greatest" seems to have been the operative motive that guided much of what was done to produce this "story": greatest expense, greatest actors, greatest vistas, greatest reverence. Initially "greatest length" might also have applied, since in its initial release it ran 4:20, but, after a series of re-edits, was cut down to about 3:10, still no candidate for a *Reader's Digest* condensation.[3]

George Stevens, who directed and cowrote the screenplay, was a success-ful producer of the day, with *Shane* his most notable work. It would be of value to watch *Shane* and other Stevens films prior to seeing *Greatest Story* in order to discern any trends in theme, characterization, or visual style. Directors often come to be known for their films' "look," tone, or by the themes they treat. In the classes we have taught on these Jesus films, we, the authors, have used, for example, a series of television commercials by the same director to see if any patterns are discernible. The commercials are thankfully much shorter than full-length movies but still provide multiple examples of a person's work for the sake of comparison and for developing one's visual literacy.

Perhaps by now the reader/viewer is beginning to see a pattern in these movie portraits of Jesus, or at least some points for comparison and con-trast. We are not suggesting that each successive film is an immediate reac-tion to the one immediately preceding it, resulting in a sort of cinematic tennis match made up of a series of celluloid volleys. But there is a dis-cernible rhythm or trajectory. From the very traditional emphasis on Jesus' divinity in *The King of Kings,* we moved to a countervailing emphasis on his humanity and struggles toward social consciousness (in the Hollywood pro-duction of *King of Kings*) to a smaller-scale and more angry, rugged, and radical view of Jesus *(The Gospel According to Saint Matthew)* back to a major motion picture emphasizing Jesus' divine nature *(Greatest Story)* without quite returning to the piety of *The King of Kings*. Baugh observes that Jesus' "identity [in *Greatest Story*] as Son of God is clear to him and it is clear to us."[4] Thesis, antithesis, synthesis—the process of interpretation and reinterpretation goes on and on.

In *Greatest Story,* the pendulum makes numerous "adjustments" from its predecessors. A couple of these are worth noting here, even though they are treated more fully later. From the "social action" message of Jesus in *King of Kings,* in *Greatest Story* Jesus moves inward to demonstrate personal reflection and personal sacrifice, from reforming the world to reforming the self.[5] From the desire to secure Jesus in a historical context in *King of Kings,* this film is more concerned about locating Christ in the spectrum of faith. The opening scenes of these movies, which create contexts for all that follows, communicate these different perspectives ever so clearly.

The Sermon on the Mount scenes from the two films also capture the different essences of these films. In *King of Kings* the sunburned, wind-blown, bare-headed Jesus is moving about the hillside, in the midst of the crowds, looking this way, then that, responding to individuals' questions or challenges. It is a much different setting in *Greatest Story*. Baugh describes the scene in *Greatest Story* as an example of "static artificiality."[6] Everything is neatly arranged, the crowds listen quietly as if transfixed by Jesus' words. Instead of Jesus' interaction with the crowds dominating the scene, as in *King of Kings,* Jesus' diminutive place in the vast landscape is emphasized. Other such comparisons, film-to-film, are left for further examination until after viewing the films, or for the viewer to detect. Those questions, however, that drive these comparisons and that the viewer should take to the film are, "What is the effect of this scene; what are we left with at the end of the scene; and/or what message do these visuals convey?"

Another important element of the "look" of *The Greatest Story Ever Told* is the series of cameo appearances made by virtually every major actor in the Western world, at least of that time. There is a message in this to be sure, a powerful subtext. One could be cynical and say this was intended to draw audiences. On the other hand, one might also claim that a story so important to world history (the greatest story ever told) demanded the highest-power cast. The question is, how did this decision actually impact the viewing of the movie?

Clearly then, *The Greatest Story Ever Told* is a major production with a story to tell, put together with a clear view of Christ and his mission in mind. It makes claims about the work of Jesus the Christ but also reveals something of the times in which it was produced and of the people who created the film.

Movie Preview: Questions and Suggestions

1. *Describe the mid-1960s. What was going on in American society at the time? How did it differ from the late 1950s and early 1960s?*

2. *Who were the pivotal characters in* The King of Kings, King of Kings, *and* The Gospel According to Saint Matthew? *Who are they in this movie? Compare them to the pivotal characters in* The Greatest Story Ever Told. *How are they different in this movie from the earlier ones you have viewed? How does the director use the visual vocabulary to portray the qualities of these characters?*

3. *Watch for the image of the kingdom of God. Where is it? When does it come?*

4. *What portions of the gospels are most prevalent? What elements are least used or missing altogether?*

Movie Viewing

Movie Review: Questions and Responses

1. *What tone, mood, or underlying message is set in the opening scene, or what is the context created for this greatest of stories? What are you left with in the closing scene: a challenge? resolution? summary?*

2. *Who is the Jesus in this movie: his qualities, personality, strengths, image? How does he compare to the Jesus in* King of Kings *played by Jeffrey Hunter? to the Jesus played by H. B. Warner in* The King of Kings *or Enrique Irazoqui in* The Gospel According to St. Matthew?

3. *What was the role of women in this film compared to the previous two that were viewed?*

4. *How did you respond to the many cameo appearances of star actors? How did it influence your response to the movie?*

LENS ONE

Having left the European, socialist vision of Pasolini, we turn to the work of George Stevens. In so doing, we reconnect with a portrait of the life and teachings of Jesus that stands in the tradition of the great American epic. The development of this tradition is evident as one moves from DeMille (1927) to Ray (1961), and then to Stevens (1965). It is an evolutionary process that increases in breadth and depth, yet does not abandon certain fundamental assertions about the Christ of faith.

Recall again that Cecil B. DeMille created a Jesus whose image was shaped by popular piety and contemporary morality. His basic literary source was the New Testament, from which he produced a Christ who was decidedly more divine than human. Some thirty years later, Nicholas Ray found a more human Jesus within the same literary sources. This portrait of Jesus was of a teacher of social values whose sources were located both in the New Testament and in the writings of the historian Josephus.

With DeMille's portrait of a Jesus who was essentially divine in nature serving as the baseline measure for the films we are reviewing, Ray's Jesus, most clearly human in nature, stands as an antithesis. It seems only natural, then, that Stevens should now offer a synthesis of these previous perspectives. Indeed, he provides a firm argument for the humanity of Jesus, yet a humanity that bears the form of divine possibility. A close contemporary of Ray, Stevens is quick to accept much of Ray's counterculture Jesus. Yet Stevens carefully casts his own hero within much of DeMille's popular imagery. In the language of New Testament students, the Jesus that Stevens offers is semidivine in nature, a "god-man." It is an image that closely resembles the Jesus found in the Gospel of Mark, to the extent that Mark is permitted to tell the story apart from references to Matthew, Luke, and John. The early church believed that Mark should not be the sole gospel voice. So too, Stevens has supplemented his god-man figure with materials from across the entire collection of New Testament Gospels.

For the moment, it is sufficient to note that a blend of visions is evident in the film. It is a blend that should be seen against the backdrop of the ancient record of Israel's Old Testament prophets. This is a new twist that gives a personal stamp to Stevens's contribution to the epic vision. It is one of several trends or themes that deserves further consideration.

Back to the Prophets. In *Greatest Story,* for the first time in the evolution of the Jesus saga, the question of Old Testament background comes into play in a serious way. The traditional Christian approach toward the writings of ancient Israel has been to subordinate the revelation of pre-Christian authors to the interpretation of the early church witness, that is, the New Testament. Christianity offers a distinction between an "Old Testament" and a "New Testament" understanding of the words and actions of God. Christians read the Old Testament through the lens of the New Testament. Western culture has been dominated by this understanding for almost two millennia. This tendency is evident in the work of DeMille, Ray, and Pasolini, and it continues with Stevens. By the mid-1960s, a time when respect for minority cultures was coming to awareness on college campuses and within American consciousness, North American biblical scholars began to take seriously the Jewish setting in which the first-century Jesus lived and preached. Within this growing consciousness, *Greatest Story* stands as a testimony to its times.

Stevens is careful to spend extended effort to establish the biblical setting that influenced Jesus' early vision of his mission. From the beginning of the film we encounter numerous Old Testament references and allusions: from the discussion among Herod the Great's advisors about predictions of the coming Messiah to Joseph and Mary's return from Egypt (Mt 2); from the baptism of Jesus in the Jordan River to Satan's temptation of Jesus in the wilderness (Lk 3–4). Especially prevalent in such scenes is a reliance on the Psalms and the writings of the prophets (Isaiah, Hosea, Micah). The Psalms stand as a natural backdrop for Jewish worship—the traditional hymns sung by a people of faith. They are the words of praise that Jesus presumably heard on a weekly basis as a youth. The writings of the prophets, as Stevens hints, develop into even more for Jesus, however. It is in these texts that Jesus seems to hear the voice of God speaking, directing him toward a specific understanding of his special mission. Perhaps no clearer an example of this influence can be found than in the consideration of texts from Isaiah that Jesus ponders during his wanderings and wonderings in the wilderness during the temptation episode.

The observant viewer soon becomes aware that the mission and message of Jesus are only appropriately understood when seen as a response to the call of Israel's early prophets. In many ways, Jesus assumes the guise of a prophet. His central message, thoroughly prophetic in tone, utilizes the words of Hosea 6:6: "I desire mercy and not sacrifice." Stevens employs this theme on three separate occasions in reference to three distinct audiences: to those who witness the baptism of Jesus by John the Baptizer at the Jordan River; to those who hear the teachings of Jesus at the synagogue of Capernaum; and to those who experience Jesus' rebuke of the money changers at the Temple in Jerusalem. In each instance a specific action accompanies the expression of that theme: at the river, Jesus submits to baptism as a sign of his acceptance of God's will; at the synagogue, he heals a lame man as an expression of the power of God's authority over the evils of the world; and at the Temple, he "cleans house" in defiance of the policies that Israel's corrupt religious leaders have brought to the holy sanctuary. The acceptance of divine will, the employment of miraculous powers, the challenge to evil intentions—these are all characteristic features of ancient Israel's prophetic voices from the past.

There is one element of the ancient prophetic voice that Stevens's Jesus does not accept—a cry for the coming destruction of society by God's hand. Jesus chooses instead to focus on an element of hope. He insists upon the need for salvation of all who will turn and listen to God, and the possibility of restoration for an Israel that has lost its way. Jesus represents a beacon shining upon a glorious future for God's kingdom, not a sword pointing toward a deadly end for society.

History and Tradition. One of the most intriguing aspects of Stevens's vision is his creative (at least for the 1960s) combination of Christian concerns and social assumptions with respect to the Jesus saga. He accepts the testimony of the gospels as the framework for his story and tells that story with elements borrowed from each gospel witness. With the Gospel of Luke, he offers Satan as the motivator behind much of what happens to Jesus—from the temptation in the wilderness at the beginning of Jesus' earthly ministry to the instigation of mob cries for crucifixion, which eventually end that ministry. With the Gospel of John, Stevens envisions several trips by Jesus between Galilee and Judea (only one trip is alluded to in Matthew, Mark, and Luke), and portrays a hero who, though given over to the temporary will of Roman power, shines with the assurance that he is above the events of passion week because of divine guidance. With the Gospels of Matthew and Mark, the evidence of Jesus' teachings and his connections to first-century Jewish society are preserved and serve as a chain of episodes upon which the ongoing saga can hang.

Of course, like Ray, Stevens incorporates specific testimony from Josephus as well. This is true in two specific cases: the Jewish revolt against Roman symbols in Jerusalem, which occurs early in the film (*Antiquities of the Jews* 17.6.2–4), and the slaughter of the gathered Christians by Pilate's troops outside of the Fortress Antonia (north of the Temple), which comes toward the end (*Wars of the Jews* 2.9.4). Stevens does not include these elements for the sake of history alone, but as tools to explain and illustrate the Jesus story. The former incident leads to information about why the first-century Jews anticipated a messiah at all; the latter gives occasion for Jesus' early followers to "turn the other cheek" against overwhelming odds.

Stevens moves beyond his literary sources with a subtlety reminiscent of Ray, but perhaps with more life. For example, the dialogue of the film is scriptural in tone but more in the way of allusion than quotation. The listener *seems* to hear scriptural words and see biblical scenes, but with a certain cinematic license. Sometimes sources are combined. The apostle James identifies the tax collector Matthew as his blood brother, presumably because James is called "son of Alphaeus" in Mark 3:18 and Matthew (though here "Levi") is called "son of Alphaeus" in Mark 2:14. Jesus holds conversation with Lazarus in the role of "the rich young man," although Lazarus is a character specific to the Gospel of John, while the episode of Jesus' debate with the unnamed rich questioner comes from Matthew, Mark, and Luke. Finally, before the Last Supper episode, Jesus is "anointed" with oil both upon his head and his feet, a combined view of parallel episodes in the gospels, one form of which depicts the anointing of Jesus' head (Matthew, Mark) and the other, of Jesus' feet (Luke, John).

This is more than a combination of literary sources. Stevens feels free to employ traditional interpretations of the texts, which have more basis in historical speculation than in the Scriptures themselves: The woman caught in adultery is assumed to be Mary Magdalene, although this episode in Scripture (found only in John 8) makes no such association. Further, she is depicted in red clothing, an indication of her status as a prostitute, while the text in John lists her simply as an adulteress, which does not necessarily assume a life of prostitution. Nicodemus and Joseph of Arimathea are introduced as members of the Sanhedrin; this is certainly a possibility, but is nowhere specified in the gospels. Finally, the Magi who visit the baby Jesus at Bethlehem include an African member. This assumption is a popular tradition but, once again, is not supported by Scripture.

Elements of a Unique Message. There is an aspect of Stevens's Jesus that combines the visions of DeMille and Ray but moves beyond them as well. The details of this new offering are difficult to blend into a single, coherent picture. Yet the contours of those elements become evident when temporarily removed from their context for examination.

First is the consideration that Stevens gives to the "miraculous." Clearly, Stevens appeals to scriptural texts but avoids those events, stories, or references that might seem difficult for the modern mind-set to accept. Thus, when God's message is revealed to characters in the story line, it is related through the narrator, never directly through heavenly intermediaries. This is especially obvious whenever the text of Matthew is used early in the film.

Likewise, Jesus performs miracles, but only of healing. Even these he attributes to the faith of those who have been healed. He never performs what might be called "nature miracles" (walking on water, multiplication of the loaves, stilling the storm). Such stories are reported indirectly by rumor and speculation. There are two exceptions to this avoidance of miraculous events: the cure of the man born blind and the raising of Lazarus. Even in these cases, however, Jesus never provides comment. The viewer must decide what is at work here. Curiously, we hear nothing more from or about Lazarus. The blind man offers testimony at the trial of Jesus which, though it acknowledges that Jesus has enabled him to see, is certainly less than a satisfactory confession concerning the status of Jesus as the Son of God.

Along with this avoidance of the miraculous are the attempts to ignore predictions about the future. Biblical texts that speak of the coming of God's kingdom or the return of the Son of Man (see Mk 13; Mt 25) are not represented. Indeed, when Jesus speaks of the kingdom of God (a theme that stands at the center of the New Testament Gospels), this kingdom is specifically identified as coming to each person from within—not from some transcendent source. Although many biblical texts suggest that such a kingdom is indeed existential to the human experience, others suggest the contrary. Stevens clearly prefers the former interpretation.

Quite curious in Jesus' preaching is his explicit use of material from the apostle Paul! As Jesus offers a discourse on his own forthcoming death (after the cleansing of the Temple), he refers specifically to the importance of "faith, hope, and love." This trio of themes sounds natural enough on the lips of Jesus, and certainly is in harmony with what he has said elsewhere. The tradition by which these themes are linked, however, actually comes to us through the preaching of Paul (see 1 Cor 13). Paul never attributes these words to Jesus, and most scholars believe that the coupling of these traits is Paul's own work. In *The Greatest Story Ever Told,* George Stevens has provided us with a vision of Jesus that represents a unique and highly synthetic contribution to the development of the Jesus saga in film.

Finally, Stevens has made a most interesting adaptation of Acts 1:18, which may be a commentary on the death of Judas Iscariot. The author of Acts, whom most biblical students now believe to have been the author of the Gospel of Luke as well, observes that Judas eventually bought a field with the silver he received for his betrayal of Jesus. It was in this field that he fell and died. (Compare Mt 27:3–10, which states that Judas *hung* himself and the chief priests took *his* blood money to purchase a field as a place to bury foreigners.) In agreement with Acts, Stevens depicts Judas as falling to his death, but not in some remote field. Instead, he thrusts himself into the sacrificial fires of the Temple. The imagery is most intriguing since, on the one hand, this action may be taken as a self-sacrifice of distress made to God in the moment of a sinner's repentance. On the other hand, perhaps it is the ultimate reprisal for the betrayal of God's Son, the hurling of the deceiver into the fires of hell. In either case, the imagery of final destruction for Judas is an intriguing variation of the Acts narrative.

The Gospel of John at Work. More than any other film we have thus far encountered, the work of Stevens is a continuous blending of different gospel accounts. Stevens often uses the story of Jesus as told by Mark, only to turn to a combined narrative about the ministry of Jesus from Matthew and Luke. Interspersed throughout are references and episodes from John, as well as allusions to Acts and Paul. All of this is laid out on a canvas of Old Testament prophetic parallels. The bottom line, however, is that Stevens has not used his texts with equal consideration.

As with the early church, which seems to have shown the least preference for the Gospel of Mark among the various gospel accounts, Stevens gives less attention to Markan versions of scenes and sayings. As already noted, in a certain sense Stevens depicts Jesus as a god-man, without the glowing presence of divinity, yet with something more than the average mortal. This view of Jesus is characteristically Markan. But the early church wanted more than this, and so it added Matthew and Luke to its collection of gospel witnesses. A Markan Jesus is somewhat disturbing and stark, both for the ancient Christian and for the modern one (as we shall see in *The Last Temptation of Christ,* to be discussed below). Stevens perhaps wisely chooses to incorporate Matthew and Luke as well.

The Matthean/Lukan view of Jesus is typically a happy one for the modern American Christian. This view presents a more complete story about the origins of Jesus and the conclusion of his ministry through the resurrection narratives. It includes sayings and miracles (as well as parables, which Stevens, like DeMille, Ray, and Pasolini before him, chose to ignore). It shows Jesus at work in and around Galilee. It tempts Jesus in the wilderness, calls the disciples from their various life tasks, arrests and executes John the Baptizer under the compulsive influence of an old man's lust for his wife's dancing daughter, and confesses, through the same rock-solid disciple (Peter) who later denies that he ever knew the man, that Jesus is the expected Christ. What the modern American Christian looks for from the biblical narrative is found within the confines of Matthew and Luke: concern for the poor, directions for a pure form of ethical living, instructions for the church community, forgiveness for the hopeless, condemnation of the self-righteous, praise of God, and hope for the future. Stevens offers all of this, just as do Matthew and Luke. But despite this array of elements, something was lacking. Something bigger and grander was called for. It is then to the Gospel of John that Stevens turns for the heart of his visionary genius.

More than any director before him, Stevens is immersed in Johannine texts and thoughts. He opens his film with a reading from John 1:1–5: "In the beginning was the Word, and the Word was with God, and the Word was God...." Much of what the popular modern imagination considers to be vital to the story of Jesus comes directly from John's account; Stevens gladly taps into this repository of material. For example, we hear Jesus identified as the "good shepherd" (10:14) and the "bread of life" (6:51). We learn that John the Baptizer himself believes that he is only a forerunner of Jesus' own message (1:30) and that belief in Jesus leads to eternal life (3:15). We see the woman who was caught in adultery (8:1–10), hear rumors of water turned into wine (2:1–11), learn that Jesus is validated not only by the works of God, which he carries out (10:37–38), but by the people who benefit from them (9:13–25). We thus come to understand that Jesus lives as the light of God (12:35–36). Finally, we see much of the last week of Jesus' earthly ministry prior to his crucifixion in Jerusalem through the lens of John's account of his passion.

There is one overriding feature of the Johannine vision that dominates the story, a feature unique to John's narrative framework. Most scholars observe that the Gospel of John has two primary parts. Part one depicts the ministry of Jesus' teachings and deeds as signs of God's glory, made evident through the work of Jesus on earth. These events are included in chapters 1 through 11 of John's Gospel and conclude with the greatest miracle ever attributed to any prophet, the raising of a man from the dead (in this case, Lazarus). Prior to the intermission, Stevens concludes the first part of his own story with this same event. This high point stands forth, both in John and in *Greatest Story,* as a moment of significance. But in each case there is something else to come, of which the raising of Lazarus is only itself a pro-leptic glimpse or foretaste: that of Jesus' own resurrection.

In John, the second part of the story continues through chapters 12 through 20 (with chapter 21 as an additional account of resurrection episodes). Stevens likewise covers these same materials in the second part of his film. Any account of the Jesus saga demands some presentation of the passion narrative, which concludes with the crucifixion and some render-ing of the resurrection. And Stevens naturally offers this as well. But in par-ticular consideration of John, he brings the viewer to a foretaste of the glory of that event as it is prepatterned in the raising of Lazarus. This is uniquely Johannine.

In conclusion, there is a final way in which Stevens remains true to the telling of all Jesus stories: he concludes with a version of Matthew 28:20. There is, perhaps, an element of hope here that seems too good to omit. Once more, Stevens adds his own touch in the telling. While Matthew 28:20 instructs the disciples of Jesus to teach others about the Messiah who has come, Stevens draws upon two other texts to serve as the essence of that teaching. The first text is John 13:34 ("I give you a new commandment, that you love one another...."), a teaching to which Jesus has made reference on occasion throughout the film. In some sense, this is the essential message of Jesus, and Stevens has made use of the final episode to reiterate its impor-tance one last time.

The second text is Matthew 6:33–34 ("...strive first for the kingdom of God and...do not worry about tomorrow...."), which invites the viewer to look within for God's presence and to turn away from concerns about the future, which false preachers may emphasize. This viewpoint—looking within and focusing upon the day—has been raised throughout the film as central to the gospel message.

There is a definite twist to Jesus' preaching here that builds upon the visions of DeMille and Ray. It is a twist that sets the stage for films to come: What God intended to do in the life and death of Jesus of Nazareth is meant to be shared in Christian love and the living of life in God's kingdom today and every day.

LENS TWO

In Lens Two sections, we have typically started by discussing the film's opening scene in order to make some initial assessments about its image of Jesus and the context in which the narrative takes place. In the case of *Greatest Story,* the film's opening scene *is* of an image, an image or painting of Christ on a cathedral ceiling. This same image is also the last scene of this movie. Unlike the concern of *King of Kings* to place the narrative in a historical context, here the concern is to place the work of the film in the context of faith. We are searching for the Christ of faith, not the Jesus of history. That is the first conclusion we can draw about this film's image of Jesus, but there is much more yet to be observed or "read" from the visual vocabulary of *Greatest Story.*

Greatest Story digs deeply into cinematic methodology to create its image of Jesus: characterization, setting and scenery, camera angles, editing, and lighting. All of these combine to produce a monumental image of an ascetic Christ figure not unlike that of *The King of Kings* (1927).

The film opens with an apparent bow to the institutional church, reassuring the viewer that this movie takes place within the purview of the established ecclesial realm. The opening scene is a view of a *christus* figure painted on a cathedral ceiling, assuring the viewer that the church has survived and prospered since the life and death of Jesus. No scandal here, no antiestablishment reconstruction will take place. This film takes place within the contexts of respect for a traditional, orthodox, noncontroversial view of Jesus and of the church. In order to reinforce this notion one last time, the film also ends with this same scene—the same place where it began. We have, in a narrative sense, gone nowhere; no change has taken place from beginning to end. The film becomes a way of filling in the details that led to Jesus becoming revered enough to be painted on a cathedral ceiling. There is little suspense here; we begin and end with a static, known, and, dare we say, two-dimensional image of Christ.

As suggested earlier, characterization is always an important consideration: what the qualities and characteristics of the various figures will be and who the actors will be who portray them. The choice of actors is a significant element in this film. Indeed, the film might be subtitled *The Greatest Cast Money Could Buy.* The cameo appearances of nearly every major actor of the time comprise a production feature one cannot miss. In fact, as a cultural/historical artifact, this feature becomes somewhat distracting—the viewer is continually tempted to try to identify these now aging or deceased actors in their earlier prime. But to abandon the discussion with this admittedly catty observation would be to miss the subtext of possible *reasons* for the choice of these well-known actors.

Why employ these actors, with all the star-power they represent, for often rather minimal roles? Just to generate sales at the box office? Possibly. But the magnitude of an enterprise is communicated by the choices one makes about those who are chosen to participate. If you want your dinner party to have an air of importance, you invite important people to attend. This is an important story and an important movie; look at who is playing all the parts! Unfortunately, it is hard to separate the cast members' previous (and later) roles from the roles they play in this movie; they bring, perhaps unintentionally, a great deal of baggage to these assignments.

Interestingly, the one instance in which the choice of actors departs from surefire celebrity status is in the casting of the actor who plays Jesus. Perhaps Stevens recognized the dangers in identifying or transferring the qualities of a well-known actor to the person of Jesus. Unlike the protagonist in *King of Kings,* in this movie Jesus is played by an actor with relatively few (at the time of this movie) celebrity credentials, at least for American audiences—Max von Sydow. Von Sydow portrays Jesus in a fashion that is largely restrained and understated, especially in comparison to Jeffrey Hunter's freer and more youthful portrayal several years earlier in *King of Kings.* In some ways, von Sydow's portrayal harkens back to *The King of Kings*

(1927). His gaunt look, often melancholy demeanor, and ascetic detachment from people and place are common to both.

Jesus seems to be the most gnostic in this film, seeming to know beforehand the whole trajectory of his life, discerning the significance of crosses even as an infant. About halfway through the movie, Jesus is speaking with a group gathered around a well. Someone urges Jesus, "If you are the Messiah, say so plainly." In a rather obvious device, Jesus steps out from behind a roughly woven veil into the light and says, "I say unto you, the prophecy is now fulfilled. The Spirit of the Lord is upon me, because he has anointed me to announce good news to the poor, to give recovery of sight to the blind, justice and delivery to the afflicted. I have come to proclaim the year of the Lord's favor." This "wise man" image is further reinforced by Jesus' costuming; frequently he is wearing a hood or shawl over his head, giving him a severe, monastic look. Compare this to the bare-headed, wild-maned figure of Jesus in *King of Kings* played by Jeffrey Hunter.

The close observer of credits may also note that Joseph Schildkraut acted in both *The King of Kings* and *Greatest Story,* as Judas in 1927 and as Nicodemus in the current film. One would certainly not want to make too much of this particular observation, but it may be suggestive of Stevens's point of view in this project and of the sources to which he was looking for material and inspiration. Perhaps Schildkraut's presence in *Greatest Story* is a subtle *homage* to *The King of Kings.*

Another noteworthy character study is the devil, played by Donald Pleasence. It is interesting that the devil is seen on various occasions throughout this movie overtly and covertly manipulating the events that lead to Jesus' crucifixion. The devil, if he is portrayed at all in movies, is rarely portrayed in such a personal way as in this Jesus movie. Compare this to, for example, *King of Kings,* where we encounter only a voice, creating some doubt whether the devil is a real being or only an internal voice. Stevens's decision certainly implies something about his perception of evil and its role in the story of Jesus. The devil is unassuming, not nearly as seductive a character as in *The King of Kings,* but convincing nonetheless.

Setting can serve an important role in creating mood and a sense of psychological space. In this movie there is an ongoing contrast between the huge, red-rocked, butte-filled, wide open spaces of the American Southwest and the stagey, angular, sparse but often massive, grey interiors. When Roman soldiers come to take John the Baptist prisoner, the Romans are lined up high above him on the ridge overlooking the river. One cannot help but be reminded of Indians about to attack some poor innocent settler.

Note how small the characters often are in comparison to the surrounding scenery, whether indoors or out. This would be even truer when the film is seen in the theater, with its wide screen. Mary and Joseph are mere specks as they make their way across the desert. Both at the start and end of the temptations' sequence, Jesus is silhouetted against vast vistas. The people seem overwhelmed by their surroundings. The same is true indoors, where we find Herod Antipas seated on his throne in the midst of dark, towering walls and columns. He demands little respect in the setting and less in the narrative. He is small and weak. The setting communicates this to the viewer.

Occasionally, the settings and voice-overs overlap unnecessarily. For example, when the speaker is talking about sheep, we see a shepherd with sheep overlooking a canyon, and when children are spoken of, it is children that we see.

In *King of Kings* we made some observations about the color red as a symbol of power. In *Greatest Story,* which is largely monochromatic, that is, shot in shades of grey (indoors) or browns (outdoors), color plays little role—except for, again, red. Here, however, red is worn largely by evil people: notably Herod Antipas, Mary Magdalene in her role as adulteress prior to her conversion, and Matthew the tax collector before his repentance and conversion.

The cinematography, or use of the camera as a tool, in this film is a bit more refined and subtle than in *King of Kings.* This reinforces the more refined image of Jesus that is portrayed as well. The settings and backdrops seem more stylized, more restrained. Often the camera seems closer to the action. There are more close-ups and medium shots than in *King of Kings.* As Babington and Evans have noted, "...vast cinerama landscapes are often set off against intimate pastoral moments."[7]

Camera *angles* are important. Notice that the camera is often looking slightly up at Jesus, putting the viewer in an inferior position, making Jesus seem tall or more dominant. The movement within the frame is often from lower left to upper right. This is very classic composition for still and film photography, subtly underscoring the traditional feel of this film—no boundaries are broken, or even approached.

Although this could be considered as part of editing, the camera work contributes to the slow pacing of the film. There are frequent long pans across the vistas, and slow pull-outs, as the camera zooms back to assume a wider angle of view.

Editing also contributes to this slow pace. Transitions from scene to scene affect the pace. Notice, in the opening sequence, for example, the number of slow dissolves, that is, where one image gradually disappears as a new image gradually appears.[8] These "dissolves" create a slower pace than if they were simply "cuts" from one scene to another, that is, if one scene were instantaneously replaced by another. These different transitions imply different meanings, different senses of elapsed time, different moods and tones. When the disciples are gathered listening to Jesus under a bridge, the use of dissolves implies a long passing of time. Had the editor used cuts, the sense would have been of a much shorter duration of time from image to image. Compare this speech segment to Pasolini's segment of the Lord's Prayer, which uses cuts but with varying light conditions to confuse or make irrelevant the passage of time for the monologue. These are not random choices made by the flip of a coin. As one's visual literacy increases, these devices become more powerful, more evident, and more communicative.

Lighting is a powerful tool of communication in this film. Overall, the lighting is quite subdued, even dark, especially in comparison to *King of Kings,* and is much less harsh and dramatic than in *The Gospel According to Saint Matthew.* There are many, many scenes in which lighting is subdued and many others in which people are in shadows. Great attention is paid to who and/or what is in the light and in the dark or in the shadows. For example, when Jesus is in the synagogue, the room is dark except for Jesus, who is somehow fully lit. This is no coincidence, of course, no oversight by the lighting director. When Lazarus is brought back to life, the already sunny skies get even brighter. Often in the dark (literally and perhaps figuratively) are the Roman armies. During Jesus' encounter with the devil, the devil is backlit, creating a silhouette against the cave opening; Jesus is standing in the light. In addition, the Garden of Gethsemane also takes on a light/dark significance beyond the fact that the event takes place at night. Jesus asks, "Why now do you come and take me in the dark?" The implied question is obviously, "Why don't you arrest me in broad daylight?"

This film scores no marks for originality in sound effects or use of music. Only one instance is a bit curious: the way the Hallelujah Chorus is used at several points as a signpost that Jesus has apparently done something significant and indicative of his divinity. We hear it at the raising of Lazarus, which seems quite inappropriate, just prior to the intermission, and then later at the resurrection and ascension.[9]

All in all, while this is clearly a grand film, produced on a large scale, with major actors, large set pieces, and magnificent locales, it is strangely subdued, even quiet when compared to its predecessors. Characterization, lighting, editing, and the other elements of the visual vocabulary have all helped to create this tone. They say something about the image of Jesus that the director sought to portray, but they also reveal something about the director and the time in which the film was made.

LENS THREE

If Nicholas Ray's *King of Kings* was a Hollywood auteur's response to a 1950s postwar ideology, then George Stevens's *The Greatest Story Ever Told,* made for United Artists, is a product of 1960s diversity and postmodernism. Based on the 1949 best-seller by Fulton Ousler and originally sold to Twentieth Century-Fox for a mere one hundred thousand dollars, *The Greatest Story Ever Told's* Ultra-Panavision 70mm Technicolor cost over twenty million dollars, making it the most expensive life of Christ ever filmed. After long-time epic adapter Philip Dunne rejected the project, the picture was turned over to United Artists and George Stevens (who produced, directed and cowrote it with James Lee Barrett). That deal was only the beginning of a long, winding road.

Among other production features, *The Greatest Story Ever Told* boasted of more cameos and guest stars than any other epic: Dorothy McGuire as the Virgin Mary, Claude Rains as King Herod, Sidney Poitier as Simon of Cyrene, John Wayne as the centurion, and even the young pop idol Pat Boone as the angel at the tomb. Max von Sydow, a classically trained Swedish actor associated with the intense, searching cinema of Ingmar Bergman (who had caught Nicholas Ray's eyes for his own production of *King of Kings* a few years earlier), would play Jesus. Von Sydow's presence also guaranteed another bonus for United Artists: it played to the growing American interest in foreign films. Indeed, integrating von Sydow's foreign and mystical persona of Jesus is certainly one of the most interesting aspects of *The Greatest Story Ever Told,* and, for an American movie about the Savior, begins to suggest broader cultural tendencies in 1960s cinema. Such an exotic depiction of Jesus as a kind of Euro-wise guru reminds us, once again, of the global expansion and diversification of the 1960s and, further, Hollywood's attempt to secure a highbrow audience for its epic production.

In addition to the all-star international cast and the promise of fabulous, super wide-screen projection, the choice of the director also bestowed some prestige to the picture. The person of George Stevens brought a well-known, dependable director to a movie about Jesus that was supposed to be the biggest super-spectacle of them all. Stevens's career stretched as far back as the 1920s, first as a cameraman for Hal Roach and the Laurel and Hardy comedy shorts, and then, more recently, as the director of outdoor pictures such as *Shane* (1953) and *Giant* (1956). He also had a reputation in the industry for perfectionism and would often labor with shot after shot from multiple angles and conceived from every possible direction. Above all else, Stevens insisted on authenticity: from the biblical "look" of Utah and Arizona, where the film was shot, to the evocative Leonardo da Vinci *vivant tableau* of the Last Supper.

With an already expensive budget, the preproduction for *The Greatest Story Ever Told* became almost preposterously excessive, with Stevens himself personally retracing Christ's steps in the Holy Land. The scrupulous director even conferred privately with Pope John XXIII and David Ben-Gurion. But the studio's promotional promises to filmgoers went even further. As an unusually philosophical United Artists promotional description explained, the goal of *Greatest Story* is "to challenge one's own image of Christ—an image derived from a word, a panel of stained glass, a Gothic-lettered Christmas card, a burst of organ music...."[10] Some sixty years after photographing the Oberammergau Passion Plays, the Savior on the silver screen would appear to have reached its peak with this latest entry by United Artists.

Despite all its elaborate production values, however, *The Greatest Story Ever Told* did not do very well. Certainly, the exorbitant length was unwieldy for the average filmgoer. After almost five years of production and postproduction, *Greatest Story* was released at four hours and twenty minutes and then, after a poor box-office showing, cut to just over three hours. In addition to the viewer endurance factor, much of the commercial motivation for the biblical epic was centered on showcasing technical features, establishing an important alliance between the formal nature of the biblical genre and the technological growth of the film industry. It was no accident, for instance, that Twentieth Century-Fox's Cinemascope process was first launched with the production of *The Robe* (1953), a film that deals with the people and events immediately after Christ's death. But by the mid-'60s, the demand for large-scale epics about Jesus was passé, even as the demand for wide-screen productions was also dwindling. Indeed, the late '60s and early '70s saw the rise in more naturalistic, even improvisational film making, in part influenced from the off-beat cinema of the French New Wave. In fact, in 1961, Rank studios in Britain produced a somewhat low-key, allegorical film, *Whistle Down the Wind,* starring Alan Bates as an escaped prisoner who is discovered by children in a stable and taken to be the Savior himself.

Casting Decisions. The biggest commercial problem with *The Greatest Story Ever Told,* however, centered on Stevens's intent on assembling an all-star cast, to what most agree were disastrous results. Indeed, the film looks like a great big apocalyptic get-together for everyone's favorite movie stars from the Classical Studio era. Any number of critics and filmgoers complained about the distracting use of big-name stars to portray well-known biblical characters. A few years later, Felix Barber wrote a retrospective in the *Evening News* (8 April 1968), about seeing, among other things, Shelley Winters in a brief showdown with leprosy, and that "no one blames Hollywood stars for wanting to arrange a little personal atonement. But couldn't George Stevens the director see that this sort of casting was death to sincerity and realism?"[11]

The matching of characters from book to film has never been an easy problem and is always fraught with risks. One thinks, for example, of the deluge of correspondence that producer David O. Selznick received when he was casting Rhett Butler for his adaptation of Margaret Mitchell's best-seller, *Gone with the Wind.* Matching Rhett with the immensely popular Clark Gable certainly worked for a variety of reasons (just as the relatively unknown Vivien Leigh succeeded in her portrayal of Scarlet O'Hara). Such "matching" of characters from a novel into a film can be either successful or unsuccessful by accident of personality. Such a phenomenon occurred with George Cukor's casting of W. C. Fields to play the part of Micawber in *David*

Copperfield, or John Huston's use of Bogart as Sam Spade, along with the other Warner Brothers character actors chosen for his adaptation of Dashiell Hammett's *The Maltese Falcon,* which Andrew Sarris and James Naremore rightly call a casting coup.[12]

The perceptive reviews for *Greatest Story* remind us of the danger of a film engaged in adapting a biblical text into a culture-text, particularly if the production deploys a kind of "hyperstardom." Such deployment of "star power" in *The Greatest Story Ever Told* is an instance in which traditional Hollywood production values strained the verisimilitude of the biblical text. Since stars possess their own unique cultural codes and modes of expression, the method of adapting a familiar (biblical) story into a movie also becomes a "star text." Thus, critics were reacting to the fact that more so than in any other biblical epic before or since, the audience for *Greatest Story* was left in the unfortunate position of matching their favorite characters in the Bible with familiar stars, some of whom only appeared in cameos. It was as if the stars only showed up in order to be identified and then retreated to their Beverly Hills mansions. After all, what are we to do when John Wayne, in a vocal style that can only mean "John Wayne," makes his notorious remark as the centurion, as if he had just walked off the set of a John Ford western: "Truly, this man was the Son of God."

The Cultural Divide. In addition to the traditional problems of adaptation, there were other, more profound factors indicating that the traditional Hollywood methods of "text into film" were untenable in the mid-'60s and would begin to influence the fate of the Jesus epic for years to come. American culture had changed drastically since the early Jesus movies. The "authenticity" of the production of *The Greatest Story Ever Told*—thought of as a real selling feature for United Artists—was something of a problem for a more sophisticated American audience. Although George Stevens followed the classical Hollywood tradition of deploying the evocative memories of famous representations, or a *vivant tableau,* in order to evoke familiar images of Jesus and his world (recall the film's opening scene), the diversified, media-educated audience was not impressed. The picture looked artificial, even pretentious to some critics. *Variety* said that the priests of the Temple were "fussy," and Fred Myers in the *Christian Century* remarked that there were "thousands of Jews massed in public squares reciting Psalms from the Revised Standard Version of the Bible and sounding like Presbyterians in an elocution class."[13]

It is easy to sense that the filmmakers struggled for a way to represent Jesus and his world in 1960s America. From a philosophical point of view, traditional ways of religious experience and even modes of knowing were eroding in the 1960s. In fact, Americans were reinventing all sorts of different approaches to the ways they thought, believed, and acted. Historians often point to the early '60s as the time in which Americans, after long years of post–World War II fragmentation, lost their unity as a nation and became a culture of loosely politicized movements and social networks. In some ways, this zeitgeist is an oversimplification about the period, which became the site of a culmination of many historical conflicts involving race, gender, generation, power, and religion, all of which had complicated origins in American culture. Popular anecdotal representations of the 1960s today remind us that those were days in which few people agreed on anything—the contentious war in Southeast Asia perhaps being the most obvious example. For our purposes, these social features call into question the business of cultural representation or, more simply put, how a historically bound society agrees to cast and "re-present" its images of people, places, and things.

For decades the culture industry had been representing Jesus in more or less traditional ways because that depiction of Jesus could be drawn from a certain class or a homogeneous network of people. In fact, DeMille's epic of Jesus helped to galvanize a collection of working-class, European immigrants into a well-defined ideological space. As we have seen, that coherence of spectatorship helped to create a solid reputation for DeMille, and for Paramount as well. But all these factors and more changed in the 1960s for countless reasons, mostly due to a condition we now call "postmodernism." Postmodernism cannot be defined simply, but what we can say for certain about this fascinating cultural formation—which almost certainly has its origins as early as the end of World War II—is that postmodernism is the result of a loss of what French philosopher Jean-Francois Lyotard and others have called a social "grand narrative." This "meganarrative" is the way in which the dominant culture agrees to tell its own story and find its meaning.

It is easy to see, for example, that World-War-II America had a single "metanarrative": win the war! Hollywood was able to establish a strong bond with the Office of War Information beginning as early as 1938, helping this agency to develop certain propaganda strategies in order to unite the country in victory. But technology and the global economy and expansion since World War II have altered the ways in which cultural narratives are disseminated, and, further, the way that knowledge is ascertained by their telling. That legacy is still with us well into the twenty-first century. With the emergence of the Internet in the 1990s—with its seemingly endless menus, chat rooms, and so on—we have only one of the many indicators that American culture is deeply fragmented into countless personal narratives.

The telling (if not defining) moment of this era occurred during the production of *The Greatest Story Ever Told.* When President Kennedy was assassinated on 22 November 1963, television accomplished what Hollywood could never have done: provide us with live coverage of a national tragedy. Moreover, television, which had always boasted of its "live camera" action, was already developing the technology that would allow the audience of the 1960s to see on network news the Vietnam War as it was being fought. Television is the instrument par excellence for the postmodern audiences. Its appeal to a disparate public, its very informality (which suggests a spectatorship based not on a captive-audience situation but, rather, on a casual glance), and, finally, its personal, domestic setting, remind us of the slow disappearance of the homogeneous, immigrant audience into multiple spaces.

Robert Venturi would express his view of postmodernism in the 1960s in his book, *Learning from Las Vegas* (1977).[14] There he claimed that the famous Nevada city was an invention of postmodernism—in a word, a *bricolage* of meanings, a copy or even a parody of styles that lacked a unifying center or theme. There was no all-encompassing, grand narrative for Las Vegas, just disparate styles—classical here, romanesque there—and none of these original, but a pastiche of other artistic conventions.

Clearly, the mission of the Savior on the silver screen during the first half of the twentieth century was something like the implied function of a modern city: to help organize the whole population or create a grand scheme or narrative that would integrate a population under a single hegemony. Given what we know about the 1960s, we might want to ask: Was there a place for an Ultra-Panavision Technicolor Jesus in this more diversified, highly politicized, eclectic world? Probably not; or at least, only minimally. It should not surprise us, then, that when *Greatest Story* premiered, critics and audiences sensed not only that this was not "the greatest story ever told," but that the biblical epic genre itself was exhausted. The traditional form of the Jesus movie had, it seemed, finally played itself out. The fact of the matter is that, as far as some critics were concerned, *The Greatest Story Ever Told* had become *The Hardest Story Ever Filmed.* As far as industry related causes are concerned, the studios that, ironically, had created the Production Code to shape a middle-class sensibility could no longer count on what the public expected from a film about Jesus.

The mid-'60s audience was educated by Hollywood feature films as well as television, which was also repeating these movies on the networks. Americans were becoming media savvy and, in a way, like Las Vegas itself: coexisting with various forms of representation simultaneously. Hence, as Barber and others have pointed out, the all-star cast becomes comedic, even parodic, to such a spectator. The audiences for the film might have said to one another, "There is Claude Rains as Herod! Didn't I just see him on TV last night in *Casablanca?* Look how old he is!" In a certain sense, the difficulty with "matching" biblical characters to actors in *Greatest Story* is not only a resulting collapse of realism but an expression of a failure through excess. The truth is that the stars in the film, like so much within the milieu of postmodernism, appear to be "recycled." Indeed, even United Artists would itself become obsolete and, in a sense, recycled, as the financially troubled studio became assimilated into larger conglomerates during the 1960s.

When seen in the light of a multifractured society with growing inclinations toward countless diversified personal stories—rather than a grand narrative—*The Greatest Story Ever Told* represents a botched attempt at unity. It is the last gasp of the modern epic Jesus film in the postmodern age. The real problem with *Greatest Story* is that it is an artifact that tries to achieve at least two things: On the one hand, with its depiction of first-century Palestine as a smattering of groups without a unified center, the studio attempted to appeal to a postmodern, diversified audience. On the other hand, the film seems also to revert to a distinctly Western mythology, deploying Jesus as a frontier hero who offers the fundamental American value of limitless freedom.

Besides the more obvious example of attracting the art-house audience by deploying Ingmar Bergman's star actor, Max von Sydow, or using familiar stars for the older generation of moviegoers, the first indication that United Artists was aware of a changing 1960s spectator was its announcement that "the film, and the portrait achieved by the represented Christ, do not so much attempt to answer Pilate's question, 'What is truth?' as to intensify each individual's desire to discover that answer for himself within his own experience, past and future. A play, a film, a single performance—any work of art—undertakes to provide answers from within the beholder." There is more than a hint here that United Artists was attempting to appeal to a broad range of experiences. Further, the claim to more or less encounter Jesus "from within the beholder" suggests a kind of pop philosophy one occasionally associates with the 1960s and beyond, with the rise of more relativistic forms of Western epistemology during this period.

Indeed, many of the foreground issues in *Greatest Story* appear, like the 1960s era itself, eclectic, diversified, and open-ended. In this context, George Stevens's film makes an interesting contrast to that of Nicholas Ray, released only four years earlier. We might recall that in *King of Kings* there was no doubt as to the signification of the Romans/Nazis as the oppressors of the Jews. In certain ways, Ray was a modernist and his film crucially depends on historical memory and its ability to tell and remember a cohesive metanarrative. Ray's film functions inwardly and precisely as a metanarrative in order to create and establish quasi-allegorical references to educate the post-Holocaust world.

On the other hand, Stevens's film often seems drained of the past. For instance, the Romans are simply represented as a loose collection of politicos. Notice how many debates occur within the course of the film. Both Herod Antipas (Jose Ferrer) and Pontius Pilate (Telly Savalas) are bewildered and perplexed city politicians. They make wrong decisions, not because they are evil but (the film suggests) because of a corrupt environment. To see von Sydow's Jesus engaged with his disciples is to see a kind of counterculture guru enlightening the uninitiated in the great outdoors. Jesus reminds us less of a rabbinical teacher and more of a world-weary professor taking his wide-eyed students for an outing—not to pray to the Father, but to encounter Mother Earth.

The Greatest Story Ever Told has something to say about the 1960s conception of the Savior because it is also a film about the '60s counterculture, which sought solutions to the existential questions raised years earlier in utopian communities and by those espousing avant-garde sensibilities, such as Jack Kerouac and the Beat poets. That counterculture tapped into a long-standing American tradition that represented the city as corrupt and the wilderness as salvific. Ten years before the release of *Greatest Story,* Allen Ginsberg wrote in "Howl" of the "Nightmare of Moloch...whose buildings are judgment! Moloch the vast stone of war!/ Moloch the stunned governments!/ Moloch whose mind is pure machinery? Moloch whose blood is running money!...whose eyes are a thousand blind windows! Moloch whose skyscrapers stand in the long streets like endless Jehovahs!"[15]

Mythic Structures. Perhaps the single most dominant feature in *Greatest Story* is the way it attempts to organize what it imagines as a unified spectator into a mythic structure. It portrays Jesus as a kind of Western iconoclastic outlaw hero, an individualist who becomes associated with profoundly ingrained American values. Thus, *The Greatest Story Ever Told* is a kind of '60s spiritual Western whose hero champions not so much Christian ideology, but the frontier. We have an only slightly different vision of dichotomies present in the Western genre.

The Desert	**Jerusalem**
freedom	confinement
small-group learning	institutional bureaucracy
internal, mystical knowledge	external formulas
self-possession	confusion
apolitical	political
purity	contamination
moneyless	money

Generally speaking, the pattern here for the Western genre depends on the bifurcating tendencies of the frontier versus civilization. The signifiers for the city in the film are, for example, Herod's palace—cold stone ruins. Such scenes as Herod's encounter with John the Baptist are dark and filled with shadows. The wilderness, however, is free from such trappings. Virtually the first two hours, or more than the first half of *Greatest Story,* is a juxtaposition between the confined, dark night of the city of Jerusalem and the free, open sky of the Galilee country. Where Jesus becomes emblematic of the countryside, Pilate appears early on in the film and becomes associated with the corrupt political world of the city. The activities, behavior, and environment of the two men are compared and contrasted until, at last, they come together (even as the plot does) in Pilate's praetorium. There, Jesus is done to death by the city and its corrosive infrastructures, the false trappings of civilization.

The Savior, like the so-called Western unofficial hero, is allied with the frontier and, indeed, depends on an encrypted representation that is independent of the trappings of domestication and civilization itself. Unlike the official hero who takes his place with society, the unofficial hero is a *natural* man. Typically, as in the opening shots of *Shane,* the unofficial hero is often showcased as a kind of outlaw who appears from an unknown place and even out of nowhere. He can be dangerous and has hidden powers. His past and origins are repressed. Jesus' own origins, of course, are somewhat veiled and threaten to be revealed throughout the course of the biblical narrative. He is mysterious; he is an outlaw. With his head covered, von Sydow looks enigmatic and stereotypically mystical, rather like a precursor to Ben (Obi-Wan) Kenobi in *Star Wars,* especially during Jesus' curing of the crippled Uriah (Sal Mineo) in the synagogue.

Again, the film's cinematography serves to heighten the Western form. There are long sequences in *The Greatest Story Ever Told* where we glimpse the seemingly unfathomable desert. This is especially true during Jesus' temptation in the wilderness. Stevens spends a great deal of time on Jesus' personal encounter with nature. The Savior's ultimate victory over the Dark Hermit (Donald Pleasence) in the desert suggests several things. First, Jesus struggles less with the temptations themselves than with a kind of dark side and, indeed, the desert itself. The trial for this "natural" man is that he must climb a large mountain and make friends with raw nature. His temptations occur, rather incidentally, on a bluff and in a cave. Perhaps more than any other Jesus epic, the temptations sequence in *Greatest Story* reminds us of the vast solitude in the wilderness and, ultimately, of the importance of the Emersonian ideal of self-reliance, so important not only to American literature and ideology but to the Western movie genre as well. Jesus tames the frontier not because he overpowers it but because he is its intimate. In a way, he is the son of nature before he is the Son of God.

The Savior in *The Greatest Story Ever Told* is a natural, intuitive superman in the tradition of Robin Hood and, like Thoreau, he would go to jail rather than pay taxes. Here, Jesus is crucified rather than become domesticated, civilized, or, like Pilate, politicized. Jesus is a hero, not of the status quo, but of the American heartland, who comes to reveal the inadequacies Americans have mistrusted all along: politics, legalism, corporations. Max von Sydow's Jesus, then, shows a remarkable departure from that of his predecessors, notably Hunter and Warner. Hunter was a Jesus of the people, even a moody idealist who, as we have suggested, becomes precisely associated with a particular ideology of liberation. Then again, Warner's Jesus is a man of status-quo intentions and inclinations, part of hearth and home. Warner's Jesus purges a corrupt society from its loose ways. One of his first miracles is to domesticate his most passionate follower, Mary Magdalene. On the other hand, von Sydow's Jesus relates to women in the city in order to teach them the ways of nature. This is particularly true of his relationship with Mary Magdalene, whom he educates in order to return her to the more innocent ways of nature. Mary and Martha are also part of the city, but, because they are friends of Jesus, live in the outskirts of Jerusalem, albeit in a fashionable villa. Here, once again, Jesus the celibate coexists nicely with the man of the frontier West: he is a man of the wilderness, which, like him, is untamable and unknowable.

To follow this paradigm is to suggest that Jesus was killed, not so much for being the Son of God, but for being Mother Nature's Son. Ultimately, Jesus is a Son of the West and shows us the importance that the 1960s placed, not only on flight from the city, but on grass-roots ideology: it is spirituality without dogma. Having been crucified, Jesus rises and, as the film reveals, returns to his painting. Like the Man of the West he is, Jesus returns to his mysterious origins, unconfined and uncontaminated by civilization, yet, ironically, telling his disciples to "teach all nations." Ray left us with a bewildered group of disciples and a call to action. Stevens's Jesus returns to his origins. Finally, one wonders, does this Savior on the 1960s silver screen have anything prophetic to say to so many diversified nations?

NOTES

1. Lloyd Baugh, *Imaging the Divine*, 24.
2. Ibid., 5.
3. Kinnard and Davis, *Divine Images*, 161.
4. Lloyd Baugh, *Imaging the Divine*, 25.
5. Babington and Evans, *Biblical Epics*, 139.
6. Lloyd Baugh, *Imaging the Divine*, 29.
7. Babington and Evans, *Biblical Epics*, 141.
8. Ibid.
9. Lloyd Baugh, *Imaging the Divine*, 31.
10. United Artists promotional for *The Greatest Story Ever Told, George Stevens Collection, The Greatest Story Ever Told.*
11. Felix Barber, "Too Many Faces," *Evening News*, 8 April 1968. Quoted in Babington and Evans, *Biblical Epics*,148.
12. Andrew Sarris, *The American Cinema: Directors and Directions, 1929–1968* (New York: E. P. Dutton, 1968), 156. James Naremore, "John Huston and *The Maltese Falcon,*" in *The Maltese Falcon*, ed., William Luhr (New Brunswick, NJ: Rutgers University Press, 1995),149–60.
13. Fred Meyers, *The Christian Century* (21 April 1965), 492.
14. Robert Venturi, Denise Scott Brown, and Steven Izenour, *Learning from Las Vegas,* rev. ed. (Cambridge, MA: MIT Press,1977).
15. Allen Ginsberg, "Howl," in *Selected Poems 1947–1995* (New York: HarperCollins, 1996), 54–55.

FIFTH FEATURE

Jesus Christ Superstar (1973)

"Jesus Christ Superstar, do you think you're what they say you are?"

Directed by: Norman Jewison

Produced by: Norman Jewison and Robert Stigwood

Screenplay by: Norman Jewison and Melvyn Bragg

Lyrics by: Tim Rice

Music by: Andrew Lloyd Webber

Actors Include: Ted Neeley (Jesus), Carl Anderson (Judas), Yvonne Elliman (Mary Magdalene)

Running Time: 107 minutes

Introduction

The thought of watching another long, luscious, powerful, reverent, deeply moving, big-screen, commercial rendition of the life of Jesus may seem overwhelming at this point. Not to worry; an alternative has arrived in the form of *Jesus Christ Superstar,* a significant change of pace from those movies viewed so far in the series. There is a well-known line from one of the songs in the movie, the quote that stands at the top of the chapter: "Jesus Christ Superstar, do you think you're what they say you are?" This is a pertinent question. Indeed, what does this *film* think it is? Where does the film fit in the scheme of things? And then, within the context of the film, who does Jesus think he is? Whether any of these questions is resolved becomes an important factor in the discussion of yet one more Jesus movie.

First of all, recall that *Superstar* was originally only a collection of musical numbers created by Tim Rice and Andrew Lloyd Webber. Then it became a full-blown musical stage performance. Only later did it become a film. More than twenty-five years later the play is still being performed, with some of the same actors who performed in the film, namely Ted Neeley as Jesus and Carl Anderson as Judas. Keep in mind, too, that this is a play-within-a-play. It is the story of a troupe of actors putting on a passion play somewhere in the desert. One needs to determine perhaps whether the "real" story here is about Jesus or about an actor who plays Jesus. This will then influence how one watches this film and subsequently how one evaluates it.

Translating a performance piece from one venue or medium to another is fraught with challenges and sometimes insurmountable difficulties. What was designed as a stage performance may not move comfortably outside the confines of the proscenium arch, nor outside the theater, nor outside into a vast, hot desert with ruins and scaffolding as the primary scenery. Baugh points out that in stage design, "realism is not the crucial element. The setting must above all support the spirit of the music and song and the tone of a given scene or major number."[1] Since, as the communication truism goes, context determines content, if the context is changed, the content changes as well. In addition, to reprise a Marshall McLuhan theme contemporary with the film, the medium is the message (or massage). The message/massage of the stage is different than that of the movie screen. They provide different experiences and ask different things of their respective viewers, and particularly allow for different degrees of participation. In the process of translation (or better, transduction, converting one form or medium of energy into another), something is inevitably lost, but also something is always gained in the process. Some of the message is lost or distorted, and some new data are inadvertently added. It is simply a part of the process, a factor to be reckoned with. It is unavoidable.

If the problem of moving from stage to desert is not serious enough, one need only remember that this is a musical with no spoken words. While the actor typically serves the music in stage musicals, the needs of cinema generally call for more depth of character, a fuller and more subtly rendered persona for the actor to live into or out of. The actors need not project their voices, gestures, and images to be seen/heard by those in the back row. This need for a more refined, nuanced style of acting is made necessary, in part, by the requirement of extended and more intimate camera work.[2]

The view of the actor necessarily changes from wide angle to close-up, if only for variety's sake. We see characters from different vantage points, different points of view, even through different eyes. The nature of cinema is to supply more of the information for the viewer. Any inadequacies or gaps become more evident in film. This is quite unlike the stage, where we see everything from that one seat, that one vantage point, often around or between the heads of those sitting in front of us. In stage performances, the viewer supplies more of the information, automatically filling in where more details are called for, either because of the nature of the set, because of gaps in characterization and plotline, or because one simply cannot see what is going on. Somehow we can tolerate or compensate for having only one fixed point of view in stage performances, but we would find it intolerable in cinema if we had one wide-angle shot for an entire two-hour movie. It is hard enough coping with the popcorn munching and whispering going on three rows behind us. Such fixed visuals would be deadly.

In addition to the production challenges that go with converting any musical stage performance to film, there are many additional ways in which *Superstar* departs from its predecessors. There is little pretense here about producing a "realistic" image or portrayal of Jesus. In fact, the film seems intent on bursting the bubble of the pretensions of its predecessors. In previous features, we have seen several distinct images of Jesus portrayed, but they were all serious efforts to create an image that did not seek to undo Jesus himself, but rather to overcome previous inadequate or incomplete *images* of Jesus. In the process, this film seems to tinker with the traditional image(s) of Jesus and thus seems to be irreverent. In so doing, hopefully the viewer realizes that the image of Jesus in this film, as well as all of the other films, is a construct, a collection of pieces. When the construct of Jesus' image is largely similar to our own construct of Jesus, its nature as a construct is less obvious. In *Superstar,* our image may clash dramatically with that of the movie and thus highlight both our own values and those of the movie.

One need not probe too deeply to recall that the mood of the time was one of challenge: challenge any and every truth and authority in sight. Every icon was defaced, every tradition deconstructed, every truth questioned, every hope quashed, every traditional value violated. The reverent, traditional views of Jesus suffered as well.

Jesus Christ Superstar was not unique in its attempt to create a musical life of Jesus. *Godspell,* also a play before it became a film, circulated for a time. It seems not to have had nearly the influence or endurance, although it is a more complete rendition of a gospel. Set in contemporary New York City, Jesus is portrayed as a clown figure who gathers a troupe of would-be wrong-righters. While the entire movie is artificially sweet at points, it certainly has a more positive tone than *Superstar.* There are a couple of decent musical numbers. We have not found it available on video, however, and therefore have not included it for more extensive treatment in this book.

While *Jesus Christ Superstar* is clearly dated by its outlandish costumes and sometimes syrupy, sometimes raucous music, unexpectedly, it has been one of the more popular movies in the classes we have taught. The music still has some appeal, energy, and power. For some viewers it has provided a trip down Nostalgia Lane, evoking memories of a freer and more rebellious time when those viewers were slim and audacious enough to sport their own hiphuggers or actually performed this play or *Godspell* in church basements. For younger viewers, the movie is so stylized, so camp, that it seems to maintain a novelty and an aura of cache that have survived for over two decades.

Perhaps also, it presents a view of Jesus who, in these increasingly conservative religious times, is more accessible, more personal, more human, and certainly more fallible than the one currently in vogue, that is to say, someone with whom it is easier to identify. There is frequently a countervailing spirituality that runs alongside the prevailing spirit of the day. Popular piety often serves as the outlet for these countervailing tendencies. What the mainline theologies cannot provide, populist, even underground, gatherings will.

If the movie has sustained a popularity, perhaps in part because of its obviously dated look, how was it received at the time of its debut? It met with mixed reviews. *Variety* wrote, "*Superstar* blares with the shallow impact of an inferior imitation of Isaac Hayes. The erratic filmization in the picture's last half will strike some as inhibiting the full dramatic potential of the climax."[3] Later the critic adds, "The entire music score is on the thin side." None of this would qualify as high praise. Other reviews of the time have little to add. It is nevertheless worth noting that this film, or more likely the play, does remain popular long after others have faded away.

Movie Preview: Questions and Suggestions

1. *Describe the cultural setting in the United States at the time this movie was produced. What was being protested?*

2. *What do you know about this movie, even if you have not yet seen it? Which of the songs do you recognize?*

3. *Watch for the use of visual effects: setting, camera technique, costume, and such. Do they help or hinder the telling of the story?*

4. *As you watch this movie, try to keep track of the points where you find your image of Jesus challenged by what is happening in the film.*

Movie Viewing

Movie Review: Questions and Responses

1. *How would you describe the tone of this film, its premise, its point of view?*

2. *Describe the roles of women in this film. How do they differ from the roles they have filled in previous films?*

3. *Describe the image of Jesus in this movie. How does it compare and contrast with its predecessors? How does it compare with your image?*

4. *What portions of Scripture have been emphasized; which significant passages or events have not been used?*

5. *Did you find the visual approach of the movie a help or a hindrance in watching it?*

6. *What happens to the actor who portrays Jesus at the end of the movie? What feelings are you left with at the end of the movie?*

LENS ONE

The prospect of a musical messiah surrounded by singing and dancing disciples might well lead one to question whether any serious, historical value could be derived from Norman Jewison's *Jesus Christ Superstar.* The viewer may wonder: Where is the story about Jesus' birth or the teachings of his ministry in Galilee? Where are the miracles that demonstrate Jesus' authority and power? Where, indeed, is the resurrection? Of course, we do not find a "Jesus saga" here at all. This film is most definitely not a musical rendition of the New Testament Gospels, with their summary of Jesus' origins, earthly ministry, and crucifixion. As a result, the viewer may be led to think that, since there is no attempt to retrace the historical events of Jesus' life, this film shows no interest in historical questions. This conclusion would be premature...and wrong.

Superstar, while not a comprehensive review of the life of Jesus, is a recollection of the last events of Jesus' final days in Judea, during the week of his passion and death. These events are recorded only at the end of the New Testament Gospels in materials referred to as the "passion narratives." Of course, what appear here are only a few important moments drawn from the experiences of a single week. Is it possible that this brief story, the memory of that time when everything seemed to go bad for Jesus, his ministry, and his movement, could serve as the focus of an entire plot? Jewison appears to think so! Indeed, the early church, as witnessed in the gospels, certainly seemed to believe so as well. For much of the primitive church, the passion narrative, alone and without elaboration, served as the earliest understanding and encapsulation of what God had done through Jesus of Nazareth. It may be helpful to look briefly at how the oldest gospel, the

Gospel of Mark, has employed this theme of Jesus' death before we investigate how Jewison himself handles the story.

Many biblical students believe that before the Gospel of Mark was written, its author already possessed some earlier form of passion narrative. The mystery of Jesus' death and the events associated with that occasion certainly intrigued the imagination of early Christian thinkers prior to Mark. We need only recall the apostle Paul, who preached about the death and resurrection of Christ Jesus as the basis for faith. So, with some form of passion narrative in hand, the author of the Gospel of Mark soon collected stories about Jesus' ministry in Galilee, intended to serve as a prelude to the final week of events in Judea, as well as a means to preserve examples of Jesus' teachings. The passion narrative became the climactic moment in a longer story about Jesus' life and ministry in Palestine. The story, as we now know it from the Gospels of Matthew, Luke, and John, became much more developed than Mark originally portrayed it. But in each case, the central element is the final week of Jesus' passion and death.

With this in mind we can then ask about the nature of that body of data that stands at the core of Mark's passion narrative, that is, before any alterations were made to that material's "memory" of the events. It is difficult to be certain, but several events must be included. It is certain that the passion narrative that Mark received included comments about Jesus' arrest, his trial, and his execution. This three-part framework is revealed in the materials of Mark 10:32–34, an occasion when Jesus spoke to his disciples about the days ahead.

To this simple structure other elements can be added, items that are preserved by Matthew, Luke, and John as well: the anointing of Jesus by a woman (variously identified among the gospels); a supper shared by Jesus with his closest followers; a plot to turn Jesus over to the Temple authorities; the execution of this plot in the form of a betrayal by one of Jesus' followers; and a denial of Jesus by one of his friends. Each of these events is preserved in some form by the gospel stories, and each is included by Jewison in his own work. Curiously, these events focus upon the actions and conversations of characters who are central to the basic plot of the story, namely, Jesus, his followers, and his opponents. It is easy to see what Jewison does with his sources when we investigate these characters individually.

Judas Iscariot. We begin with Judas since he appears first in the film. In the gospel stories the Judas character only plays a significant role in the passion narratives. His sole function is to betray Jesus to the Temple authorities. Otherwise, the author of John mentions in passing that Judas carried the common purse for the disciples (Jn 13:29), an element which Jewison preserves. We have no other information about Judas.

Because Jesus was betrayed by one of his own chosen followers, the early church was left with confusion about the way in which this was permitted to happen. Was Jesus the Messiah somehow (inconceivably) duped by a person whom he had personally picked? Was one of his privileged followers somehow turned by the powers of evil? Or was Judas specifically selected with the knowledge that this was to be the person through whom God's purpose for Jesus' life and death would be realized?

The gospels offer no clear, unified answer to these questions. Neither Matthew nor Mark give any indication about Judas' motivation. Both authors seem unaware of the theological problems caused by the fact that Jesus had chosen his own betrayer. Luke and John, however, state that Judas was in some fashion turned by the power of evil (Lk 22:3, "Satan entered into Judas..."; Jn 13:2, "The devil had already put it into Judas's heart..."). Viewed from this perspective, Jesus could hardly be responsible for the selection of a "bad disciple." Following the writing of the gospels, Christians offered an explanation that carried more theological consideration, namely, that Judas was chosen in order to serve as the tool by which Jesus would die. Judas's very existence was part of a larger plan to sacrifice Jesus for the salvation of the world.

Of course, these proposals have not ended the conversations about Judas. We already have seen DeMille's suggestion that the betrayal was an act of revenge against Mary Magdalene, who had spurned the attentions of Judas in order to follow Jesus. Later film directors fortunately have chosen not to pursue this route! Ray and Stevens returned to the idea that Judas was a pawn in God's ultimate plan for salvation. As a result, they raised the obvious question: was Judas not, therefore, in some sense a sacrifice to this larger plan, a person who was himself a puppet to the divine will? This offers an interesting ethical consideration about why Judas should be held accountable for his actions while under the sway of God's power.

Jewison is plainly aware of this dilemma. Yet he is also under the influence of popular speculation during the 1960s that Judas had misunderstood Jesus' ministry to be that of an earthly, worldly messiah. By such standards, Judas is often portrayed in the literature of the period as a zealot for global power who saw Jesus as a probable sympathizer to his own goals. Judas either betrayed Jesus in order to force him to take the reins of this power, or his betrayal came with the realization that Jesus was a fraud (at least according to Judas's definition of *messiah*).

Jewison confronts both of these considerations (pawn or zealot), but offers his own solution to the puzzle. From Judas's opening song we find that there is a sense in which Jesus and Judas are extremely close: Judas (not Peter) is Jesus' "right-hand man" (already suggested by Ray and Stevens). It is Judas who recognizes that the crowds have begun to place Jesus at the center of their adoration and have forgotten about his teachings—Jesus' personality has replaced his message. Judas is close enough to Jesus to understand that each hearer must "separate the myth from the man" when considering who Jesus really is. He speculates whether Jesus has not been deluded by his own success. He is concerned that the crowds who gather around believe that "all is well," while he (and Jesus) realize that this is hardly the case.

With all of this in mind, Judas comes to a simple conclusion that no other director offers. Judas will betray Jesus in order to force him to admit publicly that the people have deluded themselves about who Jesus is as the Messiah (a cosmic savior from God), and thus draw them away from any direct, self-destructive conflict with Roman power. Judas sees his actions as noble, even if they have a sort of ignoble feeling when the Temple priests become involved. His solution is a means by which both Jesus and his followers can be delivered from a catastrophic end. Yet, ultimately, this is not Judas acting alone. Jewison sees Judas's actions as part of God's own plan. While Judas is sacrificed as part of this larger plan into which he stumbles in his confusion over Jesus' true character and purpose, eventually there is salvation even for him (notice that the earthly Judas is dressed in red as a sign of his dubious character as a betrayer, while the "heavenly" Judas is dressed in white, surely a sign of his redemption—he has been faithful to God's plan after all).

Jewison fully realizes that Judas is one of the gospel story's most enigmatic and problematic characters. Although Judas remains confused at the end of *Superstar,* there is no question that his motivations have been carefully considered. He remains confused, yet does his duty. The final question, of course, is: what has been achieved?

Mary Magdalene. Like Judas, Mary Magdalene is associated specifically with the passion narrative. In the Gospel of Mark she appears only as one of the first women to find the empty tomb after the crucifixion. In Matthew and John, she is also the first person to see the resurrected Christ. It is Luke alone who offers any additional information about Mary, a text on which Jewison is heavily dependent. "The twelve were with him, as well as some women who had been cured of evil spirits and infirmities: Mary, called Magdalene...and many others, who provided for them out of their resources" (Lk 8:1–3). So Mary (and many other women) first appears in *Superstar* as one of those who provide for Jesus "out of their resources."

In this movie, the relationship between Mary and Jesus is obviously close and highly suggestive. DeMille already had hinted at such ties in 1927, although his repentant Mary turned appropriately to the virtual trappings of a nun. Her relationship with Jesus became a way to separate herself from human, personal expression. With Jewison there remains the potential for an open, emotional bond between Jesus and Mary, platonic or otherwise. This bond is perceived as scandalous to Judas and perhaps to the viewer as well. But in a new way it suggests an element of real humanity for the character of Jesus that was not investigated in previous films.

Of equal importance for Jewison, Mary's close association with Jesus permits her to assume the role of many "Marys" from the New Testament Gospels. For example, we come upon Mary as she anoints Jesus, although the Mary who anoints Jesus in the gospels (see Jn 12:3 only) is the sister of Martha and Lazarus, not Mary Magdalene! So too, we find Mary dressed in red (a color traditionally worn by prostitutes in antiquity) and hear Jesus ask Judas whether he would throw stones at her (an allusion to the woman caught in adultery; Jn 8:1–11). But, of course, this assumes that Mary Magdalene must be associated with the woman caught in adultery, a connection that the gospels do not themselves make! Finally, at the end of the film, Mary is in mourning at the foot of the cross. This image from John 19:25–27 is certainly scriptural, though curious, since John mentions her as one of three or four women present (Mary Magdalene; Jesus' mother Mary; and Mary the wife of Clopas [possibly Jesus' aunt?]). In John's vision, it is certainly the mother of Jesus who is the focus of the narrative, not Mary Magdalene!

Our Mary is thus many Marys. In her relationship to Jesus she functions as nurturer (mother), potential lover, and rescued sinner. The person of Mary Magdalene is a poorly known figure from Scripture whom Jewison has utilized to raise a host of attendant issues to which the gospels offer no answer. Much like Judas, Mary remains confused throughout our film, although she does her best to understand what is happening, and her intentions are honorable (even if her motivations are a bit murky). She sings, "Could we start again, please?" Is this a reference to her relationship with Jesus, to the events of Jesus' life, or to the play about Jesus' life, because the way the plot is moving is not what she had hoped for?

Simon Peter and Simon the Zealot. Consistent with the vision of DeMille, Jewison basically portrays the twelve apostles (except for Judas) as "the good sheep." Their participation in the development of the passion plot is minimal. Only two figures stand forth from this bland and general portrayal: Simon Peter and Simon the Zealot.

The Gospels of Mark, Matthew, and Luke agree that Simon Peter is the leader of the apostles. He rises above the other disciples of Jesus in these gospels as the spokesperson for the group. It is he who confesses that Jesus is the Christ; it is he (with James and John) who is chosen to attend Jesus at the transfiguration and at the Garden of Gethsemane; it is he who receives the keys to the kingdom. But in the Gospel of John, while Peter remains important, he is no longer central. That position is reserved in John for the unnamed "beloved disciple" (traditionally presumed to be John, son of Zebedee). So it is that a mixture of these images—the centrality motif of Mark, Matthew, and Luke, together with the understated position of John— comes to define who Peter is in *Superstar.*

Peter, like the other disciples, is mostly a happy follower of Jesus. He is surely a leader of this band in many respects. He stands physically taller than the others. Together with Mary Magdalene, he is permitted to sing of his confused response to the presence of Jesus. Most importantly, however, his role is defined by the requirements of the passion narrative—he denies his association with Jesus during the trial! This alone is Peter's place in *Superstar*'s rendition of the passion story. It is a splendid example of the confusion that reigns among the disciples about who Jesus is and what his death means.

The inclusion of Simon the Zealot is an interesting move by Jewison. In a historical sense this character is shaky. The designation "zealot" appears only in Luke 6:15 and Acts 1:13, two texts written by the same author. In Mark and Matthew he is known as Simon the Cananaean, while in John he remains unnamed. His place among the disciples, somewhere between Peter and Judas, undoubtedly is inspired by the common name of Simon. He, like Peter, is yet another Simon. In the gospels he traditionally is listed as the last of the apostles prior to Judas, whose own father (according to Jn 13:2, 26) was named Simon.

With respect to Scripture, Simon the Zealot makes no appearance in the passion narrative. With respect to the plot of *Superstar,* he becomes a lightning rod to attract all claims of "zealot" or "resistance fighter" away from Judas Iscariot. As noted above, Jewison does not make the claim (popular among biblical students in the 1960s) that Judas was active among the Jewish resistance to Roman domination. Instead, and perhaps correctly, Jewison lays this burden at the door of Simon the Zealot who, unlike Judas, Mary, and Peter, holds no confusion about the true identity and capabilities of Jesus—although Jesus notes that Simon is completely misinformed!

Caiaphas, Herod, Pilate. Both in the gospels and in Jewison's film, these three figures stand united as the opponents of Jesus. Once again, in each instance there is an element of confusion about who Jesus is and what he wants.

Caiaphas is firmly convinced that Jesus is dangerous—dangerous to the power of the priesthood, dangerous to the stability of the Jewish people under Roman rule, and dangerous to his followers, whose simple minds can be easily misled. As in the gospel narrative, the machinations behind the demise of Jesus lie with Caiaphas. Yet, what Caiaphas sees clearly (that Jesus must be eliminated) never clearly transcends his need to be reassured by those with whom he controls Judaism's religious structures. His motivations are mixed. He is concerned both for the people and for his priesthood.

The interrogation before Herod Antipas (known from Lk 23:6–12) is a farce from the outset; Herod's depravity and perversion are clear. His bent toward self-indulgence is blatant. Obviously he has heard much of "the myth man" Jesus and expects to be entertained by miraculous feats of power. Of course, none is forthcoming. Herod seems confused (not that his lack of belief in Jesus as the Messiah was ever in question), becomes violent, and then demands justice from Rome in response to Jesus' insulting presence in his court. He gets that justice when Jesus is given thirty-nine lashes. It becomes painfully clear to him in that moment of scourging that only a misguided fool would submit his body to physical pain in the light of some more lofty, unseen goal. To Herod, Jesus is a complete mystery.

Pontius Pilate is troubled from the beginning as a result of his dream about Jesus' trial (recorded in Mt 27:19 as the dream of his wife). Pilate's aristocratic, effeminate mannerisms suggest that his authority must surely come from elsewhere. This is both a blessing and a curse. On the one hand, the far distant power of Rome and the all-too-near threat of Jewish anarchy require him to condemn Jesus to death. On the other, his reluctance toward the matter and his conviction that Jesus is an innocent puppet compel him merely to have Jesus beaten and released. Pilate's path is set, however. His indecisive confusion and personal concerns give way to other pressures, and the preparations for Jesus' death continue.

Jesus of Nazareth. Though Jesus obviously is the central figure of *Superstar,* his character as portrayed does little to offer clarity to the plot. If one permits the passion narrative of the Gospel of Mark to speak solely on its own, the identity of Jesus is unclear here as well. To enter Mark's passion narrative is to enter a world where Jesus' origins are left without comment, where Jesus' earthly ministry is a given fact (though without explanation), and where God's plan after Jesus' death is never explicitly delineated. The likely original ending of the Gospel of Mark occurs at 16:8: "So [the women] went out and fled from the tomb, for terror and amazement had seized them; and they said nothing to anyone, for they were afraid."

Jewison's Jesus is the Jesus of the Gospel of Mark in a form largely untainted by the imagery of Matthew and Luke. Jesus is one of us, truly human. He feels the vision of God, but he never offers a clear understanding of the details, either to his followers or to his opponents. In the same way that the great mystics say that God may be defined only by what God is not, so Jesus gives hints of what his mission is only in terms of what it is not: it is not earthly power; it is not overwhelming personal charisma; it is not common Jewish (or Roman) images of what a king and savior should be.

In many respects, Jesus is the great catalyst of this story, but a catalyst who cannot be defined with precision. He is the eye of the tornado, the center of the vortex. Everything happens around him and because of him. Yet whenever the characters turn and point to him, they are unable to identify the object of their concern. His closest friends—Judas and Mary—are confused. His staunchest enemies—Caiaphas, Herod, and Pilate—are baffled. His army of followers—Peter, Simon the Zealot, the apostles—are convinced by their own visions of who Jesus is, but ultimately have no more lucid an understanding than does anyone else. Even Jesus himself sings, "What's the fuss? Tell me whatsa happening."

As a result, then, we must ask what it is that Jesus himself offers in this effort to clarify God's plan for his life and death. Unlike the firm assurance of Jesus as depicted by DeMille, Ray, Pasolini, and Stevens, the Jesus of Jewison, like the Gospel of Mark, is opaque. There is no question that this Jesus hears the voice of God, a voice that others either do not hear or cannot decipher. But it seems to be a muffled voice providing little direction and offering little in the way of answers. The only clear element of the message is that Jesus must die, and that through his dying something good will result.

When we examine the passion narrative apart from Jesus' life and works, we see God's message to the world in the *person* of Jesus rather than in his teachings. This was the focus of the apostle Paul's early preaching (Christ crucified and resurrected); this is also the focal point of modern Christianity. The message is stark but clear. One man died according to a divine plan so that all people could have the chance to live according to the divine intention. The passion narrative contains the elements of the plot by which this death occurred. The narrative contains the names of those who functioned within that plot. What the text does not offer is the answer to myriad questions that might be raised about the motivations behind the activities and decisions of these players. In this sense, the gospel narrative does not meet the usual expectations of a novel or short story.

It is at this very point that Jewison delves into the Scriptures. He offers the traditional elements that we expect to find (anointing, supper, betrayal, etc.). He provides a cast of characters who enable the story to function. But he disturbs our sensibilities by spotlighting the very elements that make the passion story so bothersome, that is, the total lack of comprehension about the plot and its direction, as demonstrated by each of the characters. For Jewison the motivations are inexplicable. Confusion is endemic. The required activities of God's plan are clear, but the rationale for those events remains hidden. Jewison's Jesus, like the Jesus of the passion narratives in the gospels, offers the viewer little help. Both Jewison and his characters respond with one basic question: What does it all mean ultimately? The answer is left to the viewer with the movie's open-ended closing.

LENS TWO

It does not require an astute observer to detect that this film is not cut from the same cloth as its predecessors in this study of the Savior on the silver screen. In terms of overall look or style, characterization, visuals, and audio elements, it takes a major step away from the Hollywood films thus far viewed, as well as away from the Pasolini rendition. Yet, there are some points in which the movie follows a trajectory or path created by its predecessors. It is not completely discontinuous with the others we have viewed thus far in the series, plus it anticipates elements, themes, and techniques that we will see again in the films that follow.

In terms of opening and closing scenes, both scenes make clear that this is a play within a play, a theme that will recur in *Jesus of Montreal*. Ironically, unlike the more "realistic" films which we have watched thus far that were not shot in Israel, *Superstar,* the film with the least visual verisimilitude, was indeed shot in the Negev Desert of Israel. In the opening scene we see, off in the distance, a cloud of dust and soon hear raucous music; eventually we see the rickety bus, and discover a band of roving actors about to put on a musical in the ruins and reconstructions of an archaeological site, perhaps the ruins of contemporary society or, symbolically, of traditional expectations. From the beginning, then, we are clear that this film presents a pretense of sorts, not a biography, but a play about the life of Jesus.

In the closing scene the actors get back on the bus, most seemingly unaffected by the drama they have just performed. The actors portraying Mary Magdalene and Judas are the exceptions as they look with longing glances back to the site of the play. "Jesus," however, is absent. He does not get on the bus. The movie closes with a simple shot of the empty cross on a hill with the setting sun in the background. The camera pulls back farther and farther, the cross gets smaller and smaller. Faintly, we see a shepherd with some sheep down the hill from the cross. Is this "Jesus," that is, the actor, who has somehow been transformed by the role he has played? Why did we not see Jesus get on the bus with the others? We are left, certainly intentionally, with nagging questions. What happened to Jesus? What happened to the actor? The movie, unlike the play, closes open-endedly, that is, without clear resolution of all the questions. This, as suggested in Lens One, is exactly the situation or the question that the gospels, especially that of Mark, leave with their readers. We are left in *Superstar* with only a possible biblical reference, not a spectacle. The last moments of the film speak to us rather tentatively about faith in the age of doubt. What, indeed, happened to Jesus?

Baugh suggests that this shepherd could not possibly be a visual reference to Jesus or to the actor because other shepherds have been present in the film and had no metaphoric value.[4] But, it seems too obvious at the end to ignore, even if it is ambiguous. It is the last image with which we are left. Indeed, in the earlier scenes of sheep and shepherds, prior to the Last Supper, for example, the sheep/shepherd image (intercut into the walk of the apostles to the garden for the picnic/Last Supper) seems again too obvious an image to ignore, begging for some interpretation. The scene of the sheep and shepherd would seem to be totally gratuitous if it did not serve some narrative or symbolic value. The image is certainly symbolic in Scripture! Exactly what that value of the image is must be left to the viewer to interpret.

That is also how one encounters Scripture, with the role of interpreter clearly in mind. What do we read into the texts, the images, the stories? What does the reader bring to the reading? This is referred to as the hermeneutic circle where the reader/viewer interprets the text (book or film), but the text also interprets the reader/viewer by evoking the sort of preconceptions and responses that are brought to the reading, or, in this case, the viewing. One does not come to a text neutrally. In this case, if the shepherd is not the actor, we are still left to wonder what happened to him and perhaps to the others as well, as the bus returns to wherever it came from.

Again, the immediate setting for the play is an archaeological site replete with scaffolding or staging on which the Sanhedrin regularly gathers for council and to issue ultimatums. The only other constructed set is Herod's floating pleasure island, where he cavorts with his cohorts. A few props here and there around the rocky landscape create settings for the other scenes of the movie. It is very sparse, but quite effective in developing the various "spaces" where the scenes take place. Because we are essentially watching a play-within-a-play, we make allowance for the contrived, minimalist sets. If the same approach had been used in, for example, *The Greatest Story Ever Told,* the effect would have been more discordant.

At the same time that the basic sets are minimal and theatrical, there are some interesting special effects used. Several of the musical numbers are quite elaborately choreographed, suggesting the movie's stage origins, and use some "camera magic" that was probably effective two decades ago but looks a little underpowered these days with the advent of computer "morphing." Several of the dance numbers, for example, employ stop action, letting the dancers hang midair for a moment. Cute but not especially effective.

Overall, the camera work is very harsh, sometimes too close, sometimes with too much movement, all certainly intentional, somewhat in the fashion of Pasolini's *The Gospel According to Saint Matthew,* though not quite as artistic. The effect is to create, or rather to avoid creating, the seamless flow of events so typical of the Hollywood movies. There are good shots making use of the characteristics of telephoto lenses in the mode of Dustin Hoffman's race down the street with the telephone poles at one side in *The Graduate.* He ran and ran and ran but seemed to make no progress. The lens's compression of space, effected by the telephoto lens, makes this possible.

In the case of *Jesus Christ Superstar,* one scene that exemplifies good creative use of lenses pictures Judas alone in the desert. Suddenly in the background several "poles" come into view, coming up over the hill. They seem to get taller and taller. Because the telephoto lens compresses space, the cannons on the tanks, as it turns out, look much closer than they really are. Eventually the poles crest the hill, and we see the rest of the tanks lumbering toward Judas. Initially, we do not *hear* the tanks, an example of video-anticipating-audio; when their engine noise finally comes in, it is abrupt and loud. They seem to be chasing Judas, at least that is what Judas seems to think.

At other points the camera is uncomfortably close to the characters. If the goal of classic Hollywood productions was to keep the audience from even thinking about the camera work, in *Superstar,* the goal is quite the opposite: Jar the viewer with abrupt shifts in camera angle, harsh and abrupt edits, loud music, and other disquieting effects. A sort of audiovisual whiplash is induced. In something of an act of *homage* to *King of Kings* perhaps, a camera has been mounted to the top of the cross during the crucifixion scene. As viewers, we look down on Jesus hanging, as the cross is lifted to an upright position. It seems just another effect without the narrative contribution it had in *King of Kings.* With this and other camera tricks, one wonders what is the intended effect? Do they add to the narrative? They add interest in many ways, but often do not ultimately contribute much to the plot of the movie. The effect is evocative of the person who has a new video camera and feels obliged to use all of its features every time it is taken out of its case—zooms in and out, titles, dates in the lower corner, fades, and so forth. Too much! Perhaps the jarring or the whiplash is all that is intended in *Superstar:* Make the viewers uncomfortable; do not let them get settled; keep them rocking and rolling (or reeling). Again, the medium may be the real message.

We have already mentioned the editing. It is noteworthy because it is so obvious. Discontinuous action, strident and abrupt cuts, sudden intrusion of music and sound effects, and other similar devices. Editing does more than just connect scenes and shots. It helps to create pacing as well as the mood we have just suggested of an unsettled, tumultuous time in which values and expectations were changing, even being overthrown.

Much has been written about two of the three chief characters: Jesus and Judas. Basically the reviewers conclude that Ted Neeley is too weak to make a good Jesus. He whines a lot, seems to have no motivating vision of his identity as the Christ. His voice is strident as he angrily sings, "I must be mad thinking I'll be remembered." He is simply not a very attractive person. The viewer might hope he would listen to Mary Magdalene's suggestion, "Try not to get worried, try not to turn onto problems that might upset you. Don't you know everything's all right...." One inevitably wonders why Neeley was chosen for the role. Were the director and others responsible for casting oblivious to these factors? That is doubtful. So, then, what was the point?

What did the director want to communicate by choosing Neeley and directing him in the way that he did? What does the film, by its choice of actors, say about the role, person, and image of Jesus?

Finally, the viewers must make these interpretations for themselves, but this should be an intentional step in the discussion and analysis of the movie, judging its effects and its message. It is not sufficient to say that the actor was not very good. What is the effect on the movie? And why would the actor characterize his or her role in the way he or she did? As mentioned above, Neeley continues to play his role in stage versions of *Jesus Christ Superstar*. Is there a sustained appeal for the Jesus he portrays, or is it just the novelty of seeing the film actor onstage? Has he been transformed by this work? Or is it just a job?

The comments about the actor and his portrayal of Judas have nothing to do with his ability, nor the role per se, but about the fact that an African American was chosen to play Judas the betrayer. Choosing to cast the betrayer as African American might seem to be insensitive and politically unsavvy. Clearly, the Judas role is bigger than Jesus' role, however. Judas is also a more attractive character than Jesus. Judas is the catalyst that keeps the film moving. Jesus both seems mostly to respond or react to what is going on around him. Judas and some of the disciples, on the other hand, have plans or desires for Jesus, both personal and political. The concerns about this casting choice, while not unimportant, seem ultimately to be groundless. Judas is an important figure in the plot, and seems to have been redeemed in the end, having served his role in the salvation story.

The character of Jesus, on the other hand, is another story, as has already been suggested several times. Jesus angrily responds at one point, "Why should you want to know? Don't you mind about the future. Don't try to think ahead. Save tomorrow for tomorrow." Jesus, in *The Greatest Story Ever Told,* makes a similar comment, but does it with great calm, wisdom, and equanimity, giving an entirely different meaning to the words. In *Greatest Story* one is left with a confidence about the future and Jesus' part in bringing that future to fruition, whereas in *Superstar,* the result is just the opposite. Jesus is a frustrated "loose cannon" with little sense of direction and little hope for the future and little sense of his role in that future, whatever it might be. Certainly this latter Jesus represented the feelings of a great many people of that time: frustrated, verging on hopelessness, and angry about the dark future that seemed evident on the horizon.

We would be remiss not to comment on the costumes in *Superstar;* they beg for some sort of comment. First, they fit right along with the play-within-a-play concept. The costumes seem mostly very make-do, as though a youth group went to a secondhand clothes store to get whatever they needed and their directive was twofold: use your imagination and don't spend too much money. In this sense, the philosophy (admittedly too grand a term) of the costuming is similar to *The Gospel According to Saint Matthew,* which also has that makeshift, make-do, church-basement-play "look." The costumes in *Superstar* are an anachronistic mixing of times and images: camouflage pants, dimestore helmets, and purple tank tops on the Roman guards. Black pants, black bulbous headgear (upside down plastic flowerpots?) for the Sanhedrin. Tie-dye and India throws for the disciples. Only Jesus seems dressed in appropriate "Jesus-like" clothing. For what purpose? As Lens Three will discuss more thoroughly, this was a time of revolution, clashes of values, and transitions between old and new. How better to express the chaos of the time than to have a chaotic, mixed-metaphor array of costumes? Only Jesus remains the constant, the hingepin around which the rest of the activity swings, or, as mentioned in Lens One, the center of the vortex.

The props also are anachronistic, mixing pikes with tanks and machine guns and other modern military hardware. This could be a trite gimmick, but it also is a way of bringing the person of Jesus into the "present" of the 1970s, creating a clash of values and times. It is a way of posing the question, "What place does Jesus have for us today? Is Jesus relevant for the 1970s and the 1990s? Does his message intersect in any way with our behaviors and values? In what way does Jesus' message confront us here and now?" In the Temple scene in which Jesus throws out the "money changers," there is little reminiscent of traditional religious symbolism that is being sold and bartered but much to which modern societies look to for security: sex, modern weaponry, and other such symbols. Whether one agrees or not with the connection, this scene becomes more than a gimmick but, rather, an obvious social and possibly religious commentary on the status and direction of "establishment" values of that time.

Finally, what role does the music play in the film? We have already noted that the music existed before the film. Indeed, the music is what drives the film. In our increasingly conservative religious environment, the music may be as controversial now as in the 1970s. "I don't know how to love him," sung by both Mary Magdalene and Judas, is suggestive enough to raise more than a few eyebrows about the intended nature of that love. Other lines have been quoted above. It is very likely that we learn much of our theology through religious music—especially in a church context through our hymns. Similarly as we continue to hum these tunes of *Superstar* long after the videocassette has been put back in its box, the influence subtly continues. The music is what lasts from this film. The lyrics linger, lines stick in consciousness and repeat themselves again and again. To what effect? That would be hard to say. "He's just a man. He's just a man," is heard over and over. Does it impact our own theological view of the person and work of Jesus? Whether we accept the concept or actively reject it, we have been forced to engage it. The music is good to listen to; it carries the message of the movie more than any other element in the film. And it seems to have lasted well beyond the actual movie. What brought the movie into existence now lasts well beyond it!

LENS THREE

Keeping in mind *Jesus Christ Superstar*'s origin as a rock opera, it is easy to see how the phenomenon of a rock messiah might have emerged out of the late '60s. Searching for his identity as the Son of God, Jesus' status in *Superstar* suggests a cultural transformation informed by radical late 1960s politics, the emerging drug and youth culture, and commercialization of a hip, secularized Christianity. From the point of view of cinema history, the rock opera reveals a complete revision of traditional studio approaches to the Savior on the silver screen. In its various transformations from vinyl to stage to film, we see a superstar Jesus born of the social divisions created and then embedded in the Vietnam era, as well as in the political and gender liberations of the late 1960s. The late 1960s became notorious for the various despairing, existentialist undercurrents popularly proclaiming the "death of God." In the troubled days after 1968, America would fashion a very different kind of Jesus, one that the world had not seen before.

As we have already noted in our investigation, the invention of "Jesus Christ" for the American film audience has typically enabled Hollywood film makers and studios to create an ideological, technical, and, indeed, commercial space for their audiences. Over the years, the Savior served the interest of the Hollywood feature film in multiple ways. As more and more foreign films were imported into the American market, Pasolini's radicalized Jesus in *The Gospel According to Saint Matthew* made a self-conscious break with middle-class expectations of the Hollywood Savior. It was precisely because of Pasolini's ability to subvert traditional expectations about the Lord that the film achieved success as an art-house picture in the mid-1960s. But *Jesus Christ Superstar* was far from esoteric and would accomplish for the American mainstream what European cinema could never do: challenge and, hopefully, realign middle-class expectations of the Savior. No wonder that *Superstar* grossed over twenty million dollars and that the picture earned an Oscar nomination for André Previn's musical direction.

At the same time, *Superstar* shows how traditional Hollywood audiences change over time and, by the late 1960s, came to expect something different from its film culture. A politicized audience demanded more provocative subjects from the culture industry. Our expectations of what a screen Savior is supposed to do is also transformed in the process: instead of a Jesus who gathers a homogeneous audience to himself, we find in Ted Neeley a rather screechy, reluctant Messiah with a rocketing falsetto. Rather than previous versions of Jesus who, as in DeMille's *The King of Kings,* gain some control over the world and even subdue wild, female energies, this superstar seems overwhelmed by his environment and is himself lulled into passivity by the stirrings of the pop single "I Don't Know How to Love Him," sung by Mary Magdalene (Yvonne Elliman).

More significantly, though, this latest Savior lacks significant origins and, much like Stevens's failed epic of Jesus, does not articulate a "grand narrative" about God's plan in salvation history. The Webber/Rice *Superstar* Jesus seems to exist as a postmodern Christological phenomenon: He is there, not to show us the way to the Father, but to his own identity. *Superstar* is very much a part of the mainstreaming of countercultural views and products that emerged in 1970 alone. A revisionist stance on formerly unquestioned aspects of American life was itself taken for granted in films like *MASH, Five Easy Pieces,* and *Little Big Man,* to name a few. If military doctors, the American male, and the history of the West could be reimagined, then why not Jesus Christ?

Jesus Christ Superstar displays none of the comforting elements we expect from stories of God, or indeed, have come to expect from biblical narratives on film. The experiencing of *Superstar* jars us from a predisposed textual tradition about the life of God's Son; it is Jesus as we have never imagined him; it is not the established narrative of the infant God growing toward either divine Son or hesitant, crucified prophet. Like Andy Warhol's famous observation about the short-lived status of fame, *Superstar* is a play about a mere week in the life of the Messiah—the last days of Jesus' life. The opera is perhaps ambiguous as to whether Jesus even rose from the dead. Jesus comes into his generation in a flash and, seemingly, vanishes just as quickly. Much of the originality of the film production owes its success to its focus on transforming, not faithfully matching, the source text. Since our investigation depends heavily on the emergence of Jesus as popular "Superstar," this section will follow closely the genesis of the new Savior, tracing the Superstar from his beginnings in the late '60s to the film production in 1973.

Formula for a Superstar. In the late 1960s and early 1970s, tumultuous events in three highly significant areas—the political, the cultural, and the commercial—transformed Jesus into a Superstar. From a political point of view, Jesus was ready to be a martyr for the Left. In the pivotal year 1968, shock waves regularly rocked middle America and most of the world. Each day brought news of more and more disruption, either at home or elsewhere: students revolted in the streets of Paris, demonstrators were teargassed at the Chicago National Convention; Martin Luther King, Jr., was gunned down in front of his motel room in Memphis; and Robert Kennedy was murdered in a California hotel lobby while campaigning against Richard Nixon for President. The war in Southeast Asia escalated to ferocious proportions and was being televised regularly for the nation. The My Lai Massacre cast a huge shadow over the military, even for the Right. Racial protests and demonstrations resulted in riots in 168 towns and cities.

Movements that began in the 1950s were becoming highly organized political instruments and some, like the Black Panthers, were gaining a reputation for violence. The assassinations of Martin Luther King, Jr., and Malcolm X further galvanized African American interests. Additionally, another wave of feminism had been sweeping the country, and women were demanding and attaining powerful positions in American society. The revolutionary status of countercultural movements, from gay liberation to the Jesus movement, afforded many formerly silent voices a chance to be heard. America was becoming much like its contemporary fashion industry: loud, colorful, and diverse.

The moderately cynical attitude that helped influence the lyrics and music of *Jesus Christ Superstar* was also very much part of post-1968 America, a period unmistakably shaped by the course of politics, particularly of the Left. As an album, *Superstar* had a special place in America (but did not, however, enjoy much success in England), perhaps because of the controversial nature of the subject matter appearing late during the Vietnam War, when more and more Americans were searching for a peaceful solution to the conflict. Especially after the Tet offensive in 1968, in which a cease-fire was shattered and a bloody spectacle created for television audiences, Jesus' hip, antimilitant stance in the album seemed to fit well in the late 1960s youth culture. This was a Messiah who seemed to be a refuge from hawkish establishment values.

Superstar is, after all, a musical less about Jesus' divinity or miracles than a portrait of a man pitted against the established order, hypocrisy, and violence—in short, a man espousing the values that the counterculture held dear. In fact, during the late 1960s and early 1970s it was commonplace to speak of the "Jesus Freak" movement, of which Stephen Schwartz's *Godspell* (which opened a few months before the Rice/Webber rock opera in an Off-Broadway production) and *Superstar* are spin-offs. In theological circles, a social gospel was gaining acceptance, one that articulated a collapsed eschatology of peace on earth—but not in a utopic paradise. Liberation theology was making its way into mainstream thought, and a "Preferential Option for the Poor" was proclaimed by the Catholic Bishops in Medellin in 1971. Far from the site of middle-class values and status quo existence, any messiah after 1968 had to be socially conscious, youthful, and antiestablishment in order to be credible. More than any other Savior invented by the culture industry, this Jesus had to proclaim peace.

The new constructions of Jesus Christ had some precedence in other, more secular representations. Demythologizing and politicizing middle-class values for a more youthful America could not be more evident in the films in the late 1960s and early 1970s. For the first time in the history of Hollywood, an X-rated film *(Midnight Cowboy)* won an Oscar for best picture of the year (1969). Who could forget the ending of *The Graduate* (1967), in which both characters reject middle-class marriage for a more radical alternative? Or we might remember the savage and shocking picture of the wilderness in *Deliverance* (1972), or the look at corrupt, dirty nostalgia in *McCabe & Mrs. Miller* (1971). Americans favored moody, off-beat performers with an edge. These actors inherited the mantles of Marlon Brando, James Dean, and Montgomery Clift. Thus, Jack Nicholson, Dustin Hoffman, and Robert De Niro brought with them culturally assembled images of what it meant to be an American male: They were not just smoldering like their predecessors, but eruptive and violent toward an unjust society.

The appearance of a rock album about the last days of Jesus' life seems logical in a decade in which just about everything in American society was in the process of being rethought and reinvented. It is well known that in the 1960s, traditional notions of institutionalized religion were unsatisfying to many young people, who began to discover an interest in diverse spiritualities, many of them originating in Eastern philosophies. In a certain sense, the multidimensional, countercultural movements helped to feed the new concepts of Jesus Christ as a guru-passivist. If mind-induced meditations were not enough, the drug culture suggested that a psychedelically induced state could enable anyone to be "born again." Led Zeppelin, The Who, and the Moody Blues, among others, extended that invitation to thousands and thousands of youth. Additionally, the culture at large was becoming more and more enamored of youth status, which had been gaining cultural capital since the 1950s. The cultic status of the energetic playboy (another 1950s invention) flourished throughout the 1960s in the popular James Bond films. New fashion designs emphasized a youthful, less traditional look. Middle-class America had inherited and tamed the legacy of the 1950s Beat Generation.

Yet despite the 1960s "revolution," selling God remained a gamble for the culture industry. Nobody would have guessed that the rock opera produced by Decca Records and released in October 1970 would have been such a smash in the United States. Neither did Tim Rice and Andrew Lloyd Webber, who met each other in 1965 and who collaborated on two other successful musicals, *Joseph and the Amazing Technicolor Dreamcoat,* (1968) and *Evita,* (1976). But the reviews of the album indicated at once that *Jesus Christ Superstar* was special, and that there was an interest in this new Jesus. Indeed, *Superstar* seemed to have everything going for it. One critic compared the new rock opera to Handel's *Messiah,* but also perceived *Superstar* as a more sophisticated version of The Who's *Tommy.* Even seasoned reviewers sensed that there was something very original here. Chris Van Ness wrote in the *Los Angeles Free Press* that "*Jesus Christ Superstar* has to be the greatest pop recording since the first African pounded a drum....It is a synthesis of music that goes as far back as Bach and yet it is as recent as the Rolling Stones...."

Furthermore he raved that it was "potentially the single most important recording since Edison waxed his first cylinder." *Newsweek's* Hubert Saal said the recording was "brilliant."[5] By February 1971, *Superstar* had hit the top position in all three major trade magazines *(Billboard, Record World, and Cashbox)* and made music history by returning to the number one spot in all three magazines twice.[6] Even beyond its huge acceptance in the United States, it was said that Tim Rice wondered how the record became so successful in Catholic countries such as Italy and Brazil. Vatican Radio gave the record glowing reviews and programmed it.

After broadly considering its significant political, cultural, and economic components, some still might wonder today how a rock album about Jesus could have been so successful. In the 1990s, the record is celebrating a twenty-fifth anniversary with re-recordings and enjoys a kind of "retro" popularity. High school and religious groups, dinner theaters and Broadway traveling companies perform *Jesus Christ Superstar* annually.

It is clear that the album's success (and later, the film's) was due to its careful and shrewd placement within the intricate fabric of American culture. Webber and Rice's musical emerged at the crossroads in which popular rock music could exploit new inventions of the Messiah. *Superstar* appeared at a time when the quality of the new was charged with a mystique, even an aura. A year before *Superstar*'s release, America had put a man on the moon. As suggested earlier, the older screen messiahs were at an end. At the end of the 1960s, the case for a complete break with older versions of Jesus became evident. Undoubtedly, part of the appeal of a "superstar" is iconoclastic: the very content of the album has shock appeal. Jesus is portrayed as a human being struggling with a message most people ignored; he is depicted as a whining hippie who was frustrated with the status quo. Like a mournful rock star, Jesus' soulful lamentations in *Superstar* resembled what the "typical" youthful American imagined as his or her own Savior: a figure fed up with authorities, government, and war.

The musical takes pains to situate Jesus within a youthful moment, precisely to capitalize on a disoriented Savior in crisis, a marginalized Messiah trying to discover his identity. Like so many Americans, Jesus the Superstar is weary of domesticated, bourgeois living and is looking for an alternative. Jesus is even weary of being a superstar. The rock opera makes Jesus so utterly legible in the early 1970s because he, like so many Americans, was filled with cultural anxiety and worry about self, society, and even about God.

With ever increasing international fame, fueled by controversy in an age that thrived on crisis, the album was a natural for Broadway and, beyond that, Hollywood. With the musical now even more in the mainstream (there have been at least fifty recorded versions of "I Don't Know How to Love Him"), *Superstar* becomes a fascinating example of an album adapted into a play and then a movie. But this was no ordinary adaptation, as the iconoclastic status of the album already suggests. It bespoke a serious religious ideology and image, now deconstructed and placed into the realm of the popular. Like *Godspell, Jesus Christ Superstar* functioned as a kind of carnival, much like the medieval mystery plays, and even like the Oberammergau Passion Plays.

In fact, the rock opera struggled to find its way to more or less highbrow audiences. Robert Stigwood, a savvy British producer (who, as an independent, had worked with Brian Epstein and the Beatles and had staged *Hair* and *Oh Calcutta!*), wanted to bring *Jesus Christ Superstar* to Broadway by the spring of 1971. But those efforts failed (including a preview on September 27), but the production finally opened on 12 October 1971 at the Mark Hellinger Theater on West 51st Street in New York City, with Tom O'Horgan directing. Although *Superstar* was a hit, a New York stage production still faced the problem of being overly "popular," with small production companies touring in some sixteen countries already by 12 July 1971 (at the Civic Arena in Pittsburgh). While the Broadway production has long since closed, *Jesus Christ Superstar* continues its legacy, recycled and adapted to countless variations today.

It cost $3.5 million to bring the rock opera from Broadway to Hollywood, thereby placing *Superstar* in a tiny sub-subgenre of rock religious musicals. Hollywood has had an interesting relationship with rock music, extending as far back as the mid-1950s with feature films like *The Girl Can't Help It*

(1956), and as evidenced by sound tracks for numerous "teen pics." We dare not fail to remember an entire run of Elvis movies that were spawned as well, beginning in 1957. Norman Jewison, who directed and coproduced the film *Jesus Christ Superstar* together with Robert Stigwood, had recently finished another musical (*Fiddler on the Roof,* 1971), was quick to pick up on the energies and highly original qualities of *Superstar*'s stage production. He also energized the film with the intensity that one often associates with rock cinema, say, for instance, the frenetic movement in *A Hard Day's Night* (1964).

A Rock Gospel. Jewison has not received much credit for a production that was both original and provocative. By casting relatively unknown actors, Jewison also helped to showcase the film as a low-key play-within-a-play, and not as a spectacle. All things considered, it was a daring move. The acting troop subtext worked to the production's advantage, since that kind of youthful, spontaneous group get-together or "happening" is rather evident throughout rock cinema, an energetic pulse that, typically, frustrates the established order. We might think, for example, how much *A Hard Day's Night* relies on the wiry contrast between the brash, lively Beatles and the somewhat stodgy London establishment they upset throughout the course of the film. It is as if the old guard is on slow speed, and the Beatles are a virus out of control, infecting their fans with frantic energy.

Similarly, from the very beginning of *Jesus Christ Superstar,* the film's fast-paced music is associated with a group of late-teenage actors and follows their vibrant (highly choreographed) action throughout the course of the film. Jewison often uses quick cuts and tracking shots to match the music in *Superstar,* especially evident in Judas's first monologue in the desert. Jewison owes a lot of his style here to his previous work in television, as does Richard Lester, who directed *A Hard Day's Night.*

That the old tradition of Jesus films was being revised could not be clearer than in Jesus' relationship with Mary Magdalene. Yvonne Elliman's Mary is sympathetic, tender, and comforting. In her most popular number from the film, Mary puts Jesus to bed and then sings her famous lyrical monologue, "I Don't Know How to Love Him." Jesus is asleep in a tent as the camera beautifully and lovingly tracks Mary's movements and inner longings about her relationship with the Messiah. Their relationship! For the first time the Jesus film states boldly that the Son of God might even have a long, substantial relationship with a woman. Instead of DeMille's Sinner Woman transfixed by the Messiah's gaze, which domesticates and silences, this Earth Mother Magdalene comforts her Superstar Savior. It is clear that even from the point of view of the most elemental aspects of this sequence—the woman speaks while the Savior is silent—we are in a far different cultural frame than we were in the late 1920s. Women now have a voice, a sexuality, and desire and are not punished for these "offenses."

Although commercially the most successful of the musical religious pictures, the ideological effect of *Superstar* on some conservative film audiences was mildly disastrous. The National Jewish Community Relations Advisory Council condemned the movie because it was anti-Semitic. The liberal establishment felt that they had cause to complain, especially about racial issues. Casting Carl Anderson, an African American, as Judas was condemned by many. It remains an interesting contrast with Sidney Poitier's rescue of the falling Jesus on the Way of the Cross as Simon of Cyrene in *The Greatest Story Ever Told,* which today seems patronizing. Yet one would be hard pressed to call Norman Jewison a racist, whose *Soldier's Story* (1984), a decade later, would disclose racial tensions in an army barracks during World War II. Further, *Superstar* is sprinkled with a diverse group of singers and dancers, several of whom are black performers. Jewison is careful to position other black actors as Jesus' apostles close to his side, especially in the Savior's major confrontation with Judas in Gethsemane.

In fact, when viewed in the larger perspective of the film industry in general, the black Judas in *Superstar* is not unlike the whole host of black performers who found themselves as stars of Hollywood feature films in the 1970s. From *Shaft* and *Superfly* to *Sweetback* and even *Blacula,* the film industry attempted to revise old stereotypes of African Americans, while charging them with a contemporary aura. (That 1970s African American "look" is especially true when the dead Judas returns in a white pantsuit and sings a gospel-type revival version of "Jesus Christ Superstar.") The 1970s interest in the black performer was still driven by white constructions of African American stereotypes, but the newly revised image of many minorities, including women, provided them with an active, even angry voice, a way to speak out against long years of repression.

Strangely, *Superstar* has been more or less ignored by critics. In *Biblical Epics as Sacred Narrative in the Hollywood Cinema,* Bruce Babington and Peter William Evans simply name *Superstar* in a list of several controversial films (including *Bonfire of the Vanities*). But the fact remains that *Superstar* was popular and continues to undergo revivals today, either in serious church and theatrical affiliations or as retro-reprises of the 1970s. How can we ignore the popular manifestation of the Savior? Regardless of the controversy surrounding it, *Jesus Christ Superstar* is an important cultural artifact. Thus, *Superstar* has a great deal of material to recommend to our attention and reminds us, once again, of the changing construction of Jesus in Hollywood for a diverse America.

NOTES

1. Lloyd Baugh, *Imaging the Divine*, 33.
2. Ibid., 34.
3. 27 June 1973.
4. Lloyd Baugh, *Imaging the Divine*, 41.
5. Both quotes cited in *Jesus Christ Superstar: A Resurrection*, "Rock Opera: The Making of *Jesus Christ Superstar*," Part 8. Available at: http://www.geocities.com/Broadway/2596. It is interesting to see that the very long production history of *Jesus Christ Superstar* has been recorded in considerable and lengthy detail. But beyond the rock opera itself, the function of the Internet and the "construction" of "Jesus Christ" raise still further, provocative questions about how the Savior has been recycled—now on the computer screen.
6. Ibid.

Photo courtesy of the Academy of Motion Picture Arts & Sciences. Used with permission of Photofest.

SIXTH FEATURE

Jesus of Nazareth **(1977)**

"Open your eyes and your heart."

Directed by: Franco Zeffirelli

Produced by: Vincenzo Labella

Screenplay by: Anthony Burgess, Suso Cecchi d'Amicho, Franco Zeffirelli

Actors Include: Robert Powell (Jesus), Olivia Hussey (Mary, Jesus' mother), Anne Bancroft (Mary Magdalene), Ernest Borgnine (Centurion), Stacy Keach (Barabbas), Rod Steiger (Pilate)

Running Time: 382 minutes

Introduction

It is our assumption that, if you have been viewing these films in conjunction with reading this book, you have seen the preceding films on videocassette, that is, on a videocassette recorder and television set, and not at the movie theater. Keep in mind, however, that all of the movies previously discussed were designed to be projected in a movie theater on a vastly bigger screen with a greater width-to-height ratio. In order to "fit" onto a television screen, some part of the original picture had to be "cut off," that is, edited out. We are not seeing the big picture—literally—when watching these movies via videocassette, nor even the whole picture. We are seeing only a portion of the original shot.

Beyond the sheer size of the picture, there are other compromises or changes of environment that come with the change of medium. The picture resolution of television is, in current technology, greatly inferior to film; television can handle neither subtleties of color nor fine detail as well as film can. Improvements in the video/television technology are visible on the horizon but not widely available in the United States. The intense blue of the southwestern sky and the rich ochre red of the rocks in *King of Kings* become bland and ordinary on the television screen. Color differentiation and gradation suffer as well. Bright reds suffer especially, sometimes looking fuzzy around the edges. Recall that red has often had a very symbolic role in the preceding movies.

The kinds and mix of camera shots used will differ somewhat from film to television as well. Because television's resolution or clarity is not as fine as film's, there will be less emphasis on details in the television shot. Because television's picture size is so much smaller, there may be fewer panoramic landscape shots, fewer vistas of the American Southwest or the deserts of the Middle East as we saw in *King of Kings*. We will see no Roman armies marching into the far distant horizon on television programs. Those massive, stark, dark grey film interiors appear drab and trite on television. The detail is simply lost. Subtle shifts in color will be undetectable. Again, this situation will change when digital television becomes widely available, but, for the moment, television presents a major sacrifice in picture quality.

What we have watched thus far are films "squeezed" onto a television screen. We have lost some of the beautiful and grand images that directors worked hard to design and capture on film. The effect of Jesus' blue eyes as he faces off with John the Baptist in *King of Kings* is diminished when those "orbs" are less than life-size, whereas they had been one thousand times bigger than life in the movie theater! The impact of the opening fresco in *Greatest Story* is diminished, and the stark lighting contrasts in *The Gospel According to Saint Matthew* are softened on the television screen. We have not seen the film as it was intended to be seen by its creators. While you may have liked or disliked these films (the image of Jesus presented, the quality of the acting, the narrative structure, the use of Scripture, etc.), we, the viewers, have lost something in the translation process, that is, in seeing the film on a television screen.

That situation changes with *Jesus of Nazareth,* which was produced for the medium of television, with the (mostly American) television audience in mind. What production adjustments would accompany such a change of medium? What assumptions about the viewer would one need to change? In other words, how is television different than cinema? That is certainly one matter for discussion as one becomes a more observant viewer of the evolving image of Jesus on the silver screen of whatever size.

While you, the viewer, are invited to detect some of these changes as you watch *Jesus of Nazareth,* a few initial suggestions may be in order. First, because there will be fewer dramatic landscape shots, the impact of the setting will likely change. There may be less emphasis on the vastness of the setting, so the impact of the locale on the movement of the narrative will have to change. If the locale is intended to be a vast one, we are more likely to see hints of it than actual panoramic pictures. The long-running show *Dallas* took place in Texas, but instead of prairie vistas, we saw mostly the interiors of the show's luxurious estate setting.

Traditionally, plots revolve around or are motivated by conflict. If there is no conflict, there is no reason for a plot! Three sources of conflict in plots are typically cited: human against human, human against self, and human against nature. To some degree, we have eliminated the third one, which involves locale or setting. So, if locale is gone, what will be left? The emphasis necessarily moves to the interaction of the various characters and the characters' internal motivation. Of course, this is important in films as well, but it becomes more important, more dominant in television. The overall scale of the settings becomes smaller as well. We rarely see characters in designed-for-television programs encountering vast landscapes. Even in nature programs, the emphasis is more on "close-up" matters: reproduction habits of wildebeests, lions killing water buffalo, young antelope frolicking, hummingbirds feeding, and so forth. When humans are involved, although we will certainly see shots of the plains of Africa or the wild rivers of America, we will see more about life in the safari camp, the impact of wild elephants on the local villagers, or the equipment that the adventurers employ to conquer nature.

The change in medium influences the raw-picture quality (size, resolution, color sensitivity, etc.). Picture quality in turn influences the scope of the narrative, the sorts of settings in which the characters are able to interact, and even the plot itself. We will likely see more character interaction than human/landscape interaction. Further, when humans are encountering the landscape, it is often phrased as a human-against-self situation—overcoming danger, fear, or obstacles. With these observations and suggestions in mind, how do you suppose the character of Jesus will be different in *Jesus of Nazareth* than in the previous films? How will television have influenced the telling of the gospel story and the presentation of the person of Jesus? To call upon Marshall McLuhan one more time, how does the medium influence the message?

We can assume that this movie has had a lasting impact on viewers. It was well received at the time of its initial showing and continues to be broadcast, frequently at Christmas and Easter. Assuming that the primary reason commercial television exists is to make money, the movie's continuing rebroadcast is a sign of its continuing popularity among current viewers as well as its ability to attract viewers. It may well have taken the place for television audiences that *The King of Kings* had for over thirty years with cinema audiences, nearly defining (or redefining) who Jesus is for viewers, taking on nearly canonical authority.

Movie Preview: Questions and Suggestions

1. *How are your expectations different when you watch television and then go to the movie theater? List some of them.*

2. *How is the experience of watching television (not videocassettes, but television!) different than watching a film at the theater? What special considerations does broadcast television introduce that do not apply to film? Further, how does watching a television miniseries affect your viewing of the show?*

3. *List some of the differences you have noticed between movies designed for film and those designed for television.*

4. *How many times have you seen* Jesus of Nazareth? *Do you have favorite sections? What are they? Why are they memorable?*

5. *What are your memories or impressions of the late 1970s? What were the national issues, the mood, the hopes of that time?*

Movie Viewing

Movie Review: Questions and Responses

1. *Did you notice any differences in the overall "look" of this movie designed for television as opposed to those intended for viewing in a movie theater?*

2. *What influences do you think the medium of television seemed to have on the story line in this movie? on the character of Jesus?*

3. *Which familiar elements of the gospel narratives have been included and which are absent?*

4. *Describe the image of Jesus in* Jesus of Nazareth. *List elements of his persona, his work, and his mission that seem critical in the movie's portrayal. How does the image compare/contrast to previous images of Jesus?*

LENS ONE

With Franco Zeffirelli's *Jesus of Nazareth,* we find the most developed of the great American Jesus sagas. If for no other reason, the sheer length of the film speaks to Zeffirelli's attempt to provide a comprehensive view of the life and ministry of Jesus. Of course, Zeffirelli could not possibly have included in this movie everything there is to know about Jesus of Nazareth from our literary sources. But his presentation is without question more expansive than that of DeMille, Ray, or Stevens. His attempt to portray the world of ancient Israel and its pressing concerns under the first-century occupation of Rome far exceeds previous investigations into Jesus' activities in Palestine.

With respect to sources, Zeffirelli has superbly managed to weave three complementary strands into a cohesive tale that is attractive to the average American viewer. Included here are investigations into ancient Judaism (a la Stevens), historical details of first-century Palestine (a la Ray), and developing Christian traditions (a la DeMille). In order to combine these elements, Zeffirelli has borrowed freely and frequently from the New Testament Gospels and from the Hebrew Bible (Old Testament). He has included episodes from the scriptural witness, as well as inserted newly constructed scenes as a means by which to "flesh out" that witness. The film offers much for discussion, both with respect to Zeffirelli's use of sources and the image of Jesus that he develops.

Let us ask from the outset, "Why does this movie feel so comfortable to the average Western viewer, at least from the perspective of biblical sources?" The answer to this question is clear: Zeffirelli has offered his audience a Lukan/Matthean Jesus. But what does this mean?

When biblical students delve into the images of Jesus that the New

Testament Gospels present, giving each gospel a fair chance to speak in its own voice, distinctions become apparent. For example, the Gospel of Mark offers a Jesus story that is short and challenging to twentieth-century faith. This gospel contains no depictions of the birth or youth of Jesus, nor are there any resurrection appearances, assuming, of course, the Gospel of Mark's presumed original ending point (16:8). The text contains only five parables and a limited number of sayings. There is no Sermon on the Mount. There is no focus on the importance of the disciples within Jesus' plans nor upon those elements that suggested the divinity of Jesus to early Christian believers. This view from the earliest history of Christianity's origins apparently, however, was seen from within the ancient church as limited and deficient. To read Mark apart from the remaining gospels is to encounter a story of Jesus of Nazareth that omits much of later Christianity's literary heritage. Subsequently, Zeffirelli opts to make little use of those materials exclusive to the Gospel of Mark or that bear a distinctly Markan flavor (see the table of scriptural references).

The Gospel of John, on the other hand, offers an understanding of Jesus that is almost otherworldly (supernatural) in its perspective. According to the author of John, the Word became flesh only after it had served as the agent through which God created the world. Jesus, as the Word, openly performs wondrous "signs" of various types—the healing of sinners, the reversal of laws of nature, the raising of the dead! The message of the good news is less about the coming of God's kingdom and more about who Jesus is in relation to the Father, that is to say, the Son is humanity's way to salvation. This Jesus always appears to be in complete control. Nothing happens in John's story that Jesus has not anticipated or that does not conform to the divine plan for salvation.

The early church was much intrigued by this spiritually oriented view of a divine Jesus, although it continually struggled to harness its understanding of "Jesus as the Word" within the boundaries of its own worldly experience. Zeffirelli too is drawn to this perception of the Christ. As with the modern church, we see that Zeffirelli comes to rely more and more upon the Gospel of John as the film approaches and enters into the passion narrative events. Beyond Mark and John, *Jesus of Nazareth* is dependent primarily upon those gospel texts emphasizing Jesus' message about the coming kingdom of God and the responsibilities of the church within that kingdom.

Most importantly, Zeffirelli desperately wants to identify Jesus with that understanding of the coming messiah that the ancient prophets of Israel had anticipated. These three elements (kingdom of God, church foundation, and predicted messiah) are particularly evident in the Gospel of Matthew and, even more so, in the Gospel of Luke. Indeed, it is within these gospels that Zeffirelli spends the majority of his time. It is also here that the modern, mainline Christian in Western society tends to be the most comfortable. Several characteristics of this peculiarly Lukan/Matthean vision of Jesus warrant further discussion.

At the outset of the film we are engaged in the "birth narratives" of Jesus, the traditional beginning of the saga, at least as viewed from modern eyes. On the one hand, Luke provides the concerns of the Virgin Mary about the forthcoming birth of Jesus. At the same time, Mary shares in the joy of the barren Elizabeth over the impending birth of John "the Baptist." As a complement to this Lukan scenario, Matthew includes the story of Joseph and his stressful decision about whether to "divorce her quietly" (1:19). Luke then speaks of the taxation that leads Joseph and Mary to travel to Bethlehem, and includes in this presentation the adoration of the baby Jesus by the shepherds. Matthew speaks of the visit by "wise men" to that place where the guiding star has led them, and adds information about the slaughter of Bethlehem's children by Herod, which forces Joseph and Mary to travel to Egypt. Notice that none of these elements is mentioned by Mark or John. They are unique to the Lukan/Matthean accounts. Zeffirelli, like so many modern Christians, blends all of them together into a single, homogeneous story.

While such episodes are evident from the beginning of the film, there are yet more subtle ways in which the Lukan/Matthean perspective permeates Zeffirelli's vision. Notice, for example, that Jesus is continually concerned for the poor and the outcast, for prostitutes and tax collectors, for the sick and the disadvantaged, and for the rightful place of women in society. While such considerations receive passing notice throughout all of the New Testament Gospels, it is specifically in Luke that they find their greatest focus and expression. Clearly, Zeffirelli's Jesus is a Lukan Jesus. He is concerned for those whom society and religious tradition have rejected as undesirable or impure. He debates with scribes and Pharisees in order to influence the daily affairs of the religious authorities themselves. In a very Lukan sense, Jesus journeys with a distinct goal in mind: "it is necessary" (a typically Lukan phrase) for him to go to Jerusalem, that place where the prophets of God (and he himself) ultimately meet death. Here, then, are three prominent threads in the broader Lukan tapestry.

At the same time, Zeffirelli's Jesus also has a Matthean flavor. Throughout the film we hear references to the fact that Jesus is the fulfillment of the words of Israel's ancient prophets. There are continual allusions to Old Testament passages that speak of a coming savior of Israel who will suffer for the people of Israel and lead them to salvation. This is quite typical of Matthew's view of Jesus, that is, a view of prophecy and fulfillment. Included here are materials from the Psalms, Isaiah, Micah, Malachi, Zechariah, Jeremiah, Hosea, Amos, and Jonah. But these scriptural witnesses about God's Messiah are not applied to Jesus by the characters (and narrator) of the film alone. It is often Jesus himself who preaches these passages in reference to himself to whomever will listen. And how Jesus speaks! He talks constantly, offering sayings and parables, telling illustrative stories about the kingdom of God, and intervening in the daily lives of those around him. He is a very verbal Jesus, that is to say, a very Matthean Jesus.

It is evident then that Zeffirelli focuses on a Lukan/Matthean Jesus who is a very familiar and comfortable figure for the modern American Christian. This is the Jesus that modern pulpits portray on a regular basis—a preacher and teacher, a man who is human like us yet distinctly unlike us in his vision of God, a miracle worker who deeply cares for society's outcasts, an active intercessor between common humanity and the authorities of the religious tradition, the fulfillment of ancient prophecy, God's Messiah who possesses an almost mystical charismatic power and can freely forgive the sins of sinners. We have seen where he is from; we anticipate where he is going. This is the Christ who speaks words we have come to expect and who does supernatural acts in a very natural world. This is the Christ who possesses a sure vision of his task. This is the Jesus who bids, "Come, follow me."

In his effort to bring this image of Jesus to the screen, Zeffirelli leans upon several specific background supports. As suggested above, three of these props deserve review: a Jewish world; a historical emphasis; and a background of traditional Christian vision. We examine each of these supports in turn.

A Jewish World. We have already found a significant development of perspective about the Jewish world when we moved from the work of DeMille to that of Stevens. It is a movement from a blatantly caricatured picture of Judaism to a dependence upon selected Jewish Scriptures as the foundation for first-century Christian expectations. As an attempt to engage Judaism and its sources, this movement marks a milestone within the development of Jesus saga films. Yet, the transition does not provide a complete understanding of Judaism. While Stevens does look to Jewish Scripture, he has overlooked important Jewish traditions and customs. This is to say, Stevens correctly observed that it was expedient to seek out the literary basis of early Christian beliefs about Jesus as God's Messiah, but he has neglected the context out of which that literature came and in which it was used.

This development of consciousness concerning early Judaism, however, provides an avenue for the intentions of Zeffirelli. In *Jesus of Nazareth,* Zeffirelli incorporates, on the one hand, the literature of ancient Israel (the Old Testament) as well as the contexts for the usage of that literature within first-century Judaism. We often see Mary and Joseph or Jesus and the disciples at worship within the synagogue. We witness the rituals of the betrothal and then of the wedding between Mary and Joseph. We are present at the rite of circumcision both for John and for Jesus. We see the Bar Mitzvah of Jesus as he comes of age. We find the conception of John to have occurred during the Jewish month of Tishri, use of the shofar horn to call Jews to worship at the Temple, and refusal of the Jewish leaders to enter Pilate's residence during a religious festival (see John 18:28). Constantly we hear the ruminations of rabbis and priests about the Torah and its implications for daily living. The best example here, perhaps, is the instruction that Joseph receives concerning the requirements of the Torah with respect to a betrothed woman who has lain with another man (death is required; Dt. 6:24–26). This story is replete with the important trappings of Judaism and the background of Jewish settings. By incorporating all of this, Zeffirelli has advanced the context for his Jesus saga significantly.

Perhaps Zeffirelli's single misstep in this process is the very way in which he has read Judaism. He has read Judaism as a Christian! His view of Judaism is decidedly Christian in tone and orientation—perhaps a happy circumstance for modern Christians, though certainly not for Jews. This is nowhere more evident than in the words of Nicodemus, who, late in the film, offers these words: "The coming of the Messiah is the heart of our faith. Why should he not come now?" This is a decidedly Christian sentiment ("Christian" meaning "Christ seeker").

While such a perspective may have been true for those persons within first-century Judaism who were seeking the Messiah according to their reading of the prophecies of Isaiah, it was decidedly not true for Judaism in its other forms. Indeed, the scribes and Pharisees observe that the first commandment is "...the Lord is one....love the Lord your God with all your heart...." (Dt 6:4–5), to which Jesus adds "...you shall love your neighbor as yourself..." (Lv 19:18). Unquestionably, it was to this theme that first-century Judaism most commonly appealed, not to a search for an anticipated messiah. Zeffirelli himself pays subtle homage to this fact, since he chooses to use this text from Deuteronomy on four separate occasions in the film.

Zeffirelli's work is certainly more "Jewish" in tone, more aware of Jewish matters, than previous motion picture attempts to portray the life of Jesus. Yet the viewer should not remain ignorant of the fact that it is also markedly Christian in its Jewish perspective, a feature that shades the way in which the director appeals to Jewish Scriptures and traditions.

Historical Emphasis. Unlike the films of Ray and Stevens, Zeffirelli does not rely specifically upon the historical witness of the ancient Jewish historian Josephus. There is no entry of Pompey into the Temple precinct; there is no destruction of the Roman eagle standards by the Jewish mobs; there is no mass crucifixion of the Jews along the roads of Judea. Yet, there is a definite sense that Zeffirelli is interested in a high degree of historical authenticity.

The very nature of settings and clothing is, if perhaps slightly stylized, certainly reminiscent of first-century Palestine. The hills have the familiar

Palestinian look, mostly barren, sparsely covered with olive trees and clustered, whitewashed villages. The people have the poise of a society that spends much of its time outdoors: they are constantly outdoors at work and play. Society is baldly segregated between the sexes: the women worship at synagogue in a separate area from the men; men are present at the circumcision events while women remain on the periphery. Zeffirelli's props all seem to be in place.

But, despite these obvious visual features, Zeffirelli is occasionally at pains to smoothly provide his audience with important historical information of which the average viewer might be unaware. The narrative itself does not always provide occasion for the seamless integration of this context-setting information. The director resorts to asides and virtual "post-it" notes stuck onto the fabric of the movie in order to provide needed data. For example, Herod the Great and his Roman superiors engage in a brief discussion about the customs and beliefs of Judaism, including the Jewish desire for a messiah from God to save them (as predicted by the prophets of old). The three kings who search for the infant Jesus share a conversation about the significance of such an event, and come to an agreement among themselves about the signs that have anticipated this moment. The application of particular Jewish laws to specific daily circumstances is meticulously explained, first by the rabbi in Nazareth, then by the scribes and Pharisees throughout Palestine, and finally within the council of the Sanhedrin in Jerusalem. This sort of approach to solving plot inadequacies is typical of television sitcoms but seems a bit obvious and out of place in such a major enterprise, especially given its six-hour length.

Nevertheless, Zeffirelli has taken care to make his setting and sources speak to his audience. He does not assume that the modern viewer is knowledgeable about first-century Jewish customs and beliefs. There is a concerted, if sometimes strained, effort to make the events of the Jesus story both natural and reasonable, both Jewish and historical.

Traditional Christian Visions. From the time of DeMille we have observed that the telling of the Jesus saga has been permeated with the rise of later Christian traditions and interpretations of the story not directly supported by the biblical witness. To some extent this is only natural and inevitable. This situation is a product of two basic facts: the human mind seeks to include as much information as possible from different sources and blend them into a single unified picture; where there are gaps in the telling of a story, required details (often speculative) become incorporated. This is how memory works. Memory, both individual and corporate, is fluid, imaginative, and constructive.

The mother of Jesus is a good example to start with. Here is an actress who bears all of the marks of the traditional Christian view of Mary. She is young and, hence, likely to fit the traditional interpretation of the prophet Isaiah about the mother of the Messiah, a virgin. She remains youthful in appearance even at the end of the film! She is often dressed in blue, the traditional garb of the Virgin Mary as depicted in later Christian art. She is passive, in complete acceptance of the special nature of her son. She acts as an intermediary between Jesus and those who seek him. She is, in a phrase, the ultimate disciple. Of course, from the biblical material we have no evidence for any of this except for what is provided in the perspective of Luke 1 and 2. The true nature of Mary, at least from the historical materials, is almost completely lost to us.

Even less is known about Joseph. We encounter Joseph as a carpenter, a responsible worker who is surrounded by children (his own by a previous marriage?), whom he teaches and guides in a fatherly way. He comes to accept the child Jesus as his own (presumably) legal son. He dies in a passionate scene that seemingly prefigures the eventual death of Jesus himself (see the table of scriptural references). But what we really know about the historical Joseph amounts to precious little. He probably was some kind of laborer; that is the sum total of our information about Joseph. The biblical text refers to brothers and sisters of Jesus, but the tradition—in its quest to keep the nature of Jesus distinct from all other people—has often referred to these persons as "half siblings" or "cousins," which Zeffirelli suggests in a subtle manner here. Of course, after the beginning of the Gospel of Matthew, we hear absolutely nothing further about Joseph, his life and work, or his eventual death. All such speculation comes from tradition alone.

To these opening traditional views about Mary and Joseph we can quickly add other examples. There are *three* kings in search of the baby Jesus (two named Melchior and Balthasar, one of whom is African), but this is purely tradition based upon the presentation of three gifts and the fertile imagination of the ages. The woman who provides a stable to Mary and Joseph in Bethlehem is named Abigail, but of course, no woman is even mentioned in the scriptural record of the episode, which is found only in the Gospel of Luke. Peter is married (see Mk 1:29–31 regarding Peter's mother-in-law), but he must choose to leave his wife and children in order to follow Jesus. Mary Magdalene is a prostitute, but Scripture nowhere endorses this idea. A woman wipes the face of Jesus as he carries his cross to Golgotha, this in support of one of the "stations of the cross" that line the Via Dolorosa in Jerusalem today but which has no specific biblical referent. Finally, we discover that it is John, son of Zebedee, who stands as the "beloved disciple" at the foot of the cross with Jesus' mother Mary. While this, of course, has a strong tradition within Christianity, it does not have the specific endorsement of Scripture.

It seems important for Zeffirelli to tap into both traditional interpretations and modern perceptions of the biblical sources. And he does so successfully. He is careful to respect the opinions of a broad variety of Christian denominations, and offers characters who do nothing to challenge the cherished beliefs and assumptions of the ecumenical twentieth-century Christian church.

In summary, then, we find some basic ideas about sources at work in this film. Zeffirelli attends to Jewish concerns but in a very Christian way. He is historical in a generally informed sense. He is traditional in the acceptable norms of Christian iconography. Perhaps what is most unsettling about his presentation of the historical literature is that so much of what disturbs us within the gospel texts has been omitted from this attempt to provide a complete Jesus saga. As with the Jesus who appears in the Gospel of John, Zeffirelli's Jesus is in complete control. The movement of the plot often appears to be a progression from one misunderstanding to another about just exactly who Jesus is, from Peter to Matthew, from Judas to Barabbas. Yet, all of this is presented as God's will, as Jesus hastens toward the ultimate goal of death and resurrection. Jesus recognizes this divine will while all others remain blind.

Notably absent here is any hint of a future coming of the Son of man upon clouds of glory (see Mt 25 and its parallels). Zeffirelli's Jesus (much like that of Ray and Stevens) is truly concerned for the present coming of the kingdom of God. While this view is likely comfortable for the majority of modern Christians, it omits an entire perspective within the New Testament Gospels about the coming of God's *future* kingdom. Indeed, we need find no tension between the present kingdom and the future kingdom of God, as is suggested throughout early Christian literature.

Also absent here is the basic daily humanity of Jesus. True, the gospel records provide little of this. But we assume that the gospels are a carefully honed selection of stories and teachings, whereas Zeffirelli has specifically endeavored to give his audience an authentically Jewish and historical context of events. The tone of the film (like the gospels) is heavy. Jesus is nothing but serious, with little hint of the enjoyment of life and the value deriving from casual human relationships. This Jesus most certainly is not the Jesus whom we find, for example, in Jewison's *Superstar.* It is a single-and-narrow-visioned Jesus, unencumbered by questions or even curiosity about his nature and purpose. We may well ask, is it an image of Jesus that serves to address the demanding and difficult questions of our times?

LENS TWO

Given the length of this film, it would seem that there should be a great deal to say about its use of the audiovisual toolbox to produce its image of Jesus. But the very nature of television imposes certain limits and constraints on what one can do. The matter of differences between cinema and television has already been raised in the introduction of this chapter. Generally, there are more close-ups and fewer panoramas. This necessarily limits the scope or scale of the movie, making television a more intimate medium than cinema, made even more so by the fact that we usually are watching television in our living or family rooms. The very names of those spaces connote greater intimacy, even if it is not actually the case. There is typically less large-scale action on television. Any action that takes place happens on a smaller scale, in tighter surroundings, for example, the many "cop" shows that involve people running after criminals rather than entire armies engaging one another in pitched battle.

Big-screen thinking does not work on a little screen, even as that little screen has gotten bigger. Although as television screens have gotten larger, resolution has not increased. With high-definition television on the horizon, many of these generalizations will become obsolete. In this movie, note that we more often see people inside buildings than in the middle of vast deserts. There are no legions of Roman soldiers marching about. When there are "longer," more panoramic shots, they typically move quickly to zoom in or cut to a "closer" shot, rather than the reverse, from close-up to long panorama. The long shot simply and quickly provides a sense of the setting; it is not where the action takes place. A good example is the opening sequence in this movie. We start with views of a village but quickly cut to the interior of a synagogue where the initial action takes place. Much of the action of this movie takes place in con-fined spaces: houses, courtyards, synagogues. The final scene of the movie is not the apse of a large church, nor a beach scene. Instead we see the postresur-rection Jesus talking with the disciples, followed by a shot of the empty tomb over which the credits are then rolled. Smaller-scale shots predominate in this movie because it is for television. The symbolic image of Jesus, however, is made proportionately smaller as well.

With current television technology, colors are reproduced poorly on tel-evision screens in comparison with cinema, resulting in duller colors and less differentiation of, for example, shades of red or blue. *Jesus of Nazareth* almost has a "monochromatic" look compared to the more colorful *King of Kings,* for example.

Nevertheless, Jesus' blue eyes are an important feature of this movie, as in the earlier films *King of Kings* and *The Greatest Story Ever Told.* At one point in the early stages of this book, we thought of subtitling it "The Blue-Eyed Boy of Bethlehem," so prominent is this feature in several of the Jesus portrayals. In *Jesus of Nazareth* we first encounter "the eyes" during Jesus' reading of Scripture when he is still a boy. Thereafter, the viewer is fre-quently provided with interminable close-ups of the young Jesus' ice-blue eyes gazing precociously and knowingly at whomever he encounters. The eyes appear again when Jesus meets his cousin, John the Baptist, just prior to Jesus' request to be baptized. From this point on there are countless shots of Jesus' face as he coolly encounters either his friends or enemies, typically with his face centered on the screen looking out at us or just to the left or right. The faces of the other characters are not always centered; they have space on the screen to look into. This is sometimes ungraciously referred to as "nose room."

As was noted above, Jesus frequently speaks in this movie; that also suggests by implication that there is little action. This leaves the director with an important question: if there is no action, what is left to portray? The answer is *relationship,* something television can do well, showing close-ups of faces, milking dialogue for all it is worth, switching back and forth between characters' faces, when, on film, most likely both characters would have been present in the same shot. The use of the camera forces our attention on the individual characters and their relationships with one another. We first encounter Mary, not through dialogue in this case, but with a close-up of a warp on a loom with Mary's face veiled behind the many homespun threads forming the warp. Much is communicated with this simple scene of private domestic activity. We rarely see more than two or three people in a scene talking with one another. Our eye is freer to wander both in stage performances and in large-screen cinema. However, relationship and characterization become the twin engines that drive this television film. We see it play out mostly in shots of faces, revealing the characters' reactions to what is happening in the scene.

Of particular importance is the characterization of Jesus. Some interesting choices were made here. Surely, Powell looks like the current operative image of Jesus. But it seems that his aristocratic British accent is quite out of place for a peasant figure. Given that actors often assume accents other than their own natural manner of speaking, why did Powell assume this "voice"? It seems rather "upper-crust" for a Jewish peasant. The question comes, how is Jesus being portrayed in *Jesus of Nazareth*? What are his qualities and characteristics? He seems, as already suggested by the ice-blue color of his eyes, to be a rather "cool" and mildly remote figure, stereotypically British. We can only speculate how the portrayal would "feel" if the actor had assumed a Cockney accent instead. Or a Jewish accent. There is here little of the fire of Pasolini's rendition, little of the rebellious streak of Ray's Jesus, little of the fatherly warmth of Jesus in DeMille's *The King of Kings*.

Editing in television poses a peculiar problem for screenwriters, editors, and directors that cinema does not have to deal with, at least not in the movie-theater forum. That problem is commercials. Television requires plotting and scripting a show to allow for a string of commercials to be inserted at least a couple of times within every half hour. This results in a rather predictable and episodic rhythm of scenes. Immediately before a commercial break it is wise to end with unresolved action or a measure of suspense so that the viewer stays tuned to the channel. At the same time there needs to be a resolution when the commercials are over and the movie begins again. Several times every hour this must happen. In addition, ideally nothing too gruesome should happen just before the commercials so that viewers are not too upset to think about the products being advertised. This amounts to a complex set of demands on any screenwriter.

In *Jesus of Nazareth,* when the picture fades to black, we can feel a sequence of commercials waiting in the wings, so indoctrinated are we into the rhythms of television. Relatedly, since this was initially a miniseries, the writer had to allow for a stopping point that both brought some resolution or closure at the end of each segment but also left some suspense to bring the viewer back the following week or following evening for the next installment. Interestingly, of course, we already know how this film is going to end. There is no suspense or uncertainty about that, even the first time we watch it.

Also, as a matter of scripting and editing, there seems to be a regular rhythm of scenes in *Jesus of Nazareth* that are set in dark interiors alternating with more evenly and brightly lit exteriors, and then back to dark interiors with light beaming through windows or coming from the flames of torches. The shadows created by these sources of light in the interiors create some visual interest and provide occasions to spotlight certain actions and characters. Back and forth the scenes go, light to dark and back to light.

One additional function of editing is the need to create a pace, either fast or slow, for a film. In the case of *Jesus of Nazareth,* the pace seems to be deliberately slow. For example, the many, many gazes that the characters exchange seem to be overly drawn out. Some of our sensitivity to this may be due to our frequent viewing of these films. But it must be said that this is surely an intentional factor in the creation of a film, that is, its basic pace. As viewers who are not always aware of the devices of the visual vocabulary and as first-time viewers, we may not always be aware of the use of the audiovisual vocabulary, but it is present nevertheless.

Sound or audio is another tool available to the director. In *The King of Kings,* for example, even though it was a "silent" movie, the soundtrack played an important role with its use of familiar hymns. Music also played an interesting role in Pasolini's *The Gospel According to Saint Matthew,* with its interesting mix of black spirituals and Russian choirs. Audio seems to play a rather minor role, however, in *Jesus of Nazareth.* Certainly we need to hear the steady diet of dialogue and pronouncements from the main characters. But the audio simply does not stand out. This is not necessarily a criticism.

Sometimes "standing out" is not desirable. Perhaps this situation exists in part because the speakers on the television sets of the 1970s were small and of remarkably poor quality. Now, of course, much has changed with the advent of better audio tracks, even stereo, on broadcast television, not to mention on videocassettes. The equipment, necessarily, has also improved in order to take advantage of the improved soundtracks. The music of *Jesus of Nazareth* serves to set mood, but in a low-key fashion. Were this movie made today, the audio qualities might likely have a much more lively role to play. We have become used to "big" sound, even on television. Let those subwoofers vibrate the rafters!

Jesus of Nazareth has been influenced by the very medium used to tell the story. While a superficial watching might not detect major differences between this and other cinema portrayals, the medium itself has influenced the telling. Both what is pictured and how it is pictured have been dictated to an important degree by the nature of the medium. Even the settings themselves are shaped by use of the small screen. Finally, the scope or scale of the story or narrative has been "downsized" because of the nature of television. The medium affects the message and the shape of the content it seeks to communicate.

LENS THREE

Pilate asks Jesus, "What is truth?" By now, the reader/viewer should have suspected that portraying the absolute or "gospel" truth about Jesus by means of cinema is not possible. There is the matter of scriptural interpretation, then the challenge of creating the person of Jesus by means of the cinematic vocabulary. Further, we know that those very images or representations become even more difficult to decode when technology, ideology, and culture continue to create an *aura* of authenticity or realism on that image as "true" rather than as an interpretation. "Jesus of Nazareth" has become a cultural icon. "Deconstructing" contemporary iconography in popular culture can be a daunting task. We are still rather close to the ideology that made Franco Zeffirelli's multimillion-dollar production, *Jesus of Nazareth,* so wonderfully admired. Echoing a host of Christian and secular journals, Roy Kinnard and Tim Davis, in *Divine Images: History of Jesus on the Screen,* conclude that Franco Zeffirelli's *Jesus of Nazareth* is the "finest adaptation of Jesus' life ever made."[1] The high ratings that *Jesus of Nazareth* continues to receive certainly suggest that the popular imagination took this representation of Jesus very personally and seriously. This longest, most beautifully and elaborately produced life of the Lord is still clearly important and influential. But, again, what is truth?

We look first at the elements in popular culture that contributed to *Jesus of Nazareth*'s success, and then consider the overall narrative strategy. Additionally, we consider briefly the place that *Jesus of Nazareth* holds as a miniseries, as a pricey picture book, a recycled holiday celebration on television, and, finally, a production subsequently transferred to videotape.

Popular Culture. A multinational, collaborative production between

Britain and Italy, *Jesus of Nazareth* was made for NBC television and broadcast during the Easter season in April 1977 in two parts (a little over six and a half hours). Since then, the program has also been reedited into several configurations. The script is cowritten by the very literary Anthony Burgess, who wrote one of the most controversial novels of its day, *A Clockwork Orange.* Finally, *Jesus of Nazareth* was directed by an Italian known for his opulent, theatrical style, and who began as an actor on the stage with Luchino Visconti, and then became that filmmaker's assistant before moving on to make a career as a costume and set designer and director of operas. His films have run the gamut from *Romeo and Juliet* (1968) and *Hamlet* (1990) to *Endless Love* (1981).

It is hard to imagine that *Jesus Christ Superstar* and *Jesus of Nazareth* could have been made within five years of each other, still less that both depictions of Jesus seemed credible and interesting to spectators at the time. That divergent representation suggests, once again, the culturally inflected status of the face of Jesus. This range of options was characteristic of America in the 1970s. In the most general terms, the radicalization of America in the 1960s was made possible by an increasingly unpopular war. After South Vietnam fell to the Communists in 1975, the country moved into a period now notable for its swing toward conservatism and even a movement away from political action.

With the war at an end, now the journey of America in the mid-to-late 1970s into the 1980s became a process of rewriting the past—deradicalizing, and, to some extent, dehistoricizing. Watergate gave the average American yet another reason to despise politics. In addition to its postwar disgust with foreign entanglements, growing economic concerns, together with domestic debates on affirmative action (in 1978 the Supreme Court upheld *Bakke v. University of California*) and the nuclear accident at Three Mile Island, America kept its attention—and its soldiers—at home. To this more domestic and apathetic America, subcultures like the "punk rock" phenomenon, with its outrageous behavior and dissonant, brash music, functioned as countercultural nostalgia, a la the 1960s.

Related to a decline in political activism was the rise in evangelical, even "muscular," Christianity. Although Jimmy Carter was elected as a moderately liberal democrat, he was also a born-again Christian. By 1979, Reverend Jerry

Falwell would establish the "Moral Majority." The current interest in "spiritual-ity" is, to some extent, a legacy of the 1960s, with its ashrams, incense, and mantras. Certainly, the rise in fundamentalism suggests not only a depoliti-cized national agenda, but a dehistoricized one as well. The 1960s interest in Eastern forms of spirituality, meditation, and doctrines of self-awareness played an important role in transforming the late 1970s into what we now call "New Age," an amorphous, somewhat gnostic movement. New Age, with its extraordinary range of associations, appears concretely to emerge out of the 1960s and, like so many of the cultural progeny of that decade, to have extended well beyond its radicalized borders.

It is not surprising, therefore, that American film culture in the late 1970s and into the 1980s has been labeled "escapist." With the turn toward independent films in the late 1960s and early 1970s, it appeared as if Holly-wood was reinstating the "social problem" film, a genre common after World War II. Even television was beginning to approach social problems in a more daring way by the late 1960s. For example, in 1968 *Star Trek* aired an episode showing an interracial kiss. *All in the Family* (1971–79, CBS) sati-rized Archie Bunker, a lovable, blue-collar bigot. On the other hand, Holly-wood's overall tendency during the period just before the Reagan administration was to replace the troubling human interest story, which often focused on a difficult individual or relationship (i.e., *Klute,* 1971 or *Five Easy Pieces,* 1970), with a fairy tale formula or mythic spectacle, usually based on an empire lost and then found.

Narrative Strategy. A seminal moment occurred in American film culture with the release of *Star Wars* (1977), which was written by George Lucas. He derived his story, about a young man's quest for enlightenment and the search for his father through the trials and sufferings of experience, from Joseph Campbell's popular study of mythology. Campbell, an aca-demic trained in comparative literature, transformed globalized mythology into self-help, self-discovery tools for moderns. He published a series of essays in *Myths to Live By* that applied stories found in antiquity to the day-to-day developmental journey of contemporary men and women.[2] Lucas fashioned his protagonist, Luke Skywalker, out of Campbell's paradigm of the hero's journey of testing and sacrifice for a nearly mystical goal. Under these auspices, the hero must overcome certain obstacles in order to follow his bliss. Campbell himself became a celebrity when PBS broadcast a series of interviews on *The Power of Myth* with journalist Bill Moyers, taped at George Lucas's home during the early 1980s.

Variations of the Campbell/Lucas formula have been used for narrative plots for millennia, but now, after the defeat in Vietnam and the shame of Watergate, Hollywood was interested in rediscovering more than ever before the mythological imagination of defeat and rebirth. In words from *Rambo:* "Do we get to win this time?"

Released at the end of 1978, *Superman* became the top grossing movie in 1979. The nostalgic look at the 1950s in *Grease* and the quasi-sci-fi movie *Close Encounters of the Third Kind* were the top-grossing films in 1978, and suggested to the film industry that year just how little social problems, or even history itself, had to play in contemporary film culture. American popular culture seemed interested mostly in repressing history for the sake of a kind of cultural recovery narrative, or the projection of an idealized, utopic space. The playing out of one's destiny in late-1970s America became precisely the abandonment of history to the journey inward toward self-actualization. Roy Neary's intuitions about the extraterrestrial in *Close Encounters* gifted him with spiritual friends and magical insight into other worlds. So too, in *The Hero with a Thousand Faces*, Campbell says that "The hero, therefore, is the man or woman who has been able to battle past his [or her] personal and local historical limitations to the generally valid, normally human forms."[3]

Ultimately, we might say that the turn toward mythic structures and the repression of history allowed for a commercial exploitation of America's loss in Vietnam based on denial. In terms of film culture, then, the technical advances of the blockbuster apparatus were destined for a mythical plot. With the inclusion of special effects, colorful tie-ins, and endless replays by young teenagers, such megahits would set the blueprint for the future. Rerun again and again, first as features and then as videos, the mythic plot promised endless returns.

"America has a rendezvous with destiny," said Ronald Reagan, and that refrain was echoed in thousands of different ways, even in representations of the Savior on the big silver screen—or, for that matter, the tiny screen. Although the picture was produced abroad, *Jesus of Nazareth* was very successful in the United States because of the film's position in the late 1970s, a time when America was rediscovering religion, the voyage of self-discovery, and winning through denial. Mythic spectacle, translated through the newly emerging miniseries, advanced the process of naturalization, as it did for so much of American film culture after the Vietnam War. When seen in the light of a post-1960s, inner-directed, therapeutic American culture, the myth of the hero becomes attractive, even seductive, and extremely powerful. When *Star Wars* appeared on thousands of movie screens across America, many could not help but note the religious and liturgical parallel in the now famous phrase, "the Force be with you." *Star Wars* borrows religious language to convince us of its sincerity; *Jesus of Nazareth* deploys mythological signification to guarantee authenticity to a pluralistic audience.

By using a highly effective, cultural mythology, the television production of Jesus' life did not need special effects: it had 6½ hours and Zeffirelli's artistic sense. He assembled the footage like a montage of fine Italian masters. Much was made of Jesus, a hero with one of a thousand faces. What matters for Campbell might also be said for Zeffirelli, not that the gospels have their roots in a historical faith community and witness, but that those texts have produced another variation of the heroic myth. As Campbell told Moyers in his PBS interview, "I don't have to have faith. I have experience...when you are awakened at the level of the heart to compassion and suffering with the other person, that is the beginning of humanity." We are not claiming that Zeffirelli followed Campbell's paradigm, but clearly the direction of popular narrative in American culture was moving toward an ahistorical, mythic paradigm with which *Jesus of Nazareth* shares certain features.

Like several other films in the period it would anticipate, *Jesus of Nazareth* takes a decidedly mythic approach to narrative, in which the journey/quest motif and Judeo-Christian history are easily entwined. Zeffirelli makes it clear throughout the film that his Messiah has probed "infinite space" and has, as it were, a "rendezvous with destiny." It might even be said that, after the (nonbiblical) death of Joseph in *Jesus of Nazareth,* the rest of the narrative takes Jesus on a quest for his father, much like Luke Skywalker.

In the end, Zeffirelli's Jesus finds his Father, even as he faces the actualization of his own powers as well as his suffering and death. In the curious alchemy between the revealed tradition and the mythology of the journey, the hard edge of history and the Gospel is blunted, indeed naturalized into something beautiful and tasteful. *Jesus of Nazareth* portrays a hero for middle-class America—in love with his own destiny.

Dehistoricizing the Gospel. How does the mythology discourse play itself out in *Jesus of Nazareth?* A case in point is the annunciation. In *Divine Images,* Roy Kinnard and Tim Davis say, for example, that the annunciation sequence of the Virgin birth (mistakenly identified as the immaculate conception) shows Zeffirelli's thoughtful approach and conveys "an intense spiritual quality too often absent from other films of this type."[4] Perhaps. We are not questioning the dramatic or artistic quality of the sequence, but the unreflective deployment of the word *spiritual* by its critics and its displacement of historical and even textual knowledge. Zeffirelli shows Mary's annunciation as a silent encounter with shadows and mystical light in the moonlight.[5] This aspect of spiritual awakening by light in a room is probably what reviewers typically refer to as "good taste." Mary looks out the window at a beam of light while her mother looks on; the young girl says, in words familiar to us, "How can that be? No man has ever touched me....I am the handmaid of the Lord, be it done to me according to your Word." Mary then prophetically tells her mother that Elizabeth is going to have a son and that she must visit her. Like a Renaissance painting, perfectly balanced in its perspective and source of light, Zeffirelli (in the long tradition of the *vivant tableaux*) has managed to bathe the announcement of Jesus' birth in an aura of respectability, what some call "restraint."

If the scene is supposed to be portraying the annunciation, however, then we might expect that the sequence would begin to suggest God's very abrupt and inconvenient entry into our world, the fulfillment of a historical promise, the embarrassing appearance of an angel. Mary's response to that unique invitation to be the mother of God is the Magnificat, which itself is a hymn that gathers and celebrates salvation history—a messy history in the harsh light of day. The gospel reckons the annunciation as a Jewish hymn to the Father and a rapture over the chosen people of Israel. But the film sequence is far from fair to Jewish history, and Mary, with her fair skin and delicate Anglo features, is hardly a Jewish peasant girl.

Although the issue in the incarnation is at its core a historical event, what we have in this allegedly "spiritual" representation of the annunciation is a very beautiful, quiet, white English woman engaged in a psychodrama overseen by her worried mother. If we were not familiar with the source text, would the scene suggest a faith narrative written by a small group of Jewish followers of the Jesus event? From the point of view of physical representation, dialogue, and action, the annunciation sequence could have been about anything from a 1960s visionary to a religious hysteric. It is disarming how non-Semitic Mary appears. This representation should not surprise us, however. Zeffirelli's composition recalls the visual tradition in humanist painting representative of the gospel in the West, together with a rather seamless appropriation of contemporary notions of spirituality.

Consider again the conversation of the three astrologers, after they meet together, as if arranged by providence, by the guidance of a cosmological sign:

> CASPAR:...as Balthazar has said, I follow that star, wherever it leads.
> BALTHAZAR: But what will we find? All my calculations show that there was to be a new heavenly creature, a new star. It was even precise as to place and time. So I made up my mind to set forth to see what they would hold.
> MELCHIOR: You did not know?
> BALTHAZAR: Only that it would be something wonderful. The stars are not distant and aloof, cut off from the lives of men. The rising of a new star shows an immense labor in the heavens which always has its counterpart on earth. The Universe is about to bring forth a protégé beyond our understanding.
> MELCHIOR: Your star, my brother Balthazar, is indeed a sign of wonder. The divine Zoroaster says the next prophet will show himself in a foreign land. And the truth he will reveal will be at first only for his own people.
> CASPAR: But there is only one truth.

> MELCHIOR: And there is only one God; all the rest are vain or
> parts of him.
> CASPAR: The people of Israel know this. Many of his wise men
> have been close to him. And their writings confirm my calcula-
> tions. A king is about to be born.
> BALTHAZAR: A king?
> MELCHIOR: A king who will free us from the evils of this world.
> BALTHAZAR: Where will he be born?
> MELCHIOR: The sacred writings point to a town in Judea called
> Bethlehem, Ephrata.

Shot of Bethlehem with star above.

The scene is interesting as it manages to bring into a synthesis astrologi-
cal signs (Balthazar), esoteric religion, agnostic beliefs (Melchior's Zoroastrian-
ism), and the Hebrew Scriptures (known by Melchior and Caspar) in less than
five minutes. The dialogue speaks of signs (such as the ubiquitous star) presumed to indicate a wonder, and then concludes that the Hebrew Scriptures
and prophets agree with the heavenly signs. Here, Balthazar represents an
unrevealed spirituality (we, of course, recognize Balthazar as the voice of the
infamous Darth Vader, James Earl Jones), which brings into its domain the
historical tradition of Judaism. In a certain sense, the negotiation of the astro-
logical and the historical is not unlike the overall project of *Jesus of Nazareth,*
namely, the blending of a mythic process of self-discovery with the historical
Jesus. Finally, that the film was so widely acclaimed and accepted shows how
successful 1960s forms of popular spirituality have been mainstreamed by
middle-class Christianity.

In *Jesus of Nazareth,* traditional biblical characters play key signifiers
inviting us into a world of a generalized, popular spirituality. Mary, and later,
Jesus himself, function not only as biblical characters but as codes that suggest
a kind of fate or destiny. The gospel, in other words, has been transformed into a
plot, not as the fulfillment of God's promise to Israel, but as a self-contained,
Westernized narrative moving to an ending toward which now Jesus, and even
Mary, are demonstrated to be moving. Zeffirelli has help in creating this self-sus-
taining plot, of course, since he had already developed the rhetorical trope of

destiny in his portrait of the star-crossed lovers Romeo and Juliet in 1968. But all adapters of the gospel for theatrical purposes have an advantage here: the audience shares Mary's knowledge of her future; we know this story well. So it is that Mary harbors more than the Word at the annunciation; she also contains the secret knowledge of the plot, of the Lord's destiny. We are aware of her struggle against those who do not believe her. We know she is right and share her point of view. We become insiders, participants, instead of merely viewers. Like good gnostics everywhere, we share in a special knowledge.

Jesus of Nazareth takes an established rhetorical strategy that searches for an ending and the narrative is thus framed dramatically in precisely this way: the insiders versus the outsiders, who, in turn, vitiate the initiates. We can see how well the dynamic works, particularly with an adaptation of a well-known biblical story, since we are collectively aware of the plot and the destiny of the characters before the first shot. Zeffirelli works the spectators' familiarity with the story as a culture-text to his advantage. In *Jesus of Nazareth* the audience has been aligned with the insiders (Mary, Jesus, John the Baptist, and others), who are at odds with the outsiders (the Romans, Jewish officials, and everybody who does not believe Jesus is the Messiah). In turn, we are drawn into sympathy with the initiates, who must be convinced (first Joseph, then the disciples) of Jesus' miraculous virgin birth, and then of his messiahship. Besides using a strong plot device, Zeffirelli hints at the secret side of Christianity, which requires initiation into its mythological story as a requirement of membership. The plot trajectory reminds us of the hero's drive toward self-discovery, into which we have been drawn and vicariously share.

A Savior for All Seasons. With its mixture of a Christian, biblical tradition and a narrative of mythic destiny unfolding before us, it should be no surprise that the Savior in *Jesus of Nazareth* would find himself in the same company as Luke Skywalker and even Superman. Indeed, in his television interview, Joseph Campbell himself told Bill Moyers that many biblical figures, including Moses and Jesus Christ, perfectly fit the hero model. Zeffirelli makes much of Jesus' mysterious, even dangerous, origins, and his subsequent adventure toward self-sacrifice and death. Zeffirelli's Jesus is the "perfect" mythic hero, free from the constraints of his own psyche and society.

Most importantly, as a mythic hero, Zeffirelli's Jesus has less to do with accepting the cross than having his consciousness transformed.

Given the many options open to a director in fashioning a film about the life of Jesus, it is fascinating to notice how much Zeffirelli's Jesus fits an altogether mythic characterization of the spiritual hero: his heroic birth, dangerous infancy, the recognition of his call, and then his journey toward maturation, death, and the final return. No other movie about Jesus pays as much attention to the Savior's preadulthood or his coming messiahship than *Jesus of Nazareth,* or, for that matter, showcases the boy Jesus as the "special one." The boy Jesus witnesses a political incident in the village in which the Romans oppress Jewish citizens. The camera picks Jesus out of the crowd and then there is an extreme close-up of the boy's piercing blue eyes as he gazes thoughtfully on a man who is on his knees screaming, "How long?" Later, the child wonder preaches (again, with that dreadfully inappropriate upper-crust British accent) to the elders at the Temple and gazes at the wondrous smoke. After Mary and Joseph find him, he explains, "Don't you know I must be about my father's business?" Then, as if we had not gotten enough hints already, there is a somewhat inexplicable cut to an old rabbi reading the Hebrew Scriptures about the coming Messiah; he too then exclaims, "How long?" (apparently a common refrain for first-century Palestine).

As with all the scenes of Jesus as a young child, the mise-en-scène is luscious and inviting: the young boy with the lamb on his shoulders (another hint); the mystical Temple; and the old man under celestially seasoned sunlight reading the prophetic scriptural account, "Behold I will send my messenger before me...a messenger...." Get it? Jesus, blue-eyed and beautiful, is the messenger.

The adult Jesus inherits all the younger boy's qualities, including the "Oxbridge" accent and the intense, luminous blue eyes. These extraordinary physical properties have long been associated with the extraterrestrials— whether good or evil. They are also indicative here, of course, of Jesus' ongoing special destiny—and our recognition of that fate. But from a social point of view, it is peculiar that a Semite would have such a rich English accent and be so blue-eyed and fair skinned (a usual complaint about the Jesus movie). Powell's Jesus is an Anglo-Saxon aesthetic wonder, to be sure, but are we to take aesthetic beauty for divine wonder?

Like his depiction of Romeo nine years earlier, Zeffirelli pays special homage to male beauty. A Semitic, dark skinned Jesus—even disfigured, according to Isaiah—is hardly a product for twentieth-century consumption, with its idealization of whiteness and youth culture. But it is certainly one of the most lingering ironies that God's entry into history would be repressed, his Son made over into a British movie star for television, and the gospel of justice homogenized into a generalized New Age spirituality. Then again, all this has been the story of the Savior on the silver screen: God made over in our idealized image in order to be consumed. We might look at these representations like so many figures on a Grecian urn and ask: "Is beauty truth—truth beauty?" Students of the Savior on the silver screen must continue to ask why these culturally constructed aesthetic features are so important to our identifying Jesus as the Messiah. To put that another way is to ask a dangerous question: What would an ugly Jesus look like? A suffering servant perhaps?

The fact that Jesus is not only a male beauty but also so very British helps us to consider our own cultural constructions of the Son of God in more specific ways. Endless representations depict the upper-class British to be stoical, even repressed. But that reserve carries a certain cache. When the urbane Sir Alec Guinness was cast as Obi-Wan in *Star Wars,* his sophisticated portrait of that mystical Jedi knight was also characterized by a cultivated restraint, which neatly summoned the Force's strength to do his bidding. Guinness had a long tradition of playing otherworldly idealists—as, for example, the unyielding Colonel Nicholson in *Bridge on the River Kwai* (1957), to name only his most famous role. He was reserved, even secretive, without being snobbish.

The same can be said for the British Jesus: he is stoical, but friendly and inviting; he is unknowable and harbors (divine) secrets, which are (we know) for a noble (transcendent) cause. The British Jesus can suffer in a manly way on earth, but he is connected to the cosmos. In a certain sense, from the point of view of film culture, we were prepared for Powell's Jesus by Guinness's Obi-Wan. Between them both there is a blurring of the historical with the mystical, the gospel with New Age discourse. With his hood often up, Jesus is a self-aware (but unknowable) Jedi knight and mystic, approaching his own destiny with stoical caution, teaching others the hidden secrets of the universe. By the end of the film, Jesus of Nazareth becomes, like Obi-Wan, an ethereal voice of experience, a helper to the underdogs who remain behind. Our notions of what it is like to be British once again help to naturalize our conceptions of the Messiah.

Jesus on the Miniscreen. What makes *Jesus of Nazareth* unique is its television format. We raise again the matter, how is the film constructed so as to accommodate the inevitable commercial breaks? That rupture might seem a tearing in an otherwise seamless robe, but we might remember that feature films are based on a different "philosophy," that is, invisible editing and continuity techniques that veil such divisions. Moreover, the television/video format puts in the foreground *Jesus of Nazareth*'s potential for interaction and pedagogy, something utterly lacking in mainstream, theatrical releases. It is well known that the miniseries, which appeared in the 1970s, was television's answer to literary adaptation, or the media's perennially problematic challenge of fitting a two-hundred-page novel into a two-hour feature film. But consider the adaptation of Irwin Shaw's *Rich Man, Poor Man* (1976, ABC) or Alex Haley's *Roots* (1977, ABC), both early and very successful miniseries.

The commercial advantage aside, the miniseries offers many possibilities for religious discourse, particularly representations of the Bible. When *Jesus of Nazareth* was broadcast, families and friends gathered and watched the movie together in their living rooms. During commercials they talked, discussed, walked about—glanced at Jesus on television. Between the days of the broadcast, it is well known that people discussed *Jesus of Nazareth* with friends and coworkers. The visual dynamic of television/video positions *Jesus of Nazareth* in the sphere of a community event in which people might raise insightful, faith-filled questions about representations of God. With the segmentation of a long video program of 382 minutes, we are hardly in the position of film spectators, left in the dark for two hours, held captive by an image. In light of this, *Jesus of Nazareth* is a very useful catechetical instrument, opening up a window to further discussion about our own constructions of the Savior, communal and individual.

NOTES

1. Kinnard and Davis, *Divine Images*, 187.
2. Joseph Campbell, *Myths to Live By* (New York: Bantam, 1973).
3. Joseph Campbell, *The Hero with a Thousand Faces*, 2nd ed. (Princeton, NJ: Princeton University Press, 1968),19–20.
4. Kinnard and Davis, *Divine Images*, 189.
5. Lloyd Baugh, *Imaging the Divine*, 75.

Photo courtesy of the Academy of Motion Picture Arts & Sciences. © Python Productions. Used with permission.

SEVENTH FEATURE

Monty Python's Life of Brian (1979)

*"Don't pass judgment on other people,
or you might get judged yourself."*

Written by: Graham Chapman, John Cleese, Terry Gilliam, Eric Idle, Terry Jones, Michael Palin

Directed by: Terry Jones

Actors Include: Graham Chapman, John Cleese, Terry Gilliam, Eric Idle, Terry Jones, Michael Palin

Running Time: 94 minutes

Introduction

Caution. Put on your hard hat and safety goggles, and fasten your seat belts. We are now entering the danger zone of films about the life of Jesus. Strictly speaking, however, this is *not* a film about the life of Jesus, despite frequent and ugly rumors to the contrary. Therein lies the danger: to judge this movie as something that it was never intended to be. Some would gladly label *Monty Python's Life of Brian* as an obscene and tasteless parody of the life of Jesus. It is certainly meant to rile audiences, even to poke fun at cherished notions and practices, to stomp on sensitive toes. But that is the nature and definition of parody. So what is it that is parodied in the movie? On what (or how many) levels is the movie operating? This is the important question. To dismiss the movie too quickly may mean foregoing some revealing insights into our own individual, corporate, and cultural character. As one layperson observed to a potential preacher for his congregation, "Preaching is one thing; meddling is another. Meddling is when you get too close." Similarly with humor and parody, when the object of the parody is too close, too dear, or held too tightly, it is suddenly not so funny. The instinct to laugh is replaced by the instinct to defend or attack.

There was some question about whether to include *Life of Brian* in this collection. Because of the widespread perception of this movie as a life of Jesus and because of its positioning in relationship to the genre of films about Jesus' life, it seemed important to include it in our discussion of the Savior on the silver screen. In our seminars and classes with seminarians, clergy, and lay people of numerous denominations, this movie has generated some of the most intense and serious discussion about the nature of the historical church. Further, in these same classes, after a brief checking of signals, the reputation of the film as dreadfully obscene or even evil was judged to be somewhat exaggerated and a matter of hasty analysis or simple unfamiliarity with the film. The film is, however, surely intended to parody, even ridicule, certain tendencies in the institutional church, or any institution for that matter. It is devastatingly incisive on that point. The comedic, at times even slapstick, nature of the film does not dull its sharp edge. Indeed, it may make the film even more pointed.

In particular, *Monty Python's Life of Brian* is the story of a hapless fellow named Brian Cohen (*cohen,* in Hebrew, means "priest"). Brian has the great misfortune to be born in the manger right next to that of Jesus. The movie becomes a narrative rendition of "There, but for the grace of God, go I." Yet, from the beginning of his life, events seem to conspire to move Brian into the reluctant role of savior. While his life does *parallel* the life of Jesus in certain ways, Brian is clearly not a replacement for Jesus. Indeed, Jesus does appear briefly in the film, but he is not parodied. To limit the description and discussion of this movie to a parody of Jesus' life would be unfortunate and would result in missing its central point, and indeed, the truly challenging aspect of the movie. More than a parody of Jesus, this movie serves as a caustic critique: first, a critique of the often pretentious and sanctimonious Hollywood-style lives of Jesus; then, a critique of the institutional nature of the church, which includes the established institutional church as well as those sects who position themselves as over and against the established institutional church; and finally, a critique of all those who uncritically follow leaders of any stripe.

Many have been scandalized by this film; some of those have seen the film and some have not. In the 22 August 1979 edition of *Variety,* a reviewer made a safe prediction: "Irreverent *religioso* spoof should top previous Monty Python pics. Probably will rile churches." Probably indeed. Upon its opening, it was panned (condemned) by various Catholic, Protestant, and Jewish leaders. Indeed, it is not a film one would likely screen in a Sunday morning education class, at least not without ample explanation. However, while it is surely intended to be irreverent, humorous, even scandalous, it poses some pointed challenges to our understanding of the nature of the church, where we look for authority, and at the characteristics and requirements of discipleship. Again, as mentioned above, in classes and workshops we have taught, which have included students of many faiths, ages and theological positions, lay and clergy, Catholic and Protestant, this film has generated some of the most serious discussion about the nature of the church and the nature of discipleship. The nature of the film itself seems to recede in importance and controversy. The questions the film raises or the points it seems to make take greater importance in the discussion following the viewing.

The film is a little difficult to become engaged in initially because the actors, all veterans of the English Monty Python troupe, play multiple roles. It is disconcerting to see the same face playing several characters. It takes just a few minutes, however, to get beyond this facet of the film. Also in connection with its English cast, it is hard for American ears to decipher some of the words because of the heavy accents. Finally, some of the English humor is simply alien, if not offensive, to our American sense of propriety. For example, cross-dressing, homosexuality, and speech impediments are frequent vehicles for English humor beyond the immediate confines of this film, but, indeed, are frequently employed here. These are not subjects that form part of the catalogue of stock topics for American humor.

The word *postmodern* will be used to describe this movie. It has become a commonplace description in many arenas of discussion these days, but may need some definition for this context. *Postmodern* typically refers to the last twenty to thirty years, a time in which most authority figures have been challenged or toppled; when an uncritical reliance on science, technology, or other forms of human ingenuity to solve all the world's ills has proven to be an inflated expectation; when optimism in an unending future of progress has proven an idle wish for much of the world; when hope has turned to doubt, if not despair. The "first world" is recognized to have made its advances, to a large degree, at the expense of the rest of the world. Oppression has been a frequent tool of those who have "made it," whether as individuals or as nations. In this sense, *Monty Python's Life of Brian* may well be described as postmodern.

Another casualty of the film's postmodern perspectives is the hero: there is none. At least the role of the hero is redefined as someone who is not seduced by false values and false optimism and who is at least true to him- or herself, since there are no larger, overarching value structures to which one can appeal or, more accurately, there are too *many* value structures to which one can appeal. There is no single structure. There is a recognition, even a proclamation, in this film that life contains a large measure of absurdity. Such being the case, one should not be surprised by that, nor stymied by it. Authorities (and heroes) have often failed our expectations of them, and perhaps it is our fault for putting too much trust in them. This same theme runs throughout the Monty Python films. Other films by the Monty Python troupe include: *Monty Python and the Holy Grail* (1975), *Jabberwocky* (1977), and *Monty Python's The Meaning of Life* (1983).

So, employ a little "willing suspension of disbelief" and watch one more Jesus movie.

Movie Preview

1. *What have you heard about this film ? What are your expectations?*
2. *Define* parody *for yourself. Why do people use humor to make points or to present unpopular ideas?*
3. *Describe the issues and concerns of society in the late 1970s. What was going on in the world; what events were still in the cultural memory of the time?*
4. *What other films were popular at this time?*
5. *What do you see as shortcomings of the institutional church, either the mainline denominations or smaller expressions of the institutional church?*

Movie Viewing

Movie Review

1. *Did the film match your expectations? In what ways? If not, in what ways was it different from your expectations?*
2. *What is the image of Jesus that is created in this movie? Describe the character of Brian. How does Jesus' image compare and/or contrast with the image of Brian?*
3. *Describe the opening and closing scenes. What context is established in the opening scene? What image(s) or what message are you left with in the closing scene?*
4. *How does God "fare" in this movie?*
5. *Write a sentence or two describing what you think the theme of this movie is, and then what you think the theme is for the movie's creators.*

LENS ONE

A quick glance at the opening scene of *Monty Python's Life of Brian* and the viewer recognizes that this is an entirely different approach to the question of Jesus. As reflected in the very title of the movie, the Monty Python troupe does not offer an overt consideration of Jesus as the subject of the film, but rather of a fictional character named Brian.

So then, what do we have here? For many viewers, as suggested already, this film appears to be a poorly conceived attempt to make fun of the historical Jesus as well as of the Christian faith, which has arisen over the last two thousand years as a witness to the belief that Jesus of Nazareth was and is the Messiah of God. But a careful viewing of the Python approach actually reveals a much more deeply crafted understanding of the whole Jesus issue (plus, as Lens Three will suggest, a devastating cultural critique). Perhaps the best way to approach it may first be to examine the two heroes of the story in order to answer the question of what this film seeks to achieve and to further justify its inclusion in our review of "Jesus movies."

A Tale of Two Saviors. *Life of Brian* is actually the presentation of two heroes or twin subjects. The first is Jesus of Nazareth himself, who appears in but a single scene toward the beginning of the story where he preaches his famous Sermon on the Mount (see Mt 5–7 and Lk 6). Do not be mistaken! This briefly glimpsed Jesus is very much that same Jesus who was portrayed to varying degrees by Ray, Stevens, and Zeffirelli. Indeed, if the Python troupe had wished to continue with this image as the subject of the film, the title could easily have been *Life of Jesus*. The resulting work undoubtedly would have closely paralleled those great Jesus sagas that preceded it but with a comedic edge. But, of course, this is not the case. The

Jesus of Ray-Stevens-Zeffirelli is provided, on the one hand, to offer a context, a historical and geographical setting for the film and the film's agenda. At another level, however, Jesus is provided as the commonly envisioned figure of traditional Christian piety against which our second protagonist is to be contrasted.

Our second protagonist, then, is Brian of Nazareth or Brian Cohen. He stands as a sort of common man of the street, rational in thought with the typical concerns of any struggling first-century Jew in Roman-ruled Palestine. We learn that his father was a long-absent Roman centurion (a charge made about Jesus himself by the second-century pagan author Celsus). His mother is believed by his followers to be a virgin, though she herself refuses to address the issue "out of modesty."

Brian stands as a type of "counter-christ" figure but certainly not an antichrist. He desires to be a good Jewish patriot and to resist Roman domination in an active way. To this end, he joins a local Jewish zealot group and works to harass Roman power whenever practical. Curiously, he takes the very route that Zeffirelli's Judas Iscariot desires for Jesus, that is, to be an active leader in the zealot movement against Rome. But Brian certainly does not seek to become a leader. He has no desire to develop his own religious following. In fact, quite the opposite occurs. A religious movement finds *him,* and quickly his several followers request his words of guidance, seek signs and miracles, and ultimately offer adoration of his crucifixion as a symbol of his devotion to them and their cause of resistance against Rome.

These are the two figures operative in this film, both hastily sketched. One is visible throughout the film, one mostly hidden in the background. We discover that neither protagonist can truly be said to function as the central character of the film. The Christian viewer already has an uneasy sense about this, whether clearly defined or not. The film claims to focus upon Brian of Nazareth, but the nature of Brian's teachings and the response of the crowds suggest that there may be a concern here for Jesus of Nazareth (as known from Scripture and tradition). Yet, we have only an isolated portrait of Jesus offered in a single scene, hardly enough footage to justify the contention that the movie is about Jesus.

The reality is that *Life of Brian* is neither about Brian nor Jesus, but is instead, as suggested above, about *us* and the tradition of the institutional church. Unlike the previous Jesus sagas, this is not a film about an ancient figure who speaks words of wisdom or leads people to faith. It is a film about those people who once sought (and who now seek) teachers of wisdom in an effort to have their faith inspired and their salvation assured. It is not about the speaker (whether Jesus, Brian, or the street preachers of ancient Jerusalem), but about the hearer. The contention of the Monty Python troupe is repeatedly presented in one scene after another. The hearer is rarely merely a listener, but is instead a seeker who already brings the baggage of what he or she hopes to hear from any teacher. The result is, of course, that the hearers hear exactly what they wish to find. In a real sense, this is an assertion that offers bold challenges to the church and its catalogue of beliefs and practices.

Source Materials. With the question of the hearer in mind, we turn directly to the issue of sources. Of those biblical texts that Monty Python clearly makes use, there is a primary focus upon only three commonly known passages. First, the story begins with an obvious reflection of the birth narratives of Jesus as borrowed from Matthew and Luke: the birth in a manger, the presence of the bright and unusual star, the appearance of the wise men (astrologers) and shepherds. As with most Jesus stories, we find the Matthean account brought into harmony with the Lukan version of the birth.

Unlike most presentations, however, the two are not harmonized. The appearance of the wise men at the home of the newborn babe (from Matthew) is applied to the birth of Brian. We observe that the wise men are happy to praise the newborn Brian and to offer their gifts, despite the protestations of Brian's mother. In other words, they are determined to see and accept only what they believe to be true. When the wise men discover the error of their ways, they reclaim their gifts and hasten to the site of the stable, its manger, and the newborn Jesus, surrounded by adoring shepherds with their sheep (from Luke's story). We laugh at the mistake that they very nearly made. But a new doubt is raised, of course. From the start, their determination to worship Brian was every bit as sincere and self-directed as their resolve to worship Jesus undoubtedly will be! Are we ourselves so easily fooled or misguided?

The second scenario comes shortly thereafter in which we come upon the setting for the Sermon on the Mount (with a preference for Matthew's vision versus that of Luke) and hear the words of Jesus as he speaks the Beatitudes to the crowds. At first we encounter these well-known teachings of Jesus from close by, but the camera pulls back and we are gradually pulled away from the speaker to the far edges of the scattered listeners. In a starkly clear context we once again see the Python troupe focus on the hearer instead of the speaker. While Jesus speaks of blessings upon the *peace-makers,* the distant crowd misunderstands these words to be blessings upon the "cheesemakers." The confusion and variety of interpretations that are associated with this misinterpretation are hilarious on the surface. But the physical fight that ensues is classic, almost slapstick, irony. While Jesus speaks blessings upon those who make peace, those who have come to hear him preach are engaged in violence over their own petty prejudices, interpretations, and lack of tolerance toward one another. The history of the church is riddled with comparable events.

At the conclusion of the film we find Brian at the site of the trial and cru-cifixion: his name serendipitously arises during the Roman prefect's offer to release a prisoner to the crowds; we witness a stranger's offer to carry the cross of a condemned man; Brian is visited by Judith, a female friend/fol-lower, while he struggles on the cross. These trial and cross episodes are broadly attested in scattered scenarios among the New Testament gospels. Yet, while the gospels place each episode within the experience of the trial and crucifixion of Jesus, Monty Python offers similar parallels from the expe-rience of Brian. Here is perhaps the most immediate challenge to the church's interpretation of the death of its Messiah. For Brian, who has no desire to die, the forthcoming death is very real, unjust, and tragic. It is made all the more so by the fact that his so-called friends and followers praise him for his actions; they interpret his death by their own vision, for their own needs.

The crowning moment in the entire charade comes in the closing song, whose words, "...always look on the bright side of life," soon shift to "...always look on the bright side of death." For Brian, this situation is absurdly ludicrous. For his followers, the situation is wonderfully desirable— someone else is dying for their misdeeds! It is desirable in the same sense that the early church needed some means, some lens, through which to interpret and understand the tragic death of their Messiah, Jesus. The unanswered question, of course, is: what was *Jesus'* actual view on the entire situation? (Compare the Garden of Gethsemane scenes of the gospels with the interpretations of this event among the previously viewed films.) To all this one might add a question about *who* it is that decides what God's will is that necessitates the whole crucifixion scenario, and *how* it is that the death of Jesus managed to provide salvation for those who "believe" in the mystery of that saving event. How did we Christians come to claim these beliefs? This is not a matter of doubt or faithlessness, but a willingness to examine the development of the historical details of our various theological statements and proclamations, of our Creeds and our creeds. They did not drop out of the sky but were hammered out over a long period of time.

There is a second layer of biblical allusions that is more subtle in nature and requires some limited explanation. The first allusion involves Brian's encounter with a "former leper" whom Jesus had healed in some unseen setting. This leper may be an intentional allusion to one of several episodes preserved by the gospels (Lk 17:11–19 is offered in our appendix as a likely possibility). What stands out is that (1) Jesus healed this particular leper through Jesus' own volition and without prompting, and (2) the leper subsequently lost a competitive edge at his only known means of livelihood, begging for alms. While thrilled about the first point, the leper is understandably chagrined about the second.

The ensuing conversation between Brian and the leper raises questions about motivations and consequences that our gospel authors never attempted to address, since their own concerns were for the implications of Jesus' healing miracles as indicators of the validity of his message and his true character. Indeed, what happened to those who are healed, or, in the case of Lazarus, who were raised from the dead? How were their lives changed? The closing lines of the conversation provide the Python message in a nutshell, however. After the leper complains about the meager contribution Brian gives to him, Brian responds, "Some people are never happy." To this the leper retorts, "That's exactly what Jesus said!" The unasked question for the viewer becomes whether the "some people" to whom Jesus (supposedly) referred were meant to indicate his enemies or (and much more likely from the Python point of view) his followers! Some people are never happy; at least they are happiest when they are unhappy.

The second example really is a combination of two scriptural considerations melded into a single context: Brian's preaching among the prophets on the streets of Jerusalem. First is the address of the prophets themselves. These men are fiery, impressive preachers who evoke the imagery of God's coming wrath for the end times (with clear allusions to Revelation and Ezekiel). As contrasted with one individual in their midst, a prophet whose mild words and seemingly rationally considered and practical sayings draw virtually no listeners, the prophets of doom attract numerous spectators. Modern counterparts are the "preachers' corner" of Hyde Park in London and the endless rounds of cartoons with the bearded prophet holding up signs with some pronouncement or another in the *New Yorker* and other publications.

The prophet of doom has become a stock character, usually to be derided, but always attended to. Words of doom and fear (whether in antiquity or modernity) gather great numbers of hearers. Is it because such words carry more value than practical, daily wisdom? Not at all! It is because such imagery has a deeper appeal to the common imagination. The doomsday imagery has greater pathos. Such concerns naturally form the (un-)happy playground of audiences far and wide who would rather be frightened by doomsayers than to engage in the difficult and gritty business of engaging life's trials and struggles. This world of doomsayers flourishes because there has been and presumably always will be an ample market of "buyers" for such goods in the world.

Against this backdrop of apocalyptic (and basically nonsensical) prophets appears Brian, who has literally "dropped out of the blue" into his new role as preacher and teacher. In an attempt to avoid the suspicions of Roman sentries who seek him among the crowds, Brian begins to teach, using a series of sayings reminiscent of materials found in the Gospel of Luke. It is all quite practical on a literal and ethical level: do not judge and you will not be judged yourself; if God takes care of birds and flowers, then God surely will take care of you; God gives to those who use their gifts. The teachings sound familiar to our ears, and we readily accept them within the framework of two thousand years of Christian interpretation. But Brian's immediate audience has further questions about what it all means and whether Brian is just "making it up as he goes along."

Unlike us, who have been trained to accept the teachings of Jesus through the authority of centuries of ecclesiastical and scriptural tradition, Brian's audience needs to have some practical and tangible answers to its immediate questions. As a result, they never quite perceive the meaning that Brian's words offer for the living of life. They feel confused, in need of some further clarification—not about the words (which they really do not understand anyway), but about the nature of just who this Brian is that he claims the authority to speak at all! The issue of the authority to speak is always pivotal, whether in the Bible or on television talk shows. Who has it? How do we get it?

They miss the meaning of the words, but that does not mean that Brian is rejected. Quite the contrary happens! Brian is hailed as the Messiah, for no good reason, except that his audience seeks a messiah. Within ten minutes this band of religious enthusiasts, caught up in their own uncritical zeal, does four crucial things: (1) They form a new cult based upon their own proclamation that Brian is the Messiah, with no prompting from Brian himself. (2) They divide into three groups who argue for *five* different ways in which Brian should be followed—either follow the sign of the sandal, together with its three different forms of interpretation; or follow the "holy gourd of Jerusalem"; or stop to consider the great significance of what Brian's coming may mean—with only one follower, this is clearly the least popular of the three approaches! (3) They appeal to Brian for miracles and interpret his every word and gesture as revelatory of some greater truth. (4) Finally, they eagerly identify and persecute a perceived heretic. In these four steps we see a rather revealing rendition of the history of Christianity from a nonfaith perspective: religious enthusiasts proclaiming a messiah, dividing into groups along the lines of their idiosyncrasies of interpretation and belief, pursuing miracles to justify their faith, and persecuting anyone who stands in disagreement with the message they preach.

Exasperated by his followers' pursuit of their new messiah and his "wisdom," Brian, in a very telling scene, finally confronts the crowds and offers the very wisdom that the Monty Python troupe wishes to deliver as the central message of the film:

> Look, you've got it all wrong. You don't need to follow me; you don't need to follow anybody. You've got to think for yourselves. You're all individuals; you're all different; you've all got to work it out for yourselves. Don't let anyone tell you what to do....

This is an outsider's point of view. It stems from the belief that the faithful are so intent to hear what they wish to hear, to see what they wish to see, to find what they wish to find, that they completely ignore the plain and simple reality standing before them. Curiously, this is not only a comment upon the value of the teachings of Jesus and whatever his original message may have been; it is also a comment on the way that Jesus' hearers (both then and now) have transformed his image into a gilded object of faith and reverence. To appeal to New Testament witnesses and writings from early church history in support of the *historical* events of Jesus' life is not necessarily convincing, since by the time of the composition of the biblical texts the memory of what Jesus did was already being influenced by who they believed Jesus to be. We can conclude then that *Life of Brian* treats its sources quite freely and even loosely, since to assume that the sources themselves are a careful preservation of historical facts would be unwarranted.

This is a broad look at the sources (minus some smaller details) that "Monty Python" has used and the loose way in which those sources have been employed. We must also, however, consider the question of the themes as they relate to the texts and their interpretation. These themes may be clearly distinguished according to two phrases used throughout the film in different contexts: "you lucky bastard," and "bloody Romans can't take a joke." Both phrases appeal to the question of interpretation.

Loaded Labels. The words "you lucky bastard" are applied only to Brian and only in situations where the concept of "lucky" would hardly seem to apply. When first thrown into prison by the Romans he is addressed in this way by a fellow inmate who is manacled to the wall. After Brian falls from a tower into the hold of an alien spacecraft, chased through space by a Dr.-Who-variety war cruiser only to crash in a pile of wrecked metal and dust at his very point of origin, he is addressed once again as "you lucky bastard" by a casual observer (a reflection of John the Baptist's testimony in John 1:1-18?). Finally, the manacled prisoner accosts Brian with these words one more time as Brian is led away with numerous others to be crucified.

A new consideration must be brought to bear here. Brian in fact is a bastard, as his own mother confesses. Yet, in a real and practical sense, by worldly standards Jesus of Nazareth also fits this category. Jesus is *not* Jesus *ben* (son of) Joseph, but Jesus *ben* God. He is the Son of a divine Father (according to Christian sources), though his mother is legally engaged to a human husband. Thus we read words that are attributed to Jesus in John 8:54: "....it is my Father who glorifies me, he of whom you say, 'He is our God....' " (and this reference is clearly not to Joseph!). Are we thus intended to transfer the theme "you lucky bastard" from Brian to Jesus? Why not? For despite the hardships and cruelties that befall both of these characters in their respective and parallel lives, the ultimate result as determined by their followers will be that both Jesus and Brian are the focal points of salvation. Their deaths (though tragic for them personally) will stand as the center of faith for myriad other believers. The memory of who they were and what they did will be their salvation. And therein lies their *luck*.

The words "bloody Romans can't take a joke" are applied by all manner of characters to any representative of Rome throughout the film. We can easily apply this to ancient Rome. There is no risk in that application. A riskier but more likely interpretation would be to apply these words to the church, its history and theology. While the obvious connection is between "Rome" the Empire and "Rome" the Roman Church, it is certainly intended that "Rome" should extend to all facets of any denomination of the institutional church. It is within these walls, after all, that Jesus of Nazareth has become deified, worshiped, and quite probably interpreted beyond the boundaries of his immediate followers' original experiences with him. Indeed, the charge that the church possesses little ability to look at itself with a critical eye and to stand in constant true reflection upon what it is and whom it serves ("can't take a joke") may well be "Monty Python's" most cogent and devastating critique. What the movie says about the church is one matter, of course. What the church says about the movie, however, reveals as much about the church as about the movie.

There is more that could be said about *Life of Brian* with respect to its use of sources and traditions. One thinks, for example, of the movement of statues around Jerusalem as a casual reflection of the Emperor Caligula's desire to have his own statue erected in the Temple (see Josephus, *Antiquities of the Jews* 18.8.2). The stoning of the blasphemer contains shades of John 7:53—8:11; that scene where a woman who is caught in adultery is brought to Jesus prior to her imminent stoning (in both cases there are no people without sin—either in the spiritual or legal sense—who should carry out the decree of stoning). We observe the claim by the followers of Brian that he had been "taken up" before they then discover that he simply had walked away. There is also the realization that the followers of Brian, much like those of Jesus, make no serious attempt to rescue him at his very moment of need upon the cross (plenty of talk, but little action).

In sum then, our consideration of sources in *Life of Brian* comes to something like this: unlike other Jesus films, which struggle with who Jesus was and what he said, Monty Python struggles with who he was *not* and what his followers have chosen to hear him say regardless of what he may actually have said. We clearly see in this film that Brian does not want to be anyone's hero, yet he becomes the sacrificial victim and martyr of his followers' own cause. It leads to a provocative but perhaps inevitable consideration: whether, in fact, Jesus could have been a martyr to his followers' own needs as well.

LENS TWO

Given the role of parody and humor in this movie, one might expect some equally "over the top" approach to the visualization of the story. For most of the visual aspects of the movie, this is not the case. Is the film playing with our sensibilities one more time, toying with our expectations, a twist upon a twist? Probably. This movie, however, plays the visualization side of things in a fairly straightforward fashion, with several noteworthy exceptions.

The opening scene, for example, begins just as many of the Jesus movies begin, with a slow pan of the arid, dusty Judean countryside eventually settling on a picture of Jesus proclaiming the Beatitudes. However, along with this average, expected opening scene, comes a little twist: captions labeling this as "Saturday afternoon" and "Tea Time." That is the tip-off, or shall we say kickoff, for what is to follow.

This rather unexpected and therefore disarming production trick of the film is, indeed, its realism, that is, the visual verisimilitude of the costumes and locale. If the viewer were to turn the sound down, this would seem to be a pretty respectable, straightforward rendition. While one certainly expects a spoof or a parody from a film by the Monty Python troupe, there is little to visually betray that this film is a parody. The scenery, sets, and costumes in *The Gospel According to St. Matthew* and *Jesus Christ Superstar* are far more stylized, caricatured, distinctive, even odd. Unlike that of *Saint Matthew,* the lighting is very naturalistic. *Life of Brian* has the look of a Hollywood production, although the scale is not as grand. From the beginning, then, we are toyed with a bit; our expectations are put into a tizzy. What genre is this film? How am I supposed to "read" this film? A good question, indeed. Visually, there is little to betray the movie's agenda.

Of course, there are those several moments in *Life of Brian* when the late twentieth century comes comically and anachronistically rocketing into the scene. This occasional juxtaposition of very contemporary idiom and issues with the realistic sets and scenes creates an unbalanced and comic atmosphere throughout the film and may result in a case of cultural whiplash for the viewer. *Comic* need not always mean *funny,* however. James Hopewell refers to Northrup Frye, who defines comic plots as those that seek to find a higher or bigger reality in which seemingly antithetical, contradictory, or conflicting elements can find a place in which all the elements fit or make sense. The goal, according to Frye, is not necessarily humor but a happy ending (Take note of this movie's closing scene!). Along these same lines, Hopewell further comments: "Created in misinformation and convoluted by error, a comedy is resolved by the disclosure of a deeper knowledge about the harmonious way things really are."[1] This is exactly how *Life of Brian* ends. This device becomes one more trick to draw the viewer into the chaotic and cluttered world of the movie that is ironically held together by, of all things, absurdity. Similarly, in *The Meaning of Life,* the answer to the unstated question of where is the meaning of life is, "There isn't any."

Another element of visualization has been mentioned previously—the actors themselves, or the characterization. Knowing that this is a Monty Python production clues the viewer into certain aspects about this film. This is not going to be a solemn, sober presentation. Certainly, no one should be surprised by the antics and sight gags, although surely many viewers have been scandalized by the perception that this is a parody of the life of Jesus. One would have to say, however, that a certain minimal amount of restraint was exercised at least by utilizing Brian as the subject of this film and not Jesus himself. Few others are spared!

Having actors play several roles is not an unusual theater practice; it was, of course, common in Greek drama and Shakespearean plays. Yet it defies normal cinematic conventions: we expect precise differentiation of characters in movies. In *Life of Brian,* however, conventions are meant to be broken. Men act as women, men act as men acting as women, and men even act as men. Women act as women. Plus, each actor plays several roles. What does this method of characterization do to the viewer's engagement in watching the movie? Is it harder to become "lost" in the viewing of the film? Does it keep you on the edge of your seat, or just simply on edge?

While the British accents in *Jesus of Nazareth* tended to be rather "upper-crust" (especially that of Jesus himself), the accents in *Life of Brian* are far from that. They are rough, street-worn, urban, lower-class accents. They are an indicator that this movie is a look at Christian history from a very different point of view. It is a look from the outside at the "underbelly" of religion and discipleship. The accents are another warning that this will not be the usual respectful, reverential look at Christian faith.

Although the overall "look" of the movie (with the exception of the actors themselves) seems fairly pedestrian and straightforward (again, were one to turn the sound down), there are several visual devices that call for some comment. First is the use of animation. After the initial nativity sequence, the animated sequence announcing the title and credits is audacious and silly but does fall in line with (or maintains) the mood of irreverence for the remainder of the movie. It creates or reinforces a mind-set that shapes the viewer's watching.

There are all sorts of visual puns and allusions evident throughout the sequence that reflect and point to the culture in which this and obviously other films of the day were produced. The image of God from the Sistine Chapel is pictured, for example, with arm extended. The one theme that runs throughout this animated sequence is that all of the buildings pictured seem to be crumbling; great Roman arches tumble down, fall up and reform, then fall again. This is certainly a commentary on the entropic movement of history, particularly religious history: one era building on the ruins of the previous era, only to crumble in turn. Finally, the angel figure, a la Icarus, flies too close to the sun and goes down in smoke. The music throughout the sequence is an obvious spoof of the James Bond movies of the time, a character who carries more cultural weight as hero than Jesus the Christ. Another icon becomes grist for the Monty Python mill.

The other notable interjection of modernity is, of course, the scene in which Brian falls off a parapet into the passing rocketship. Brian is apparently saved by alien beings, only to be returned to his take-off point. In the process, Monty Python lampoons our fascination with space travel and the popularity of the mythlike narratives of space odyssey films of the time, which, like the Bond films, provide heroes for the viewer's consumption.

There is a tacit recognition that institutions have done some good. As the members of the People's Judean Front plot to kidnap Pilate's wife, Reg asks rhetorically, "What have the Romans ever done for us?" As it turns out, the rebels create quite a list of good things: aqueducts, wine, and more. But the list is not convincing enough to dissuade them from their desire for revolt. The decision has already been made; facts will not deter them.

If the film's message is, as Brian says, "You don't need me....You've got to work it out for yourselves," what are we left with in the last scene—a song-and-dance crucifixion? The song proclaims, "Always look on the bright side of life...," which then becomes, "Always look on the bright side of death." Is it too sarcastic? Perhaps. But it is not so far from Paul's statement, "For me to die is gain." And if life is as absurd and chaotic as Monty Python movies surely proclaim, why not look on the bright side? The suggestion here is not that one need to like this film, not even that one must agree with the film, but at least allow it to speak for itself by examining the devices it uses to make its point.

The movie asks us to take a step back to see what is going on. A scene in which this point seems to be implicit is that in which Brian is caught painting graffiti on the fortress walls. The Roman soldier has greater concern that the grammar be correct than for the revolutionary content of the message! How often do we fail (to use that old cliché) to see the forest for the trees? Monty Python would like to destroy the forest so that only trees are left. One could easily miss the absurdity that the Popular Front of Judea (as opposed to the People's Front of Judea) has only one member (not really so popular, after all). Everything is perception. Image is everything; at least that's how it appears. Even a one-person sect can be a "popular" movement. Words mean nothing or, at best, they mean only what we want them to mean. Thomas Merton has observed that we must become disillusioned, that is, we must get rid of our illusions if we are to make any progress in the life in Christ. In a sense, and from outside the Christian faith, *Life of Brian* urges the same.

LENS THREE

The scene is as familiar as last year's Christmas card: a cloudless night on the outskirts of Bethlehem. In the distance, a sweet light comes from a cave at the base of a mountain. A tired father has just raised a lantern to behold the infant God and his mother near a manger. From frosty hillsides come the shepherds and their beasts of burden to pay homage. As the brilliant star burns in the sky over Judea, three wise men from the ancient East journey to offer their gifts of gold, frankincense, and myrrh. "Peace on Earth, Good Will to All," shout the angels. God has come to dwell among humanity. But hold on just one more moment.

ANGELS' CHOIR: [Sort of chant to the Star of Bethlehem]
BRIAN: Uhuhlk!
CASPAR: Hrmhrm!
Mother falling off stool: [Crash]
MOTHER: Ohooh! Who are you?
CASPAR: We are three wise men.
MOTHER: What?
MELCHIOR: We are three wise men.
MOTHER: Well, what are you doing creeping under a couch
    at two o'clock in the morning?
BALTHASAR: We are astrologers.
MELCHIOR: We have come from the East.
MOTHER: What is this some kind of joke?
CASPAR: We wish to praise the infant.
MELCHIOR: We must pay homage to him.

MOTHER: Homage? You're all drunk! It's disgusting!
   Out! Come on, out.
CASPAR: No.
MOTHER: Barge in here with tales about all the ancient fortune-tellers.
   Come on, out!
CASPAR: No, no, we must see him!
MOTHER: Go and praise someone else's brat! Go on!
MELCHIOR: We...we were led by a star!
MOTHER: Led by a bottle more like! Go on, out!
MELCHIOR: Well, well, we must see him, we have brought presents!
MOTHER: Out!
CASPAR: Gold, frankincense, myrrh!
MOTHER: Well, why didn't you say so. He's over there....

This irreverent scene from the opening sequence of *Life of Brian* is typical of the Cambridge-educated, young British wits and members of the brilliant and notorious performing society, *The Footlights Club*. In 1969, Graham Chapman, John Cleese, Eric Idle, Terry Jones, Michael Palin, and Terry Gilliam (who was an American expatriate, and cartoonist for the humor magazine *Help!*) assembled their talents to form a group called Monty Python's Flying Circus. Their outrageous, satiric comedy show was broadcast on the BBC between 1969 and 1976. In America, that series was subsequently rebroadcast by PBS and featured in two ABC late-night specials in 1975 (with a video release in 1988).

The team also became famous for its feature films. Their second movie, *Monty Python and the Holy Grail* (Gilliam and Jones, 1975) was a spoof of medieval knights, which included (among other hilarious bits) a talking torso, a gay prince who does not want to be rescued by Sir Lancelot and a killer rabbit. Some have suggested that the film was a "send-up" of medieval movies, but the film goes beyond that to tease us about the very notion of legends and sacred myths. The dismantling of what our culture holds important becomes further clarified at the end of *The Holy Grail* when the story is interrupted by a squad of modern policemen. This burst of chaos and other skits like it suggest the often bizarre, surreal quality of Monty Python films.

Directed by Terry Jones, *Life of Brian* went too far, at least according to the Religious Right and other organized religious groups; they labeled it "iconoclastic," even "blasphemous." The son of a Roman centurion and a Jewish woman, Brian Cohen is misidentified as the Messiah. After a number of mishaps and scenes that obviously exploit the gospels, Brian is chased by authorities for his antigovernment graffiti on the walls of Jerusalem. He is subsequently crucified with a number of others as they sing from their crosses, "Always look on the bright side of life." In an article in the *New York Times* (30 August 1979), the Archdiocese of New York took the position that the film was a "mockery of Christ's life." The film was perceived as offensive to more than just Christian churches and was condemned by no less than three rabbinical organizations as "a crime against religion." Apparently, not many people were scandalized, since the film grossed $80,529 in one week, and made $60,277 in its first five days alone.

Orion/Warners was quick to defend the film, calling *Life of Brian* a satire and a spoof and maintaining that it should be viewed in that context. Indeed, the film mocks throughout what Vincent Canby called the "toga-and-sandal epics."[2] On the other hand, it is easy to see how *Life of Brian* would appear offensive, since it was intended to offend the middle class. In an interview for *Playboy* (November 1979), Terry Gilliam said that *Life of Brian* had nothing at all to do with religion but was an "allegory about suburban England." In the same interview, Michael Palin said that the send-up of the biblical epic was the perfect area for the Python group to work in, "the ludicrous power itself, authority, the trappings of authority—and the extraordinary length to which authority must go to preserve its credibility."[3]

In considering issues surrounding the politics of surrealism, parody, and genre, exploring *Life of Brian* forces us to deal with a generational split, which asks: Why are some utterly offended by the movie, but others, particularly religious youth, seem to enjoy the film without scandal or suggestion of "blasphemy"? To deal with this question is to face, once again, the inevitable interplay of technology upon the religious space we construct, the images we create, and the beliefs that guide us.

A New Britain Emerges. The Britain that emerged out of the 1960s and 1970s was a substantially different country than it had been for centuries.

The class system had not collapsed, of course, but the country had faced squarely some of the issues surrounding cultural stratification. The British Labor Party directly sponsored a strong contingent of 128 members of Parliament in 1975. The unions dominated political party formation and, through the Employment Protection Acts (1975 and 1979), increased the union strength in England to over half the workforce. But nothing shows the shift in attitudes toward class in Britain more than the increase in film roles for working-class men and the stars associated with them.

Over the years, British films had tended to project a conservative image of the country, long associated with colonialism, quaint verbiage, and class trappings. Despite some exceptions, the British film industry's lack of response to contemporary issues was generally true even in the period in which American, French, and Italian cinema were interested in social problems, antiheroes, and neorealism. In addition, other cinemas fueled the reconstruction of what it meant to be "English." Hollywood had long imagined the real British hero in terms of upper-class codes of refinement and stoicism. Only Ronald Colman's refined accent could take Sidney Carton to the guillotine in the closing lines of *A Tale of Two Cities* (1935): "Tis a far, far better thing I do...." The film industry had long identified genteel and manly behavior with British imperialism, evident on a remote outpost in India (*Gunga Din*, 1939), and Balaclava heights in the Crimea (*Charge of the Light Brigade*, 1936), and later, on the River Kwai with Colonel Nicholson (1957).

But in the 1960s, British cinema came out of a dormant period that politicized the film industry in that country. For instance, the superspectacle *Lawrence of Arabia* (1962) brought to light the complicated issues of Arabs falling under British colonial hegemony. Further, more and more scripts, as well as the novels from which they were adapted, handled the problems of the "underclasses." In 1960, Albert Finney mythologized the working-class man in an adaptation of Alan Sillitoe's *Saturday Night and Sunday Morning*. Michael Caine developed a working-class playboy with a cockney accent in *Alfie* (1966); and Sean Connery made a Scottish accent elegant in his long-running stint as James Bond.

The early 1970s in Britain were years that continued to feed off the energy of the late 1960s. But the Britain of 1979 was in crisis (partly, some would say, because of labor unions); social and economic concerns hastened the election of the Conservative Party that year. The Thatcher government was attempting to reinforce the traditional values of imperialism, nationalism, and monarchy. They hoped to create a government that articulated "Englishness" during the 1980s, moving toward intense nationalism, middle-class institutions, and the mythological structures in Britain. But it was all beginning to erode.

The fracturing of these nearly monolithic entities (such as colonialism, which had existed in England since 1660) became apparent, paradoxically, during a decade that had insisted on their value. There was an unfavorable reaction to the unseemly and aggressive military activity in the Falklands. In this and in other affairs, the British press was quick to seize upon the unraveling of the monarchy, with its loss of credibility, power, and prestige. There were other signs of weakness as well. The strong movement both in cultural studies and in poststructuralism during the late 1970s and 1980s within the academic community suggests some efforts at deconstructing a language that had long been rooted in cultural imperialism and racism. A few films, such as *My Beautiful Laundrette* (1985), even dared to explore the political and stratified atmosphere of Margaret Thatcher's England—and became successful.

A form of an outspoken political legacy of the 1960s survived in popular culture, namely, in television. Despite the gains of the film industry in the 1960s, and the success of a handful of auteurs, British television had long eclipsed the native movie business, which tended to be dominated by Hollywood imports. Some have gone so far as to argue whether there is any English "national cinema." Yet, it was television, with its fluid, eccentric projections of the many facets of British life—history, class, and literature—that allowed popular culture to form a kind of national idiom. Those television exports also projected an "Englishness" to the rest of the world, although not one necessarily endorsed by the Tory Party. After all, when we think of the influence of British popular culture in America, certain series come to mind: *Masterpiece Theater* serializations of British literary classics like *I, Claudius* or, then again, *Upstairs, Downstairs'* portraits of classes in Edwardian England; and *Monty Python's Flying Circus's* surrealistic look at modern life.

Monty Python's Origins. The Monty Python troupe was invariably shaped around their early days at Cambridge, the obstreperous university life of the 1960s. Their humor, much like the age in which they lived, became political, satiric, and surrealistic. Surrealism, with its subversive attack on the middle class, has long been associated with comedy. The surrealist relies on comedic anarchy in order to perform an act of self-observation or a new awareness. The project of the surrealist, in other words, is to shake the status quo into consciousness. Although the classic modernist period (in which André Breton declared in his famous *Second Manifesto of Surrealism* [1929] that his purpose was "to provoke, from the intellectual and moral point of view, an attack of conscience") had passed, it is easy to see how comedic anarchy might have emerged out of the 1960s, with its radicalized values and dismantling of a middle-class sensibility.[4] The surrealist of any age wants to free the mind of logic, unleashing its hidden powers.

Interestingly, *Monty Python's Flying Circus* had its roots in earlier television shows in Britain, such as *Till Death Us Do Part* and *That Was the Week That Was*. While we would not call these shows efforts at radical subversion, *Monty Python's Flying* Circus, in particular, functioned as a surrealistic enterprise in attempts to satirize or, more severely, to "lay waste the ideas of family, country, religion."[5] The purpose of surrealism, then, is intended to lift us out of comfortable, conventional expectations, out of the "suburbia" of the mind. As the country turned away from the radical 1960s and moved toward conservatism, that project became more and more vital, even for middle-brow, avant-garde groups like Monty Python. The absurd humor was invasive, the cross-dressing outrageous, the attacks on genteel living ubiquitous. Cartoonist Terry Gilliam's often violent, upsetting, and nightmarish illustrations for the television series and feature films remind us, once again, of the group's efforts at the often class-related politics of surrealism.

Monty Python's comedic use of anarchy—a force that ruptures narrative space—is perhaps one of the group's most effective features, as in "The Spanish Inquisition Sketch":

CHAPMAN: Trouble at mill.
CLEVELAND: Oh, no—what kind of trouble?
CHAPMAN: One on't cross beams gone owt askew on treddle.
CLEVELAND: Pardon?
CHAPMAN: One on't cross beams gone owt askew on treddle.

CLEVELAND: I don't understand what you're saying.

CHAPMAN: One of the cross beams has gone out askew on the treddle.

CLEVELAND: Well what on earth does that mean?

CHAPMAN: I don't know—Mr. Wentworth just told me to come in here and say that there was trouble at the mill, that's all—I didn't expect a kind of Spanish Inquisition.

(Dissonant music as the door suddenly opens and Cardinal Ximinez enters with Cardinal Biggles [with goggles] and Cardinal Fang)

XIMINEZ: *Nobody* expects the Spanish Inquisition! Our chief weapon is surprise. Surprise and fear. Fear and surprise. Our two weapons are fear and surprise. And ruthless efficiency. Our three weapons are fear, surprise, and ruthless efficiency. And an almost fanatical devotion to the pope. Our four. No—Amongst our weapons. Amongst our weaponry... are such elements as fear, surprise. I'll come again. (Exit)

CHAPMAN: I didn't expect a kind of Spanish Inquisition.

(The scene repeats, somewhat like before)

The sketch is not unlike many of Monty Python's routines: a conventional exchange, often class related (here, the language difficulty between Chapman and Cleveland suggests this), is punctured by a bizarre interruption (often coded as a repressive authority: police, government, church). The result is an interplay of associations and forms that calls our attention to class conventions of language, ideologies, and the power structures that inform them.

Like the ending of *The Holy Grail,* in *Life of Brian* there are continual breaks in our expectations, such as the prison guards who are chatting in very normal, civil voices until the officer arrives, at which point they become suddenly stupid and unable to talk. We are jolted out of what we expect. The film reminds us of the rupture of what Freud called the "thin veneer of civilization," or the potentially fragile state of mythic language and narrative. Just as in *The Holy Grail,* the satiric force is not directed at medieval movies (that really serves no social purpose). The lampoon in "The Spanish Inquisition Sketch" is not directed specifically at the church (would anyone defend the Spanish Inquisition anyway?). Rather, the absurdist, indeed anarchical, context heightens the social reality of class and language. What really is at stake in the sketch, then, is not the Spanish Inquisition or the values of the Catholic Church but the fate of middle-class British politics, language, and power. As is so often the case in literary history, allusions about the past provide the occasions for satire about the present. Hence, much of Monty Python's project is an antiauthoritarian allegory directed against bourgeois, comfortable English living and that class's methods of garnering and retaining power. Thus freed from the logical, conventional demands of plot, Monty Python's work forces the audience out of a more or less linear spectacle into the challenging conditions of multiple associations, a kind of "metalanguage," or language about language.

In *Life of Brian,* religious orthodoxy and history also function as a commentary about the present in a metalanguage: they provide a context to involve us in a satire not so much about religion, but about human behavior and ways of thinking in contemporary society. The film wants to cast a political light on the dark side of the late twentieth century, particularly capitalism and class privilege. The Roman soldiers suggest a pointed allegory about bureaucracy, the ruling class, and colonialism. The silly populous of Israel is nothing but a group of willing followers who misunderstand, misidentify, and follow what anybody tells them. Brian is swallowed up in arcane red tape and constructed as a messiah by fools who exist in an apparent state of false consciousness and self-delusions.

In *Life of Brian,* then, what often seems like a burlesque of church and gospel is a cultural critique of something more appealing to Monty Python's sensibility, namely, contemporary British society. What is clear from the opening sequence, showcasing the wise men to the unfortunate Brian and his surly mother, is a look at greed in the suburbs ("Gold, frankincense, myrrh!" "Well, why didn't you say so. He's over there."). Another clear example of serious politics masquerading as religious lunacy occurs when the reluctant Brian goes to the window to address a large crowd. Like the pope speaking to his audience on Sunday afternoon in St. Peter's Square, Brian comes to the window dressed in white (including zucchetto). He tells the large gathering, "You are all individuals." They respond together, "Yes, we are individuals." He tells them again, "Don't let anyone tell you what to do...otherwise...." At which point Brian is summarily grabbed by the ear by his annoying mother and taken away. This short scene is hardly meant to be a message to Catholics not to obey the pope (could this ever be a strategy for a highly politicized Monty Python in a Protestant country where few people regularly attend religious services?). Rather, the religious context becomes the occasion for a bigger, political statement against the established order, which often hides behind religious (epic) conventions and (biblical) traditions.

With the gathering Conservative forces in England by the late 1970s, the recognition of the collapse of the long reign of colonialism and the continual deployment of an empty royalty to marshal power and prestige, *Life of Brian* is a satiric instance of social criticism of Britain at the edge of the 1980s. Further, *Life of Brian* appears to anticipate the Orwellian vision of Terry Gilliam's *Brazil* (1985), as well as the absurd *Monty Python's Meaning of Life* (1983). It is not coincidental that these films get more and more bleak during the high noon of Thatcher's England. In a certain sense, much of Monty Python is guided by the paranoid, surrealistic, shocking awakening of the protagonist in the opening lines of Kafka's *Metamorphosis*: "As Gregor Samsa awoke one morning from uneasy dreams he found himself transformed in his bed into a giant insect."

American Reactions. In America, of course, Monty Python's humor was received somewhat differently. Like Britain, America faced a similar trend toward conservatism that would lead to a decade dominated by "Reaganomics." Having survived a period of European anti-Americanism in the1970s, the country returned to a pre-1960 nationalist mode, with its president revisiting the language of the Cold War. Not that the Cold War had ended, but Reagan proclaimed in mythic language that the United States was the "city on the hill" and portrayed the USSR as the "evil empire." We might recall that just a few years earlier, Hollywood was experimenting with independent films and young filmmakers. But after the matchless turnout at the box office for *Star Wars* (1977), the film industry became driven by studio mergers and production deals, the special effects' blockbusters, commercial tie-ins, and the tendency toward "theme park" integration. Moreover, the country now found itself patriotically and somewhat nostalgically defending American soldiers in Vietnam at the hands of corrupt bureaucrats in blockbusters like *First Blood* (1982) and *Rambo: First Blood Part II* (1985).

It is no wonder that Universal Studios insisted on cutting more than fifteen minutes from Gilliam's *Brazil,* a dark vision of life in the future. Things were a bit different a few years earlier for *Life of Brian,* since the satiric edge of the biblical comedy could be read by an American audience not so much as a political weapon against British governmental practices—or a Kafkaesque plot devouring the human subject—as much as a parodic send-up of biblical epics. After appearing regularly on PBS stations across the country and on some of the major networks as guest comedians, Monty Python had their American fans. In addition, a Hollywood audience would have been quite at home with Monty Python's intertextual references to past cinema practices and conventions. Generations had grown up on movies produced by the Classic Studio System; film studies were by now part of the college curriculum. Interestingly enough, *Life of Brian* was hardly the only film released in the late 1970s that focused America's attention on past film tradition. It appeared during a period in cinema history in which traditional film genres were being transformed, even reinvented. As critics such as John Cawelti have noticed, by the late 1960s and well into the 1970s, Hollywood was producing "darker" detective pictures (*Chinatown* ,1974) and gangster movies (*Bonnie and Clyde,* 1967 and *The Godfather,* 1972).[6] Parody plays an important role in determining the way the American audience looked at cinema and consumed it—as a kind of "retro style"—especially in regard to the horror film (*Young Frankenstein,* 1974), the western (*Blazing Saddles,* 1974), musical (*Pennies From Heaven,* 1981), and, of course, the "biblical" epic *(Monty Python's Life of Brian).* Parody is a complicated artistic formation which, in the popular imagination, tends to be a "send-up" or a lampoon of a familiar work of art or tradition. It is well known that there is certainly an aspect of the comedic to parody, but there is a serious side to this fascinating literary practice as well. For example, parody was deployed most substantially in the twentieth century by James Joyce's rereading of Homer's *Odyssey* in his masterpiece, *Ulysses* (1922). While there are very funny elements to *Ulysses,* Joyce was also taking Homer quite seriously, and the modern novelist was attempting to forge or transform a genre with another kind of epic in prose fiction.

That a large group of feature films in the 1970s relied on intertextual references should tell us something about the culture that surrounded them.

Many of the cultural artifacts produced in the late 1970s remind us of other forms of parody: from disco (ballroom dancing) to television *(Happy Days),* to the ways in which film genres parodied themselves. American culture was becoming an intertextual landscape, a pastiche of styles, a caricature of itself. In terms of film culture, Americans were getting very good at reading films, or at visual literacy. Even before video technology became widely available, old Hollywood movies were regularly being recycled on late night television.

But the transformation of established film genres should recommend deeper issues for our consideration. In a certain sense, when legible generic conventions are parodied, a whole way of looking at the world is called in question because the established genre (that is, the Western or biblical epic) solidifies or institutionalizes a certain way of looking at the world. In a certain sense, the late 1970s in America was a culture driven toward parody. After the edge of the 1960s began to dull, and the war in Vietnam ended, Americans were left with the cynicism of Watergate. The American military left Saigon, and Richard Nixon resigned his office in humiliation and disgrace. Americans elected Ronald Reagan, a movie star from the old Hollywood studio system. In a way, Reagan, former president of the Screen Actor's Guild, was himself a transformed, recycled cultural product—a reinvented character, a movie star reconfigured as a politician. Technology has changed the stakes in political discourse, as it will continue to do throughout the twenty-first century. Electronic systems (the emergence of the sound byte as a kind of language all its own, together with its ability to duplicate an aura) force us to think self-consciously, intertextually, and parodically.

Recycled image? Parody? If technology has shaped the course of politics, then it will continue to transform our image and expectations of the Savior and the silver screen. What does the "postmodern Jesus" look like? How does technology compel us to come to terms with our image of God? That is the question that faces us in these days of endless parody, the age of pastiche. To this end, *Jesus of Nazareth,* with its more or less gnostic strategy of evacuating historical meaning, makes a fine contrast to *Life of Brian.* Where the miniseries drew in its audience by a series of established conventions, Monty Python's appeal is to a postmodern, anticonvention audience comfortable with irony. Ostensibly, there is nothing "scandalous" about *Jesus of Nazareth,* but, accusations of "blasphemy" notwithstanding, perhaps it is *Life of Brian* that might engage students more fully in a discussion of our images of Jesus.

In terms of religious education, we have noticed that objections to *Monty Python's Life of Brian* tend toward a generational division. An older generation was positioned to see the Savior as middle-class spectators; Jesus himself even endorsed conservative values. In the past, however, Hollywood was able to establish a singular aura around Jesus. Usually, Hollywood spectatorship insists on positioning the movie viewer firmly within institutionalized genres such as the biblical epic. Religious institutions and modes of epistemology tend to be firmly tied to genre conventions. The fact is that younger people, nurtured on hours and hours of MTV, recycled television shows, and so on, are also comfortable with parody and the politics of surrealism. That *Monty Python's Life of Brian* should be condemned as a scandal carries very little weight for postmodern children born in the post-Watergate world. The deeper question that the film seems to raise, then, is what does the aura of Jesus mean to young people. Again, is it possible to be a disciple of Jesus and still watch *Life of Brian?* The 1960s began to chip away at established ideologies and, together with the deployment of new technologies, helped reinvent our ways of inventing God. The legacy of the 1960s is still with us today and likely will remain in the days to come.

NOTES

1. James F. Hopewell, *Congregation: Stories and Structures* (Philadelphia: Fortress, 1987), 58.

2. Vincent Canby, "Gospel of Lunacy," *The New York Times Film Reviews 1979–1980* (New York: *New York Times* & Arno Press, 1981), 17 August 1979, quoted in Baugh, *Imaging the Divine*, 49.

3. *Playboy* (November 1979): 161, 216, 218.

4. André Breton, *Manifestoes of Surrealism*, trans. Richard Seaver and Helen R. Lane (Ann Arbor: University of Michigan Press, 1972), 123.

5. Ibid., 128.

6. Cf. John G. Cawelti, "*Chinatown* and Generic Transformation in Recent American Films," in *Film Genre Reader*, Barry Keith Grant, ed. (Austin TX: University of Texas Press, 1986),183–201.

EIGHTH FEATURE

The Last Temptation of Christ (1988)

"Fear. You look inside me and that's all you'll find."

Written by: Paul Schrader (based on the novel by Nikos Kazantzakis)

Directed by: Martin Scorsese

Actors Include: Willem Dafoe (Jesus), Barbara Hershey (Mary Magdalene), Harvey Keitel (Judas), David Bowie (Pilate)

Running Time: 163 minutes

Introduction

We arrive at the most vilified of all Jesus movies. Storms of controversy accompanied this film even before its showing. It is the film version of the novel by Nikos Kazantzakis. The film opens with a quotation from the novel:

> The dual substance of Christ—the yearning, so human, so superhuman, of man to attain God...has always been a deep inscrutable mystery to me. My principal anguish and source of all my joys and sorrows from my youth onward has been the incessant, merciless battle between the spirit and the flesh...and my soul is the arena where these two armies have clashed and met.

This quotation from the novel is then followed by a disclaimer, or perhaps it is more in the nature of a proclamation: "This film is not based upon the Gospels but upon this fictional exploration of the eternal spiritual conflict." The film, in this way, identifies what its alleged intentions are, even if many have accused it of being something much different, including many who have never seen the film or read the book.

It is true enough, however, that films based on books go through an inevitable transformation process while moving from one medium to another. In addition to the different demands and characteristics of print versus cinema, there are the filters provided by the screenwriter and especially by the film's director, in this instance Martin Scorsese. The film is a separate artifact. While comparisons are inevitable, one must recognize that it is a bit like comparing apples and oranges. The content and intent of the book cannot be equated with the content and intent of the movie. Just as the reader of a novel fills in data from his or her own experience or expectations, so the director inevitably infuses his or her own vision and values into the film, even in a lengthy film. Editorial decisions must be made about what is included and what is excluded. Further, the director controls how the material that is selected is pictured or portrayed. The manner in which the director employs the cinematic vocabulary can shade meaning in one way or another. The director may also choose to add material not in the book in order to create a more cinematic vision of the events being considered. Movies, then, are not reproductions of a novel, but heavily filtered, creative interpretations of a theme or of an event recorded in the book.

Even with those initial disclaimers, many have labeled *Last Temptation* as a film that flagrantly attacks basic Christian values. Michael Medved has written: "The urge to assault cherished recollections of even universally esteemed figures in our culture reached its most infamous expression, of course, in *The Last Temptation of Christ* (1989) [sic]."[1] Religious groups from around the world protested the movie's release. Medved observes that:

> Christian leaders identified more than twenty elements in the finished film that offended them deeply, ranging from an early scene in which Jesus crouches by the bed and watches with voyeuristic intensity as Mary Magdalene has sex with ten different men, to a later conversion in which the Apostle Paul confesses he doesn't really believe in the Resurrection and admits that "I've created truth out of what people needed and believed."[2]

The film industry apparently relied on claims to First Amendment rights to dodge the brunt of the criticism. However, it must be noted that commercial media exist for one purpose and one purpose only: to make money. Lloyd Baugh, however, concludes that in "spite of Scorsese's written disclaimer before even the title and the opening credits of the film...this is a film about Jesus the Christ."[3]

If any part of this is true, why include this movie in our considerations of the Savior on the silver screen? Because it has become part of the genre, it requires some consideration. It has a gravity that makes it unavoidable. The movie is an obvious counterpoint to the perhaps overly pious Hollywood versions that preceded it. Scorsese has attempted to create the feel of rugged Palestine. The actors do not adapt a neutral style of speech but often have a rather rough edge. Some critics have complained about Harvey Keitel's rough New York accent. But is this any more out of place than the upper-crust, aristocratic British accents adopted in several of the other Jesus films? Baugh adds that Scorsese is a respected filmmaker with many worthy film credits to his name and that "the seriousness and tenacious dedication he devoted to the project oblige us to treat the film seriously."[4] This does not at all suggest that we recommend the movie. Whether one watches it or not, whether one likes it or not, the place of the movie in the chronology of "Jesus films" warrants comment.

Medved claims, "In my opinion, the controversy about this picture is a lot more interesting than the film itself."[5] As it turned out, the movie was not profitable and did not garner a large audience. Precisely because of this, then, we believe the film has a place in our examination of the Savior on the silver screen. We hope to provide some analytical framework by which one can judge *The Last Temptation of Christ* both as a film and as one more image of Jesus.

Movie Preview: Questions and Suggestions

1. *What have you already heard about this film? Are you willing to employ a "willing suspension of disbelief" during your viewing of the film?*

2. *Have you read Kazantzakis's novel? What are your impressions and recollections of the novel?*

3. *Have you noticed any trends in the evolution of Jesus' image over the course of viewing the previous films? How has Jesus' image or character changed over time? What is being more emphasized or de-emphasized?*

Movie Viewing

Movie Review: Questions and Responses

1. *How did the film compare to your expectations? How does the film compare to the novel?*

2. *How would you describe the "last temptation"?*

3. *What seemed to bring Jesus' life into greater focus?*

4. *If you have seen other Scorsese films, in what ways is this film similar and/or dissimilar?*

LENS ONE

With *The Last Temptation of Christ* we arrive at a film whose presentation and purpose are clearly distinct from those that we have thus far examined. Martin Scorsese provides us with those two already mentioned propositions that, in the words of Kazantzakis, clearly serve as the primary issues behind the production: "The dual substance of Christ...." and "This film is not based upon the Gospels but upon this fictional exploration of the eternal spiritual conflict." These two emphases—struggle and fiction—begin our discussion.

Jesus, the One Who Struggles. It is, perhaps, the element of "struggle" that most bothers the modern American viewer of this film. Kazantzakis takes seriously the claim of the Council of Chalcedon (A.D. 451) that Jesus Christ was both fully human and fully divine. Inherent to that reality is the probability that Jesus, *man* of Nazareth, had to undergo some element of personal discernment, struggle, and decision throughout his years in Palestine. This is an acknowledgment that it was not in the Garden of Gethsemane alone that Jesus wrestled with his mission. Instead, the wrestling of the spirit was an ongoing process. Part of the purpose of Kazantzakis is to speculate about the nature of this struggle and to offer Jesus of Nazareth—the Messiah of Christian faith and theology—as that figure who can best illustrate how we ourselves may undertake the struggle within ourselves and succeed in that venture. In this way the figure of Jesus becomes a model for all human introspection, the ultimate arena in which the competitive forces of good and evil, sacrifice and desire, God and the devil may be viewed in conflict. For Kazantzakis, regardless of whether most audiences realize it, good and sacrifice do indeed become victorious in the Jesus story.

The element of struggle in the psyche of Jesus is rarely acknowledged in gospel literature. It is, perhaps, even consciously avoided in our scriptural texts, with the possible exception of the Garden of Gethsemane. Kazantzakis is thus left with no choice but to offer a fictional construct of what that struggle might have been like. It is all the more shocking to join both him and Scorsese as they open the film with a mature Jesus at work in his carpenter's shop, an individual who is deeply perplexed by his own process of self-discovery. We are permitted an (admittedly fictional) entrance into the mind of Christ. It is an exploration of a tortured spirit, the view of a first-century holy man whose tendency to look deeply into the common elements of existence and to find there the intimate realities of life cause him to stand apart from his friends and family. This is a man who is confused, tempted by the desire for home and family, emotional in his feelings for other people, and afraid of who he may be and where he may be going. This is also a person with great potential, but who has not yet come to realize the significance of how that potential is to be employed.

What we find in this opening vision is a man, Jesus the laborer, who is at work immediately prior to the opening of the Gospel of Mark. Unlike the Gospels of Matthew, Luke, and John, Mark tells us nothing about the life of Jesus before the preaching of John the Baptist. We simply come upon a fully mature Jesus who has been drawn into the wilderness to be baptized by John. Scorsese takes us to this gospel scene soon enough, but prefaces the Markan story with some background as to how Jesus came to John in the beginning. Hence we are introduced to the tortured motivations of Jesus.

The Role of Fiction. To provide his own introduction for Jesus is, of course, convenient for Scorsese. Many details of the story may be conjectured in such a setting. For example, it is suggested in the movie that Jesus and Judas have been friends for a long time, a theme present in previous Jesus films as well. Judas is concerned for Jesus, and Jesus constantly turns to him for support. Indeed, Jesus even desires that Judas (as his closest friend) ultimately "betray" him to the authorities as a means to the fulfillment of God's plan for salvation! We also "discover," for the first time in any of our films, that Mary Magdalene too was a childhood companion of Jesus. She has desired Jesus as they have grown. His rejection of what she wants in life (his love, his attention, his children) has led to her "fallen" state as a prostitute. Finally, Jesus' mother is stereotypical of first-century (and modern) mothers throughout Palestine; she is concerned that Jesus be responsible, a family man, a solid member of the local Jewish community. Naturally she desires to hold onto "her boy," even as he gradually takes the reins of his own life and pulls away from home and hearth. All of this is fictional, but it broadly fits, or at least does not conflict with, the facts of the New Testament Gospels as well as any other movie presentation thus far. The movie, however, collides with our common piety, often not securely based on data from the New Testament.

Certain theological divergencies that Kazantzakis and Scorsese choose to include perhaps challenge us even further. For example, at several moments in the story Jesus freely proclaims to friends and followers that he is the Son of God, the Messiah for whom all have waited. This is little supported by Scripture. In fact, in the New Testament Gospels, Jesus refers to himself only as the Son of man; it is always other characters in the story who honor him with titles such as Son of God, Son of David, King of Israel, and Lamb of God. Indeed, the claims of the gospels that Jesus only rarely spoke to others about his true nature help us to explain why he was so often misunderstood by the multitudes who followed his ministry.

Christian claims about Jesus' identity have become second nature to us; we easily forget the long history of conflict that accompanies many of our doctrinal statements about the nature of Jesus. We are less comfortable, however, with the forces that Jesus identifies as those against which he, as God's Messiah, struggles. When he enters into the wilderness to contemplate his life, Jesus believes that the Devil is tempting him with the words: "You're not the son of king David, you're not a man, you're the Son of man, and more, the Son of God, and more than that, God!" Jesus struggles with his own belief that Lucifer might lead him to think of himself in a blasphemous way, namely to identify himself with God! In other words, he identifies the very claim of later Christian theology (that Christ is God, the second person of the Trinity) as a temptation from Lucifer. Certainly, this is not part of the traditional picture of Jesus' patterns of thought.

As a second example, in the movie Jesus casts doubt upon institutional religion and the norms of society. For him, although the intention behind religion and society may be valid, they have become perverse. Home and family are fine, but they are the way of common humanity. Safety and security are okay, but they function as supporting crutches for the poorly disciplined masses. Worship of God through sacrifices and offerings is the usual daily fare, but (in the words of Israel's ancient prophets) mercy and love are what God really wants. What Jesus is—an unpredictable holy man, a social loner, a prophet with vivid visions and an incredible depth of feeling who can excite the crowds and whose actions are unpredictable—is the very thing that both institutional religion and society fear the most.

Jesus is a "loose cannon" who follows the beat of a different drummer and who wants more for religion and society than what is perceived to be the acceptable status quo. It is as Pilate himself summarizes: "It's one thing to want to change the way the people live, but you want to change how they think and how they feel...either way it's dangerous; it's against Rome, it's against the world...we don't want them changed." It is Jesus' call for change that leads to his death. We moderns (or postmoderns!) can feel comfortable with Jesus' call for change in a first-century context, of course. What is bothersome is the message that the same call is issued to us, even now, in a Christian society some two thousand years later.

The Role of Scripture and Tradition. If we can allow ourselves to step past the fictional aspects of Kazantzakis's view of the struggling Jesus (certainly not an easy task, and perhaps impossible for some), the subtlety of Scorsese's use of scriptural texts becomes interesting. If there ever was a story that took the Gospel of Mark seriously within a non-Western setting, this is it. Apart from the inherently fictional aspects of *Last Temptation,* it is the fact that the Gospel of Mark itself serves as the backbone of the plot that is potentially troublesome. In Mark, we begin our tale with a mature Jesus, whom we see as a preacher and teacher, ultimately crucified and with no confirmation of any resurrection (apart from that which Jesus predicts, without details, throughout his ministry). Indeed, there is some talk of resurrection and salvation, but this is the preaching of Paul of Tarsus in his efforts to spread the new Christian religion among potential followers.

There are no stories of Jesus' birth or promising tales of angelic revelations to his mother about the coming of a messiah. There is no blessed assurance that this is a divine messiah, whose certainty of purpose and ominous ability to look into the future and know the outcome of his actions dictate all that he says and does. There is no walking on the water, no multiplication of loaves, no calming of storms. No potential disciples simply drop their work when Jesus says "follow me" as he passes by them. There is no glorious transfiguration, no firm instructions for the regulation of a future church, no plan for how this whole situation will work itself through according to the vision of God.

Yet there is something! There is a man who hears God's call to stand up and be counted as someone who has a special task. There is a man who, much like other wonder-workers of antiquity, can heal those with diseases and wounds, soothe those who are possessed by demons or evil spirits, and assume the stigmata of human suffering. There is a man who rejects home and family, who accepts that he is different, a leader and not a follower. There is a man who reads meaning behind the everyday experiences of life, who has extraordinary visions about God and the Tempter, who hears voices and footsteps that others do not perceive, who witnesses the comfort of an angel during his most fretful moments in the Garden of Gethsemane.

The story of Mark provides certain elements that later tradition has often bathed in the soft light of romance and acceptability, elements that actually are exceedingly harsh by modern standards. So it is that Jesus goes forth to find John the Baptist, truly a man of God, a prophet of olden times, who wears coarse camel-hair clothing, as did his ancient predecessors. But John's act does not stop there, for his own hair is wild and unkempt, and his preaching is dramatic, filled with words of destruction and terror, words of condemnation and threat. It is to such a person that Jesus goes, together with many others who surround John, in the ecstasy of undisciplined religious passion, an enthusiasm expressed in free-form dance and wild yells of bloodcurdling euphoria. It is a medicine show of sorts. And it is to such a person that Jesus goes? Worse yet, could it be that it is by such a person that Jesus is greatly influenced in the vision that he has for his own purpose in life and in death? That is indeed what Mark suggests and what Scorsese portrays. It is not necessarily pretty, but religious conviction often is not.

Most disturbing in this film, however, is that Jesus appears to be a messiah whose vision of his mission is a "work in progress." As Judas says: "Every day you have a different plan; first it's love, then it's the axe, and now you have to die! What good can that do?" Indeed, the ministry of Jesus takes different shapes as his experience progresses and his vision clarifies. He begins with the message of love and the realization that the kingdom of God is present even now for those who will possess it through their love of God and their love of neighbor. Curiously, this aspect is *not* a particularly Markan message. It resides firmly in Matthew, Luke, and even John, but it is not Markan. Yet Scorsese does not wish to abandon this teaching, which we now consider to be central to the message of Jesus. Indeed, it becomes the focal point, the primary pillar of Jesus' earliest revelation of who he is and what he is to preach. This message is never lost throughout the film, but with time its urgency is reduced.

The "message of the axe," the threat of coming destruction, the call for all who hear to save themselves through active participation in God's plan for the faithful, comes to Jesus next under the influence of John. This is certainly Mark's foundational "good news" within chapters 1 through 8. Here are the incredible miracles of healing, the message that inspires others to follow the rising star of the Messiah, the clear divider between those who choose to follow the old, traditional ways of Israel's laws and priesthood and those who place their hope in a message of change and of challenge to see more than others see. While these visions stem from Jesus himself, and not necessarily from his followers, his disciples seek to share in his convictions to the extent that they can understand them. In this image of action and rebellion, the crowds that follow Jesus' little band come to identify what they themselves are seeking in a messiah—someone to cast off the yoke of Roman domination and to establish religious and social security within the land. There is an appeal here. There is a seduction here. There is some promise here. But this is not yet the final message.

Jesus finally reveals to his followers that the time for revolution is not upon them. Instead, the time *to die* has become manifest! This final message comes to guide the last actions of Jesus as he moves in and around Jerusalem. It is the immanence of his death that now becomes Jesus' message. This seems to be the case in the New Testament Gospels as well. When Jesus finally "turns toward Jerusalem" (in the case of Mark, at 8:31), the narrative begins to focus on the forthcoming crucifixion and its implications for the followers of Jesus. Issues of love and charity are mostly forgotten, as are concerns for revolution and the axe (though portents of future devastation are neatly collected into a running narrative in Mark 13). It is now the cross that is of concern, because this is the climax of the Markan gospel—cross (and resurrection).

Each of these elements—love, axe, cross—certainly resides within the gospel accounts, but they tend to be subtly interwoven among scenes. This artful tapestry is perhaps better illustrated in the more developed visions of Matthew and Luke than it is in Mark, which suggests that the story of Jesus has been given more thought and consideration in these slightly later texts. But, Scorsese asks us, are not these scriptural presentations of Jesus actually massaged retellings of that old, old story, adaptations and recreations concerned less with the historical sequencing of individual events than with the theological meaning that the early church saw in the life and death of Jesus? Indeed, this undoubtedly is the case; hence the variations that exist among the gospel narratives.

Scorsese seems to suggest that the mixture of elements in the New Testament Gospels is the work of authors and editors who wanted to make the story palatable for a first- and second-century audience. Why must Jesus necessarily be an individual who was constantly driven by a uniform and unchanging understanding of who he was as the Messiah of God? This kind of speculation certainly stands as an affront to modern theology and piety—but is it an affront to the historical facts? There is no objective evidence by which to make such a decision.

Remaining Matters. This brings us finally to certain scattered issues that Kazantzakis and Scorsese raise that creep like little gnomes of concern around the focal elements of struggle and fiction. These issues remain in our discussion as disparate points, perhaps with no real connection except for the way in which they challenge us individually.

The early church apparently was quite concerned about the Gospel of Mark and charged that its Christology was adoptionistic, that is, that the author of Mark thought that Jesus of Nazareth was "adopted" as the Son of God as a reward for his faithful response to God's call. Some interpreters believed that this adoption came with Jesus' baptism at the hands of John; others thought that it came with Jesus' resurrection after his death. Could Kazantzakis's story be any less subject to the charge of an adoptionistic theology? Certainly not, and thus his interpretation may be the most closely attuned to Mark's own views. Indeed, Kazantzakis's vision may bother us modern faithful in the same way that Mark's views often disturbed the ancient faithful.

Our Jesus in *Last Temptation* is truly human, but like Mark's own vision, he is a "God-man." There is no denial here that Jesus could perform miraculous feats of healing and power. The problem for modern piety is that our film Jesus does not seem to limit these feats to spiritual messages. He changes water into wine at Cana (Jn 2:1–11), but without the comment of the author of John that this was a sign performed in order to reveal his glory (Jn 2:11), it takes on the aura of a parlor trick. The wine of the Last Supper actually transforms into blood as the disciples drink from the common cup, but no specific rationale or purpose is ascribed to this change. Jesus heals the ear of the high priest's slave at the arrest; he reveals the stigmatic marks of crucifixion before their time; he heals those who follow him without comment about their own faith. Jesus is a doer! He is a wonder-worker! He is full of the spirit! He speaks aloud to those around him that he is the Son of God, the long-awaited Messiah.

But he is not perfect by human standards. He asks forgiveness of Mary Magdalene (a prostitute!) before he goes to the wilderness to pray. He tells others that he is afraid of everything and, indeed, that his god is "fear" itself. After he rejects the message of John the Baptist about God's forthcoming anger at the day of judgment, he admits that he himself does not know what God's true message must be. He apologizes to his mother at the cross for the fact that he has been "a bad son." Jesus is, as the early church interpreted him to be through the words of the prophet Isaiah (chapter 53), a man of sorrows who was "wounded for our transgressions." He makes the crosses, ties on the belt of affliction, withstands the rocks and curses of the crowds, refuses the pleas of his mother, withstands the spittle of a prostitute, and carries the loads of those who have been condemned to death. He bears the sins of others. When Judas asks, "How will you ever pay for your sins?" Jesus responds, "With my life, Judas. I don't have anything else!" Jesus may not be sure just what the tune is, but he is certain that in the end the bell will toll for him.

Curiously, neither Kazantzakis nor Scorsese confront either Rome or the Jewish authorities in their consideration of Jesus' death. While previous directors, in compliance with scriptural accusations, have implicated either one or both of these adversaries to Jesus' ministry, such is not the case here. This is not to say that Rome and Judaism have no role in the course of events. Instead, it is to admit that other elements are of more immediate concern.

One surely wonders what those elements might be. We must consider issues of the struggle between the forces of good and evil within the human heart; we must recognize that God directs the movement of history without clear recognition of that movement even by those who believe; we must accept the harsh reality that historical fact and historical interpretation are rarely the same, since each person's historical remembrance and understanding creates some new diversion from the cold facts. Kazantzakis and Scorsese do not seek to identify opponents or culprits, devils or scapegoats in their presentation of the life of Jesus. Such approaches to Scripture have often been attempted and too easily achieved in Christian history. Instead, there is a desire to look at the core of the issue, Jesus of Nazareth, the Son of God, and to seek there the deepest motivations that ultimately led to his crucifixion.

The gospel story does not end with the crucifixion, of course. In the last temptation, the dream sequence in which Jesus is tempted to find his reward for faithful service and suffering in the arms of happy hearth and home, we find the near catastrophe that occurs with the seductive choice to let our religious devotion culminate in the crucifixion instead of in the resurrection. When Jesus is tempted to abandon the cross and accept some final consideration for himself and his own personal desires, all seems to go astray. She whom he loved (Mary Magdalene) dies before birth is given to their child. He settles for other women. Those who followed him (the disciples) now rebuke his weakness. He tries to explain his situation. The world as he has chosen to accept it (common, daily living) turns into the chaos of the Jewish wars of A.D. 66–70.

It is at this point that he comes to realize that he has been tricked. The choice to abandon the cross is not God's payment for a life lived in service to the divine, as suggested by the "angel," but the chicanery of the Devil. Just as Jesus has rejected the symbolic apple of Adam's first fall, just as Paul of Tarsus has preached about the hope that lies within the resurrected Christ, just as Jesus has foreseen that he has been chosen to bear the sins of the world without any significant appreciation for his efforts by common humanity, so all of this must come true through his death on the cross. As Kazantzakis has so correctly translated his native Greek tongue, "It is completed!" With Jesus' final choice to remain on the cross, so it is.

LENS TWO

The controversy concerning this film, that is, its operative image of Jesus and its speculations about Jesus' character, has tended to obscure or overshadow discussion of the film *as* a film, that is, how it works as a movie, or as a story. Included within this latter discussion would be observations about plot, characterization, setting, editing, use of the camera, and other visual and audio elements. Yet, as we have noted many times before, these are the very tools at the director's disposal to create, in this case, the image of Jesus. These are the tools by which the director crafts or forms the message, substance, or "stuff" of the film. The dialogue of the film is shaped, colored, contextualized, even formed by these other elements. It seems appropriate, even necessary, to address some of these elements at the same time, even before, one seeks to form judgments about the message of the movie.

The overall look of this film certainly is very gritty. There has been no attempt to sanitize the events of the movie. It is dusty and dirty with very little color, except red, blood red, which we see as the background color for both the opening and closing credits. Additionally, the viewer is exposed to an unusual amount, for this series of Jesus films anyway, of blood and gore.

One might well conclude that blood is a motif evident throughout the film. Blood spurts into Jesus' face as he helps Romans nail criminals to crosses early in the narrative. Blood runs into gutters where dogs lap it up. Bleeding stigmata appear twice on Jesus' hands. During the temptation in the desert, an apple that Jesus bites into runs bloody from his mouth. We see people blithely walking in the blood of sacrifices, and then the film cuts immediately to the scene of the Last Supper, where Jesus speaks of the bread as his body and of the wine as his blood; the earlier bloody scene is still vivid in our mind's eye. The wine in the cup at the Last Supper appears to have actually become blood. There is no absence of blood in the film. Surely it is a motif that builds and builds until the ultimate sacrifice is made as Jesus returns from his dream and assumes his rightful place on the cross to proclaim, "It is completed." Today in sermons, we may also frequently hear preachers speak forcefully but abstractly of the "bloody sacrifice" when speaking about the crucifixion. Scorsese has visualized this phrase and the events behind the phrase quite forcefully. It is not pretty, but it is powerful.

Characterization is certainly one of the most obvious elements to observe. Who has been chosen to play what character and to what effect? There are two characters who seem to attract most of the attention: Jesus and Judas. We have already commented on the critique some have made of Harvey Keitel's portrayal of Judas with a Brooklyn accent. Yet, again, this must surely be less ludicrous than the upper-crust British accents of Jesus and others in earlier films—less ludicrous but also less acceptable.

Viewers should surely assess how Dafoe's Jesus differs from those of previous films. The answers are long, emotion laden, and controversial. But beyond how Dafoe's portrayal of Jesus may conflict with the image in other movies or with our own image of Jesus, can we identify with this character at all? Does the portrayal hold together within the context of the film? Already noted and to be further discussed in Lens Three, this image is a much more human image of Jesus, reflecting an evolving sense of mission after a time of significant confusion, anxiety, and doubt. Yet how does the director create and/or reinforce this character or image, beyond raw dialogue? For example, how does Scorsese communicate Jesus' internal turmoil; as a viewer, how do I recognize or identify his inner turmoil? Dialogue helps. The meanings of words, however, develop nuance and color as they are spoken. Dafoe's tone of voice and gestures must also communicate this in a fashion consistent with the dialogue he carries on with the other characters. However, even more obvious is the use of an "off-camera" voice. We hear Jesus' inner thoughts at points throughout the film, usually thoughts of doubt and uncertainty. The quality of Dafoe's voice in these situations is more intimate-sounding, softer, as though he is closer to us, closer to the microphone, even inside our own heads. They are thoughts to which we have become privy; the rest of Jesus' world has not heard them.

One especially interesting example of this inner voice comes from Jesus while he is on the cross. We hear Jesus' inner thought, "Father, forgive them." Of course, had these words been only Jesus' inner thoughts, presumably they would not have become part of the gospel record. It is an interesting twist on the gospel's record of the crucifixion and subtly raises the issue of the degree to which the precise details of an event are remembered or supplied in order to fill out the memory? Memory, after all, is a very fluid and creative process, often filling in and/or dropping out details in order to complete the picture of what one experienced, or even hoped or expected to experience. If Jesus is portrayed in very human, even tortured, fashion, he nevertheless has prescient moments. On his first trip to the desert to seek clarity about his mission, he visits with an abbot who we soon discover has died the night before and who later reappears in the person of John the Baptist.

Camera angles reinforce this tone of turmoil. Often the camera assumes a position high overhead, looking straight down on Dafoe as he writhes and twists in dreams. The opening scene of the movie takes just such a vantage point. One wonders whose vantage point this might be.

Many critics have concluded that, although they may or may not agree with the basic substance of the image of Jesus, even in terms of the film, his character does not evolve convincingly. The character seems to vacillate back and forth, making little progress in insight until that very last moment when he "returns" to his place on the cross. The viewer suffers through an endless series of Jesus' changes of mind or spirit and may finally weary from character-evolution whiplash. Yet, at the end, Jesus does seem to have developed clarity, but one wonders from whence it came.

It seems obvious that Scorsese has attempted to give women a more prominent place in the ongoing narrative of this film than in most of our previous films. Yet Mary Magdalene assumes center stage initially with much the same role that she had in *The King of Kings*. In *Last Temptation*, however, it is her relationship with Jesus, rather than with Judas, that is explored as a means of pushing the plot along toward its conclusion. Mary and Martha, too, assume unexpected, untraditional roles. After all is said and done, however, one may wonder how progressive the role is for the women of this film. They play more prominent roles, but they seem to remain subservient to Jesus, waiting for him to make up his mind, seeming to have few positive, creative, independent alternatives. While this was certainly true of first-century Palestine, more could have been said and done in this regard. While Mary and Martha become Jesus' wives only in a dream, it is perhaps unfortunate that Jesus seems to view them as little more than servants who attend to his various needs.

The viewer may observe that the camera shifts in its perspective throughout the movie and occasionally assumes some unconventional angles. As a reminder, this is against the grain of typical Hollywood protocol, which seeks to minimize attention drawn to the actual work of the camera. The viewer should, instead, become lost in the story. Sometimes the camera takes a neutral point of view, assuming a straight-on point of view. Other times it takes a perspective high above and immediately over the action, usually with Dafoe as the object of interest. Other times it seems to become one of the participants in the ongoing action of a scene: moving, shifting to get a better view of what is going on.

An example of camera movement echoing several earlier films occurs after Jesus has been nailed to the cross. As the cross is raised into place, the camera seems to be attached to it, rising with the cross to the vertical position. At some points the camera seems uncomfortably close to the figures or action on the screen. There is an impulse to move back.

The film employs a variety of visual effects. Included here would be the use of a style of "dissolve" on at least two occasions to suggest the passing of time. The images overlap as they are dissolved one into the other. The first occurs when we see a herd of camels settling down to their knees, presumably to be unloaded of their cargo or for a rest. The other occurs when we see Jesus' disciples approaching along the lakeside. As they get closer, several dissolves indicate them making their journey toward the camera, suggesting a long period of time. Is this symbolic of something or just a piece of camera magic? The question here is whether this particular effect is necessary, that is, does it contribute to the evolution of the narrative? It would seem not, since the actual elapsed time was rather minimal to warrant this special effect.

Other effects may contribute more solidly to the narrative. For example, recall that Jesus takes his heart from his chest, a scene not included in the novel but with highly evocative power within Catholic piety. One might also list the various embodiments of the temptations in the desert: the serpent with Mary Magdalene's voice; the lion with Judas's voice; the flame as the archangel, with a Darth Vader-like voice in "reverb"; the apple tree, possibly a symbol of the original fall and the first temptation in Genesis. Jesus' death on the cross is the last special effect the viewer sees. It is an attempt not so much to portray Jesus' death, but to signal its fact. Lights, colors, flashes, bells tolling—all signal the end.

This scene is reminiscent in some ways of DeMille's use of Technicolor to picture the resurrection in *The King of Kings.* The director, in both cases, employs something nonliteral, something beyond mere description and straightforward portrayal, pulling out all the technological stops in order to evoke the sense of the magnitude of the event. There is nothing more to be seen, heard, or said. It is accomplished. The credits roll. Of course, the viewer may still have some questions about what has just been accomplished. The answers to that question have been the stuff of theological reflection for the last nearly two millennia.

Although it is somewhat outside the purview of this lens, it is worth noting that, for DeMille, it is the resurrection that warrants the extra special effect, whereas for Scorsese, it is Jesus' death, or more properly, Jesus' decision to die. This makes sense in terms of the narratives as they evolve in each of the films, but there is an important theological statement implicit in the difference. There is no reference to the resurrection in *Last Temptation* because it is outside the confines of the self-defined plot. We can only note that it is absent, but not necessarily what its absence means.

Less a matter of special effect than of directorial choice, *Last Temptation* brings an unusual realism to the portrayal of first-century life in Palestine. For example, it makes clearer than any other film the terrible odor that would presumably have accompanied the miraculous raising of Lazarus after his death two days earlier. Martha explicitly mentions it in John 11. In this film, onlookers are visibly repelled by the stench as the door is moved; even Jesus hesitates. By restoring a sense of the real-life experience to this event, the raising feels less holy but even more miraculous than the sanitized versions so often presented in the films. The raising takes a turn to the tragic when Lazarus is killed soon after.

Later yet, Jesus' treatment at the hands of his Roman captors is visualized in greater, gory detail than in any other film, bringing a heart-sickening reminder that the events immediately preceding the crucifixion were cruel, harsh, painful, inhuman, and horrifying examples of the capacity of humanity for inflicting pain on other, less powerful humans.

Music and sound effects also play supportive roles in this film, as they do in many others. Directed by Peter Gabriel, the music throughout has a very authentic Middle-Eastern sound. Baugh notes, however, that while authentic sounding, it is inappropriate at points, particularly in regard to the wedding at Cana. The music used in this scene is apparently Arabic and based on an Islamic confession of faith that says, "I believe that there is no God but God and that Mohammed is the One Sent by God."[6] Certainly, not many viewers would catch this, but, if true, it would seem to be an affront to people of both Christian and Islamic faiths.

Sometimes the absence of sound can be used to create a desired effect. This device is used several times in the movie and creates a separation or isolation of the character from the extraneous events going on around him. For example, when Jesus is baptized by John at the edge of the Jordan River, only the sound of the water is heard, all of the remaining environmental sounds, including the voices of those present, fade out. The same device is used as Jesus trudges to Golgotha. We hear wailing voices, strident music, but no environmental sound. Lastly, while Jesus is on the cross, the environmental sound fades out and we focus on Jesus' interior thoughts and experiences. The "angel" then comes to Jesus to escort him off the cross while seemingly the events continue, somehow remotely, in his absence as the two of them depart. It has the feel of an "out-of-body" experience, which is precisely what it turns out to be. "I'm not the Messiah?" Jesus asks the angel. "No, you're not," is the reply.

LENS THREE

What is left to observe about Jesus on film? In dealing with Martin Scorsese's *The Last Temptation of Christ,* undoubtedly one of the most controversial and widely discussed religious films in recent years, we might say that its director must have faced a similarly perplexing question: after almost a century of Jesus on celluloid, what is left to be done? By the late 1980s, the realistic biblical epic had been more or less exhausted due to several different reasons.

Indeed, the factors that contributed to a decline in the familiar biblical form should be obvious to us by now. First, the advent of the new Hollywood, "restored" during the late 1960s, together with the influence of European cinema on another generation of directors in America, made showcasing new technical, religious superspectacles (such as CinemaScope's premier with *The Robe,* 1953) less desirable. Second, there was a gradual expectation on the part of American audiences (beginning in the mid-1960s) to find this new, revisionist cinema normative, a style that transformed older Hollywood genres, including biblical epics. Third, representations of Jesus could be effectively negotiated in another format (television) and became more protracted and intimate via the miniseries. Finally, and paradoxically, a less pious, secular culture on the one hand, and the rise of more and more Christian fundamentalists on the other, made financing a biblical epic too risky for Hollywood.

Martin Scorsese, however, wanted to take a gamble on a new Jesus. As early as 1972, when he reportedly was given a copy of *Last Temptation,* an insightful, controversial novel published in 1951 (translated into English in 1960) by Nikos Kazantzakis, Scorsese began to think about how he might deploy his own unique vision of Jesus within the context of the Hollywood industry. In choosing to direct a film about Christ—a project that saw years of alternating interest among frightened producers—Scorsese would abandon conventional ways of looking at the Son of God that had guided the Hollywood film industry for almost a century. With a meager production budget of 6.5 million dollars (compared to the average eighteen million dollars in 1988), Scorsese chose to imagine his version of Jesus precisely as an alternative to Hollywood.

At the same time, however, Scorsese is not avant-garde, but remains in the Hollywood film tradition. *The Last Temptation of Christ,* despite all its controversy, is still governed by long-standing conventions the director admired. In fact, in a series of lectures Scorsese gave in Britain in 1987, he explained that his inspirations and working blueprints for *Last Temptation* were older Hollywood movies about Jesus (and, as a matter of fact, his film would include more than a few citations from these older movies). He found *The King of Kings* and *Ben-Hur* somewhat boring and, as with *The Greatest Story Ever Told,* discovered that "there is no sense of real people living."[7] Scorsese was determined to deal with the human side of Jesus, an unfamiliar face in film culture.

Scorsese's first point of departure was to adapt a source text other than the gospels that represented Jesus. Kazantzakis portrays a Jesus Christ who is continually on the edge of doubt about his mission and divinity; he only gradually grows into an awareness of his messiahship. In a certain sense, Kazantzakis and Scorsese are aptly suited to one another: they are pious mavericks who take risks. Besides finding a place on the *Index of Forbidden Books,* Kazantzakis's novel is nothing if it is not one man's reflection on the meaning of the incarnation and, indeed, a fierce contemplation on Jesus' divinity. Scorsese himself approached his future production in a religious mode, claiming that his depiction of the Savior on the silver screen is "like a prayer." In other words, Scorsese freely admits that his representation is a kind of meditation on Christ's incarnation. Like the novel from which it came, *Last Temptation* engages a Christology that was not taken lightly (as has been noted already in Lens One). Despite the fact that Scorsese maintained he was adapting a novel and offering a visual theological reflection, *Last Temptation* still causes much dissonance for those who have not even seen it. What is this controversy about?

In what has become the most controversial aspect of the novel—a dream sequence on the cross in which Jesus seemingly renounces his messiahship—we find Scorsese quietly demythologizing the most important cultural icon in the history of the West. Jesus is put to the final test: the young angel leads him into the life he now has purchased: a wife, children, and old age. The cross was just a nightmare, a fiction in which he just pretended to die. As if a movie in which the divinity of Jesus was questioned were not controversial enough, we see the Messiah glimpse at carnality, a scene in which he and Mary Magdalene make love.

Scorsese, evidently a devout man who still says he is passionately Catholic (ironically making him one of the most religious directors of the Jesus film epics), went on national television to defend the film, Kazantzakis, and even the morality of temptation. Others, like Paul Schrader, who wrote the screenplay (later revised by Scorsese with consultation), argued for a dense theological viewing of the film. Schrader, who wrote *Transcendental Style in Film* (1972), one of the most intelligent books on the theology of film, told film critic Kevin Jackson that the point of *Last Temptation* was not to dismantle Christ's divinity or even his call, but to refocus the debate of the early church between the Arian heresy (which claimed that Jesus was a man who only pretended to be God) and the Docetist heresy (which said that Jesus was a God who cleverly acted as a man). That debate is a long one and extends back to the Council of Chalcedon in A.D. 451.[8]

The film becomes an apologetic, an arena in which two warring sides clash and are played out. Not unexpectedly, then, everyone from the telecast nun Mother Angelica to born-again singer Pat Boone condemned Scorsese's Jesus. The film was banned in several countries, including Israel. Twenty-five thousand people marched on Universal Studios to protest the film. The United States bishops themselves called for a nationwide boycott of *Last Temptation*—a first.

The violent condemnations from seemingly every sector suggest several things worthy of our attention. First, any attempt to justify the filmed version of *The Last Temptation of Christ* confronts a simple but powerful issue. Whether Kazantzakis's Jesus matches Scorsese's Jesus, or how they both differ from the gospel is not the point. "Jesus Christ" is a cultural icon that cannot be reduced to the problems of "novel into film." Secondly, most investigations of *Last Temptation* focus heavily on its polemical (i.e., sexual) content, but we want to suggest that there may be other issues to explore than what some critics refer to as Scorsese's heretical or "scandalous" vision of Jesus.

From the point of view of culture, then, is there more at stake in Scorsese's depiction of Jesus than either adaptation or a theological debate? In fact, as we have been suggesting throughout these chapters, a construction of "Jesus Christ" is an aggregate of many aspects worthy of exploration. Our position is that Scorsese has attempted to confront the dominance of a certain kind of prevailing tendency in 1980s America. *The Last Temptation of Christ* is a troubling, shrill, almost operatic film that wants to demythologize our cherished beliefs and, in so doing, becomes a lightning rod for criticism about morals, religion, and the culture industry. We do not necessarily intend to endorse this particular film, but rather, hope to encourage dialogue and exploration about the conditions that fostered the emergence of such a controversial cultural artifact.

In the Aftermath of Vietnam. The culture industry played an important role in the years after the Vietnam War by endlessly restating therapeutic, triumphal narratives that tended to exploit clearly established perimeters between good and evil. It is by now commonplace to refer to the 1980s as a time driven by a recovery of national pride lost, of course, in a decade overshadowed by the defeat in Southeast Asia and the shame of Watergate, and further burdened with a growing fear of the rise in terrorism. The 1980s made a myth of the "American dream" explicit by masterfully (re)articulating the possibility of expansion within the rhetoric of Republican ideals of freedom and biblical motifs of the "chosen people." Reagan's vision of imperialism was certainly nothing new—just old material repackaged for a different age.

Reagan began his presidency at the end of the Iran hostage crisis. The 1980s would be stamped by a significant increase in subversive activity in Libya and South and Central America. After 240 Marines were killed in Beirut by a suicide truck loaded with explosives, Reagan deployed American troops less than a week later on Grenada as a gesture of power. Since much of his presidency was reactionary, Ronald Reagan invested American culture with a return to the language of the Cold War. For example, Reagan's rhetoric positioned America and its (covert) subversive allies in Nicaragua as the "freedom fighters" against a government funded by the "evil empire" of the USSR. At the same time that he was condemning the USSR, however, Reagan created an image of stability, even a grandfatherly figure of reassurance. A master of media manipulation, Reagan carved out a national space based on nostalgia and a sense of superiority.

It is not accidental that the film culture of the 1980s is filled with stories about "the Other" in just about every genre or subgenre imaginable. *Alien* (1979), Ridley Scott's fascinating look at cosmic, ultrahostile terrorism, suggests the fear of "the Other" and set the tone for the decade to come. There were several notable feature films that fueled a return to a Cold War rhetoric, so much so that Soviet Deputy of Culture, Minister Ivanov, said that *Red Dawn, Rocky IV,* and *Rambo II* were downright "anti-Soviet." Then again, *The Little Drummer Girl* (1984) deals overtly with terrorism of Palestinians, while *Die Hard* (1988) wittily shows us what happens when the media capitalize on European fanatics who are foiled by an all-American maverick (what else?) cop. On the other hand, the best films of the 1980s, however, tend to blur the distinction between "them" and "us," as in *Blade Runner* (1982), a postmodern noir film that suggests that there is a very thin line between the human and the "replicant."

The cycle of Vietnam War movies exhibited throughout the decade of the 1980s enabled the country to establish a fictitious, utopic space of victory, usually based on the dynamics of "loss and recovery." It is easy to see that the legacy of Vietnam in the 1980s—now restored into a vigilante motif and an excuse for racism—would function well under the hegemony and rhetoric of nationalism and antiterrorism. Masterfully, *Batman* (1989) showed another version of a vigilante motif, with the caped crusader as medieval knight, wiping out the Joker's terrorist chaos and, at the last, handing over the batshield to the police at the end of the film in order to protect law and order. But there were some disguised triumphal films as well. From action-adventures like the *Indiana Jones* cycle (1981–89) and melodramas such as *Terms of Endearment* (1983), one would be hard pressed not to name several major Hollywood features each year that did *not* explore the dynamics of recovery in some way.

These 1980s films are, of course, a far cry from the "domestic" violence showcased in the 1970s, where evil is often frightfully positioned within our own backyard (i.e., *The Godfather I* and *II*). Even the well-known disaster movies such as *Airport* (1970), or the somewhat better *Towering Inferno* (1974), remind us that destruction comes from *within* and that the evildoer may, in fact, be one of us. After all, Dirty Harry fought "punks" in our city streets, not international terrorists.

Scorsese's important films in the 1970s focused our attention on domestic and national violence as well. His breakthrough film was *Mean Streets* (1973), a look at small-time hoods in New York City. Broadly speaking, Scorsese's efforts bridge the gap between ourselves and what we *project* as "the Other": vicious gangsters become human beings; a prizefighter is exposed by weakness and fragility; a murderous taxi driver is shown to be as lonely as we are. Scorsese tends to challenge us by narrowing the mysterious gulf between good and evil and, as is so often the case, it becomes difficult to exact a moral judgment on characters by traditional Hollywood standards.

A director with a considerable body of films to his credit, Scorsese emerged from a strong Catholic background, NYU's film school, and the new Hollywood of the 1960s. Scorsese, like Francis Ford Coppola, Brian DePalma, and their generation of directors, was able to carve a reputation out of the industry by negotiating another, more radicalized Hollywood. It was characterized by an emerging, stylistic tendency, which, on the one hand, acknowledged the classical industry conventions of the studio period (often citing them in their own work), but, on the other hand, revitalized and transformed generic conventions into something slightly new. Predictably, these directors were often products of film schools and knew the great auteurs and their films like textbooks. Thus, we find a new gangster film in Coppola's *Godfather* cycle, DePalma's violent pastiche of "Hitchcockesque" murder mysteries, and, of course, Scorsese's reanimation of the Jesus epic.

As no feeble observer of culture or Hollywood movies, Scorsese undoubtedly realized that he had to do something different with "Jesus Christ" in cinema. Scorsese would bring to bear his vast knowledge of the film industry and its techniques, together with his own unique stamp—a mark that created some of the best films about the violent imagination in America—with what he saw was lacking in the Christ film, namely a vulnerable Jesus. Scorsese recognized that from a narrative point of view, the Christ film has typically placed Jesus as the center of knowledge in the story. We share his special knowledge as we rehearse the story over and over again, albeit with different actors over the years.

Like the stations of the cross, the Christ film functions as a spectacle, even a ritual. We realize that he is given up to death, but so does he: DeMille's Savior victoriously controls his environment; Ray's Jesus triumphs as a politically astute, sensitive male; Stevens's Christ is a mystic, European seer. In a certain sense, the Hollywood tradition around Jesus suggests not only the Savior's intuitive knowledge about his fate, but that he has even read his own passion narrative ahead of time. Well scripted, Jesus is hardly vulnerable. Good and evil are distinctly drawn: we know that the story will come out okay. Judas is punished; DeMille even rewards Jesus and the disciples with living color at the resurrection.

Scorsese's Metathemes. Scorsese films have been called a cinema of loneliness, but they are really visions taken from the point of view of the cross, much like Jesus' final temptation. In a certain sense, Scorsese's roots remain linked to the early 1970s and the transformed Hollywood, with its expressions of an often violent, vulnerable humanity. For Scorsese, the ethical problem is in the present; he focuses on the choice—the "script" that one has to live out in the historical moment. The moral problem in *GoodFellas* (1990), for instance, deals with what the rite of baptism refers to as rejecting the "glamour of evil." As Henry Hill takes us through the course of his narrative in *GoodFellas,* we learn that what is at stake is not a mythical destiny or fate, but human weakness and the choice of whether to do evil. In a way, many of Scorsese's characters face a "last temptation."

Similarly, Scorsese's Jesus has no identifiable aura or series of codes that would either identify him as the Son of God or allow him to make divine decisions. Rather, this Jesus is a character who straddles the gap between good and evil within himself, and the process of the film is one in which the gap is gradually closed. Thus, from his first moments in the film, there is a reversal from what we typically expect about the character of Jesus. There is an uneasiness about the film's opening sequence. Michael Ballhaus gives us a rapid tracking shot through the woods, only to come upon Jesus (Willem Dafoe) in a fitful sleep. That segment begins to suggest our relationship with Jesus for the rest of the film: we come upon him prone, vulnerable, and alone. Instead of a calm, self-possessed individual, Jesus is disturbed by obsessive dreams. Like Kazantzakis's Jesus, our Savior makes crosses for Romans, for which he receives the scorn of his people, as well as of Judas, who calls him "a disgrace." It is obvious from this point on that Scorsese's portrait of the Savior marks a singular departure from other depictions of Jesus in the cinema. What was familiar and most comfortable—the face of Jesus—is now blurred.

Consider, for a moment, how we first meet Jesus in other films. From what we can tell, Jesus must be identifiable, indeed, distinctive, so there is often a discourse about him even before we meet the Savior, as in DeMille's *The King of Kings.* Then we find that Jesus is bathed in diffused, mystic light as seen through the eyes of an innocent child. Zeffirelli's *Jesus of Nazareth* is at pains to show how different Jesus is from everyone else; in a crowd, the Savior walks about like some exotic crane amid shallow water. Pasolini's Jesus has an aura of penetrating simplicity and disarming presence. Aware of their own destiny, the Saviors of the silver screen go to their fate as if they are acting out the familiar passion play. Scorsese, on the other hand, is at pains to shock us with the same astonishing revelation that Kazantzakis gave us: part of Jesus is just like everyone else; he lacks any overt, external aura that would identify him as the Son of God. In other words, Jesus' awareness of his messiahship in *The Last Temptation of Christ* comes from his growing interior relationship with the Father, making his account of the story of Jesus closer to the early Christian witness than the inheritor of a great tradition.

More importantly, Scorsese goes further by depriving the film audience of the traditional construction of "Jesus Christ" as well. Here, Scorsese is on more dangerous ground because he is attacking our collective, cultural memory of what we think about Jesus, a deeply held community identity that has gathered itself, ideologically, around the image of Jesus. As we have suggested earlier, "Hollywood" is a conservative cultural force that continues to reassure the audience of its collective imagination, something like the lyrics of the best-selling record of 1988: "Don't Worry; Be Happy." No wonder Scorsese received such vituperative condemnation from so many different sectors. He was assaulting not only an image of Jesus but the way we construct that image: safe, self-assured, and predictable.

Obviously, the film's most iconoclastic contribution is its representation of Jesus, seemingly violating everything we have come to cherish about him—wise, knowing, and celibate. Jesus' relationship with Mary Magdalene in *Last Temptation* is a far cry from DeMille's domestication scene.

In addition to deploying the Kazantzakis text in order to reposition our traditional expectations about Jesus, Scorsese uses acting as a way to underline his point. It would be an understatement to say that Scorsese senses the importance that the star culture had in constructing the Jesus film and is at pains to cast a film in another way. Could there be a less likely choice for Jesus than Willem Dafoe? An actor who projects earthy experience, Dafoe's training was in experimental theater. In the years before *The Last Temptation of Christ,* he became famous as Sergeant Elias in *Platoon* (1986), an intense, realistic depiction of a small group of soldiers in Vietnam. Dafoe's other notable role was *To Live and Die in L.A.* (1985), a noirish movie in which he is a sadistic villain. Is there a less likely precedent in any other Jesus film for Dafoe's volatile presence on the screen?

Further, the most successful Jesus films have managed to gain plausibility by circumventing any association between the star and the biblical character. The search for the right Jesus on the silver screen has usually been a search for the unknown actor with something a little different. But, of course, we would associate Dafoe with celebrity culture and international status garnered after his performance in *Platoon.* Here again, the film asks us to think differently about how we would ascribe an aura to Jesus. Dafoe as Jesus in *Last Temptation* challenges what we expect: he is well known and has developed an aura as an actor in certain roles. Scorsese is attempting to demythologize American culture by rupturing the Hollywood text of the 1980s.

When the infamous scene in which Jesus imagines that he is having sexual intercourse is looked at in context, it becomes less offensive, if still somewhat objectionable. Demythologizing the Hollywood Jesus means also rejecting our construction of "Jesus Christ" as the cinema has usually depicted him. Scorsese, like Kazantzakis before him, is not abandoning Jesus' divinity, but claiming his sonship and his struggle to make it manifest in the world. What Scorsese is asking us to leave behind, then, is the Docetist heresy, that is, the view of Jesus as a disguised man, the fictitious Hollywood

God who just acted like a man, but really knew he was God all along. Scorsese is asking us to find God inside of the human subject and outside of glamor.

The last temptation, then, is *our* temptation to find Jesus only in the mythology of a gnostic world, or in creating our heroic image of God who died a humiliating death on the cross. It is worth pointing out that early gnostic depictions of Jesus represent him as not actually dying on the cross but, in a kind of magical dualism, leaving his "self" behind and coming down from the cross. Sound familiar? In a certain sense, that is the triumphal, therapeutic narrative of the 1980s. The inability to admit the weakness and the failure of Vietnam and Watergate created a decade of Rambos, vengeful and invincible. In *Last Temptation,* the point of the sex scene, then, is that Jesus cannot escape himself and refuses to do so. That is the real triumph—the cross of Christ on which true God and true man dies for all humanity. The film becomes a powerful reflection on the incarnation.

Finally, Scorsese is exploring the historical Jesus in *The Last Temptation of Christ.* Here, he is not alone. For already in 1980, *In Search of Historic Jesus,* a low-budget, pseudodocumentary appeared, followed by a number of books and articles on the same topic later in the decade. In fact, Scorsese's picture provoked a discussion about Jesus in history in the major news weeklies. It is more than a little interesting that while Americans were going to the cinema in droves to see formulaic narratives dispensed by Hollywood, there was, simultaneously, a renewed interest in the historical Jesus. Evidently, more people than Martin Scorsese were interrogating the face of Christ.

From the point of view of theology, the Hollywood tradition around Jesus is guilty of a heresy—the Docetists claim that Jesus was a kind of superman, a god who just pretended to be a man and only appeared to have died on the cross. (The exception is, as we know, the Jesus of *Jesus Christ Superstar,* since the film drives home the death of Jesus by portraying the actor who plays him as missing at the end of the picture.) The gnostic Jesus would conform to any 1980s hero, except those on Scorsese's mean streets. Indeed, Scorsese's Jesus swings to the other side of the heretical divide (Arianism), and becomes a weakling, a relentless doubter. Scorsese's creation, like St. Paul's, "groans" for redemption. This discussion raises some additional interesting questions. Why, for instance, are we more comfortable with one heresy and not the other? Should we not also be disturbed at a God who never fully becomes human and shares our weakness? Perhaps seeing Jesus struggle puts our faith in jeopardy. If so, we might ask ourselves why we need for Jesus *not* to experience our humanity. Does Jesus need to be superhuman in order to conform to our national (not religious) identity? Regardless of what we might think about the artistic or theological merits of *The Last Temptation of Christ,* Scorsese's film challenges a powerful cultural mythology and dismantles traditional norms and ways of thinking in the 1980s.

We recognize that, for some, *Last Temptation* is not an easy film to watch. Yet the film is a tremendously important contribution to the study of Jesus and the silver screen, since, in many ways, it is the logical progression of "Jesus Christ" on celluloid. In *The Last Temptation of Christ,* Scorsese has reviewed the past tradition of Jesus films and produced his own commentary on them. He has given us a Christ who overcame sin by rejecting temptation. Scorsese's film should be seen as grounded in a rebellious and provocative spirit—a film that never fails to raise questions about the role of Jesus in culture and in our faith.

NOTES

1. Michael Medved, *Hollywood vs. America*, 207.
2. Ibid., 44.
3. Lloyd Baugh, *Imaging the Divine*, 71.
4. Ibid., 52.
5. Michael Medved, *Hollywood vs. America*, 47.
6. Lloyd Baugh, *Imaging the Divine*, 60.
7. Cf. *Scorsese on Scorsese*, "The Last Temptation of Christ," David Thompson and Ian Christie, eds. (London and Boston: Faber & Faber, 1989), 116–45. The chapter is an excellent discussion on the Jesus film with many insights from the director.
8. Paul Schrader, "The Screenwriter: *The Yakuza* to the *Last Temptation of Christ*," in *Schrader on Schrader and Other Writings*, Kevin Jackson, ed. (London and Boston: Faber & Faber, 1990),135–40.

Photo courtesy of the Academy of Motion Picture Arts & Sciences. © 1990 Orion Pictures
Corporation and Max Films, Inc. All rights reserved. Used with permission.

NINTH FEATURE

Jesus of Montreal (1989)

*"If you forget yourself and ask how to help others,
life becomes perfectly simple."*

Written by: Denys Arcand

Directed by: Denys Arcand

Actors Include: Denys Arcand (judge), Lothaire Bluteau (Daniel), Remy Girard (Richard Cardinal), Robert LePage (René), Gilles Pelletier (Father Leclerc), Johanne-Marie Tremblay (Martin), Catherine Wilkening (Mireille)

Running Time: 119 minutes

Introduction

We come to the final and most recently produced film considered in this book, *Jesus of Montreal,* written and directed by Denys Arcand. Even more than some of the other films, this movie, nominated in 1989 for an Academy Award as Best Foreign Language Film, is a reflection and product of the time and place in which it was created. In this case, the place and time are Montreal in the Province of Quebec in Canada in the late 1980s. The film is in French with English subtitles.

This work takes yet another step along the developing road of so-called Jesus films. Most of the films viewed thus far have clearly been lives of Jesus. The vision and values of each of the films have influenced the shape, look, and content of the film, but each is clearly intended to portray a life or image of the Jesus of faith and/or history. Exceptions to this observation include *Jesus Christ Superstar,* which is a play-within-a-play (as is *Jesus of Montreal*), and *Monty Python's Life of Brian* which, obviously enough, is about the experiences of Brian. With *Jesus of Montreal,* however, the manner or approach of imaging Jesus takes a large metaphoric leap. This is certainly the most parabolic of the films treated thus far, nearly allegorical, with its plentiful scriptural allusions to events replayed in the lives of the characters in the film.

The viewer will quickly realize that this is not simply a film about the life of Jesus. There is much more going on. There are several levels on which the film operates. First, one *can* view it simply as a filmed story, assessing how it works simply as a story about characters who interact with one another, usually around some conflict and with various successes and failures along the way, working toward some climax and subsequent resolution and denouement. Certain questions can be asked. Does the plot work? Are the characters believable? Can you identify with them to any degree? Does the climax resolve the conflict?

The stakes are raised here, however, because *Jesus of Montreal* is also a film about a group of actors reenacting the life and death of Jesus in a passion play performed in modern-day Montreal. One cannot blithely incorporate Jesus into a play without seriously considering the freight or risk that goes along with such a decision. So, one might then investigate what the film reveals about Jesus as the Christ, at least about the author/director's image of Christ. As mentioned in earlier chapters, there is no neutral encounter with Jesus. The image of Jesus is so powerful and demanding, whether one's viewpoint is based upon orthodox devotion or cynical rejection, that Jesus should only be incorporated into a story with intentionality.

Further yet, the actors themselves begin, in their lives outside the immediate performance of the passion play, to reflect qualities and events of the Jesus story they are performing. So, there is the movie, there is the passion play to be performed, and there is the offstage interaction of the actors who have been gathered to perform the play. Finally, there is an intertwining of these levels throughout the film. The more times one watches *Jesus of Montreal,* the more one is likely to detect the ways the levels interact with one another. Where is the "play"? Which play is the real one? Is anyone ever "offstage"? Who are the players and who are the viewers? Or are we all both players and viewers? Indeed, the first scene is of an actor in a play, but not the primary passion play that will come later. What we do get in this scene is a hint about the fickleness of human loyalty. If all this sounds confusing, it is not confusing in the film itself and, indeed, provides for viewer interest and viewer involvement that are less likely in the more straightforward portrayals of the life of Jesus.

The premise of the film is the revision/updating and subsequent performance of a passion play in contemporary Montreal. The play had been written thirty years earlier by a Catholic priest, Father Leclerc, who has decided that, with the help of an out-of-work actor, the play should be revitalized and performed again. This actor gathers a band of unlikely characters to help with the revision and performance. The results are far beyond what the priest could have predicted. The play is clearly a success, evoking heartfelt responses from many in the audience. The nature of that success, however, influences the lives of those involved in the play.

The film, then, may not seem to be a life of Jesus at all, but merely a film about a play about the story of Jesus' life. But as the plot unfolds, the separations between actor and character, within the context of the film, become less and less clear. While Daniel and the character he portrays—Jesus—become more and more alike, the priest who wrote the play is quite obviously only going through the motions of being a priest and is thus, in effect, only *acting* as a priest. Who is acting and who is "real" becomes difficult to identify; who is genuine and who is false becomes hard to assess. Maybe that is precisely the point.

There are many obvious and subtle scriptural allusions that the attentive viewer of the film will be able to identify. Especially after several viewings, viewers may find themselves trying to win at the game of "Guess the Bible Passage" in many of the film's scenes. Indeed, in a few places, the allusions are perhaps a bit heavy-handed. The ending of the film may qualify as the most strained allusion of all. But this notwithstanding, *Jesus of Montreal* evokes many deep, troubling, and thoughtful issues about the identity of Jesus and his influence on one's life, and, as well, provides a caustic critique of contemporary Canadian (Western) culture.

As noted above, *Jesus of Montreal* is the most parabolic of the films reviewed here, and, as with all parables or metaphors, it works by borrowing images and language from one sphere in order to talk about an object or relationship in another sphere. While throughout the Bible there are many metaphors— allegories, parables, and parabolic sayings—the parables of Jesus in the synoptic gospels are probably the most familiar. Jesus preached using many metaphors or parables. He also used metaphors when comparing himself to bread, a good shepherd, a gate, and so forth. It is obvious that, in a way, Jesus is a shepherd, even though, for example, he does not literally tend sheep and is not literally a gate or door. One needs to examine the parable to see which qualities of the sheep, the vine, the door apply to Jesus and which do not. So Jesus is a shepherd, but is more than that and *other* than that. Metaphors are used to speak of God as Father and as a mother hen.

Metaphors work by exposing not just a single quality of that which is being examined but a whole realm of qualities, unlike a simile, which only looks to one point of comparison. If we describe someone as a "mule," we are probably only referring to that person's stubbornness, exclusive of other features of "mule-ness." Yet while metaphors expose more than a single point of comparison, there is also a sense that the metaphor is not comprehensive; there is always more to be said than a metaphor can evoke.

Metaphors may be used overtly or subtly, even without our notice. Metaphors require adaptation and interpretation.

More broadly, the use of metaphors is an extremely common device employed to describe something that is otherwise difficult to describe. The metaphor never assumes it says everything there is to say. Within the comparison there is an implicit premise that the analogy is limited, that it says something important but not everything important. In the case of *Jesus of Montreal,* there is a sense in which the film is about the life of Jesus, but it is more than that. On the surface, anyway, the film is less about Jesus' life than some of the films reviewed earlier. It is ostensibly about a play, the actors who perform the play, and how they are transformed by performing the play. On the most superficial level the subject of the play is not necessarily that important. But, it is also clear that this film has something to say about the institutional church, about Jesus, and about the characters who perform the play. It is difficult to incorporate Jesus into a plot without drawing attention to that important detail: there is no neutral portrayal of Jesus! So the film is also about Jesus.

The metaphoric or parabolic value enters because it also explores the impact of Jesus' life on those who study it, who attempt, in some sense, to recreate it. "Who is Jesus?" becomes an important question. The Jesus of the original passion play? The Jesus in the revised passion play? Or the Jesus who comes alive in the person of Daniel? The belief that the church is the body of Christ becomes more than a figure of speech in *Jesus of Montreal* as Jesus comes into being in the life of the one who takes his part in the play, as well as in the lives of the actors who perform with Daniel.

In regard to the premise of the film—a film about a play about the story of Jesus' life—it might seem to bear something in common with *Jesus Christ Superstar* from 1973. However, *Jesus Christ Superstar* had a much more contrived and artificial look and feel. The artifice of the play was only present at the very beginning and end. Yet in both *Superstar* and *Jesus of Montreal,* the key character is transformed by the experience of playing Jesus. Kazantzakis, author of the novel on which *The Last Temptation of Christ* was based, also used this device in *The Greek Passion.*[1]

Movie Preview: Questions and Suggestions

1. *Read some of the parables of Jesus. How do they work? How do they create their meaning or impact in the reader or listener? How does the working of the parables compare with how a movie "works"?*

2. *Be alert to the several levels of the "Jesus" story active within the film and how and where they intertwine. This is a film about a play about a story of Jesus' life.*

3. *Watch for the backgrounds of many of the shots, especially of Montreal. Background shots provide context for the foreground action and context determines content. While the background may not seem especially important, it provides subtle information for interpretation of the scene. For example, note the many panoramic shots of Montreal. What role do these serve?*

4. *Who is Jesus in this film? Watch for the qualities of Jesus that are portrayed.*

5. *Be alert for theme statements—keys to interpreting the characters' dialogue and actions, and possibly therefore, the producer's intention.*

Movie Viewing

Movie Review: Questions and Responses

1. *Describe the opening and closing scenes. What mood or tone does the opening scene create? What are you left with in the closing scene?*

2. *What is the view of the institutional church in this film? What in the film leads you to this conclusion?*

3. *What scriptural allusions or references did you notice?*

4. *How would you describe the priest in the film? His character? His dilemma?*

5. *How would you describe the* theme *of this film? Have any of the other films had similar themes?*

6. *Who is the subject of the movie? Who is the audience for the movie?*

LENS ONE

In this our final film, *Jesus of Montreal,* we encounter what has become a foundational issue within modern studies of the historical Jesus: the question of whether the message of Jesus was directed primarily toward the concerns of the future or, instead, the concerns of the present. It is here that biblical students often divide into two distinct camps: Some scholars believe that the words of Jesus were spoken with an eye toward coming days and with the realization that the present means nothing when contrasted with the future, apocalyptic glory of God, which would destroy evil and elevate righteous believers to an eternal reward. Others find the good news of Jesus to be intended for the immediate benefit of Jesus' own disciples and their issues of common, everyday existence, with little regard for the future.

This division of thought already had proven to be a testing ground among biblical scholars in the 1800s. At the turn of the century the well-known scholar Albert Schweitzer offered a published review of popular positions on the topic in his *The Quest of the Historical Jesus* (English translation). His own conclusion was that the preaching of Jesus of Nazareth was directed toward the coming days or "end-time." According to Schweitzer, Jesus' good news looked forward to the future arrival of God's kingdom, a period when divine mercy and reward would be provided for those whom God found to be righteous in spirit and deed. The key by which this kingdom would be revealed was Jesus himself. The true core of what Jesus taught was thus directed toward what was to be, not what was. Of course, there is an ethical implication for the present times within his message, namely, that in order for believers to achieve this future reward they should take care to act correctly, both toward God and neighbor, in the present! But the kernel of Jesus' thought remained future oriented or "eschatological" in focus.

Immediately after the publication of Schweitzer's book and just prior to the great world wars of Europe, the influence of the philosopher Martin Heidegger began to gain academic ground. Heidegger's position had ramifications in a much different direction from that of Schweitzer and his followers. His thought was directed toward the present moment and the essence of being. His was a quest for whatever meaning could be found in common existence. From such concerns arose the modern movement of "existentialism," a philosophy that seeks truth within the confines of life as it is commonly shared by all people, and not beyond.

Heidegger's views ultimately influenced New Testament studies, as can be most clearly detected in the work of the German scholar Rudolf Bultmann. For Bultmann, the message of Jesus himself seemed to be directed toward the daily situation of first-century Palestinian Judaism. The reality of God is in the essence of life, not in some far-off heavenly hereafter. As Bultmann saw the situation, all talk of a future kingdom of God or the spread of a Christian faith among the nations should be attributed to the earliest level of non-Jewish Christians, fervent believers who translated their own concerns back into the words of Jesus. Thus, much of what modern Christianity has become since the days of Jesus is the product of Christianity's evolution, not simply the consequence of what Jesus himself taught.

Jesus of Montreal is itself a subtle reflection of this very struggle— eschatology versus existentialism. To the extent that existentialist thought had a great impact on twentieth-century France in the work of such authors as Albert Camus and Jean-Paul Sartre, this same consideration is translated into our film (itself produced through the eyes of French Canadians). This is not to say, of course, that existentialist thought is strictly French. Instead, it is to orient us as informed viewers to the realization that our director, Denys Arcand, has chosen to portray Jesus in a manner which happily assumes that the life and message of the Messiah were given for first-century Jews and for the times in which they lived. Even more importantly, it is to sober us to the realization that much of what Christianity has become as a religion since the time of Jesus—its liturgy, its worship, its ecclesiastical customs, its hierarchy of leadership, its theological speculation, its ethical orientation—are more the products of the development of the institutional church rather than what Jesus himself ever spoke and/or intended.

Here, perhaps, is a theme (typical of *Monty Python's Life of Brian*) that challenges the modern Christian viewer. How much of our own tradition can we (or should we) ascribe to the teachings of Jesus, and how much to the particular spin of our own popular and religious history? Can we legitimately incorporate the history of Christian custom and popular belief (a la DeMille) into our reconstruction of the life and teachings of Jesus? It is certainly within this context that we must look at Arcand's use of sources.

Existential Influence. The film opens with the presentation of an important existentialist issue, the question of death (the end of life). We come upon a scene in which an unidentified actor reaches the conclusion of a play in which he has been performing. His anguish seems to be borrowed straight from the death of Judas in Matthew 27:3–5. In discussion with a second actor, his anxiety revolves around the question of which of the two of them has killed yet a third (unnamed) character. And the words resound: "I struck him, but you're the murderer. You said, 'Man must root out the idea of God and accept mortality with no hope of resurrection. Then will he resign himself to death and stop bemoaning this short life. His love will be selfless....' " We soon discover that we are witnessing a play—far, far off Broadway. In response to his remorse, we witness the actor as he acts out his suicide (by hanging—see the Gospel of Matthew). The curtain closes.

We are left with a question that becomes the guiding theme for *Jesus of Montreal*. The question, however, is not immediately clear. But as the film progresses the question takes shape. It becomes a measuring rod (*canon,* in Greek!) by which all of the films we have viewed must be considered: who, in fact, is responsible for the death of Jesus—those persons in the first century who opposed what Jesus was or, perhaps, those persons in the twentieth century who cling to what Jesus never was?

The film continues with the actor whom we have just seen in the opening play being heralded by adoring crowds at the conclusion of his performance. He turns to recognize the actor whom he considers to be the more important, Daniel. Just as John the Baptist proclaimed the priority of Jesus in our gospels, so the story of God's salvation plan moves from the proclaimer to the proclaimed. The story of Daniel begins.

Daniel is given the task of rewriting an old, old story of the life of Jesus in the light of his own newly envisioned understanding of who Jesus was and what Jesus may mean for modern religious faith. He attempts to bring the old Jesus story to life for late twentieth-century eyes and ears. The task is undertaken with the specific permission of the church under the direction of a local priest, Father Leclerc. Just as Jesus chose the twelve, Daniel gathers those who will act with him. Together, as in the gospels, they take various meals together—Daniel with Constance at the soup kitchen; Constance with Daniel at breakfast; Daniel with his friends at dinner; Daniel with his friends at a last meal before the final showing of their play; and, of course, there is a constant sharing of bread with the audience in the revised play that Daniel and his friends perform. The eating, the sharing of bread, is a constant reminder of Jesus, who ate with and taught both his followers and his opponents.

After the actors have been assembled and the play rewritten, it is performed, fresh in format and new in insight. Two factors shine forth from within the play. In the first place, there is a heavy emphasis upon the *teachings* of Jesus, especially those that relate to the present world and the lives of the common person. It is true that some miracles are ascribed to the ministry of Jesus; at the same time, however, the more fantastic stories of miraculous events are mostly omitted, perhaps as an acknowledgment of the speculation of the times and often as the claims of false messiahs.

Nonscriptural Influences. Historical information is offered in this play that comes, not from the New Testament Gospels, but from other literature and purportedly from archaeological data of the first century. This data includes: speculation about the human father of Jesus, allegedly a Roman soldier named Panthera (compare the second-century charge of Celsus; see *Monty Python's Life of Brian*); evidence that crucifixions were numerous and that the death of Jesus would not have been unusual in its day; and the common acceptance of numerous deities in the religious thought of the Mediterranean world, as offered by Pontius Pilate. The use of this nonscriptural material parallels, yet also exceeds, the use of the works of Flavius Josephus by Ray and Stevens. It is an attempt to incorporate disparate data about the life of Jesus from a broad range of sources. There is one primary difference, however. Ray and Stevens used Josephus as a means by which to support the traditional story of the life of Jesus. Arcand uses his materials to offer optional considerations to that traditional image of Jesus that the church holds dear. The transition in intent is significant. As we will see below, the goal is no longer to support the customary view of Jesus but to offer expanded possibilities.

The first presentation of this newly refashioned play about the life of Jesus is important to the plot of our film for several reasons, both as it reflects the biblical text and as it reveals more recent speculation about Jesus of Nazareth. The play is offensive to its very producers, that is, Father Leclerc and the institutional church, which he represents. It is out of control, offering materials and ideas that do not conform to the traditional standards of interpretation as determined by ecclesiastical authority. Never mind that "the people like it" and are moved by its message! It is inappropriate to what has been deemed acceptable for consumption by the laity. It challenges the authority of the church to speak for the resurrected Christ. It points to flaws in the tradition and does little to expound on the glories of the traditional gospel message. In other words, the "official" tradition is to be protected and preserved by that institution which exists for just such a purpose—the priesthood. Undoubtedly we are to see a parallel with Jesus, who also confronted similar powers and authorities two thousand years ago, namely the Sanhedrin. As a result of Daniel's revision of the play, he is "examined" by the religious institution and found to be dangerous. He is to be silenced. He must conform or he must go!

The inaugural presentation of Daniel's passion play also provides Arcand the occasion to consider his vision. Any discussion of the life of Jesus of Nazareth ultimately must lead to the question of whether Jesus undertook his mission with a more-or-less clear vision of his ultimate goals and an acknowledgment of his likely death/execution: yes or no! The former position tends to emphasize the divinity of Jesus; the latter, his humanity. Our films have generally answered yes to this speculation about the clear vision of Jesus, as is already endorsed by the Gospels of Matthew and Luke and confirmed by the Gospel of John. With more recent films, works such as *Life of Brian* and *Last Temptation,* the answer has been no. This second position underlies the position of the Gospel of Mark.

In *Jesus of Montreal* there is no question that Daniel begins his research on Jesus with little prior assumption about the nature of his subject. Those who hear that he has taken the role have conflicting responses: some believe it to be a minor role in the world of acting; others, a great opportunity. His is a true quest for the historical Jesus—an eye-opening search for what can be known. After a first showing of the play, however, the entire plot is laid before Daniel's eyes, from ministry to death, from teachings to persecution. In other words, there is within the movie itself a revelation that suggests the broader scope of his mission and the nature of his character. Are we to understand this as a parallel to some experience in the life of Jesus? One might point, for example, to the baptism of Jesus by John, the temptation in the wilderness, or the reading from the prophet Isaiah in the synagogue. Whatever the case, Arcand manages to answer the question of vision in yet a new way: Daniel (Jesus) does not begin with a full vision of his mission or his end, but at some point in the saga he certainly acquires it with clarity. Could one not also say this about Jesus?

Scriptural Influences. Let us now consider some of the specific biblical texts that Arcand chooses to incorporate into the revised play and into the film in general. He is fair to his sources to the extent that he roams freely among the gospel texts, choosing first from Mark and then Matthew, from Luke and then John. In the play, which Daniel and his friends redesign, there is a tendency to choose practical sayings emphasizing the importance of ethics and morality. Many of these are drawn from Matthew's Sermon on the Mount: do not worry about food or clothing; do not resist evil; give both your coat and your cloak; do good to those who hate you; do not judge others.

Beyond these ethical sayings, there is some speculation among the disciples about the nature of Jesus as the Messiah of God. We find here Peter's confession that Jesus is the Christ. Arcand adds to this an interesting comment on the lips of Daniel (Jesus) about Jesus' own nature: "Never speak of me to others. Never say I am the Christ. I am the Son of Man." It is true that Jesus refers to himself in the Scriptures only as the "Son of Man," but nowhere does he forbid others to call him the Christ. Finally, the passion narrative of Jesus' death is played through: the betrayal, the interrogation, the whipping, the crucifixion. Afterward, stories of Jesus' resurrection (though in a different physical state) are spread, together with the teaching that all of us are to "love one another."

With the conclusion of the play we encounter the hostile response of Father Leclerc on behalf of the dignity of the church. The future of the play as it has been rewritten is doomed. Thereafter, we see portions of the production only twice more, and only in the first of these do we hear any further dialogue from the narrative itself. What we hear in this second viewing of the play are additional teachings about the nature of morality (do not swear, and be faithful to your oath). Certainly more important, we find Daniel (as Jesus) castigating the religious authorities as "hypocrites" for their love of high places and the best seats at feasts, for their desire to do religious deeds while neglecting ethical duties. The message (as delivered within the context of the play) fares no better with Daniel's sponsors than it apparently did with Jesus' own audience. The future of the production is now surely doomed. Father Leclerc insists that the actors return to the original old and outdated script.

Now we must step away from the play itself in order to look at the allusions that Arcand offers within the film as they relate to the movement of Daniel and his fellow actors. Remarkably, the process of gathering actors and producing the play closely follows the events of the gospel narratives. From the first, Daniel (just as with Jesus) bids the future disciples to "follow me" from their various jobs. He sits in the company of women and children; he lives in the homes of others; in them he finds what it means to possess family. Their lives and work become quite close as they learn to respect each other. They become more than fellow actors; they become friends.

There is one woman (Mireille) who gradually comes to fall in love with what Daniel is and what he aspires to be. She, of course, is a reflection of the character Mary Magdalene, whose close relationship to Jesus has been the frequent object of speculation within our films from DeMille onward. Mireille, though inwardly pure in spirit (if a little naive), comes from the tarnished background of commercialism that traditionally employs sexuality and sensuality in order to sell products. Models and others become pawns in the game of conspicuous consumption. She struggles to remain within or at the edges of this world until she is summarily released from it during the tryouts for a new beer advertisement. In an interesting mixture of settings, Daniel basically "cleans the Temple" (the tryout studio) as a hostile reaction to all that is perverse about the process of buying and selling and the marketing of goods, not to mention of the human spirit. During this cleansing Mireille (perhaps as the fallen adulteress of John 8) comes to her salvation.

But it is this "cleansing of the Temple" that places Daniel in opposition to the secular authorities, and thus Daniel finds himself opposed both by the civil government and by the religious leaders. The civil courts are much more reluctant to prosecute than are the church authorities, yet they will follow the juridical processes to the appropriate end. With great irony, a court-appointed psychologist proclaims Daniel more sane than most of the judges. The parallels to the life of Jesus are obvious but not heavy-handed.

Ultimately, the courts do not have the opportunity to prosecute Daniel for his destruction of private property; the final showing of the play leads to the accident that results in his death. In this scene, the accident on the cross, a most curious twist occurs. Although the religious authorities want Daniel gone, they do not cause his death. Although the civil authorities want Daniel to stand accountable for his destruction of property, neither do they cause his death. Indeed, it is those people who have come to see the play, those who demand that the production run its intended course, those who insist on having their own way, who "cause" Daniel's death.

We are reminded that in the gospel narratives it is the crowds, the masses (fanned by the religious authorities admittedly), who ultimately demand that Jesus be sacrificed on the cross. In Arcand's own film, then, the people themselves set into motion the events that lead to the accident that kills Daniel. Clearly, again, Daniel's life parallels the life of Jesus, the character whom he enacts in the play. As with Jesus' life, the drama's audience uses the character for its own fulfillment, whether for punishment or for entertainment. To what degree does any gathering of people both serve the group and likewise use the group for the individual ends and needs of each member?

Only after the accident, a time when the weakened Daniel wanders in a haze throughout the hospitals and subways, do we hear him speak about future apocalyptic visions of the end-times and the need to be prepared for the tragedies to come. Similarly, in the gospel texts the majority of materials about the future coming of the kingdom of God are relegated to collected sayings that appear immediately prior to the arrest, trial, and crucifixion of Jesus. It is likewise here that Arcand employs these eschatological teachings of Jesus. But by no means are these teachings either the original message Daniel taught or the cornerstone of what Daniel wished his followers to hear. They are the ramblings of a ministry that has come to its end. Daniel rants and raves: the abomination of desolation is upon us; flee to the hills and do not go inside; pray that it not be in winter; beware of false christs and prophets; you do not know the hour; be on your guard! With such warnings on his lips, Daniel dies.

Daniel's death is most intriguing. Behind the dead Daniel on the subway wall is the poster of his actor friend (from the beginning of the film) in his new role as "The Savage (or Wild) Man" (is this John the Baptist, or Judas?). From the dead body of Daniel, parts of his corpse are "resurrected" as living tissue for those who receive his body parts: eyes, heart, and so forth. Compare this visual allusion to Jesus' proclamations at the Last Supper (and subsequent eucharistic prayers) to "This is my body, which is given for you" (Lk 22:19 and parallels).

As with Jesus, many witnesses immediately seek to spread the good word about who he was and what his death may mean for others. He is praised, and institutions are planned to serve as caretakers of his memory and of his goals. One assumes that some parallel to the writing of the New Testament Gospels and the establishment of the institutional church is intended here.

All of these, however, are only surface issues. We must return to the question of existential faith versus eschatological faith. We must revisit the question of just exactly who has killed our hero. Daniel has evidently come to the conclusion that Jesus taught a message of immediate hope for those who surrounded him in first-century Palestine. It was a message of love and right actions, of respect and sharing. Those whom Daniel encounters (the church, the civil authorities, the crowds) operate under the assumption that life carries within it a message of present practicality. There is the need to live within some system of rules and convictions (however tentative at their core). These systems ultimately must be transcended by the hope of some future reward that will justify all of life in the end.

Arcand questions: Who is it that supports this message of present practicality and future hope? Who is it that supports a message of dreams and illusions, a view that often seems to run counter to the original faith and convictions of Jesus himself, the man upon whom the whole system of Christian convictions presumably is based? It is apparently everyday believers who cherish common traditions and pious hopes and who remain seemingly ignorant or unconcerned about the Jesus of history but most concerned for the Christ of their own faith!

One of the agendas of this book is to create a willingness to examine our own images of Jesus, to see them as constructs or collections of beliefs and images that have been gathered over time. Some of the elements of that construct may have become dated or obsolete but they remain influential. Some of the elements remain from childhood and perhaps should be revised in light of adult experiences and adult levels of theological reflection. This is not to say that we are to toss out our images of Jesus, nor that we need to purge the image of all childhood notions. It suggests merely the willingness to examine our own beliefs much as we have examined the image of Jesus in each of these films to find their coherence as well as their inconsistencies.

LENS TWO

Initially, this movie may not seem to contain much on which to comment in terms of production values or its use of the cinematic vocabulary. There are no obvious or spectacular special effects. The cinematography is well done but nothing beyond what we have come to expect in commercial film. Yet, the metaphoric quality of *Jesus of Montreal* carries subtly into its use of visualization, as well as in its plotting. One key to examining the director's use of the cinematic vocabulary in this film lies not in fancy, hi-tech camera tricks, not in heart-pounding audio, but in the director's use of place to communicate impressions of the biblical references and allusions that are incorporated in the film. (The list of references and allusions is contained in the appendix.) Throughout the film the director has been creative in using setting or locale to create an additional level of meaning for the surface action. The fabric of the film becomes more interesting, more textured, because it operates on many levels or layers. This is part of the parabolic nature of the film.

The nature of parable, of course, is that there is more than one thing to be said. Facets of the film's meaning may even remain unsaid or at least hidden from obvious view. We define parable as a form of metaphoric comparison in which narrative and fiction comprise the key elements. Parables are stories meant to speak about something else; they are not necessarily historic incidents. The elements of one sphere are used to refer to or evoke elements of another sphere. As is true with any metaphor, the comparison does not intend to describe or evoke everything about that which is being described. There is an "is" and "is not" quality to metaphor and parable. Jesus used parables to speak about, among other things, the kingdom of

God. The parable intends to say something important, but it does not intend to say everything!

Typically, it might seem as though setting is just the site and time where the action takes place. But if it is true (to some important degree) that context determines content, the setting or context in which the action takes place is central for "locating" the meaning of a scene. The question becomes not simply what is going on here, but where is "it" going on and why there? It might be helpful to list a few detailed examples to suggest how the director has creatively used place, not simply as a neutral setting in which action evolves, but as a tool to communicate meaning and lend texture to the interpretative enterprise.

For example, after Daniel's revision of the play proves to be tremendously successful, Daniel is taken by a lawyer and potential investor to the lawyer's office at the top of a large office building. The two chat in front of a large window from which one can see Montreal far below. This could simply be the place where such activity occurs. It has certain and obvious reference to corporate power structures in twentieth-century culture—high up in a large corporate office building overlooking a beautiful city. It is a place of power and activity, a place where business decisions are made. The world has many such buildings. Countries vie for the honor of having the world's tallest building. People have always sought high places as locations and as symbols of prestige and power.

But the high places (especially mountains) seem also to have been where the gods located themselves and where one went to encounter them. The Acropolis in Athens, Greece, is one of many examples. Moses went to Mount Sinai to receive the ten commandments. Additionally and more narrowly, might this scene also be an allusion to Jesus' temptation and his conversation with Satan, the Tempter, at the top of the Temple where Jesus is offered the kingdoms of the world in exchange for allegiance to the power of evil? Just as Jesus began his public ministry with a confrontation with the Tempter in the wilderness, so Daniel must recognize the implications of his play's success, the attraction his success would be to those who want to profit from it and, in the process, distort and pervert both the work and the one who does the work. Ironically, Daniel's followers visit with the same lawyer following Daniel's death in order to create an institution intended to preserve Daniel's work.

Likewise, Daniel's destructive anger at the shooting of a television commercial tryout clearly parallels Jesus' rampage among the money changers at the Temple. The specific parallel suggests that, in the larger metaphor, the business world is the evil tempter that desires to seduce us from simpler, nobler motives. Even seemingly pure motives can be corrupted. Only one of Daniel's troupe, Mireille, sees through the lawyer's offer of help to the seduction and surrender that are inherent. She has seen this side of the business world already, the side in which people are turned into objects and are valued merely for their various body parts.

One more example of the use of locale to create an additional layer of parabolic meaning occurs following Daniel's initial injury. An ambulance arrives at the shrine where the passion play is performing to take the injured Daniel to a hospital. General Hospital is full, however, so they take him to St. Mark's. After Daniel is released, he suffers a relapse and is taken to Jewish Hospital. Is this sequence merely coincidental? One would assume not. What is the point? That is up to the viewer, of course. But could there be some suggestion of the inadequacy of Christianity to address the ills of Western culture? Perhaps they are simply names for hospitals and nothing more.

The physical environment of the hospital, especially St. Mark's, also suggests a place not designed primarily for healing. Ironically, it is a very busy, inhospitable place with a pervasive cool and eerie blue light. There is little attention given to the needs of people and undue attention given to the forms that must be filled out before treatment can be administered. It is a hellish environment. In this eerie blue light, Daniel, in red blanket and neck brace, stands out. We have addressed the role of red in earlier films. Here again, it draws our attention. Could this be a vague allusion to Jesus' decent into hell?

As noted earlier, this is a movie about a play. Indeed, the movie's initial scene makes this fact clear. From this point on, it is often difficult to tell what *is* the play and what *is not.* A Haitian woman breaks into the performance of the passion play, confusing Daniel's portrayal of Jesus with the real Jesus. The tour guide/guard keeps breaking into the passion play. Just about the time we become lost in the play, he breaks it up to move the audience along to the next scene.

There are the multiple plots that weave their way through this movie and occasionally they intersect, even collide, with one another. For example, there is a jarring moment that comes when one sees the police arrive to arrest Daniel while he is hanging on the cross. Jesus should have been arrested *before* the crucifixion! Indeed, the same thing happens the second time police come to shut the play down—it happens during the final—crucifixion—scene. Daniel's hanging on the cross during the performance of the play is his equivalent to Jesus' time in the Garden of Gethsemane, a time of testing and betrayal, a calm before the storm. Clearly, there are many plots being played out at the same time. Clearly, there are several Jesus figures, but which is the "real" Jesus? The one of history? The one portrayed by Daniel? Daniel himself? The Jesus of faith? But whose faith? The issue here is a subtle one of characterization about who Jesus is and who re-presents Jesus. Daniel not only plays Jesus, in a very real way, he becomes Jesus, at least becomes Christlike.

One technique or stylistic element the viewer might notice is the frequent use of panoramic views of Montreal, including those from the hill of the shrine and from the office building where various characters meet with the lawyer/agent, but especially during the crucifixion scenes in the passion play. Why these frequent panoramas? To remind us that this story is bigger than Daniel and his company? To remind the viewers that this is about Montreal and not just a nice story about actors and dedication to a cause? After all, the movie is entitled *Jesus of Montreal,* not *Jesus of Contemporary Western Urban North American Culture.* One of our students watched this movie with great interest. He had lived and worked in Montreal for twenty years. He noted that at one time Montreal was the most Catholic of Canadian cities but had now become the most secular. A traditional Catholic spirituality had been replaced by a relentless joie de vivre, a constant quest for enjoyment or pleasure. The city had lost its soul, he concluded.

In high school English classes, during the study of Shakespeare's plays, many of us were introduced to the concept of "breaking the wall," or "breaking the boundary." The wall that was broken was the fourth wall on stage through which the audience viewed the play. When one of the play's characters addressed the audience, he or she would be breaking the wall. This happens frequently in *Jesus of Montreal,* especially during the performance of the passion play. The watchman clumsily moves the audience from locale to locale just about the time you forget the passion play is a play being performed. Again, during the passion play, the audience members are incorporated into the play when they receive bread being passed out by the women narrators. Indeed, throughout this play, one cannot be sure who is real and who is acting. The Haitian woman forgets that this is a play and rushes forward to pledge her help and issue a warning to Jesus.

Are names important? Again, perhaps. Is Mireille a recasting of Mary Magdalene? Is Constance the one who is truly constant? She acted in the early rendition of the passion play as well as in the revival and therefore provides continuity. She is constant, that is, faithful or loyal, to the priest in attending to his needs: "It gives him such pleasure and me so little pain." Indeed.

The final scene brings the movie full circle. Shortly after the movie starts, we see a choir practicing in the balcony of the shrine. Two young women singers are featured. They are also present for the beer commercial tryouts. These same two women reappear one last time in the final scene singing Pergolesi's *Stabat Mater (Sorrowful Mother)* in the subway accompanied by a boom box, positioned in front of the poster of the actor in the film's opening scene.[2] Their presence in these several scenes mimics the journey of faith that many have taken, from participation in organized religion to the surrender to more immediate gratification to an amorphous faith in either some guru or simply faith in faith, faith in anything.

Finally, the viewer could hardly miss the cruciform posture Daniel's body takes during the surgery that removes his organs. This is perhaps a bit too obvious as a cinematic device. It does, however, provide entrée to a discussion of how literally one is to take the "body of Christ" imagery in the New Testament and in church doctrines about the Eucharist and about the life of Christ's followers.

All in all, the director has used the cinematic vocabulary not in any dazzling way but more subtly to provide depth and interest to the plots and subplots and to engage the viewers' exploration of multiple layers of meaning. The film works as a parable with much of the interpretation left to the viewer.

This is not allegory but a metaphor creating a world in which the characters operate, rather than a simple catalog of coded references known only to the initiated. The viewer will continue to enjoy this film after many viewings, noting additional allusions with each viewing, just as the parables of Jesus continue to evoke meaning after some two thousand years.

LENS THREE

One might assume that this movie intends to communicate a hostile attitude toward the church, the Catholic Church in particular. But that would be too easy a critique. First, one should note that the Catholic Church may have cooperated to some degree in the production of this movie, giving permission to use various religious settings. Secondly, the context or thrust of the movie is not really so much an attack on the church as it is on the fickleness of much of our faith, which includes, in *Jesus of Montreal,* the fickleness of the audiences who are attending the play in the opening scene and who later attend the passion play, the fickleness of the faith of Father Leclerc, the mercenary attitude of the lawyer/agent who failed to tempt Daniel but who seemed to make points with the acting troupe after Daniel's death, and so on.

> MEDIUM SHOT: *(Young Man):* Woe to those who commit suicide...to those who destroy themselves! No one is more miserable. By damning God and life, they damn themselves. Timeless their consuming hunger...their rejection of forgiveness.
> MEDIUM CLOSE-UP: *(Young Man's feet stepping on the stool.)*
> MEDIUM CLOSE-UP: *(Fastening rope to the beam)*
> MEDIUM SHOT: *(Young Man):* They curse the God who beckons them. They wish annihilation on Him...and on all his creation. They thirst after death...and the void.
> MEDIUM CLOSE-UP: *(Young Man's feet dangling.) (Applause)*

Abject despair? Suicide? Death? What could this rather depressing scene from a Dostoyevski adaptation staged during the opening sequence of the film have to do with the Savior and the silver screen? If *Jesus of Montreal* is quite obviously not a traditional Jesus film or even a parody of one, then what is such a movie doing in our assessment?

This chapter takes up the difficult, but necessary question explicitly provoked by Arcand's treatment of "Jesus Christ" in *Jesus of Montreal*. The issues that concern us are as broad as they are complicated. If we can only scratch the surface here, we hope this will inspire an ongoing and important discussion of the future of the Savior on the silver screen and the challenge of an increasingly secular, postmodern culture that *Jesus of Montreal* poses. The movie is a unique commentary about the image of Jesus leveled at the culture industry that manufactures those representations and the world that consumes them. Thus, *Jesus of Montreal* appropriately concludes our study of the Savior and the silver screen because it does at least three things: it looks back on a history of the genre through the world of postmodernism and intertextuality; it establishes itself as a postcolonial text; and it explores future complications of the modern world that have displaced the "metanarrative" of the Christian story.

Historical Retrospective. As we have suggested earlier in this book, postmodern aesthetics question, among many things, the validity of humanist art, even the very notion of "authentic" reproduction. With the catastrophic events surrounding World War II and its aftermath, those of us on the edge of a new millennium are left with provocative, unanswered questions: What, for instance, is the moral and aesthetic value of representation after Auschwitz? With the reliance of horrific films of concentration camp victims and photographs of Hiroshima and Nagasaki as a grim legacy, we appear to reach a kind of "ground zero" for representing *anything,* let alone a picture of Jesus.

With the prospect that *any* attempt at reproduction is overshadowed by the events surrounding the Holocaust, then, postmodern art becomes a supermarket of disparate forms filled with quotations and parodic references from the past. Lava lamps, Barbie dolls, and even sentimental pictures of Jesus come to mind here as examples of contemporary chic. All of us have seen the way in which other cultural forms in fashion, home furnishings, even early religious piety have been deployed into what the French call *la mode retro—retro style.* From our perspective, *retro* suggests the loss of authentic religious aura, loss of originality and loss of the genius of the new: all with the result that the Savior on the silver screen is robbed of power. Stylized monastic habits became fashion chic; crosses were worn to slim the body, and so on.

We introduced this study of the Savior and the silver screen recalling that among the earliest representations of Jesus on film were the Oberammergau Passion Plays in 1897. Interestingly enough, after almost one hundred years of filming the life of Jesus, we would come, as it were, full circle. *Jesus of Montreal* has as its subject the staging of a passion play in Montreal and invites us to think self-consciously and self-reflectively, not only about the history of the Savior on the silver screen, but about how we image God and, indeed, consume images about God in the postmodern age of technology. When a young actor in *Jesus of Montreal,* eventually cast as Jesus in the passion play, finds himself moving away from the consumerized spectacle of "Jesus Christ" and, instead, becomes a prophetic *alter Christus* (alternate Christ). Arcand has outlined what is at stake in the clash between religious faith and secular consumerism in the postmodern world.

What are the implications here for representations of the Savior on the silver screen under the postmodern gaze? Old artifacts of film culture have been used in a thousand different ways, from decorations to commercials; they can be removed easily from their traditional, organic context and reassembled. Jesus' face becomes an artifact from another time now recycled in a parodied, ironic form. Under certain circumstances, we might say that all of the traditional biblical epics have become kitsch, or trendy art. The face of Jesus is not exempt from all this. What must H. B. Warner's representation of Jesus in *The King of Kings* look like today when we can rip such a portrait out of its contextual, "sacred" context? What if we deployed Jeffrey Hunter in *King of Kings* the way some commercials make use of Humphrey Bogart, Elvis Presley, or Cary Grant to sell products?

As a recent magazine illustration clarifies, computer technology makes it possible for a traditional representation of the Sacred Heart to have the face of Elvis. Some may consider this blasphemous. In one sense it is that, but only if we agree that there are certain representations of Jesus that carry a transcendent aura, that transcend time.

Postmodern aesthetics will never admit to such a practice and, instead, suggests that there is no aura we can all agree upon. Therefore, "Jesus Christ" as a transcendent portrait claims little authenticity for religious experience. Those representations that depict Jesus with an aura (e.g., early modern pictures of the Sacred Heart) become postmodern collectibles in the same way that crucifixes have become fashionable jewelry. Postmodern aesthetics has forced us, then, to confront an aspect of the Savior on the silver screen in a radical way: the power of technology and communication and its effect on displacing religious aura. Even beyond this, we must deal with a new generation of young people who are educated by postmodern images— MTV montage, Hollywood special effects, amorphous computer technology, and so on—and understand their worldview in relationship to the construction of another kind of "Jesus Christ." That new Savior may turn out surprisingly like the one reconfigured by Daniel in *Jesus of Montreal,* not into parody but into metaphor with its "is" and "is not" quality.

We know that before the advent of postmodernism, "religious" aura in Hollywood was well established by deploying artistic conventions in adaptation, such as the sacred *tableau vivant* and so on. But when these paintings have lost their viability, their own sacred aura in our day (after all, we can purchase copies of da Vinci's "Last Supper" for our kitchen decor), the possibility of using them to establish a divine aura significantly diminishes. Arcand is well aware of these often baffling issues in *Jesus of Montreal.*

Unlike the Hollywood depictions of Jesus (DeMille, Ray, Stevens, and Scorsese), Arcand has departed from an "adaptation" altogether so that even the source text of the gospel itself becomes secondary. Yet, at the same time, *Jesus of Montreal* wants to claim a role in a consideration of biblical epics and cinema history. It is more than just a film in which the protagonist, as a kind of "Christ figure," reenacts the passion, death, and resurrection of Jesus. In fact, from the very first moment of the film, we are drawn into a world which lets us know that the subject will be vast, complicated, and intricate: *Jesus of Montreal* is not only a thematic treatment of modern faith and life—a confrontation between the sacred and the secular—but a cultural critique wrapped in a multidimensional narrative. It is a story about how to tell the story of Christ in a society that has lost the ability to represent God in a coherent way. Thus, *Jesus of Montreal* chooses to take as its subject the very idea of the Christ film itself and, beyond that, the possibility of representing God at all.

Arcand's exploration of the Savior in the postmodern world deals with a loss of the "old cinema," the world of spectacle. In a certain sense, Arcand explores the postmodern world of the unstable image. As Arcand tells us in the prologue of his screenplay, he wanted to create a film "full of rupture." For Arcand, this means a kind of bricolage in which often contradictory, paradoxical items share the same domain. This is the arena that challenges the sacred image because the formally sacred aura, under the lens of postmodernity, has an ironic twist: we live in that world of supermarkets, Internet menus, and free associations of images. Arcand has dared to ask us to confront the image of Jesus in this context. After all, that is the very impulse of the film: to restage the old world of the spectacle (the passion play) and make it credible. And credibility becomes the driving question behind Arcand's film.

Additionally, from the point of view of star culture (a topic that has also informed our study here, especially as it relates to the aura of "Jesus Christ"), we can infer that we are being challenged to move away from the older, studio constructions of "Jesus Christ," a Savior with the aura of spectacle. Arcand deeply questions the power of the star to maintain a religious aura. Now, the director suggests, we are in a different universe, in what appears to be the unique alternative left to the filmmaker: the spectacle of "Jesus Christ" lacks authenticity, the *star* "Jesus Christ" seems to have lost credibility altogether.

Jesus of Montreal positions us in a new direction for the Savior and the silver screen: the smaller world of the "micronarrative" in which the narrative must be personalized. As the priest/producer says of the passion play at the beginning of the film, "it must be modernized." That modernization will, of course, demand Daniel's own life—not a translation into another spectacle. Thus the film's trajectory from the start reminds us that the world of the Jesus film and the creation of a divine image as a star with a religious aura are mostly illusionary. Rather, the young actor Daniel Coulombe must really "play" the role of Jesus, in the words of Paul of Tarsus, "put on Christ."

Daniel as actor appropriates not the external features of Jesus, but the Savior's interior disposition of the Suffering Servant, and finally, redeemer. Ultimately, as a person who becomes more and more like Jesus, Daniel becomes, paradoxically, a Jesus *without* a Hollywood aura, an actor without a script. In constructing a multiallegorical, intertextual narrative, Arcand has problematized the Jesus film, bringing it into a postmodern context.

We have seen that some directors, like Martin Scorsese, have been particularly good at absorbing certain stylistic tendencies in the biblical epic. *The Last Temptation of Christ* even uses certain cinematic "citations" or "quotations" which, by their intertextual nature, call our attention to other films about Jesus. As the opening of the film suggests, *Jesus of Montreal* deals with plays within plays, and, to a large extent, texts within texts; and, even further, actors inside and outside the performance frame. To this end, Arcand wants to interest us in a kind of intertextuality so inevitable in the postmodern world that it has left traditional artistic forms exhausted.

In a society dominated and controlled by the media and the entertainment industry, potentially everything can refer to something else. This intertextuality is the film's entry into piercing the illusion of religious spectacle, which is at the core of *Jesus of Montreal.* Indeed, as far as other texts we have seen are concerned, the films that most closely resemble *Jesus of Montreal* are *Jesus Christ Superstar* and *Monty Python's Life of Brian,* which anticipated the decline of the Jesus film to a great degree. We will recall that Jewison's film brought a group of actors into the "theater" of the gospel in *Superstar,* and after the show was all over, the production found itself missing the actor who played Jesus himself. As we saw Ted Neeley walking in the distant horizon with some sheep, we are reminded of Jesus' role as shepherd. In the transformation of the actor into "Jesus, the Good Shepherd," however, we sense the relationship between art and life and the mutual claims they make on each other. In *Life of Brian,* the narrative functioned parodically, mostly as a political allegory. It used our familiarity with the gospel and biblical epics as a political statement against the bourgeois structure of suburban England.

We can see a radically intertextual aspect of *Jesus of Montreal* with even a cursory look at its narrative architecture. Within the various contours of the film itself, then, we can identify the interplay between at least two different texts in *Jesus of Montreal:* the political and ecclesial world of Montreal, on the one hand, and the passion play on the other. Both texts are, of course, linked by Daniel/Jesus. Arcand's staging of the passion play with an actor who plays Jesus in art but then, interestingly, duplicates the Lord's passion in his own personal life articulates a Savior for a posthumanist world. The film takes a much different turn from any of the films about Jesus we have seen thus far. Rather than imposing a cinematic image of Jesus on the audience, *Jesus of Montreal* critiques the very aura of spectacle itself and its partner: realistic Hollywood acting.

Postcolonial Canada. Additionally, Arcand makes a nationalistic, political statement about Quebec and the possibilities of rearticulating the life of Jesus within a national boundary. Daniel becomes a singular Jesus, a personal savior—uniquely, a political one, a Jesus of Montreal—made necessary by the postmodern aesthetics of intertextuality, nationalism, and the culture of the superspectacle. What were the larger industrial and environmental contexts out of which *Jesus of Montreal* emerged, and, beyond that, what are the artistic, political, and social implications the film raises because of these social structures?

Its intertextual narrative features notwithstanding, perhaps the most important thing to observe about *Jesus of Montreal* is that it is very consciously *not* a Hollywood movie. More importantly, it remains linked to Quebec theater, church, and politics. For, in addition to calling our attention to the illusionary world of the movies, Arcand has chosen to go further and has deployed intertextual references as a cultural critique, an articulation of nationalist cinema. The Jesus film, as we have argued, performs a certain social function. In America, the Bible had been very profitable for the studio system and for guaranteeing a respectable middle-class feature. Moreover, the Jesus film helped to negotiate class divisions within an emerging film culture; it showcased its directors, stars, and emerging pyrotechnics; it projected and protected a collective, dominant (usually conservative) ideology.

The story of the film industry is quite different in Canada for a variety of reasons. That we Americans seem to know little about Canadian cinema in itself says something about the country's film industry, which has been dominated by American mass cultural imports for decades. Canada's proximity to the United States has made our northern neighbor a cultural dependent. Some data suggest that as much as 97 percent of Canada's total theater time for feature films comes from imports produced by United-States-based media transnational corporations.[3]

The problem in the Canadian film industry is complex, of course, and can be traced back to a lengthy legacy of a Canadian public that long enjoyed a constant stream of Hollywood features. Moreover, the Canadian government signed an agreement with the Hollywood studios (the Canadian Cooperation Project) that affirmed a steady stream of imported features for many years. Like so much of Canadian life, seemingly dominated by larger economic markets in the United States and elsewhere, the Canadian film world found itself oppressed by a cultural imperialism that many just took for granted.

This saturation of American-made films continued until directors like Arcand began to emerge in the 1960s, slowly giving voice to a politicized cinema. But how, then, does a national literature or a cinema establish itself through *indigeneity*—claim its own uniqueness from the country of origin? Americans had long faced the issue of developing a literature of their own, quite apart from British and European influence. More radically, is it possible to voice a national literature in a colonized space? Authors such as Herman Melville and Nathaniel Hawthorne published narratives that attempted to capture America within its own indigenous nature—sea stories, settler novels, and so on. If Americans faced such a crisis of national literature, so did the Canadians; perhaps even more so because, simply put, they were a composite of French and English identities, with the Queen Mother on its currency and America's capitalism at its borders.

In the 1960s, a time of great upheaval for so much of our contemporary world, the beginnings of a consciousness began to be unearthed, fostering a style of writing that we now call "postcolonial." Postcolonial writing recognizes that throughout human history there has remained a repressed, unarticulated voice deeply submerged under the various contours of the cultural experience. Postcolonial critics research ways that colonial settlements have come to recognize that they have been long faced with a nationalism not their own, a cultural imperialism that has muted the native writer's own unique language. In James Joyce's *A Portrait of the Artist as a Young Man* (1914), for example, Stephen Dedalus, who, by the end of the novel is destined to "forge the consciousness" of his race, realizes that even his language has been shaped by the English. As Stephen encounters his English professor at his Jesuit school, the young man as artist faces the hegemony and control of the state, the church, and language itself:

> ...the language we are speaking is his before it is mine. How different are the words *home, Christ, ale, master,* on his lips and on mine! I cannot speak or write these words without unrest of spirit. His language, so familiar and so foreign will always be for me an acquired speech. I have not made or accepted its words. My voice holds them at bay. My soul frets in the shadow of his language.[4]

Stephen's emergence as an artist would, like Joyce himself, depend on his ability to subvert the language of the English, the colonizer, and claim the newly emergent writing of an indigenous Ireland. And it was with Joyce and other writers in mind that Bill Ashcroft, Gareth Griffiths, and Helen Tiffin entitled their interesting and useful study of the practice and theory of postcolonial literatures, *The Empire Writes Back* (1989).[5]

It is no wonder that Margaret Atwood and other Canadians also began "to write back," saying to the Parliamentary Committee on Free Trade in the mid-1980s that "Canada as separate but dominated country has done about as well under the United States as women, worldwide, have done under men; about the only position they've ever adopted towards us, country to country, has been the missionary position, and we were not on top."[6] It seems clear that the media industry in Canada had been especially repressed by Hollywood and the Cooperation Project, which, in effect, dwarfed or co-opted any attempt at a national cinema. By the late 1960s, however, Canada was given the impetus to develop its own national voice in the film industry through a grant given to the Canadian Film Development Corporation of ten million dollars. Still, bureaucratic conflicts have remained such that the American imports still monopolize the film industry and, to a great extent, with governmental cooperation.

Yet the film industry in Canada has never been utterly silent, mostly due to directors like Denys Arcand. Arcand, like James Joyce, has been very attentive to the indigenous quality of his productions and is notable for his documentaries as well as his feature films. In 1965, Arcand directed the short film, *Ville-Marie,* which traced the early history of a Canadian city, focusing on the intense missionary work of the priests and sisters involved in its transformation in the mid-seventeenth century to a religious center, and tracking its later decline at the hands of the French fur traders. Twenty years later, Arcand made *The Decline of the American Empire* (1986), in which he once again took up local history (contemporary Quebec) in order to examine class and gender relationships. Clearly, Arcand is interested in the question of power, self-destruction, and the loss of spirituality. As an allegory, *The Decline of the American Empire* recalls Atwood's configuration of gender power as an image of colonial domination. Men oppress women so that marriage (or even decent human relationships) ceases to function in any other way except through appetite. Everyone is objectified and commodified. It is not hard to see that Arcand is also suggesting the oppressive power structure at work in the Canadian economy, especially the film industry, which also has functioned on the level of consumerist, secular appetite.

Allegory and Its Use. Arcand followed a similar cultural critique in *Jesus of Montreal* by using allegorical structure. The first level of this allegory, of course, is much like the familiar story of Jesus in the gospels. The film is so loaded with all sorts of fascinating allusions between the modern world of Quebec and the gospels that we note only the most obvious here. The play-within-a-play—most especially *this particular* play, the passion play—has obvious rhetorical advantages insofar as it continually calls our attention to the film's allegorical structure. Moreover, *Jesus of Montreal* begs for contrasts, similarities, and the penetration of one text into another. Like the prophet Daniel and, of course, Jesus himself, Daniel comes as an innocent to a hopelessly secular society in an attempt to redeem it. Once there, he must teach his actor friends as Jesus taught his disciples—some of whom have abandoned the theater in favor of money—and particularly confront an utterly commodified society enthralled by spectacle (pornography) and commercial profits. When touched by Daniel, his friends Martin and Constance become contemporary followers who must unlearn the ways of the world. They share a last meal with him, a moment of despair before he will surrender his life as an organ donor, which will give life to someone else.

There is another allegory at work here as well; it is more politicized because, like Arcand's early work, it suggests much about cultural imperialism and its relationship to Canada. The use of the passion play in *Jesus of Montreal* evokes the history of film and the Hollywood spectacle. Further, Arcand draws our attention to the multiple allegory when we first see Daniel after the Dostoyevski sequence. The theatrical producers and star watchers buzz flatteringly around the play's star, who spots Daniel standing silently in the wings. Then, turning to his fans, the star says of Daniel: "*There* is a good actor." The scene has both a religious and a political allegory: on one level the star is John the Baptist pointing out Jesus on the banks of the Jordan and saying that he must decrease so that the Lord must increase. On another level this is the (rare) moment in which star culture faces the craft of acting.

The scene also serves to show Daniel's distance from superspectacle (read: Hollywood) and his closeness to a simple, theatrical style. Daniel's simplicity suggests his *indigenous,* or national, life. He is a kind of folk creature, free from artifice and pretense and, of course, directly opposed to the world of bureaucracy, which has effectively suppressed the simplicity of his own world, the arena of pure theater. This could not be more obvious during the scene in which several professional actors, perfunctorily and affectedly, dub a sex scene in a studio. Daniel, the "good actor," appears out of place. Indeed, there is hardly a scene in the film that does not place an emphasis on Daniel's prophetic role as a shy, cultural Savior. Daniel drives out commercial beer producers from the Temple (theater), and these are only some of several people in the film who seem distant not only from his own sensibility, but, by extension, from the "real" Quebec.

Daniel's attempt to gather a cohort of disciples around him is a way of suggesting a more simplified Quebec free from foreign domination and unsullied by pornographic and commercial interests. Here, of course, we see Arcand involving us in a postcolonial conversation: to redeem Quebec means to urge that nation to embrace religious values, but also, to free that country from corrupt influences. Like Joyce's Stephen Dedalus, Daniel seems to want to cry out against the established hegemony in Quebec: "My soul frets with the shadow of his language." Daniel wants to redeem art, his country, and humanity. Similarly, Arcand has subverted the language of Hollywood and articulated his own *ecriture,* his own indigenous writing.

Future Complications. Finally, *Jesus of Montreal* asks us to think about so many things: the encounter of the sacred with the secular; the power of the religious image in postmodern technology; the ability of spectacle to hold us in its grasp; and the aegis of media dictatorship and its role in subverting other cultures. We could enumerate several issues in the film, but ultimately Arcand wants to provoke us into confronting the question of the future, the implications of the sudden, tragic apocalypse of humanism.

In the Bible, the Book of Daniel was written in order to account for the period of exile after the people of Judah were captured by the Babylonian king, Nebuchadnezzar. The young prophet and visionary Daniel was responsible for interpreting a vision of truth from God, unlike Hollywood's fantasy-aura. Instead, Daniel's vision is of the Son of man, who stands outside of time. It is an apocalypse that has devoured everything and leaves us at the end of time:

> I looked up and saw a man clothed in linen with a belt of gold from Ophir round his waist. His body gleamed like topaz, his face shone like lightning, his eyes flamed like torches, his arms and feet sparkled like a disc of bronze; and when he spoke his voice sounded like the voice of a multitude. I, Daniel, alone saw the vision, while those who were near men did not see it, but great fear fell upon them and they stole away, and I was left alone gazing at this great vision. (Dn 10:5–8)

Ultimately, *Jesus of Montreal* brings us to the end of things, and, indeed, to the end of the possibility of the Christian metanarrative. The "Jesus Christ" whom Arcand portrays is only a character in a micronarrative, a small story of redemption in a deeply conflicted and horribly fractured society. Daniel as "Jesus Christ" models perfect charity, not the aura of spectacle. Not unexpectedly, *Jesus of Montreal* also brings us to the end of this study of the Savior and the silver screen. The world that constructed the Jesus film is at an end because, in a certain sense, the humanist culture that assembled an image called "Jesus Christ" has disappeared. We have become a society of small communities, like the one that gathered around

Daniel Coulombe. At the same time, however, we are a world village endlessly assembling and constructing images, people, and mythologies. Hopefully, there has been a place in small faith communities for ways of thinking about God through a reflection on Jesus and film culture. There, all of us wait for redemption from the God beyond all imagining.

NOTES

1. Referred to in William Hamilton, *A Quest for the Post-Historical Jesus* (London: SCM, 1993), 4.

2. Lloyd Baugh, *Imaging the Divine*, 128.

3. See for example, *Canada's Hollywood: The Canadian State and Economic Life* (Toronto: University of Toronto Press, 1993).

4. James Joyce, *A Portrait of the Artist as a Young Man* (New York: Viking Penguin, 1993), 189.

5. Bill Ashcroft, Gareth Griffiths, and Helen Tiffin, *The Empire Writes Back: Theory and Practice in Post-Colonial Literature* (London and New York: Rutledge, 1989).

6. Margaret Atwood, *Toronto Globe and Mail*, 5 November 1987.

Appendix
Tables of Bible References and Allusions

Table 1
The King of Kings (1927)

Introduction
Mk 16:15* (see Mt 28:19)

Home of Mary Magdalene
Lk 7:21–22*

Blind Girl Is Healed
Mk 2:1–2
1 Pt 3:13*
Mk 3:17–19* (parallels)
Mk 3:2*
Lk 8:39*

Mary Magdalene Is Cleansed
Mt 7:7
Mt 8:3
Lk 8:2*
Mt 5:8

Woman Caught in Adultery
Jn 12:19*
Jn 5:18*
Mt 21:46*
Jn 7:47
Jn 8:4–5*, 7
Lk 18:11
Jn 8:10–11

Jesus Blesses the Children
Lk 8:1
Jn 13:27
Mt 26:22
Jn 16:33 (with 14:27)
Mt 20:28

Garden of Gethsemane
Mt 26:36, 38
Lk 22:42, 44
Mt 26:40–42
Jn 17:1, 4
Mt 26:48–49
Lk 22:48
Jn 18:10* (parallels)
Mt 26:52, 55*
Jn 18:8

Trial before Pilate
Mk 15:1*
Lk 23:2–3
Jn 19:10
Jn 18:37–38
Lk 23:14–16*
Mt 27:20*
Ps 15:5*
Mt 27:27–29* (parallels)

The use of an asterisk (*) indicates that the biblical reference is not a quotation of the text in question, but is either a paraphrase or an allusion. This has no bearing upon the question of context.

Mt 27:18*
Jn 18:39*
Lk 23:18*
Mt 27:22
Mk 10:14

Raising of Lazarus
Jn 11:17–44

Cleansing of the Temple
Jn 2:14, 16
Mk 11:15*
Mt 21:13, 23
Jn 2:19
Lk 19:37*
Mk 11:10
Jn 14:6 (with Mt 5:12; 11:28)
Lk 19:38 (with Mt 21:9)
Jn 6:15 (with Lk 4:30)

Temptation
Mt 4:8, 9*
Mt 16:23
Lk 4:8
Jn 18:36
Mt 6:9–10

Betrayal by Judas
Mt 26:14–15*
Mk 14:2* (see verse 1)

Last Supper
Lk 22:19 (with Mt 26:26)
Mt 26:27–28

Jn 13:33–34
Lk 22:21
Mk 15:14
Jn 19:15
Mt 27:24
Mt 27:4–5

Crucifixion
Mk 15:20 (parallels)
Lk 23:32*
Mk 15:21*
Lk 23:33*
Mk 15:23*
Mt 27:42
Lk 23:34–43*
Mt 27:45, 43*
Lk 23:46 (with Jn 19:30)
Mt 27:51
Jn 19:34
Mk 15:39
Mt 27:51

Resurrection Appearances
Mt 27:62–66*
Jn 20:11–17*
Mt 28:7*
Jn 20:19*
Lk 24:39
Jn 20:28–29
Jn 21:17
Mk 16:15 (with Jn 20:21;
   Mt 28:19)
Mt 28:20

Table 2
King of Kings (1961)

Birth of Jesus
> Lk 2:1–5
> Mt 2:1–21
> Mt 2:22–23 (parallel
> > Lk 2:39–40)

John's Messianic Preaching
> Lk 3:15–16
> Jn 1:19–23

Baptism of Jesus
> Mk 1:9, 11 (with Mt 3:14–15)

Temptation
> Lk 4:1–13 (with Mt 4:4, 10)

Call of the First Disciples
> Jn 1:35–42 (with Mt 16:18)

Imprisonment of John
> Lk 3:9–20 (parallels)

First Preaching Tour in Galilee
> Mt 4:23 (parallels)
> Mt 16:26 (parallels)
> Mt 13:36–38

Woman Caught in Adultery
> Jn 8:2–11

Choosing of the Twelve
> Lk 6:13–19 (parallels)
> Lk 15:4–6
> Mt 9:9–13
> Lk 9:10–17 (parallels)
> Lk 9:22–25 (parallels)

Death of John the Baptist
> Lk 7:18–19
> Mk 6:19–28
> Lk 7:20–28
> Mk 6:14–16

Sermon on the Mount
> Mt 4:24–5:11 (with Lk 6:20, 22)
> Mt 24:3 (parallels)
> Lk 17:20–21
> Lk 10:25–37
> Jn 10:11
> Mt 5:17, 43–46 (with Lk 6:27–28)
> Lk 5:30–32
> Mt 6:24–28
> Mt 11:28
> Mt 20:26–27, 28
> Mk 3:24, 23 (with Lk 11:18)
> Jn 10:37–38
> Mt 4:7 (or Lk 4:12)
> Mt 17:20

Mt 7:1–12

Mt 6:9–13 (with Lk 11:1)

Choosing of the Twelve

Mk 3:13–14, 16–19 (parallels)

Commissioning the Seventy

Mt 10:9–16 (with Lk 10:1; Mt 10:1)

Triumphal Entry

Lk 22:1, 2 (parallels)

Mk 14:1, 7–8 (parallels)

Lk 23:19*

Last Supper

Lk 22:7–8 (parallels)

Jn 13:21, 27 (parallels)

Jn 16:16

Jn 13:34, 36–38 (parallels)

Jn 15:13

Jn 16:21–22

Jn 14:1

Mt 26:26–28 (parallels)

Betrayal by Judas

Lk 22:3–4 (parallels)

Garden of Gethsemane

Mk 14:32–36 (with Jn 12:27)

Mk 14:43–46 (parallels)

Peter's Denial

Lk 22:56–62 (parallels)

Before Pilate and Herod

Jn 18:28, 37–38

Lk 23:6–7

Mt 14:1–2 (parallels)

Lk 23:8–11

Jn 19:1–3 (parallels)

Jn 18:39–40*

Crucifixion

Lk 23:26, 28, 32–34, 39–43

Jn 19:26

Lk 23:38 (parallels)

Mk 15:34 (or Mt 27:46)

Jn 19:30

Lk 23:46

Mk 15:39 (parallels)

Mt 27:5

Jn 19:38–42 (parallels)

Resurrection Appearances

Jn 20:1, 14–17 (with Mt 28:10)

Lk 24:13–35*

Jn 20:19–29*

Mt 28:16

Jn 21:15–17*

Mt 28:19–20

Table 3
The Gospel According to Saint Matthew (1964)
(Italian)

Birth of Jesus
Mt 1:18–23
Mt 2:1–12

Flight into Egypt
Mt 2:13–21

John the Baptist
Mt 3:1–3, 7–12

Baptism of Jesus
Mt 3:13–17

Temptation
Mt 4:1–11a

Call of the First Disciples
Mt 4:12–22
Mt 9:37
Mt 10:2–4
Mt 9:38
Mt 10:16–20, 22, 28–31,
    34–39

First Preaching Tour in Galilee
Mt 4:23–25
Mt 8:1–4

Sermon on the Mount
Mt 5:3–12

Mt 7:9–12
Mt 5:13–15, 17
Mt 6:3–4, 19–20, 24
Mt 5:38–40, 43–45
Mt 7:1–3
Mt 6:7–13, 25–34
Mt 7:13–14

Jesus' Thanksgiving to the Father
Mt 11:25–30

Eating and Healing on the Sabbath
Mt 12:2–8, 10–14, 16–21

Five Thousand Are Fed
Mt 14:13–21

Walking on the Water
Mt 14:22–31

John's Question and Jesus' Answer
Mt 11:2–23a

In Debate with the Pharisees
Mt 12:23–24, 30–31, 38–42

341

Jesus' True Kindred
Mt 12:43–45, 47, 48–50

Rejection at Nazareth
Mt 13:54–58

Rich Young Man
Mt 19:16–24

Jesus Blesses the Children
Mt 19:13–15

Death of John the Baptist
Mt 14:6–12

On Following Jesus
Mt 8:18, 19–20, 21–22
Is 15:3

Peter's Confession
Mt 16:13 (see Mk 8:27;
Lk 9–18), 14–20

Jesus Foretells His Passion Twice
Mt 16:21–24
Mt 17:22–23

True Greatness
Mt 18:1–8, 12–14, 21–22

Third Prediction of the Passion
Mt 20:17–19

Triumphal Entry
Mt 21:1–9

Cleansing the Temple
Mt 21:12–17

Cursing of the Fig Tree
Mt 21:18–22

Questions on Laws and Authority
Mt 21:23–44
Mt 22:14–39

Woe to the Scribes and Pharisees
Mt 23:1–39
Mt 24:1–2
Mt 26:3–5

Anointing in Bethany
Mt 26:6–9 (see Jn 12:4–5),
10–13

Betrayal by Judas
Mt 26:14–16, 20–25

Last Supper
Mt 26:26–29

Garden of Gethsemane
Mt 26:31–50

Peter's Denial
Mt 26:57–75
Mt 27:1–2

Death of Judas
Mt 27:3–10

Trial before Pilate
Mt 27:11–30

Crucifixion
Mt 27:31–44

Mt 13:14–15
Mt 27:45–51, 55–66

Resurrection Appearances
Mt 28:1–8, 18–20

Table 4
The Greatest Story Ever Told (1965)

Prologue

Jn 1:1–5 (with 18:5)

Birth of Jesus

Mt 2:1–10* (with Hos 11:1)

Lk 2:15–16*

Lk 1:32–33

Mt 2:11–12

Flight into Egypt and Return

Mt 2:13, 16–21 (with Is 9:6)

Ps 61:2–3

Ps 130:1–5

Ps 22:1–2, 4–5

Ps 25:2

Ps 43:1–3

Ps 72:17

Ps 135:13

Baptism of Jesus

Hos 6:6

Lk 3:1–6* (parallels)

Mt 3:11, 13–15* (parallels)

Mi 5:2

Ps 24:7

Mi 6:1

Is 43:9

Is 40:10

Is 7:11

Temptation

Lk 4:1–2, 3–4*, 5–12

Is 32:15

Is 35:5

Is 29:19

Ps 9:18

Is 60:1

Is 66:18*

Call of the First Disciples

Jn 10:14

Mt 4:18–22 (parallels)

First Preaching Tour in Galilee

Jn 6:27, 33, 51

Lk 12:22–26, 28–31

Lk 17:20–21

Mt 6:19 (with Lk 6:29–30)*

Mt 5:3, 16*

Mt 7:2*

Mt 6:28–29

Jn 1:30*

Jesus' Lament over Jerusalem

Lk 13:34–35

Rich Young Man (Lazarus)

Mk 12:28–34

Mk 8:36 (parallels)

Mk 10:25 (parallels)

Mt 6:21, 24* (parallel Lk 12:34;
16:13)
Mk 12:42–44* (parallel Lk
21:2–4)
Mk 8:34* (parallels)
Mk 10:26* (parallels)

Call of Matthew
Mt 4:12* (parallels)
Mt 9:9 (with Mk 2:14; Jn
14:9*)

Teaching in the Synagogue at Capernaum
Mk 1:21–22 (parallel Lk
4:31–32)
Hos 6:6*
Lk 17:3
Lk 6:31 (parallel Mt 7:12)
Lk 11:9–10 (parallel Mt 7:7–8)
Lk 17:19* (or 18:42*)
Jn 3:15*
Lk 5:23 (parallels)
Lk 17:19* (or 18:42*)

Arrest of John the Baptist
Mt 14:3–5 parallels (with Jn
1:15*)

Choosing of the Twelve
Jn 1:42*
Lk 7:28 (parallel Mt 1 1:11)
Mt 11:28–30
Mk 3:13–19 (parallels)

Jn 6:35
Jn 10:3*, 14
Mt 16:24 (parallels)
Mk 10:15, 14 (parallel Lk
18:17, 16)

Woman Caught in Adultery
Jn 8:3–5, 7, 9–10

Jesus Heals Multitudes
Mt 4:24–25 (with 9:20–22;
parallels)
Mt 14:13–21* (parallels)

Death of John the Baptist
Mt 14:6–11* (parallel Mk
6:21–28)

Sermon on the Mount
Mt 5:3–9, 10–11, 13–14, 16
Mt 6:7–15
Mt 9:1–8* (parallels)
Jn 2:1–11*
Mt 14:13–33* (parallels)

Peter's Confession
Mt 16:13–19 (parallels)

Warning against Herod
Lk 13:31–33

Rejection at Nazareth
Lk 4:16, 22–24, 18–19 (with
Jn 10:24; parallels)

Mt 4:7 (parallel Lk 4:12)

Jn 10:37–38

Raising of Lazarus

Jn 11:1–7, 17–38, 43–44 (with
Mt 6:7–15)

Anointing in Bethany

Ps 136:1–9

Jn 12:1–8 (with Mt 26:7, 12)

Triumphal Entry

Mk 11:7–10 (parallels)

Mk 11:18 (parallel Lk
19:47–48)

Cleansing the Temple

Mt 21:12–13 (with Jn 2:15
parallels)

Hos 6:6

Is 1:11

**Woe to the Scribes and
Pharisees**

Mt 5:17

Mt 23:3, 5–9 (with 6:5*)

Discourse on Jesus' Death

Jn 3:17, 19, 21*

Jn 12:35–36

1 Cor 13:13

Mt 18:20

On Retaliation

Ps 23:1–4, 6

Ps 24:4–8

Lk 6:29*

Betrayal by Judas

Lk 22:3–6 (parallels)

Jesus Foretells His Betrayal

Mk 14:18–21 (parallel Mt
26:21–25; with Lk 22:21; Jn
13:23)

Peter's Denial Predicted

Jn 13:33, 37–38

Jn 14:2, 5–6

Last Supper

Lk 22:19–20, 15 (with Mt
26:29; parallels)

New Commandment of Love

Jn 13:27, 31, 34

Jn 12:24

Mt 18:19

Garden of Gethsemane

Jn 18:1

Lk 22:41–42 (with Jn 12:27;
Mt 26:39; Jn 18:11)

Mk 14:37–38 (parallel Mt
26:40–41)

Mk 14:43–46 (with Mt 26:52)

Jn 18:20*

Before the Sanhedrin
> Mk 15:53–55, 61–62 (parallel
> Mt 26:57–59, 63)
> Jn 9:13–25*

Peter's Denial
> Lk 22:56–62 (parallels)

Before Pilate and Herod
> Jn 18:33, 36–38 (with Dt 6:4)
> Lk 23:6–11 (with Mt 14:1–2)
> Mi 5:2

Pilate Delivers Jesus to Crucifixion
> Mk 15:16–17 (parallels)
> Jn 19:5–6 (with Lk 23:16)
> Mk 15:6–14 (parallels)
> Jn 18:36
> Jn 19:15
> Mt 27:24

Crucifixion
> Lk 23:26, 27–31, (parallels)
> Ac 1:18*
> Lk 23:33–34
> Jn 19:26–27
> Lk 23:35, 39–43
> Mk 15:33–34 (parallels)
> Jn 19:28–30
> Lk 23:46
> Mk 15:39
> Mt 27:62–66

Resurrection Appearances
> Mt 28:4
> Jn 20:1–8 (with Mk 16:5;
> Lk 24:5)
> Mt 28:11–16, 20 (with Jn
> 13:34; Mt 6:33–34)

Table 5
Jesus Christ Superstar (1973)

Jesus Is Thought to Be Beside Himself
> Mk 3:20*
> Jn 12:6*
> Mt 13:55*

On Anxiety
> Mt 6:34* (see Jn 14:1)
> Lk 10:38–42*

Anointing in Bethany
> Jn 12:3–4, 6–7 (with Lk 7:39;
>   Jn 7:7*)
> Jn 14:5

Chief Priests Take Counsel against Jesus
> Jn 11:47–48

Anointing in Bethany (return)
> Lk 8:1–3*
> Mt 6:34*
> Mk 14:3–5 (with Jn 12:8)

Chief Priests Take Counsel against Jesus (return)
> Mt 26:3–4 (parallels)
> Lk 17:11–19*
> Mt 3:1–2* (parallels)
> Jn 11:49–50

Triumphal Entry
> Jn 12:13
> Lk 19:39–40
> Lk 6:20–23*

Temptation
> Lk 4:5* (parallel Mt 4:8)
> Mt 6:13*

Prediction of the Passion
> Lk 18:31–34*
> Mt 27:19*

Cleansing the Temple
> Mt 21:12–13 (parallels)

Sick Healed at Evening
> Lk 4:40 (parallels)

Betrayal by Judas
> Mk 14:10–11 (parallels)

Last Supper
> Lk 22:17–19*

Jesus Foretells His Betrayal/ Peter's Denial Predicted
> Lk 22:21*, 23 (parallels)
> Mk 14:26–27*, 30–31
>   (parallels)

348

Garden of Gethsemane
Mt 26:37*, 39, 40, 42
(parallels)
Lk 22:47–49 (with Jn 18:11)

Before the Sanhedrin
Lk 22:66 (with Mt 26:63–64)

Peter's Denial
Lk 22:56–61 (parallels)

Before Pilate and Herod
Mk 15:1–5 (parallels); Lk
23:6–9
Jn 2:1–11
Mt 8:1–4* (parallels)
Jn 11:1–44*
Jn 6:16–21* (parallels)
Jn 6:1–15* (parallels)

Death of Judas
Mt 27:3–5

**Pilate Delivers Jesus to
Crucifixion**
Lk 23:23–25
Jn 18:29–38 (with Lk 23:4–5)
Jn 19:4–6, 9–11, 13–15
Mt 27:24, 26

Crucifixion
Jn 19:17–18, 25
Lk 23:34
Jn 19:19 (parallels)
Mk 15:34 (parallel Mt 27:46)
Lk 23:46

Resurrection Appearances
Mk 16:8*
Jn 10:11*, 14*(?)

Table 6
Jesus of Nazareth (1977)

Introduction
Is 60:1
Dt 5:32*, 6:5*
Nm 6:24–26

Annunciation
Lk 1:26–38

Mary's Visit to Elizabeth
Lk 1:39–44, 46–49

Birth of John the Baptist
Lk 1:57–60

Birth of Jesus
Mt 1:18–19
Dt 22:23–24*
Dt 24:1
Mt 1:20–21
Nm 6:24–26
Lk 2:1–2
Is 9:6*
Mi 5:2*
Lk 2:3–7

Adoration of the Infant Jesus
Lk 2:8–18
Mt 2:1–6
Lk 2:21–33, 35
Mt 2:10–13 (with Jn 1:29*)

Flight into Egypt and Return
Mt 2:14, 16–21 (with Dan
2:44*)

Childhood of Jesus at Nazareth
Lk 2:39–40
Dt 6:4–6
Ps 31:24

Boy Jesus in the Temple
Lk 2:41–49 (with 1 Kgs
8:27–29)

John the Baptist
Mal 3:1
Lk 3:19* (parallels)
Jer 13:27
Mt 3:1–2 (with Lk 3:5)
Zec 1:3
Hos 8:13*
Lk 3:8, 10 (with Is 55:8)
Jn 1:19–25, 27
Lk 3:16–17 (parallels)

Death of Joseph
Lk 23:46*
Ps 3:4
1 Pt 3:19*
Dt 6:4

350

Baptism of Jesus
Mt 3:13–15, 17 (with Jn 1:32)
Jn 1:35–37
Jn 3:30

Jesus' Preaching at Nazareth
Lk 4:16–21
Mk 1:14–15 (parallel Mt 4:17)
Lk 4:24 (parallels)
Lk 9:26* (parallel Mk 8:38)
Lk 4:28–30

Call of the First Disciples
Jn 1:40, 43

Healing of the Demoniac in the Synagogue
Lk 4:31–33 (parallels)
Mk 1:23–27 (with 9:22)

Call of the Disciples
Jn 1:41
Lk 5:2–3, 6–7
Mt 13:44–48
Mt 4:17
Lk 11:16 (parallels)
Lk 12:54–56
Mt 4:17

Healing of the Paralytic
Mt 9:2–8 (parallels)

Call of Levi (Matthew)
Lk 5:29–30, 32 (with Hos 6:6)
Lk 15:11–32

Jairus's Daughter
Mk 5:21
Mt 10:34–36
Mt 19:27*, 29* (parallels)
Mk 8:35 (parallels)
Mt 19:30 (parallel Mk 10:31)
Mt 6:19–21
Mk 5:22–24, 35, 41 (with Lk 8:52–55)
Jn 20:24–29*

Death of John the Baptist
Is 29:20
Eccl 1:2
Is 5:20–21
Am 6:4–6
Is 40:21–23
Mk 6:19–29 (with Is 32:1, 3)

Rich Young Man
Mt 9:13* (parallel Mk 2:17)
Mt 6:25–26, 27, 28–34
Mk 10:17, 21–22 (parallels)
Mt 6:24* (parallel Lk 16:13)
Mk 10:25 (parallels)
Lk 6:44

Five Thousand Are Fed
Mt 14:13–20 (parallels)

Great Commandment
Lk 7:33–34 (parallel Mt 11:18–19)
Mt 12:10–11

Mk 2:27
Mt 7:1
Mk 12:28–30*, 31, 34
    (parallels)
Lk 10:29*

Anointing in Bethany
Lk 7:37–38, 44, 47–50

Commissioning the Seventy
Mt 10:8–11, 14–16, 19–20
Lk 1:42*
Mt 12:50

Peter's Confession
Mt 16:13–21

Sermon on the Mount
Mt 5:3–12
Mt 6:8–13

Peter Rebuked
Mt 16:22–23 (parallel Mk
    8:32–33)

Raising of Lazarus
Jn 11:3, 20–22, 21, 25, 27, 34,
    39, 41
Jn 2:6
Jn 11:25, 43–44

Betrayal by Judas
Mk 14:10 (parallels)

Triumphal Entry
Jn 12:12–18

Cleansing the Temple
Lk 19:45–46 (with Is 1:21, 11;
    parallels)
Jn 2:19

Teachings at the Temple
Lk 10:21, 23–24 (parallel Mt
    11:25)
Mt 20:26–28 (parallel Mk
    10:43–45)
Mt 11:28
Mt 25:35–40
Mt 5:44 (parallel Lk 6:27)
Mt 26:52*
Is 11:9, 6*
Is 65:19
Jn 1:29*
Mt 10:38* (parallel Lk 14:27)

Questions about Authority
Mt 21:15–16
Lk 20:1–4, 7–8 (parallels)
Mt 21:28–32

Teachings at the Temple (return)
Lk 6:27–28 (parallel Mt
    5:43–44)
Mt 5:39–40, 42, 46 (parallel Lk
    6:32, 29–30)
Mt 7:12* (parallel Lk 6:21)
Lk 6:37

Mt 5:48
Mt 7:7, 9, 11 (parallel Lk 11:9,
    11, 13)

Woman Caught in Adultery
Jn 8:2–11

Centurion of Capernaum
Mt 22:1–14* (parallel Lk
    14:15–24)
Mt 8:5–10, 13

Jesus Heals the Man Born Blind
Jn 9:1, 5, 8, 17, 18, 24–25,
    35–38, 39–41
Lk 11:15*

**Woe to the Scribes and
Pharisees**
Mt 23:13, 24, 23, 27
Mt 24:2
Is 64:10*
Mt 23:33, 39
Jn 10:30–31

Discourse with Nicodemus
Jn 3:1–4, 6–8, 16–17

Jesus' Death Is Premeditated
Jn 11:47–50, 53 (with
    Dt 18:20; parallels)

Peter's Denial Predicted
Lk 22:15
Jn 13:33, 37

Mk 14:30–31 (parallels)
Mt 26:31
Lk 22:32

Jesus Foretells His Betrayal
Mt 26:21–23 (with Jn
    13:27–28, 30; parallels)

Last Supper
Jn 6:48*, 58
Lk 22:19
Mk 14:24–25

New Commandment of Love
Jn 15:12–13
Jn 13:35
Jn 17:1, 20
Jn 14:6

Garden of Gethsemane
Mt 26:39 (parallels)

Jesus Arrested
Lk 22:47, 53, 48
Jn 18:8
Lk 22:5* (parallels)

Jesus before the Sanhedrin
Jn 18:19–21
Mt 26:61
Mk 14:59, 61–63 (with Dt 6:4)

Peter's Denial
Mk 14:66–72 (parallels)

Death of Judas
    Mk 27:5

Trial before Pilate
    Jn 18:28
    Lk 23:2
    Jn 18:31, 33, 36–38
    Jn 19:1–3 (parallels)
    Jn 19:5, 9–11
    Mt 27:15–21, 26 (parallels)

Crucifixion
    Jn 19:17–21
    Lk 23:34, 39–43
    Jn 19:25–27
    Mt 27:42 (parallels)
    Mt 27:45–47
    Ps 22:1*

Is 53:3, 4–5, 7
Lk 23:46
Jn 19:30

Guard at the Tomb
    Mt 27:57–61* (parallels)
    Mt 27:62–64, 66

Women at the Tomb
    Mk 16:1–4 (with Lk 24:4–5)
    Jn 20:14–17*, 18
    Mk 16:11 (parallel Lk 24:11)

Report of the Guard
    Mt 28:11–15*

Jesus Appears to the Disciples
    Lk 24:45–49 (with 10:3)
    Mt 28:19–20

Table 7
Monty Python's Life of Brian (1979)

Adoration of the Infant
Mt 2:1, 10–11*
Lk 2:16

Ascension
Acts 1:9*

Sermon on the Mount
Mt 5:4, 6, 8
Mt 5:9*
Mt 5:5
Lv 24:16*

Cleansing of the Ten Lepers
Lk 17:11–19*

Coming of the Word
Jn 1:1–18*

Apocalyptic Prophecies
Rv 6:1–17*
Rv 17:1–18*
Ez 21:1–32*
Ez 7:1–27*

Sayings and Parables
Lk 6:37 (parallel Mt 7:1)

Lk 12:27, 24 (parallel Mt 6:26,
28)
Lk 19:11–27*
Lk 10:25*

Ascension
Acts 1:9*

Signs and Miracles
Mt 12:38* (parallels)
Lk 9:10–17* (parallels)
Mt 4:1–11* (parallel Lk
4:1–13)
Lk 4:40–41 (with Jn 5:25)

Ministering Women
Lk 8:1–3*
Lk 1:42*, 27*
Mk 10:13 (parallels)

Trial before Pilate
Mk 15:6–14* (parallels)

Crucifixion
Mt 27:32* (parallels)
Jn 19:17–18* (parallels)
Jn 19:25–26* (parallels)

Table 8
The Last Temptation of Christ (1988)

Introduction
> Mk 6:3* (parallel Mt 13:55)
> Is 53:1–12 (with Heb 1:3)
> Ps 28:7
> Mk 3:22* (parallels)
> Lk 8:2*
> Lk 2:25–26*
> Mk 1:11* (parallels)
> Mk 1:12–13

Woman Caught in Adultery
> Jn 8:3–9
> Mk 6:2* (parallels)
> Jn 1:46*

Sermon on the Mount
> Mk 4:3–9 (parallels)
> Jn 13:34
> Mt 5:4–5, 6, 7, 10, 12
> Lk 6:24, 25
> Mk 1:19–20 (parallels)
> Jn 13:5*

Choosing of the Twelve
> Mk 3:13–19 (parallels)
> Lk 6:29*
> Mt 12:43–45* (parallel Lk
>   11:24–26)
> Mk 4:30–32* (parallels; with
>   Gen 3:6–7; 1 Cor 15:45)

John the Baptist
> Mk 1:4–6 (parallels, with Is
>   40:3)
> Mt 3:13–15
> Mt 7:19

Temptation
> Lk 4:1–13
> Gn 3:6–7*
> Jn 3:30
> Mt 7:19*

Mary and Martha
> Lk 10:38–40
> Mk 6:17–29* (parallel Mt
>   14:3–12)

Jesus' Messianic Preaching
> Mt 16:13–19* (parallels)
> Lk 3:15–16* (parallel Mt 3:11)

Conditions of Discipleship
> Lk 14:25–26 (parallel Mt
>   10:37–38)
> Mk 8:31 (parallels)

Sick Healed at Evening
> Mk 1:32–34 (parallels)
> Mk 8:22–25 (with Lk 17:14)

Marriage at Cana
Mt 22:1–14* (parallel Lk
14:15–24)
Jn 2:1–9

Ministry in Galilee
Mk 1:14–15 (with 8:11–12)
Mt 6:19–21 (with Lk 12:33–34)
Lk 13:24
Mk 6:1–3 (parallels)
Mk 3:31–33 (parallels)

Raising of Lazarus
Jn 11:17–18, 39, 43–44

Cleansing of the Temple
Mk 11:15–17 (parallels)
Mt 5:17–18*
Mt 10:34
Jn 2:19*

Plot against Lazarus
Jn 12:9–10*
Is 53:4–5, 7

Triumphal Entry
Jn 12:12–13 (parallels)
Mk 11:15–17* (parallels)
Jn 2:19*

Last Supper
Mk 14:22 (with 1 Cor 11:25)
Jn 13:27–30

Garden of Gethsemane
Mk 14:32, 35–36 (parallels)
Lk 22:43
Mk 14:37, 43–46 (parallels)
Mt 26:51–52 (with Lk 22:51)

Trial before Pilate
Mk 15:2, 4–5 (parallels)
Dn 2:31–34
Jn 18:36

Crucifixion
Mt 27:27–31 (parallels)
Mk 14:66–69 (parallels)
Lk 23:27, 33–35
Mk 15:33–34 (parallel Mt
27:45–46)

Temptation-Dream Sequence
Gn 22:1–14*
Acts 22:3–16
Lk 1:26–38*
1 Cor 15:3–5, 20–28*
Jn 20:19–29*
Lk 15:11–22*

Crucifixion (return)
Jn 19:30

Table 9
Jesus of Montreal (1989)
(French)

John the Baptist
> Mt 27:3–5*
> Mk 6:24*
> Lk 3:15*
> Jn 1:29*

Adoration of the Infant Jesus
> Lk 2:13–14*

Choosing the Twelve
> Mt 8:20* (parallel Lk 9:58)
> Mt 9:9* (parallels)
> Mt 4:18–22* (parallels)
> Mt 7:1–5* (parallel Lk 6:37–42)
> Jn 1:40–42*
> Jn 1:1–5, 9–10*
> Lk 8:1–3*

Trial before Pilate
> Jn 18:29, 33–34, 36, 38 (with 15:13)
> Lk 23:13–15*
> Jn 18:14, 38
> Jn 19:1, 16

Jesus' Early Life
> Lk 2:21*
> Mk 2:28* (parallels)

Mt 13:55*
Mt 2:13–21

Miracles and Sayings (Play)
> Mt 14:25, 29–31
> Mk 8:22, 25*
> Mt 6:25, 27 (parallel Lk 12:22, 25)
> Mk 5:41–42
> Mt 6:25, 34
> Jn 13:34
> Mt 5:39–40
> Mk 10:23 (parallel Lk 18:14)
> Mt 6:21 (parallel Lk 12:34)
> Lk 6:27, 32
> Lk 14:13
> Mt 21:31
> Mt 7:1
> Lk 9:18–21 (parallel Mk 8:27–30)
> Mk 11:33 (parallels)
> Jn 13:36

Arrest, Trial and Crucifixion (Play)
> Mt 26:47–56* (parallels)
> Jn 19:1 (parallels)
> Mk 15:22–23 (parallel Mt 27:33–34)
> Jn 19:28–30

Jn 19:34
1 Pt 3:19*
Mk 14:15 (parallel Mt 26:56)

Resurrection (Play)
Jn 20:2
Mk 16:12 (parallel Lk
    24:13–35*)
Jn 13:34
Lk 17:21*

First Temptation
Lk 4:3*
Mk 2:28* (parallels)
Mt 16:13–15* (parallels)

Cleansing of the Temple
Lk 8:1–3*
Lk 10:1*
Jn 2:14–15
Mt 7:6*

Sayings (Play)
Mt 5:33–34, 37
Mt 23:1–7, 8–9, 11–12

Arrest and Trial (before Pilate)
Mk 14:1–2* (parallels)
Jn 18:12*

Mt 27:24*
Mk 14:66–72 (parallels)
Mk 14:62*

Before Herod
Lk 23:8–9*

Second Temptation
Lk 4:5–6*
Jn 21:18*

Last Supper
Lk 22:15*
Jn 18:1*
Jn 8:1–11

Jesus Arrested and Crucified
Mt 26:47–50* (parallels)
Lk 23:23*

Death of Jesus
Mk 15:34* (parallel Mt 27:46)
Mk 13:2, 14–18, 21–22, 33
    (parallels)
Mt 27:45 (parallels)

Burial and Resurrection of Jesus
Mt 27:57–61* (parallels)
Jn 20:1*

Reading List

Aland, Kurt. *Synopsis of the Four Gospels.* United Bible Societies, 1982.

Arcand, Denys. "Jesus de Montreal." In *Best Canadian Screenplays*, edited by Douglas Bowie and Tom Shoebridge. Translated by Matt Cohen. Kingston: Quarry Press, 1992.

Arijon, Daniel. *Grammar of the Film Language.* Los Angeles: Silman-James Press, 1976.

Armstrong, Karen. *A History of God.* New York: Ballantine Books, 1993.

Ashcroft, Bill, Gareth Griffiths, and Helen Tiffin. *The Empire Writes Back: Theory and Practice in Post-Colonial Literature.* London and New York: Rutledge, 1989.

Babington, Bruce and Peter William Evans. *Biblical Epics: Sacred Narrative in the Hollywood Cinema.* Manchester: Manchester University Press, 1993.

Baugh, Lloyd. *Imaging the Divine: Jesus and Christ-Figures in Film.* Kansas City, MO: Sheed & Ward, 1997.

Bordwell, David and Kristin Thompson. *Film Art: An Introduction*. 4th ed. New York: McGraw-Hill, 1993.

Breton, André. *Manifestoes of Surrealism*. Translated by Richard Seaver and Helen R. Lane. Ann Arbor: University of Michigan Press, 1972.

Campbell, Joseph. *The Hero with a Thousand Faces*. 2nd ed. Princeton, NJ: Princeton University Press, 1968.

Clark, Clifford E. Jr. "Ranch-House Suburbia: Ideals and Realities." In *Recasting America: Culture and Politics in the Age of Cold War*. Chicago: University of Chicago Press, 1988, 171–91.

Couch, Richard A., and Edward J. Caropreso, with Helen B. Miller. "Making Meaning in Visuals: Creative Thinking and Interpretation of Visual Information." In *Visual Literacy: A Spectrum of Visual Learning*, edited by David M. Moore and Francis M. Dwyer. Englewood Cliffs, NJ: Educational Technology Press, 1994, 277–92.

Hamilton, William. *A Quest for the Post-Historical Jesus*. London: SCM, 1993.

Hasenberg, Peter. "The 'Religious' in Film: From *King of Kings* to *The Fisher King*. In *New Image of Religious Film*, edited by John R. May. Kansas City, MO: Sheed & Ward, 1997, 41–56.

Hopewell, James F. *Congregation: Stories and Structures*. Philadelphia: Fortress, 1987.

Johnson, Paul. *Modern Times: The World from the Twenties to the Eighties*. New York: Harper & Row, 1983.

Kawin, Bruce F. *How Movies Work*. Berkeley: University of California Press, 1992.

Kinnard, Roy and Tim Davis. *Divine Images: A History of Jesus on the Screen*. New York: Citadel Press, 1992.

Malone, Peter. "Jesus on Our Screens." In *New Image of Religious Film*, edited by John R. May. Kansas City, MO: Sheed & Ward, 1997, 57–71.

Marcus, Millicent. *Filmmaking by the Book: Italian and Literary Adaptation*. Baltimore: The John Hopkins University Press, 1993.

May, John R. *New Image of Religious Film*. Kansas City, MO: Sheed & Ward, 1997.

May, Larry A. "Apocalyptic Cinema: D. W. Griffith and the Aesthetics of Reform." In *Movies and Mass Culture*, edited by John Belton. New Brunswick, N.J.: Rutgers University Press, 1996.

McDermott, Jim. "Is It Possible to Portray Christ in Film?" *Christianity and the Arts* 1 (1994): 20–22.

McLuhan, Marshall. *Understanding Media: The Extensions of Man*. New York: New American Library, 1964.

Medved, Michael. *Hollywood vs. America*. New York: HarperPerennial, 1992.

Muffoletto, Robert. "Representations: You, Me and Them." In *Visual Literacy: A Spectrum of Visual Learning*, edited by David M. Moore and Francis M. Dwyer. Englewood Cliffs, NJ: Educational Technology Publications, 1994, 295–310.

Naremore, James. "John Huston and *The Maltese Falcon*." In *The Maltese Falcon*, edited by William Luhr. New Brunswick, NJ: Rutgers University Press, 1995.

Rivette, Jacques. "On Imagination." In *Cahiers du Cinema: The 1950s: Neo-Realism, Hollywood, New Wave*. Cambridge, MA: Harvard University Press, 1985, 104–6.

"Rock Opera: The Making of *Jesus Christ Superstar*." *Jesus Christ Superstar: A Resurrection,* Part 8. Available at http://www.geocities.com/Broadway/2596

Sarris, Andrew. *The American Cinema: Directors and Directions, 1929–1968*. New York: E. P. Dutton, 1968.

Scott, Bernard Brandon. *Hollywood Dreams and Biblical Stories*. Minneapolis: Fortress Press, 1994.

Stern, Richard C. and S. Rhonda Robinson. "Perception and Its Role in Communication and Learning." In *Visual Literacy: A Spectrum of Visual Learning*, edited by David M. Moore and Francis M. Dwyer. Englewood Cliffs, NJ: Educational Technology Publications, 1994, 31–51.

Venturi, Robert, Denise Scott Brown, and Steven Izenour. *Learning from Las Vegas*. Rev. ed. Cambridge, MA: MIT Press, 1977.